Democracy in Desperation

Democracy in Desperation

The Depression of 1893

Douglas Steeples *and* David O. Whitten

Contributions in Economics and Economic History, Number 199

Greenwood Press
Westport, Connecticut • London

Library of Congress Cataloging-in-Publication Data

Steeples, Douglas W.
    Democracy in desperation : the depression of 1893 / Douglas
Steeples and David O. Whitten.
        p.   cm. — (Contributions in economics and economic history,
    ISSN 0084–9235 ; no. 199)
    Includes bibliographical references and index.
    ISBN 0–313–27943–8 (alk. paper)
    1. United States—Politics and government—1893–1897.
    2. Depressions—1893—United States.   3. United States—Economic
    conditions—1865–1918.   I. Whitten, David O.   II. Title.
    III. Series.
    JK231.S74   1998
    320.973'09'034—DC21   98–11162

British Library Cataloguing in Publication Data is available.

Copyright © 1998 by Douglas Steeples and David O. Whitten

Library of Congress Catalog Card Number: 98–11162
ISBN: 0–313–27943–8
ISSN: 0084–9235

First published in 1998

Greenwood Press, 88 Post Road West, Westport, CT 06881
An imprint of Greenwood Publishing Group, Inc.

Printed in the United States of America

The paper used in this book complies with the
Permanent Paper Standard issued by the National
Information Standards Organization (Z39.48–1984).

10 9 8 7 6 5 4 3 2 1

Dedicated to our wives,
Chris *and* Bess,
with love and appreciation,
Douglas Steeples *and* David O. Whitten

THE DECADE of the nineties is the watershed of American history.
—Henry Steele Commager
The American Mind, 1950

Contents

Tables

1

The Panic in History

The depression . . . [caused] greater loss and more severe suffering than ever before.

—Otto Lightner, 1922

The panic of 1893 and its accompanying depression marks one of the decisive crises in American history. Henry Adams reflected its crushing impact when he wrote, "Everyone is in a blue fit of terror, and each individual thinks himself more ruined than his neighbor."[1] Hard times provided a lurid setting for sullen outbursts from the unemployed, violent strikes, the climax of the Populist and silver crusades, the creation of a new political balance, the continuing transformation of the country's economy, significant changes in national policy, and far-reaching social and intellectual developments. At the center of events, the business contraction was the crucial force shaping the tumultuous decade that ushered out the nineteenth century.

Contemporaries dated the depression from the onset of panic in 1893. Polemical intent and oversimplification often shaped explanations of and recipes for recovery from the crisis, which fell at the end of a generation of declining prices and bitter contention over the gold standard and monetary policy. Disgruntled Southern and Midwestern farmers, mining interests, urban workers, and others were certain that an inadequate money supply had caused the disastrous collapse. Their cure was inflation, preferably through the unlimited coinage of silver dollars. Adherents of contemporary financial orthodoxies disagreed. For them the growth of inflationist sentiment and a precipitate fall in the Treasury's gold reserve threatened to destroy the national credit and a gold standard of payments, arousing first apprehension and then panic. Conservative fiscal and monetary policies and a due regard for the sanctity of contract and the rights of property would restore prosperity. Others pointed to underconsumption as an important brake on enterprise, or to overspeculation and a consequent need to purge "unsoundness" from the economy. Some pointed to the operation of inscrutable economic laws that dictated periodic depression. Not a few blamed government extravagance for a loss of confidence in the national credit. Each remedy proposed flowed from the diagnosis of the illness.[2]

The scholarly literature produced sharp differences of interpretation. *Causes of the Panic of 1893* by William Jett Lauck, published in 1907, was the earliest extensive attempt to consider the origins of the crisis. Lauck's book, a model of illogic and misconstrued evidence, reflected the simplistic approach characteristic of many who had experienced the event. He described conditions of depression in the countries with which the United States had closest commercial ties, but he concluded that foreign conditions were essentially sound; thus, the sources of trouble must be found in this country. There followed a familiar story. Inflationist agitation and the passage of the Sherman Silver Purchase Act in 1890 had combined to produce widespread fear that the nation would be forced off the gold standard. There was a run on the Treasury to obtain specie, and as Treasury reserves fell, apprehension mounted and culminated in panic. If Lauck's argument was oversimplified and incorrect, it nevertheless accorded with prevailing financial theories and was enshrined as the standard explanation of the crisis.[3]

In time other views came to light as students probed more perceptively into the antecedents of the contraction of the 1890s. Expanding a work originally published in 1896, *New York Times* financial columnist Alexander Dana Noyes offered in 1906 a more balanced account in his *Forty Years of American Finance*. Still viewing fears of "the undermining of the Treasury" and of the gold standard as primary, Noyes added a European depression, unhealthy speculation, and agrarian distress as factors in the downturn. Frank Paul Weberg's careful *Background of the Panic of 1893*, which appeared twenty years later, confirmed and elaborated Noyes's findings. Weberg showed that European depression had helped precipitate contraction in this country by curtailing overseas markets for American produce and by deflating securities prices as foreigners repatriated holdings of American shares. Assigning labor strife some blame for the panic, he also noted excessive public expenditures. High spending after the McKinley tariff had impaired customs receipts, caused federal deficits, and compounded the threat that declining confidence posed for the Treasury's gold reserve.[4]

In his 1932 biography of Grover Cleveland, Allan Nevins offered a few paragraphs to explain the downturn of 1893. Government extravagance, erratic fiscal practices during the post–Civil War era, and "the operation of the economic cycle" were identified as underlying deflationary forces. Among the immediate causes of panic were businessmen's anxiety that the incoming Cleveland administration would implement 1892 campaign promises to reduce the tariff, and uneasiness "over the bad situation of many banks and railroads." Like earlier writers, Nevins concluded that the public's fears that the government would not maintain the gold standard were paramount. The Sherman silver purchase law increased the circulation of currency that the government had pledged to redeem in gold; thus gold exports, a falling Treasury reserve, and a declining proportion of gold in federal receipts all threatened a "crisis in the treasury."[5]

More recent students of the era have treated the depression with greater sophistication, although their comments have been brief, inasmuch as their works dealt with larger problems. In *Politics, Reform, and Expansion, 1890–1900* (1959) Harold Underwood Faulkner ranged beyond earlier writers in his treatment of agricultural depression as a leading deflationary influence. The reduced purchasing power of farmers had hurt the manufacturing and transportation industries; moreover, domestic economic weaknesses increased vulnerability to blows from abroad. Minimizing the role of silver and the public's fears about the gold standard, Faulkner asserted that a withdrawal of foreign capital attending European depression after 1890 was "probably the immediate cause of the crash." This withdrawal struck sharply at soft spots in the American economy—overextended railroads and industries, a weak banking system, a troubled agriculture—precipitating a massive contraction. Although more incisive than earlier accounts, Faulkner's few pages do not allow a detailed, comprehensive consideration.[6] The same is true of J. Rogers Hollingsworth's solid history of the Democratic Party at the end of the century, *The Whirligig of Politics*, and of Walter La Feber's impressive study of expansionism, *The New Empire*. Both Hollingsworth and La Feber offer abbreviated descriptions of the depression, but neither presents new material or adds to an understanding of the collapse.[7]

Although economists have paid scant attention to the depression of the 1890s, their attention to business cycles in general has produced a growing body of technical and theoretical writings. Observers were aware of the rhythmic ups and downs of business activities long before Adam Smith's *Wealth of Nations* (1776) marked the beginning of modern economics and serious attention to the phenomena. The Frenchman Clement Juglar concluded that business cycles, part of a continuum of economic development, comprised three phases—prosperity, crisis, and liquidation—which always followed in the same order. He rejected the hypothesis that panics or depressions were special, isolated events, holding instead that they could best be understood as incidents in continuous, wavelike economic fluctuations. By comparing the statistical series of commodity prices, interest rates, and bank balances with the records of business activity, Juglar sought to identify conditions characteristic of different phases of the business cycle. His *Brief History of Panics* summarized his findings for the United States. Circumstances pointing to imminent contraction typically included excessive spending for luxuries, rising prices, a proliferation of speculative ventures, and many loans and discounts, with "a very small reserve in specie."

Although Juglar's study ended with the year 1892, its contemporary translator discerned signs of impending difficulty. There was an ominous increase in money supply against declining Treasury reserves, as the Sherman Silver Purchase Act obliged both extensive government silver purchases and commensurate issues of new Treasury notes. Furthermore, the incoming Democratic administration threatened to disturb markets and business conditions by fulfilling a campaign promise to reduce tariffs.[8]

The founding of the National Bureau of Economic Research (NBER) in the 1920s afforded Juglar's increasingly popular approach an institutional basis. The NBER immediately began collecting quantitative data and business annals on which to base systematic analyses of economic fluctuations. Concurrently, staff economists refined the definition of business cycles and began publishing a growing body of monographs and statistics that represented important advances in understanding and research possibilities. The NBER treated business cycles as the aggregate or consensus of numerous specific cycles of economic activity, as revealed in statistical series. They were recurrent, roughly synchronous expansions and contractions of many activities; some series ordinarily led, some lagged, and others ran counter to the aggregate movement. Careful examination of the relation of the parts to the whole and of the interaction, timing, duration, and amplitude of changes in different sectors of the economy could help separate cause from effect and permit a comprehensive understanding of economic fluctuations.[9]

The NBER's strategy influenced Charles Hoffmann's 1954 Columbia doctoral dissertation, "The Depression of the Nineties: An Economic History," and an extended summary article published in 1956. Hoffmann attributed the downturn to the interaction of many factors. Numerous indices of economic activity had been falling long before panic struck in 1893; among these were general investment and building construction. The repatriation of American securities, owing to European depression, dampened investment further. Consumption fell with investment. Bank reserves contracted in the fall of 1892, when a counterseasonal outflow of gold—at a time when crop exports ordinarily produced specie imports—forced many financial institutions to settle their balances or seek gold from the Treasury. Falling reserves led to a tightening of credit. Although he considered uneasiness concerning the safety of the gold reserve and the gold standard also important, Hoffmann emphasized a great transformation of the economy.

Agricultural depression, growing out of overproduction and excessive dependence on sales in a glutted world market, was a profoundly deflationary force. It spelled a restricted market for domestic manufacturers, curtailed railroad earnings, and limited earnings of foreign exchange as farmers, forced to dump surplus produce in sated markets for low prices, suffered a consequent loss of purchasing power. However, the continued expansion of mining and manufacturing during the depression pointed toward an improvement in conditions. Low costs and efficient operations permitted American manufacturers to compete even in protected European markets before the end of the decade. Moreover, as markets abroad were not glutted, manufactures could be sold on advantageous terms there. In turn, as their share in the country's exports increased relative to farm produce and thus improved the terms on which American output was sold abroad, manufactures helped place the economy on a more solid footing.

Although Hoffmann's findings have been indispensable for later students, his study is incomplete. It is largely descriptive and at times eschews interpretation, allowing the information to speak for itself. Nor does Hoffmann fully explain changes or the origins of crisis and recovery.[10]

Joseph A. Schumpeter's monumental 1939 theoretical study of business cycles reflects briefly but importantly on the depression of the 1890s, from another perspective. Schumpeter believed that innovation is primarily responsible for business cycles. Innovation in industrial organization, product development, or the application of science and technology creates new opportunities and novel conditions of competition. In time an innovation is exploited to its limits, and the new conditions it has established require extensive adjustments; enterprises unable to adapt may fail. For Schumpeter the innovation that had dominated the long half-century ending about 1890 was the railroad. A fall-off in railroad expansion slowed investment and thus dampened the economy. Agricultural difficulties and fears for the security of the gold standard were cited as additional depressive factors.[11]

Subsequent writers subjected Schumpeter's findings to close scrutiny. Rendigs Fels's *American Business Cycles, 1865–1897* is a penetrating analysis of the nature, direction, and amplitude of economic fluctuations, one that eclectically summarizes available materials and fuses elements of several views.[12] Milton Friedman and Anna Jacobson Schwartz, in their provocative monetary history of the United States since the Civil War, examine monetary factors as they related to the crisis of the 1890s. Augmenting fears for the gold standard as depressing influences were the impact of European depression and the rate of growth of the nation's money stock. By forcing price reductions, European contraction during the early years of the decade enabled foreign manufacturers to compete successfully in this country. Thus imports rose and gold flowed out; if the United States was to remain on a gold standard of payments, deflation was requisite to make American enterprise more competitive and thereby cut merchandise imports and specie shipments. Furthermore, since the Civil War the money stock had grown too slowly to meet the needs of a rapidly expanding economy, exacerbating deflationary tendencies and contributing to depression.[13]

In contrast to the differing views on the depression, considerable harmony reigned as to the sources of recovery during and after 1897. Most political observers agreed that the Republicans' election triumphs in 1896 produced stability, promised enactment of a tariff satisfactory to American industry, and secured the gold standard, encouraging a renewal of business confidence. Returning prosperity in Europe restored foreign markets for this country's produce. Rising gold output in South Africa, Alaska, and elsewhere ostensibly promoted a rapid increase in the money stock and a consequent advance in prices. The continued rapid growth of manufacturing was another expansive force. Finally, the coincidence of disastrous crop failures abroad with bumper crops in this country improved the fortunes of American farmers and stimulated railroad and industrial earnings, investment, and business in general.[14]

The qualities evident in even a brief review of the literature, including disagreement, differing emphases, and brevity of treatment, reinforce Hollingsworth's observation that "there is no adequate account of the causes of the depression of 1893–1897" or, by implication, of the crisis itself.[15] One goal of this study is to fill that gap.

Looming beyond the contraction of the 1890s is the larger question of its place and significance in American history. The perception that the depression years were a climactic turning point dates from the era itself. In July 1893 the young Wisconsin historian Frederick Jackson Turner read to a convention of his colleagues in Chicago his momentous paper on the significance of the frontier in American history. He finished with the pregnant observation that the passing of the frontier during the preceding decade had "closed the first period of American history." Turner's remarks articulated a sense of profound change that was widespread among his contemporaries.[16] Continued economic and social stress confirmed their perceptions and made it abundantly clear that the 1890s were indeed a fundamental divide.

Rapid change, an intense sense of mission, a tendency to reject Europe and a corollary tendency to think of the United States as unique, and the conviction that this country was singularly free have often led Americans to minimize the continuities and perhaps to exaggerate the discontinuities in their history.[17] Nonetheless, contemporary historians agreed that the final years of the nineteenth century marked the watershed of the nation's development. The more perceptive of the many studies of the 1890s acknowledge the depression's vital, if not altogether clear, role in shaping that great divide.

A complete statement of the thesis that the 1890s constituted the major transition in American history appeared in Henry Steele Commager's suggestive *American Mind*, published in 1950:

The decade of the nineties is the watershed of American history. As with all watersheds the topography is blurred, but in the perspective of half a century the grand outlines emerge clearly. On the one side lies an America predominantly agricultural; concerned with domestic problems; conforming, intellectually at least, to the political, economic and moral principles inherited from the seventeenth and eighteenth centuries—an America still in the making, physically and socially; an America on the whole self-confident, self-contained, self-reliant, and conscious of its unique character and of a unique destiny. On the other side lies the modern America, predominantly urban and industrial; inextricably involved in world economy and politics, troubled with the problems that had long been thought peculiar to the Old World; experiencing profound changes in population, social institutions, economy, and technology; and trying to accommodate its traditional institutions and habits of thought to conditions new and in part alien.[18]

Accommodation had been the essence of American history to that time. Until the last decade of the nineteenth century, however, adjustment had taken place in a reasonably stable social, economic, and moral framework in which the fundamental principles of democracy and the institutions of property, family, school, church, and state, while altered, were not seriously challenged. As the century closed, though, the pattern was distorted. The rhythm of change became erratic and more rapid. The old issues dividing North from South receded. The last frontier was settled. The city, riding the crest of industrialization, emerged as a new center of political power. The modern labor movement was born amid continuing conflict. Industrial growth and economic consolidation produced new conditions and problems; the Interstate Commerce Act in 1887 and the Sherman Antitrust Act passed three years later were tentative steps in the creation of a modern interventionist state. The close of the century ended an era. An American of the late 1890s would be more at home in the 1930s than a century earlier. The principal issues in the nineteenth century's final decade persisted at the end of the next century: the clash of isolationism and internationalism, rivalry between the ideals of laissez-faire and government planning, the contrasts between progress and poverty, the need to humanize urban life—whose ills took the name inner-city decay—and to protect the rights of individuals, conflict between those who needed public aid and those who would deny it, contention over use and abuse of natural resources, and ignorance of the causes and cures of economic depressions.

Significantly, the changes Commager noted occurred against a backdrop "of economic disorder, panic, and depression." Hard times pressed remorselessly, accelerating the pace of development, exacerbating adjustment, making more urgent the discovery of solutions to difficulties accompanying the contemporary transformation of the nation. Commager had little else to say on the impact of commercial prostration, though, and it remained unclear exactly how sharply and in precisely what ways it had shaped American life.[19]

Commager's theme was subsequently elaborated and qualified in such books as Faulkner's *Politics, Reform, and Expansion, 1890–1900*. Conceding that no sharp line separated the 1890s from the previous decade or from the twentieth century, Faulkner emphasized that the changes consummated during the 1890s had been long in the making and triggered an important psychological reaction during the final years of the century. It "was in the nineties that Americans first became acutely conscious of the significance of these changes," with important consequences for their thought and behavior. Remarkably, the people did not despair during these "years dominated by depression and political controversy."[20] Other students of American thought and letters, including Ralph Henry Gabriel, Alfred Kazin, and Merle E. Curti, had previously offered comparable observations about the transition of the 1890s.[21] Samuel S. Rezneck, in a learned article on the social impact of the depression, concurred that the contraction marked a turning point in popular attitudes. Rezneck concluded his essay by

quoting from an 1897 year's-end review of business in *Iron Age*, that hard times
had brought to a close the era of "happy-go-lucky methods of buying and selling
. . . and blind confidence that the future was an inexhaustible fund against which
we could draw in the way of constant multiplication of machinery and factories."[22]

Although writers agreed that the depression of the 1890s was an important
element in contemporary social, economic, and intellectual change, their studies
provided little more than a beginning toward understanding the full impact of
the collapse on national life and thought. Most treatments saw that the era
brought deep shock, intensified problems of adjustment to an emerging industrial
and urban order, or served as a setting for the social and economic transition
so widely acknowledged. There was, however, almost no attempt to trace and
discuss comprehensively the social and intellectual ramifications of hard times
or to show precisely how these affected the transformation reshaping the country.

It has long been recognized that the business contraction of the 1890s was an
occasion for far-reaching economic developments, although treatments have
tended toward the partial or specialized. Otto C. Lightner hinted at important
economic changes, recording in *History of Business Depressions* (1922) that
"the depression . . . was extremely severe on account of our large and growing
industrial population, causing greater loss and more suffering than ever before
in the history of the country."[23] Marxist Algie Martin Simons's classic *Social
Forces in American History* had, ten years earlier, pointed briefly to even more
significant effects. The depression had inaugurated a new phase in American
business history, Simons contended. Curtailed markets threatened even more
ruinous competition than in good times; thus, "the profit seekers decided to
hunt in packs instead of as individuals, and the trust appeared as a dominant
figure of industry." Domestic markets glutted by excessive productive capacity
impelled manufacturers to expand into new overseas markets to restart the
wheels of enterprise.[24]

Subsequent studies enlarged on these themes and added others. The absolute
as well as relative growth of the importance of manufacturing during the depression altered the structure of the economy and, as noted above, provided an
important stimulus for a revival of prosperity.[25] The impact of the expansion
was clarified when in 1959 Alfred D. Chandler, Jr., published an essay on the
origins of big business in the United States. The falling rate of railroad construction at the opening of the 1890s had curtailed investment opportunities in
that industry. The failure during the panic of railroads, which owned one-third
of the country's trackage, delayed a diversion of capital to other enterprises, by
requiring huge sums for the "financial and administrative reorganization" of
the stricken roads and a restoration of stability in the industry. The completion
of this process by the latter years of the decade, with a return of prosperity,
afforded a ready supply of capital just as the rapidly growing manufacturing
industries were becoming attractive investments. "The sudden availability of

funds stimulated, and undoubtedly overstimulated, industrial combination.'' To the extent that the process of merger required the services of investment bankers, their influence grew.[26]

Political historians have found in the mid-1890s other events of great moment. The importance of the Populist movement, which climaxed during the depression, was firmly established by John Donald Hicks's *Populist Revolt* in 1931. For Hicks, Populism, born in farm distress and depression, served as a bridge between a vanishing agrarian society and the emerging urban-industrial nation of the twentieth century. Its legacy was an agenda of reforms to meet the problems arising from industrialization.[27]

More general treatments of American politics during the 1890s have yielded a broader picture of the depression's political impact. Thirty years after the appearance of Hicks's classic volume, Hollingsworth wrote an incisive study of the Democratic Party at the end of the nineteenth century. He showed that the business crisis was a political influence of immense importance. Cleveland's administration and party suffered a disastrous loss of popularity as numbers of voters blamed the Democrats for the panic, which had struck shortly after the installation of a new Democratic regime in 1893. Cleveland compounded his own difficulties. As president and chief of a party that was a coalition of diverse interests and regional groupings he ought to have compromised differences to preserve party strength and unity. Instead, he stubbornly opposed rising Democratic sentiment for silver inflation as a means of combatting falling prices and hard times. His leadership was inept when the times demanded astuteness. The consequences were evident as early as the 1894 congressional elections, when Democrats ''suffered one of the most severe setbacks in the nation's history.'' The upheaval had begun which was to replace a condition of relative parity between the major parties, extant for some twenty years, with Republican predominance in the election of 1896.[28] In his 1965 doctoral dissertation on depression-era political behavior in Connecticut, New Jersey, and New York, Samuel Thompson McSeveney provided additional evidence of the magnitude of the political revolution described in Hollingsworth's pages. He demonstrated conclusively that Democratic ineptness, local issues, and above all depression cut deeply into sources of Democratic support and offered the raw material for a new political equilibrium in which the Republican Party commanded the support of a clear majority of voters.[29]

A further illustration of the variety and magnitude of developments that scholars have related to the business collapse of the 1890s was La Feber's prize-winning treatment of contemporary American expansionism, *The New Empire*. La Feber asserted that the 1890s marked ''not a watershed of American history, but *the* watershed.'' The depression, closely following the reported end of the frontier, alarmed Americans. Fearful that the frontier's close spelled a loss of opportunity, many began to consider seeking surrogate overseas markets or lands. The sense of a national mission to bring American civilization to the rest of the world, as well as a Christian missionary urge, provided added impetus for expansion. Sea power and maritime commerce were cited as vital to the national welfare. Finally, commercial prostration lent a new note of urgency. Simons's 1912 observation surfaced again as La Feber showed how there spread among businessmen, sympathetic writers, and politicians the belief that the depression was in part the result of excess industrial capacity. With the domestic market inadequate and demoralized, it appeared to growing numbers that the acquisition of foreign markets was imperative if American enterprise was again to operate at capacity and prosperity was to return. Commercial conditions thus fostered a spirit of imperialism that impelled the United States to extend into "a virtually new world which ripped up the assumptions of the previous century and forced the American people to face the inexorable consequences of a lost security and a forfeited freedom of action."[30]

Carl N. Degler's sprightly *Age of the Economic Revolution, 1876–1900* is the sole example of a general survey of late-nineteenth-century America that sets the depression of the 1890s at the center of events. Although granting the course of the business crisis but brief mention, Degler showed how the disease of depression that followed the financial panic of 1893 ignited an unprecedented wave of labor strikes, pushed class antagonism to new heights, and provoked a major realignment in politics. The Populist rebellion climaxed and subsided, but the Republican Party capitalized on depression-inspired discontent to forge a new majority. The country, meanwhile, turned to adventurism overseas. A home market insufficient to restore prosperity fueled an expansionist drive for foreign markets that eventuated in war with Spain and the annexation of Hawaii in 1898.[31]

Clearly, then, a growing fund of annals, statistical indices, and literature has attested that the depression of the 1890s was a profound influence on national life. The depression served as a setting for a transformation creating an urban and industrial society, posed grave economic and social problems demanding prompt solution, sharply tested the resourcefulness of the country's leaders and people, helped reshape popular attitudes and thought, altered the political equilibrium, and changed the direction of foreign policy. It remains, however, for these disparate matters to be treated together in detail, and for one study to trace and interpret the economic history of the business contraction in the context of national development.

NOTES

1. Adams to Elizabeth Cameron, August 8, 1893, *Letters of Henry Adams (1892–1918)*, ed. Worthington Chauncey Ford (Boston: Houghton Mifflin, 1930–38), 2:31.

2. Contemporary views are treated in detail in Chapter 6.

3. William Jett Lauck, *The Causes of the Panic of 1893* (New York: Houghton Mifflin, 1907)—interestingly, economist James Laurence Laughlin, a staunch defender of the gold standard in the 1890s, headed a committee that awarded Lauck's volume a prize for excellence; Otto C. Lightner, *The History of Business Depressions* (New York:

Northeastern Press, 1922), 186–96; Frank S. Philbrick, "The Mercantile Conditions of the Crises of 1893," *University Studies* 2, no. 4 (1902).

4. Alexander Dana Noyes, *Thirty Years of American Finance* (New York: G. P. Putnam's Sons, 1896), 189; Alexander Dana Noyes, *Forty Years of American Finance* (New York: Putnam's Sons, 1906), 179–92; Frank Paul Weberg, *The Background of the Panic of 1893* (Washington, DC: Catholic University Press of America, 1929); Davis Rich Dewey, *Financial History of the United States* (New York: Longmans, Green, 1903); Oliver Mitchell Wentworth Sprague, *History of Crises under the National Banking System*, 61st Cong., 2d sess., 1910, S. Doc. 538, 153–215.

5. Allan Nevins, *Grover Cleveland: A Study in Courage* (New York: Dodd, Mead, 1932), 524–26; James A. Barnes, *John G. Carlisle: Financial Statesman* (New York: Dodd, Mead, 1931), 216–49.

6. Harold Underwood Faulkner, *Politics, Reform, and Expansion, 1890–1900* (New York: Harper, 1959), 141–43.

7. J. Rogers Hollingsworth, *The Whirligig of Politics: The Democracy of Cleveland and Bryan* (Chicago: University of Chicago Press, 1963), 10–11; Walter La Feber, *The New Empire: An Interpretation of American Expansion, 1860–1898* (Ithaca, NY: Cornell University Press, 1963), 152–55.

8. Clement Juglar, *A Brief History of Panics and Their Periodical Occurrence in the United States*, ed. and trans. De Courcy W. Thom, 4th ed. (New York: G. P. Putnam's Sons, 1916), 1–23, 144, passim.

9. See Arthur Frank Burns, "New Facts on Business Cycles," in *Business Cycle Indicators*, ed. Geoffrey H. Moore, (Princeton, NJ: Princeton University Press, 1961), 1: 13–44.

10. Greenwood Press published Hoffman's dissertation in 1970. Charles Hoffmann, *The Depression of the Nineties: An Economic History* (Westport, CT: Greenwood Press, 1970); Charles Hoffman, "The Depression of the Nineties," *Journal of Economic History* 16 (June 1956), 137–64.

11. Joseph A. Schumpeter, *Business Cycles: A Theoretical, Historical, and Statistical Analysis of the Capitalist Process* (New York: McGraw-Hill, 1939), 1:303–41, 383–97; 2:23–30, 245–50.

12. Rendigs Fels, *American Business Cycles, 1865–1897* (Chapel Hill: University of North Carolina Press, 1959), 209–19.

The literature on business cycles is itself cyclical. It comes in waves, usually growing in intensity after a stock market collapse and declining when economic conditions normalize. The market for such studies grows when the public has reason to fear a depression or recession. Most of the authors insist that a depression is imminent. Some offer techniques for determining the coming of a downturn, with the implication that successful predictions mean great earnings from shrewd stock market dealings. (Popular books on business cycles parallel writings about earthquakes—threats increase the market and therefore the number of books.)

Although scholarly books on business cycles have more substance than their popular counterparts, they increase and decrease with the same stimuli. Most of the scholarly business-cycle literature of the last twenty-five years concentrates on long waves and prediction. Few authors even mention the panic of 1893 and those that do have little to say. The following is a selected list of recent studies of business cycles and business-cycle theory: Kim Kyun, *Equilibrium Business Cycle Theory in Historical Perspective* (New York: Cambridge University Press, 1988); Eugene N. White, ed., *Crashes and*

Panics: The Lessons from History (Homewood, IL: Dow Jones-Irwin, 1990); Robert J. S. Ross and Kent C. Trachte, *Global Capitalism: The New Leviathan* (Albany: State University of New York Press, 1990); John Kenneth Galbraith, *A Short History of Financial Euphoria* (Knoxville, TN: Whittle Direct Books, 1990); Charles Poor Kindleberger, *Manias, Panics, and Crashes: A History of Financial Crises*, rev. ed. (New York: Basic Books, 1989); Angus Maddison, *Phases of Capitalist Development* (New York: Oxford University Press, 1982); Matthew Simon, *Cyclical Fluctuations and the International Capital Movements of the United States, 1865–1897* (New York: Arno Press, 1979); John Charles Soper, *The Long Swing in Historical Perspective: An Interpretive Study* (New York: Arno Press, 1978); David Glasner, *Business Cycles and Depressions: An Encyclopedia* (New York: Garland, 1997).

13. Milton Friedman and Anna Jacobson Schwartz, *A Monetary History of the United States, 1867–1960* (Princeton, NJ: Princeton University Press, 1963), 89–108.

14. Ibid., 134–48; Faulkner, *Politics*, 141–43, 260–80, passim; Fels, *American Business Cycles*, 193–203; and Gerald Taylor White, *The United States and the Problems of Recovery after 1893* (University: University of Alabama Press, 1982), 81–90.

15. Hollingsworth, *Whirligig of Politics*, note 9, 9–10.

16. Frederick Jackson Turner, *The Significance of the Frontier in American History* (Madison: State Historical Society of Wisconsin, 1894), 27. Also see La Feber, *New Empire*, 63–95; Faulkner, *Politics*, 1, 260–80, passim; and Ray Allen Billington, *America's Frontier Heritage* (New York: Holt, Rinehart & Winston, 1966), 1–22.

17. Marcus Cunnliffe, "American Watersheds," *American Quarterly* 13 (Winter 1961), 480–94.

18. Henry Steele Commager, *The American Mind: An Interpretation of Thought and Culture since the 1880s* (New Haven, CT: Yale University Press, 1950), 41.

19. Ibid., 50, 41–51, passim.

20. Faulkner, *Politics*, 1, 278, 260–80, passim.

21. Ralph Henry Gabriel, *The Course of American Democratic Thought: An Intellectual History since 1815* (New York: Ronald Press, 1940), 144–45, 187; Alfred Kazin, *On Native Ground: An Interpretation of Modern American Prose Literature* (New York: Reynal & Hitchcock, 1942), viii–ix, 52; Merle E. Curti, *The Growth of American Thought*, 2d ed. (New York: Harper & Brothers, 1951), vii–viii, 507, 527, 606, 623–25, passim.

22. Samuel S. Rezneck, "Unemployment, Unrest, and Relief in the United States during the Depression of 1893–97," *Journal of Political Economy* 61 (August 1953), 345, quoting from *Iron Age* 60 (December 23, 1897), 19.

John A. Garraty, *The New Commonwealth, 1877–1890* (New York: Harper & Row, 1968), held that industrial consolidation and the growth of farm and labor organizations, new government functions, and reformist social attitudes anticipating an interventionist state showed that the "United States became a modern nation" between 1877 and 1890 (p. 32). Yet he assigned depression in the 1890s a "frightening impact" that sped development of new social values, while rousing a conservative defense of vested interests that "delayed the application of many of these concepts for a decade or more" (p. 355)—thus granting the crisis a signal role.

23. Lightner, *History of Business Depressions*, 186–96.

24. Algie Martin Simons, *Social Forces in American History* (New York: Macmillan, 1912), 304–12.

25. Hoffmann, *Depression of the Nineties*, 113–41; White, *Recovery after 1893*, 81–90.

26. Alfred D. Chandler, Jr., "The Beginnings of 'Big Business' in American History," *Business History Review* 33 (Spring 1959), 15–16. Chandler expanded and developed his thesis within the larger framework of a general theory of business history in *Strategy and Structure: Chapters in the History of the Industrial Enterprise* (Cambridge, MA: MIT Press, 1962), *The Visible Hand: The Managerial Revolution in American Business* (Cambridge, MA: Harvard University Press, 1977), and *Scale and Scope: The Dynamics of Industrial Capitalism* (Cambridge, MA: Harvard University Press, 1990).

See also Victor S. Clark, *History of Manufactures in the United States* (New York: McGraw-Hill, 1929), 2:1–6, 3:1–14; Fritz Redlich, *The Molding of American Banking: Men and Ideas*. Part II, *1840–1910* (New York: Hafner, 1951), 359–87; Noyes, *Forty Years of American Finance*, 276–79; and Edward Gross Campbell, *Reorganization of the American Railroad System, 1893–1900* (New York: Columbia University Press, 1938), 145–85, 233, 255, 319–42.

27. John Donald Hicks, *The Populist Revolt: A History of the Farmers' Alliance and the People's Party* (Minneapolis: University of Minnesota Press, 1931), 1–35, 404–23. Also Richard Hofstadter, *The Age of Reform: From Bryan to F.D.R.* (New York: Vintage Books, 1960), 1–101. Lawrence Goodwyn, *The Populist Moment: A Short History of the Agrarian Revolt in America* (New York: Oxford University Press, 1978), recast the story of Populism as a reply to sweeping social and economic change that prompted a fundamental transformation of the country's political culture. Even so, his analysis neglected to emphasize the depression of the 1890s as a focal manifestation of contemporary economic and social change.

28. Hollingsworth, *Whirligig of Politics*, iv, 235–41, passim.

29. Samuel Thompson McSeveney, *The Politics of Depression: Political Behavior in the Northeast, 1893–1896* (New York: Oxford University Press, 1972), 222–29, passim.

30. La Feber, *New Empire*, 67, 102, passim.

31. Carl N. Degler, *The Age of the Economic Revolution, 1876–1900*, 2d ed. (Glenview, IL: Scott, Foresman, 1967), 121.

2

Prologue to Panic

Corn . . . was commonly burned . . . in lieu of coal.

—John Donald Hicks
The Populist Revolt (1931)

As the March 1893 date of his inauguration approached, Grover Cleveland likely turned for a time from the myriad tasks of selecting a cabinet and planning an administration to reflect on the nation whose presidency he was about to assume. He may well have considered the startling changes in the United States between his entry into legal practice in Buffalo, New York, on the eve of the Civil War and the imminent beginning of his second term as chief executive. Certainly those changes merited his attention, as they did the thoughtful consideration of his countrymen. They represented a reshaping of national life and the emergence of conditions that required deep-rooted economic, social, political, and intellectual adjustments. They posed far-reaching problems, some of which tested the new administration to the utmost.

Of the developments transforming the United States, none was more visible than the extending area of settlement. In 1860, the frontier defined the limits of an expanding American society. Beginning at the Gulf Coast, it stretched north through Texas at about the hundredth meridian, swung east around the Indian Territory, then bent west again to enclose the eastern portions of Kansas and Nebraska. Settlement had penetrated the Mississippi valley to the vicinity of Minneapolis, the southern third of Minnesota, and most of Wisconsin and Michigan's lower peninsula. In the Southeast only southern Florida remained vacant, and enclaves of settlement had appeared along the Pacific coast in California's gold fields, the Bay Area, and in Oregon's Willamette valley. The following three decades saw a heroic extension of the country's railroad system open vast new regions to development. By 1890 there was no longer a clearly recognizable frontier.[1] Reserves of unoccupied land remained, but a fundamental condition of American history had disappeared.

A sweeping agricultural expansion accompanied the advance of settlement. Between 1870 and 1890 the number of farms in the United States rose by nearly four-fifths, to 4,545,000, and it increased by a fourth again by the end of the century. Farm property value mounted by three-fourths, to $16.5 billion, and by the decade's close had gained by an added fourth. A shift in the centers of production of key crops attended these developments. Between 1860 and 1890 the center of wheat culture moved from the Ohio valley to the Great Plains; of corn, from the Ohio valley to Illinois, Iowa, Kansas, and Nebraska; and of cotton, from the southeast to the region reaching from the Mississippi Delta to central Texas. Yet the farms in the states of the Old Northwest still represented half the value of agricultural property in the country,[2] indicating an important regional disparity in the distribution of farm wealth and prosperity.

The patterns in agricultural growth are notable. Establishing a new empire of wheat and corn in the Midwest and cotton to the south and southwest proved difficult; new arrivals to the plains often continued raising corn and hogs, despite a climate that dictated wheat and other more suitable crops. Even though low capital requirements made for ease of entry into farming, there was no escaping a minimum investment before commencing operations. The cost of settling a new western farm often ran from five hundred to a thousand dollars or more. Many cash-short pioneers were obliged to borrow against the croplands they were purchasing to obtain needed capital. In the South, debt rose similarly. Cramped circumstances forced rising numbers of farmers into tenancy, share cropping, and borrowing against future crops. By 1900, non-owners operated nearly half of all Southern farms.

Unfortunately, the extent of agrarian debt was unknown. Even the census disregarded outstanding debt until 1890, and for thirty-five years thereafter only the obligations of owner-operated farms were compiled. Nevertheless, it was clear that the advancing checkerboard of tilled fields in the nation's heart represented a vast indebtedness. One contemporary observer estimated 2.3 million farm mortgages nationwide in 1890, worth over $2.2 billion.[3] Kansas croplands were mortgaged to 45 percent of their true value, those in South Dakota to 46 percent, in Minnesota to 44, in Montana 41, and in Colorado 34 percent. Debt covered a comparable proportion of all farmlands in those states. Although some borrowing was speculative, most of it represented productive purchases of land, supplies, and other necessities. Interest rates had fallen by perhaps half since 1870, but in western Kansas they still ran to 8 or 9 percent twenty years later. Under favorable conditions the millions of dollars of annual charges on farm

mortgages could be borne, but when circumstances deteriorated, charges, foreclosures, and tax sales were catastrophic.[4]

Railroads opened new areas to agriculture, linking these to rapidly changing
national and international markets. Mechanization, the development of improved
crops, and the introduction of new techniques increased productivity and fueled
a rapid expansion of farming operations. The output of staples skyrocketed.
Yields of wheat, corn, and cotton doubled between 1870 and 1890 though the
nation's population rose by only two-thirds. Grain and fiber flooded the domestic
market. Moreover, competition in world markets was fierce: Egypt and India
emerged as rival sources of cotton; other areas poured out a growing stream of
cereals. Farmers in the United States read the disappointing results in falling
prices. Over 1870–73, corn and wheat averaged $0.463 and $1.174 per bushel
and cotton $0.152 per pound; twenty years later they brought but $0.412 and
$0.707 a bushel and $0.078 a pound. In 1889 corn fell to ten cents in Kansas,
about half the estimated cost of production. At such tragic lows, ''corn . . . was
commonly burned . . . in lieu of coal'' by grimly despairing farmers who could
ill afford to ship their harvests to market.[5] Even burning the grain proved a
luxury. Needing cash to meet debts, agrarians sought income by increasing their
output of those crops whose overproduction had already demoralized prices and
cut farm receipts. The farmers were trapped by debt and market glut.

Bound up with these developments on the farm and in the markets was an
unparalleled expansion of the country's transportation system. Railroads took
the lead. During the generation preceding Cleveland's second presidency, paired
bands of iron rails crossed and recrossed the continent, linking coast to coast in
1869, striking through the heart of the midwestern grasslands, penetrating the
remote fastness of the Rockies, Cascades, and the Sierra, and stretching across
the scorched deserts of the Southwest. Mileage rose from about 30,000 to
160,000; annual freight tonnage increased from less than 70 million to 591
million and passengers carried from fewer than 100 million to 520 million.
Running at speeds up to twenty-five miles per hour, the crude steam locomotives
of 1890 could pull three hundred tons of freight loaded in light wooden cars.
In contrast, two-horse teams could draw wagons loaded with a ton and a half
of freight twelve miles a day over traces through the countryside.[6]

Inexpensive, speedy rail transportation revolutionized commerce and with the
telegraph created a national market. The completion of competing lines, rapid
advances in equipment, and improved management effected a steady reduction
of rates. By 1890 the railroads dominated transport; inland water transit was
nearly obsolete, save on the Great Lakes and a few other waterways. Rail transportation offered savings on the cost of shipping goods by roads and waterways
of perhaps $560 million, or between 4 and 5 percent of gross national product.[7]
Moreover, railroad construction was an important spur to economic growth.
Expansion peaked in the late 1880s, but the roads provided insatiable markets
for coal and such manufactures as iron, steel, and rolling stock. Communications
developed apace with the rail net. In 1892 the giant of the telegraph industry,

Western Union, dispatched 62.4 million messages through twenty-one thousand offices. With seven times the business of its nearest competitor, Western Union earned profits that year of $7 million on gross revenues of about three times as much. Pointing to the future, the American Bell Telephone Company in 1892 already embraced 788 exchanges and 266,000 miles of line, and employed over eight thousand persons.[8]

The post–Civil War generation saw an enormous growth of manufacturing. Industrial output rose by some 296 percent, reaching in 1890 a value of almost $9.4 billion. In that year the nation's 350,000 industrial firms employed nearly 4,750,000 workers. Iron and steel paced the progress of manufacturing. Farm and forest continued to provide raw materials for such established enterprises as cotton textiles, food, and lumber production. Heralding the machine age, however, was the growing importance of extractives—raw materials for a lengthening list of consumer goods and for producing and fueling locomotives, railroad cars, industrial machinery and equipment, farm implements, and electrical equipment for commerce and industry. The swift expansion and diversification of manufacturing allowed a growing independence from European imports, and it was reflected in the prominence of new goods among this country's exports. Already the value of American manufactures was more than half the value of European manufactures and twice that of Britain's.[9]

The quick progress of railroads and manufacturing entailed significant structural changes in the economy. One measure of these lay in the shifting importance of agriculture, industry, and the railroads: all three areas were expanding, but at different rates. Since the 1860s farm property values had increased a bit more than 100 percent, from $7.98 billion to $16.44 billion. In the same period, capital invested in railroads rose from $1.15 billion to $10.02 billion, or about 870 percent. Meanwhile, the book value of manufacturing capital more than doubled, to $5.7 billion, during the 1880s. Agricultural property had constituted an overwhelming share of the national wealth a generation earlier; from 1870 to 1890 its share fell from 30 to 20 percent. At the opening of the 1890s, railroad and industrial property values together equaled those of agriculture; moreover, manufacturing for the first time accounted for a larger proportion of the national income than farming.[10]

Post–Civil War commerce in beef exemplifies the vital changes in the United States that culminated in the 1890s. East Coast urban population growth, diminishing local pastures, and railroad connections with the old Northwest fueled a thriving market for Western beef. Ranchers fattened cattle on Western public domain, herded the livestock to rail yards, and shipped it to abattoirs in the East. Gustavus F. Swift revolutionized the market by slaughtering cattle in Chicago and shipping dressed beef to Eastern markets—only 40 percent of the steer was dressed beef. Beyond reduced shipping expense, Swift, Armour, Morris, Wilson, Hammond, Cudahy, and Swartszchild and Sulzsburger capitalized on the economies of scale in by-products occasioned by centralized slaughtering.

Emerging refrigeration technology underlay the development and concentration of the dressed beef industry. The railroads' refusal to invest in refrigerator cars concentrated control of dressed beef shipments to a few firms able to finance specially designed railcars, branch plants, and storage depots refrigerated with ice harvested, stored, and shipped along the right-of-way between Chicago and East Coast markets. Although ice remained the essential cooling material well into the twentieth century, by the 1890s the natural product was being displaced by ice manufactured in steam-powered factories.

Western ranching to feed Eastern markets changed concomitantly with the shift from livestock to dressed beef shipments. The calamitous losses the open-range cattle industry suffered in the winter of 1886–87 when thousands of cattle died in blizzards, accelerated the decline in what was already a faltering industry. The market for grass-fed beef gave way to a demand for better cuts from care-fully husbanded, blooded cattle. Consumers, aware of a glutted market for cattle, stable or rising beef prices, and collusion among the interstate meat shippers, demanded prosecution of packers under antimonopoly legislation; consumers were unwilling to acknowledge that the market surplus was in grass-fed beef, for which there was little demand. Packers' success at pooling (the Allerton pool and Veeder pools) encouraged them to collude more efficiently by merging. The panic of 1893 frustrated the merger and led to the founding of National Packing Company, a firm owned in concert by the large packers and used as a device to justify regular meetings to divide markets. National was eventually dissolved under pressure from the U.S. Department of Justice Antitrust Division, but in-vestigations and prosecutions of the packers begun in the 1890s and extending well into the next century never led to convictions or the dissolution of the oligopoly in interstate meat packing.[11]

After general laws of incorporation were introduced in the United States in the late 1830s, the dominant form of business enterprise changed from the in-dividually owned firm or partnership to the corporation.[12] Vast capital needs placed railroads in the fore of the shift. Manufacturing changed more slowly; despite technological innovation and mechanization, capital requirements elim-inated all but a comparatively few wealthy persons. Limited liability was prob-ably the chief incentive for incorporating industrial firms: stockholders were responsible for corporate obligations only to the amount of their investments. Capitalizing on high-speed telegraphic communications, modern securities ex-changes and investment banking developed to serve the financial needs of the new corporations. Their financial expertise and control of credit placed bankers in a strategic position. After the Civil War, financial institutions progressed from advancing loans to planning and underwriting securities issues. Their interest soon extended beyond appraising the credit of client businesses to include man-aging the funds they had made available. Bankers began to penetrate corporate boards of directors, a tie that was strengthened as corporations redeposited funds in the banks. Before 1895 investment bankers had concentrated their attention on railroads; during the 1890s, they turned increasingly to industry as well.[13]

Consolidation and combination were implicit in industrialization and the rise of corporations. Mechanization and new processes boosted productivity at the same time that large fixed investments demanded increased sales. Growing output, intensifying competition, and falling prices threatened the market positions of rival corporate giants. Innovative managers sought to contain competition through informal agreements, pools, merger with or acquisition of competing firms, and trusts. Often, interested investment bankers led efforts to replace contention with cooperation and interlocking holdings. Unfortunately, combination offered unscrupulous schemers speculative profits on watered stock sold to unsuspecting investors.[14]

Nowhere was consolidation more rampant than in the railroad industry. As early as the mid-1870s roads had begun to enter pooling agreements. Within a few years fragile, force-draft agreements covered the entire country. In the meantime hundreds of roads were leased or absorbed into giant systems. By the early 1890s the Pennsylvania, Reading, Santa Fé, Great Northern, and New York Central; the Union, the Southern, and the Northern Pacific; and a few others controlled thousands of miles of track and millions in capital each. The liabilities of the Santa Fe were $102 million; of the Union Pacific, $61 million; of the Northern Pacific, $86 million. Some of the indebtedness represented grossly inflated construction costs. Heavy debt saddled the roads with huge fixed charges that spurred them to combination and fierce competition while making them liable to bankruptcy if revenues fell.[15]

If large-scale enterprise was less conspicuous in manufacturing than in rail transport when the 1890s opened, it was nevertheless well under way. "Between 1887 and 1897, eighty-six corporations capitalized at one million dollars or more were organized," recorded Harold Underwood Faulkner, "forty-six of them in the years between 1890 and 1893, representing over $1.4 billion in capital." In 1896 the securities of twenty industrial concerns were listed on the New York Stock Exchange; by 1900 the number was forty-six. Among the new industrial giants were the United States Leather Company, with assets of $80 million; the National Lead Company, with $31.2 million; and the American Cotton Oil Corporation, Diamond Match, American Sugar Refining, the Chicago Gas Trust, and the Distillers' and Cattle Feeders' Trust (the last popularly called the "whisky trust"), all with at least $10 million and all oligopolistic. Procter & Gamble, General Electric, Illinois Steel, Carnegie Steel, and the Western Union Telegraph Company exemplified advancing concentration.[16]

Changing occupational patterns mirrored the transformation of the economy. As late as 1860, 60 percent of the population had agrarian ties. During the next generation the work force more than doubled, rising to 23.7 million, but the proportion engaged in farming fell by nearly a third despite a striking increase in the number employed by an expanding agriculture. In 1890 the professions and services engaged 3.2 million Americans, or 13.6 percent of those gainfully employed, a slightly smaller share than thirty years earlier. Simultaneously the combined employment in transportation and in trade and finance had just about doubled to 15 percent of those employed—to 1.5 million and 2 million, respectively. Employment in manufacturing and hand trades grew by perhaps one-sixth, to 4.8 million, about 20 percent of the labor force. Mining, forest, and fishing occupations made varying gains.

Although real wages had risen since the Civil War, compensation remained distressingly low, and working conditions were dismal. Average annual earnings for industrial laborers in 1890 was $439, and the sixty-hour workweek was the rule. The cost of living was low, but labor lived close to subsistence. In 1890 America, two hundred thousand citizens controlled 70 percent of the national wealth. Weak bargaining power separated the individual workingman from concentrated business capital. Employers fiercely resisted workers' efforts to organize, and violent strikes punctuated late-nineteenth-century management-labor relations.[17]

The three decades of economic development preceding Cleveland's second administration wrought vast social changes. Cities had emerged as centers of population, culture, commercial and political power, and national life. Of the sixty-three million Americans in 1890, 35 percent lived in communities of 2,500 or more; a generation earlier, only 20 percent of the population had lived in communities of that size. New York, Chicago, and Philadelphia teemed with over a million inhabitants each. Finance, trade, transportation, and manufacturing had attracted large numbers from the countryside, and foreign immigrants swelled their ranks. Minneapolis, St. Louis, Baltimore, San Francisco, New Orleans, Boston, and population centers in the Ohio valley boasted over a hundred thousand citizens.[18]

Already modern America was evident in the sprawl of suburbs outside city centers, the spread of ugly tenements and slums, the rush of traffic in trading districts, acrid clouds of smoke in industrial areas, and a maze of electrical wiring overhead. Horse-drawn vehicles and surface and elevated steam commuter trains in the cities were yielding to electric trolleys. Corrupt officials and inadequate municipal services, combined with the conditions of industrial life, provoked a growing clamor for reform. The advent of depression in the mid-1890s exacerbated the stress of urban life.[19]

In January 1893 the nation's most respected business journal, New York's *Commercial and Financial Chronicle*, published its customary review of trade in the year just closed:

If we were to gather the consensus of the whole business community, the result obtained would not support the idea that this has been a conspicuously prosperous year. Consumption of almost every article of merchandise has been large and the cotton goods industry has probably thrived beyond any other; the grocery trade has likewise enjoyed a good share of activity with fairly remunerative prices ruling. On the other hand, large and important departments of business and sections of the country have shared to very small degree in the better conditions as to profitableness, while there has been almost everywhere an absence of buoyancy and an entire unwillingness to invest in undertakings at all venturesome. Stated in brief, we have apparently been in the midst of prosperous conditions, and yet as a people without achieving prosperity.

The *Commercial and Financial Chronicle* decried the disturbing influence of the recent presidential campaign, predicting that Congress would in the current session pass unwise legislation. Despite deepening worldwide recession, conferees at Brussels, Belgium, had recently failed to secure an international bimetallic monetary agreement that would have moderated the effects of inflation. A fall in railroad earnings, reduced exports of produce, and a substantial outflow of specie to Europe further depressed U.S. stock prices. Nevertheless, the *Commercial and Financial Chronicle* reflected prevailing opinion when it expressed cautious hope for the new year. A "review of business . . . during the past year . . . [was] decidedly encouraging and calculated to stimulate the belief in a rapid growth and development of industrial enterprise and general resources."[20]

Economic indicators signaling a business recession in the United States were largely obscured. Trade had ostensibly improved during the past year. Business failures had declined, and the average liabilities of failed firms had fallen by 40 percent. The country's position in international commerce was improved. During the late nineteenth century the United States had had an unfavorable net balance of payments; passenger and cargo fares paid to foreign ships that carried most American overseas commerce, insurance charges, tourists' expenditures abroad, and returns to foreign investors ordinarily more than offset the effect of a favorable merchandise balance. In 1892, however, improved agricultural exports had reduced the previous year's net unfavorable balance from $89 million to $20 million.[21] Moreover, output of non-agricultural consumer goods had risen by more than 5 percent, and business firms were believed to have an ample backlog of unfilled orders as 1893 opened.[22] Clearings—the settlement of cheques and accounts—among banks outside New York, factory employment, wholesale prices, and railroad freight ton-mileage advanced through the early months of the new year.[23]

Yet several monthly series of indicators showed that business was falling off. Building construction had peaked in April 1892, later moving irregularly downward, probably in reaction to overbuilding. The decline continued until the turn of the century, when construction volume finally turned up again.[24] Weakness in building was transmitted to the rest of the economy, dampening general activity through restricted investment opportunities and curtailed demand for construction materials. Meanwhile, a similar uneven downward drift in business activity after spring 1892 was evident from a composite index of cotton takings and raw silk consumption, rubber imports, tin and tin plate imports, pig iron manufactures, bituminous and anthracite coal production, crude oil output, railroad freight ton-mileage, and foreign trade volume.[25] Pig iron production had crested in February, followed by stock prices and business incorporations six months later.[26] These developments, too, were in part a reaction to a characteristically overenthusiastic expansion of activity during the most recent economic upswing.

The economy exhibited other weaknesses as Grover Cleveland's 1893 inauguration drew near. One of the most serious was agricultural depression. Storm, drought, and overproduction during the preceding half-dozen years had reversed the remarkable agricultural prosperity and expansion of the early 1880s in the wheat, corn, and cotton belts. Wheat prices tumbled twenty cents in 1892. Corn held steady, but at a low figure and on a fall of one-eighth in output. Twice as great a decline in production dealt a severe blow to the hopes of cotton growers: the season's short crop cancelled gains anticipated from a recovery of one cent in prices, to 8.3 cents, close to the average level of recent years. Midwestern and Southern farming regions seethed with discontent as growers watched staple prices fall by as much as two-thirds after 1870 and all farm prices by two-fifths; meanwhile, the general wholesale index fell by one-fourth. The situation was grave. Farmers' terms of trade had worsened, and dollar debts willingly incurred in good times to permit agricultural expansion were becoming unbearable burdens. Debt payments and low prices restricted agrarian purchasing power and demand for goods and services. Significantly, both output and consumption of farm equipment began to fall as early as 1891, marking a decline in agricultural investment. Moreover, foreclosure of farm mortgages impaired the liquidity of mortgage companies, banks, and other lenders.[27]

Slowing investment in railroads was an additional deflationary influence. Railroad expansion had long been a potent engine of economic growth. "During the years 1870 through 1890 gross capital expenditures by the railroads amounted on the average to from 15 to 20 percent of those of the entire nation," according to an authority on the subject.[28] Construction was a rough index of railroad investment. The amount of new track laid yearly peaked at 12,984 miles in 1887, after which it fell off steeply. Capital outlays rose through 1891 to provide needed additions to plants and equipment, but the rate of growth could not be sustained. Unsatisfactory earnings and a low return for investors indicated that the system was overbuilt and overcapitalized, and reports of mismanagement were common. In 1892, only 44 percent of rail shares outstanding returned dividends, although twice that proportion of bonds paid interest. In the meantime, the completion of trunk lines dried up local capital sources. Political antagonism toward railroads, spurred by the roads' immense size and power and by real and imagined discrimination against small shippers, made the industry less attractive to investors. Declining growth reduced investment opportunity even as rail securities became less appealing. Capital outlays fell in 1892 despite easy credit during much of the year. The markets for ancillary industries, like iron and steel, felt the impact of falling railroad investment as well; at times in the 1880s, rails had accounted for 90 percent of the country's rolled steel output. In an industry whose expansion had long played a vital role in creating new markets for suppliers, lagging capital expenditures loomed large in the onset of depression.[29]

European depression was a further source of weakness as 1893 began. Recession struck France in 1889, and business slackened in Germany and England the following year. Contemporaries dated the English downturn from a financial panic in November. Monetary stringency; the collapse of extensive speculations in Australian, South African, and Argentine properties; and a sharp break in securities prices marked the advent of severe contraction. The great banking house of Baring and Brothers, caught with excessive holdings of Argentine securities in a falling market, shocked the financial world by suspending business on November 20. Within a year of the crisis, commercial stagnation had settled over most of Europe.[30] The contraction was severe and long-lived. In England many indices fell to 80 percent of capacity; wholesale prices overall declined nearly 6 percent in two years and had declined 15 percent by 1894. An index of the prices of principal industrial products declined by almost as much. In Germany, depression lasted three times as long as the average for the period 1879–1902. Not until mid-1895 did Europe begin to revive. Full prosperity returned a year or more later.[31]

Panic in the United Kingdom and falling trade in Europe brought serious repercussions in the United States. The immediate result was near panic in New York City, the nation's financial center, as British investors repatriated American securities to obtain funds. Uneasiness spread through the country, fostered by falling stock prices, financial stringency, and an increase in business failures. Liabilities of failed firms during the last quarter of the year were $90 million— twice those in the preceding quarter. Only the normal year's-end grain exports, destined largely for England, averted a gold outflow.

Circumstances moderated during the early months of 1891, although gold flowed to Europe and business failures remained high. Credit eased, if slowly: in response to pleas for relief, the federal treasury began the premature redemption of government bonds to put additional money into circulation, and the end of the harvest trade reduced demand for credit. Commerce quickened in the spring. Perhaps anticipation of brisk trade during the harvest season stimulated the revival of investment and business; in any event, the harvest of 1891 was of signal import. A bumper American wheat crop coincided with poor yields in Europe to increase substantially exports and the inflow of specie: U.S. exports in fiscal 1892 were $150 million greater than in the preceding year, a full 1 percent of gross national product. The improved market for American crops was primarily responsible for a brief cycle of prosperity in the United States, which Europe did not share. Business thrived until signs of recession began to appear in 1892 and early 1893. Even in those years, however, the economy was operating 5 to 10 percent below the capacity revealed by peaks of employment in 1895 and 1899.[32]

NOTES

1. U.S. Bureau of the Census, *Eleventh Census of the United States: 1890, Population* (Washington, DC: Government Printing Office, 1895–1897), 1:xxiv–xxxiv.

2. U.S. Bureau of the Census, *Compendium of the Eleventh Census, 1890* (Washington, DC: Government Printing Office, 1897), 3:589–621; Charles O. Paullin, *Atlas of the Historical Geography of the United States* (Baltimore: Carnegie Institution of Washington and American Geographical Society of New York, 1932), plates 142, 143.

3. Edward Atkinson, "The True Meaning of Farm-Mortgage Statistics," *Forum* 17 (May 1894), 310–25.

4. *Eleventh Census, Report on Farms and Homes* 13:1–16, 55–134; Allan G. Bogue, *Money at Interest: The Farm Mortgage on the Middle Border* (Ithaca, NY: Cornell University Press, 1955), 2–4, 268–72, passim; Fred Albert Shannon, *The Farmer's Last Frontier: Agriculture, 1860–1897* (New York: Holt, Rinehart & Winston, 1945), 184–85; Gilbert C. Fite, *The Farmers' Frontier, 1865–1890* (New York: Holt, Rinehart & Winston, 1966), 42–48, 216–18; J. Rogers Hollingsworth, "Commentary. Populism: The Problem of Rhetoric and Reality," *Agricultural History* 39, no. 2 (April 1965), 81–85. For the South, Alex Mathews Arnett, *The Populist Movement in Georgia* (New York: Columbia University, 1922), 57–58; and C. Vann Woodward, *Origins of the New South, 1877–1913* (Baton Rouge: Louisiana State University Press, 1951), 180–84. The average western farm debt was about $1,200. Also see Jeffrey Ostler, *Prairie Populism: The Fate of Agrarian Radicalism in Kansas, Nebraska, and Iowa, 1880–1892* (Lawrence: University Press of Kansas, 1993); Thomas W. Riddle, *The Old Radicalism: John R. Rogers and the Populist Movement in Washington* (New York: Garland, 1991); Scott G. McNall, *The Road to Rebellion: Class Formation and Kansas Populism, 1865–1900* (Chicago: University of Chicago Press, 1988); Donna Barnes, *Farmers In Rebellion: The Rise and Fall of the Southern Farmers Alliance and People's Party in Texas* (Austin: University of Texas Press, 1985); Barton C. Shaw, *The Wool-Hat Boys: A History of the Populist Party in Georgia* (Baton Rouge: Louisiana State University Press, 1984); Robert W. Cherny, *Populism, Progressivism, and the Transformation of Nebraska Politics, 1885–1915* (Lincoln: University of Nebraska Press for the Center for Great Plains Studies, University of Nebraska–Lincoln, 1980); Robert Klepper, *The Economic Bases for Agrarian Protest Movements in the United States, 1870–1900* (New York: Arno Press, 1978); Philip Roy Muller, *New South Populism: North Carolina, 1884–1900* (Chapel Hill: n.p., 1971, 1972); Karel D. Bicha, *Western Populism: Studies in an Ambivalent Conservatism* (Lawrence, KS: Coronado Press, 1976); William Du Bose Sheldon, *Populism in the Old Dominion: Virginia Farm Politics, 1885–1900* (Gloucester, MA: Peter Smith, 1935, 1967); John Bunyan Clark, *Populism in Alabama* (Auburn, AL: Auburn Printing Company, 1927).

5. Three-year average crop prices were calculated from farmers' estimates of the average price, minus commissions and charges, for the season's sales (the season begins on December 1 of each crop year). Prices were lower in local markets immediately after harvests. See U.S. Bureau of the Census, *Historical Statistics of the United States, Colonial Times to 1957* (Washington, DC: Government Printing Office, 1960), 274, 297, 301, 302. Quote from Hicks, *Populist Revolt*, 56. Hicks estimated the cost of producing wheat at forty-two to forty-eight cents, corn at twenty-one cents, and cotton at seven to eight cents.

6. *Historical Statistics . . . to 1957*, 428, 429; U.S. Department of Agriculture, *Yearbook of the Department of Agriculture 1901* (Washington, DC: Government Printing Office, 1902), 690.

7. Faulkner, *Politics*, 75. See Robert Fogel, *Railroads and American Economic Growth: Essays in Econometric History* (Baltimore: Johns Hopkins Press, 1964); and Albert Fishlow, *American Railroads and the Transformation of the Ante-Bellum Economy* (Cambridge, MA: Harvard University Press, 1965). The studies by Fogel and Fishlow stimulated a torrent of economic investigations into the contribution railroads made to American economic growth.

8. U.S. Bureau of Statistics, *Statistical Abstract of the United States: 1900* (Washington, DC: Government Printing Office, 1901), 338, passim; *Statistical Abstract of the United States: 1896*, 331, passim; Fogel, *Railroads and American Economic Growth*, 17–110, 219–23; and for a critique, Marc Nerlove, "Railroads and Economic Growth," *Journal of Economic History* 26 (March 1966), 109–15; David O. Whitten, *Emergence of Giant Enterprise, 1860–1914: American Commercial Enterprise and Extractive Industries*, Contributions in Economics and Economic History, no. 54 (Westport, CT: Greenwood Press, 1983), 35–56.

9. *Statistical Abstract of the United States: 1900*, 530; U.S. Bureau of the Census, *Twelfth Census of the United States: 1900, Manufactures* (Washington, DC: U.S. Census Office, 1902), 7:liv–lvi; *Historical Statistics . . . to 1957*, 546–47; William Howard Shaw, *Value of Commodity Output since 1869* (New York: National Bureau of Economic Research, 1946), 30–64.

10. *Historical Statistics . . . to 1957*, 150–52, 258–59, 266, 284–85, 402–3, 410–12; Garraty, *New Commonwealth*, 70, 71.

11. Whitten, *Emergence of Giant Enterprise*, 89–109; Rudolf Alexander Clemen, *The American Livestock and Meat Industry* (New York: Ronald Press, 1923), 96; Willard F. Williams and Thomas T. Stout, *Economics of the Livestock-Meat Industry* (New York: Macmillan, 1964), 10; Margaret Walsh, *The Rise of the Midwestern Meat Packing Industry* (Lexington: University of Kentucky Press, 1982), 20; Mary Yeager, *Competition and Regulation: The Development of Oligopoly in the Meat Packing Industry* (Greenwich, CT: JAI Press, 1981), 54–55; Lewis Corey, *Meat and Man: A Study of Monopoly, Unionism, and Food Policy* (New York: Viking, 1950), 39; *Report of the Federal Trade Commission on the Meat-Packing Industry*, Part II, *Evidence of Combination among Packers* (Washington, DC: Government Printing Office, 1918), 14–15; A. D. Melvin, "The Federal Meat-Inspection Service," published in USDA, *Twenty-third Annual Report of the Bureau of Animal Industry for the Year 1906* (Washington, DC: Government Printing Office, 1908), 65–100.

12. Ronald E. Seavoy, *The Origins of the American Business Corporation, 1784–1855: Broadening the Concept of Public Service during Industrialization*, Contributions in Legal Studies, no. 19 (Westport, CT: Greenwood Press, 1982), 1–45.

13. Chandler, *Visible Hand*.

14. Redlich, *Molding of American Banking*, 2:359–97; Garraty, *New Commonwealth*, 97; C. Joseph Pusateri, *Big Business in America: Attack and Defense* (Itasca, IL: F. E. Peacock, 1975), 1–106; Glenn Porter, *The Rise of Big Business, 1860–1910* (Arlington Heights, IL: Harlan Davidson, 1973); Chandler, *Visible Hand*; Whitten, *Emergence of Giant Enterprise*.

15. U.S. Interstate Commerce Commission, *Twelfth Annual Report, 1898* (Washington, DC: Government Printing Office, 1899), 11–22; Henry Varnum and Henry W. Poor, *Poor's Manual of Railroads, 1892* (New York: Henry Varnum and Henry W. Poor, 1893); also, *Poor's Manual, 1895* and *Poor's Manual, 1900*.

16. Faulkner, *Politics*, 75. See also Luther Conant, Jr., "Industrial Consolidations in the United States," *Quarterly Publications of the American Statistical Association* 8 (March 1901), 207, 226; and Edward Chase Kirkland, *Industry Comes of Age, 1860–1897* (New York: Holt, Rinehart & Winston, 1961), 225–30, 216–36; *Poor's Manual, 1895*, 1, 132–93.

17. *Historical Statistics . . . to 1957*, 74, 91–92, 127, 128, 344; Charles Barzillai Spahr,

An Essay on the Present Distribution of Wealth in the United States (New York: T. Y. Crowell, 1896), 65, 70.

18. *Historical Statistics . . . to 1957*, 14.

19. An excellent general discussion of urbanization and attendant problems in the 1890s is in Faulkner, *Politics*. For reform see also John G. Sproat, *The Best Man! Liberal Reformers in the Gilded Age* (New York: Oxford University Press, 1968); and Garraty, *New Commonwealth*, 1–32, 179, 309–35.

20. *Commercial and Financial Chronicle* (January 7, 1893); and H. A. Pierce, "A Review of Finance and Business," *Bankers' Magazine and Statistical Register* 47 (February 1893), 561–72.

21. For business failures, *Statistical Abstract of the United States: 1900*, 396, and for foreign commerce data, 562.

22. Shaw, *Commodity Output*, 70–75; *New York Times* (December 31, 1893).

23. Monthly series, *Business Cycle Indicators*, vol. 2, ser. 13.2, 119–20, ser. 18.1, 137–38; U.S. Bureau of the Census, *Historical Statistics of the United States, 1789–1945* (Washington, DC: Government Printing Office, 1949), 344, 345.

24. *Historical Statistics, 1789–1945*, 342; David M. Blank, *The Volume of Residential Construction, 1889–1950* (New York: National Bureau of Economic Research, 1954); John R. Riggleman, "Building Cycles in the United States, 1875–1932," *American Statistical Journal* 28 (June 1933), 174–83; Shaw, *Commodity Output*, 64.

25. Moore, *Business Cycle Indicators*, 2, ser. 15.1, 130.

26. *Historical Statistics . . . to 1957*, 115, 296–97, 301–2; George Heberton Evans, *Business Incorporation in the United States, 1800–1943* (New York: National Bureau of Economic Research, 1948), 80; Moore, *Business Cycle Indicators*, 2, ser. 7.3, 94–96.

27. *Historical Statistics . . . to 1957*, 267, 301–3. See *Historical Statistics, 1789–1945*, 115, 231, for comparative movements of agricultural and other prices; also Schumpeter, *Business Cycles*, 1:319–23; Shaw, *Commodity Output*, 54; and Bogue, *Money at Interest*, 125–26, 261, 264–76.

28. Melville J. Ulmer, *Trends and Cycles in Capital Formation by United States Railroads, 1870–1950* (New York: National Bureau of Economic Research, 1954), 10.

29. For railroad capital outlays, see ibid., 14–24, 20; *Poor's Manual, 1897*, iii; *Poor's Manual, 1889*, vii; *Poor's Manual, 1892*, xx; and *Historical Statistics . . . to 1957*, 410. Data on rail securities yields are in *Poor's Manual, 1900*, lix; on the mood of railroad investors, in Hoffmann, *Depression of the Nineties*, 127–32. See also Fels, *American Business Cycles*, 184–90, 212–13; and Garraty, *New Commonwealth*, 86–87.

30. Willard Long Thorp, *Business Annals* (New York: National Bureau of Economic Research, 1926), 29–81, passim, offered a general view. See also Weberg, *Background of the Panic of 1893*, 3–8; and Lauck, *Causes of the Panic of 1893*, for dated accounts.

31. B. R. Mitchell, with the collaboration of Phyllis Deane, *Abstract of British Historical Statistics* (Cambridge, UK: Cambridge University Press, 1962), 472–73. See also Thorp, *Business Annals*; and Hoffmann, *Depression of the Nineties*, 41, 48–50, 288.

32. *Commercial and Financial Chronicle* (February 25, 1893, and 1891–92); Thorp, *Business Annals*; Fels, *American Business Cycles*, 173–74; Barnes, *John G. Carlisle*, 222–27; Hoffmann, "Depression," 137–64.

3

Panic

People are in a state to be thrown into a panic at any minute.
—Henry Lee Higginson, 1893

The business revival of 1891–92 only delayed an inevitable reckoning. While domestic factors led in precipitating a major downturn in the United States, the European contraction operated as a powerful depressant. Commercial stagnation in Europe decisively affected the flow of foreign investment funds to the United States. Although foreign investment in this country and American investment abroad rose overall during the 1890s, changing business conditions occasioned sharp counterflows in capital. Initially, contraction abroad forced European investors to liquidate substantial holdings of American securities; then, the rate of new foreign investment fell off. The repatriation of American securities prompted gold exports, deflating the money stock and depressing prices. A reduced inflow of foreign capital slowed expansion and may have exacerbated the declining growth of the railroads; undoubtedly it dampened aggregate demand.

A falling rate of foreign investment, manifest in the liquidation of American shares, contributed to specie outflows. Funds secured through foreign investment in domestic enterprise had been important in helping the country meet its usual balance of payments deficit; that less money was invested during the 1890s was one of the factors that, with a continued adverse balance of payments, forced the United States to export gold almost continuously from 1892 to 1896. The impact of depression abroad on the flow of capital to this country can be inferred from the history of new capital issues in Britain, the source of perhaps 75 percent

Table 3.1
British New Capital Issues, 1890–1898

(millions of pounds, sterling)

1890	142.6
1891	104.6
1892	81.1
1893	49.1
1894	91.8
1895	104.7
1896	152.8
1897	157.3
1898	150.2

Source: Charles Hoffmann, *The Depression of the Nineties: An Economic History* (Westport, CT: Greenwood Press, 1970), 193.

of overseas investment in the United States. British issues varied as shown in Table 3.1. Simultaneously, the share of new British investment sent abroad fell from one-fourth in 1891 to one-fifth two years later. Over that same period, British net capital flows abroad declined by about 60 percent; not until 1896 and 1897 did they resume earlier levels.[1]

Price movements accompanying European depression posed no less difficulty. The fall of European prices intensified the effect of overseas contraction and made American products more expensive just when conditions were impairing markets abroad; moreover, European merchandise imports could better compete in this country. As imports mounted to record levels early in 1893, the payments deficit and specie outflows increased.[2]

Gold exports and the circumstances they represented compelled major adjustments. The outflows of the 1890s compounded serious depressive influences in the behavior of the American money stock. Since the 1870s one western commercial nation after another had embraced a gold standard; rapidly rising aggregate output and the demand for gold coincided with a falling rate of increase in gold production. The money stock failed to grow sufficiently, and a secular price decline set in until sufficient gold was mined and minted to reverse conditions in the 1890s. Annually from 1879 to 1897, the U.S. money stock grew about 6 percent, and prices fell about 1 percent. From 1865 to 1896 the wholesale price index fell from 190 to 66 (1913 = 100), while the cost of living index fell from 102 to 74.

Because the United States was a minor member of the gold standard community, its money stock was subject to external control. Changes in foreign prices were transmitted to America along a complex path from fixed exchange rates through the balance of payments to the money stock, thence to a level of internal prices consistent with exchange rates. The nation might have responded to falling European prices in the 1890s by abandoning the gold standard and depreciating the dollar to reestablish parity between internal and external prices and attain a more favorable merchandise balance. The government, however, was determined to maintain a gold standard, so a downward adjustment of prices and income was necessary to prevent European prices from falling well below domestic prices, which would encourage imports, exacerbate gold exports, and drive the country from the gold standard.[3]

The recession that began in 1893 had deep roots. The slowdown in railroad expansion, decline in building construction, and foreign depression had reduced investment opportunities, and, following the brief upturn effected by the bumper wheat crop of 1891, agricultural prices fell, as did exports and commerce in general. Complaints of low profits suggest that many firms were finding it difficult to compete.[4] These weaknesses did not translate into an inevitable contraction; there might have been an adjustment comparable to the recession of 1882–85. But as Grover Cleveland's second term neared, the economy faced major threats from another quarter: because they threatened the gold standard, federal fiscal policy and the growth of inflationist sentiment spread alarm among businessmen.

The inflation movement became prominent during the depression of the 1870s. Falling prices persuaded many in both major political parties to support inflationary policies and prompted political radicals, debt-pressed farmers, and angry workingmen to form a Greenback Labor Party. Continued weak prices perpetuated agitation during the next decade, despite the party's demise after the depression. The admission during 1889–90 of six new states, all with substantial silver-mining interests, reinforced the crusade. Before the 1879 resumption of specie payments, inflationists had worked primarily to expand the circulation of greenbacks. Resumption, then the accession of new silver-mining states, added to the political appeal of inflationists and directed their attention increasingly toward seeking the unlimited coinage of silver dollars. The formation of the People's Party among cotton, wheat, and corn growers plagued by low prices early in the 1890s made the inflationist movement even more potent. These developments and the financial tumult in 1893 transformed what might have been a skirmish over monetary policy into a major struggle. On a platform featuring the free coinage of silver, Populist candidates in 1892 won a million popular votes and several congressional seats, and they scored impressively in local contests in several states. Silverites were also conspicuous among Southern agrarian Democrats as well as Republicans from mining regions.

With one exception, the federal treasury each year between 1866 and 1893 enjoyed a surplus. When Benjamin Harrison assumed the presidency in 1889, hostility toward trusts and protection led many Democratic leaders to demand that tariffs be lowered to reduce the surplus. The new Republican administration, however, preferred more ingenious methods of simultaneously eliminating the embarrassing excess of income and rewarding its supporters in business and elsewhere. Lavish expenditures—pension payments to Civil War veterans doubled in four years—that favored loyal Republican voters were adopted, and the Treasury redeemed government bonds ahead of schedule—initially at the end of 1890 to ease the financial stringency accompanying the Baring panic, and thereafter to reduce the surplus. The 1890 McKinley Tariff moved sugar, an important source of revenue, to the free list but raised some duties high enough to prohibit imports and thus further cut receipts. In that same year, Congress approved the Sherman Silver Purchase Act as part of a sectional bargain in which the Western silver-state Republicans traded support for the new tariff for "something for silver." The new measure obliged the Treasury to purchase monthly at market prices 4.5 million ounces of silver, essentially the entire domestic output. Against these purchases the government was to issue a new currency, the treasury notes of 1890, redeemable in coin; gold and silver money would be kept at parity.[5]

The effect of the new policies and the growth of silver sentiment were soon apparent. Silverites offered free coinage bills repeatedly from 1890, when the Senate approved the Silver Purchase Act. Meanwhile, the administration's actions sharply altered the Treasury's position. Led by a 20 percent fall in customs receipts, federal revenues dropped steeply after 1890, despite an increase in imports: the 1891–92 surplus shrank from $105 million to $10 million; the Treasury's cash balance fell by more than half, its gold from $182 million to $121 million.[6]

These developments aroused apprehension among domestic and foreign business interests. The center of attention was the declining gold reserve: not once since its creation to back and redeem the currency had it fallen below $100 million, the minimum and legally required reserve for safety.[7] The ominously rapid fall in the reserve was blamed on excessive public expenditures and the 1890 silver law. Silver purchases added some $50 million a year to monetary circulation, and the growth of silverite sentiment threatened even larger purchases. Doubt spread that the Treasury could maintain a reserve sufficient to support the currency and thus the gold standard. Maintaining parity between gold and silver meant that the new 1890 notes, like other government issues, rested on the gold reserve. Inflationary silver purchases and note issues threatened the reserve and encouraged redemption in gold. A fall in the price of silver, by reducing the bullion value of silver dollars and their desirability in exchange for currency, could produce the same result. As uncertainty grew, foreign investors began to convert dollar holdings to gold.

The situation was more complex than contemporaries believed. Silver purchases were an important addition to the stock of money, but after 1890 they had a deflationary impact: apprehensive foreigners were less willing to buy or hold dollars, and the resulting specie exports prevented gold and money stocks from rising as rapidly as they otherwise might have. To be sure, other factors also excited outflows, but uneasiness about the Treasury's ability to preserve the gold standard against deficits, declining reserves, and a mounting circulation of currency to support was probably the decisive marginal element. Never did a majority here or abroad believe that the United States would abandon the gold standard; yet only a small minority needed believe it would, or a slightly larger minority to conclude that the probability had risen significantly, "to produce a substantial outflow of capital." Accordingly, the flows in speculative funds shifted as "confidence in the maintenance of the standard waxed and waned."[8] When the crisis came in the spring of 1893—ordinarily the demand for funds during the fall harvest created stringency—its intensity was unwarranted by general conditions.[9]

The situation had deteriorated by mid-1892. The expansion generated by exports of the previous year's crops was nearly spent. In June, gold exports soared to $17 million and continued for a year, although crop exports normally created inflows in autumn and early winter. On July 9, the London *Economist* held anxiety over the gold standard largely responsible for specie shipments and questioned the U.S. Treasury's capacity to maintain gold payments from an adequate reserve. The American financial and periodical press evidenced similar views; one leading magazine ran five major articles on the subject in the next few months.[10]

Banks increasingly redeemed greenbacks and 1890 treasury notes in gold instead of the usual gold certificates. Treasury practices contributed to this phenomenon. From late 1890, the New York Subtreasury paid a growing share of its clearinghouse settlements in the new Sherman Act notes, to put them into circulation, and in greenbacks. Unable to obtain gold for trading from their usual source, the banks turned to paying the notes to one another in interbank transactions, and increasingly to the Subtreasury as customs monies, while holding on to their specie reserves. Moreover, when faltering confidence obliged gold exports, the banks redeemed greenbacks—ordinarily a large part of their reserves—to obtain specie to send abroad instead of drawing on their own gold holdings. The Treasury, meanwhile, continued to add to the 1890 notes in circulation and, as required by law, recirculated the greenbacks redeemed. As its gold receipts fell, claims against the Treasury's specie reserve rose. In fiscal 1893 redemption was $102 million (three times the total for 1879–90), and gold exports were $108 million.[11]

As uncertainty and specie outflows grew, credit contracted and curbed aggregate demand and investment. New York bank deposits and reserves fell abruptly in the last quarter of 1892: reserves were 17 percent below the year's average and close to the legal minimum of 25 percent of deposits. Rates for loans secured by commercial paper averaged 5.50 percent in December, about twice the level

in June. Liabilities of business failures in the last quarter doubled those in the
third quarter, indicating that deteriorating conditions had made competition more
hazardous for some firms.[12]

By early 1893, high merchandise imports, gold outflows financed through
greenback redemption, a declining Treasury reserve, and a federal deficit, had
etched an unsettling pattern:[13] business failures continued to rise, money remained tight, and securities prices drifted downward. Secretary of the Treasury
Charles Foster considered a bond issue to replenish the gold reserve but after
consulting with the cabinet and bankers, decided to take such a step only as a
last resort. In the meantime, New York banks replied to requests for aid by
exchanging $6.4 million in specie for greenbacks. An effort was launched to
repeal the Silver Purchase Act before Congress adjourned in March. The Senate
approved, but the House defeated the proposal, offered by Senator John Sherman
of Ohio as a rider to the Sundry Civil Appropriations Bill. All the while, Foster
was sharply criticized for "his openly expressed view . . . that his responsibility
ended with the fourth of March [the end of Harrison's administration] and that
he cared only to avert a catastrophe up to that date. . . . Such a low standard of
duty has never been adopted by any previous Secretary of the Treasury."[14]

The failure of the Philadelphia and Reading Railroad in the third week of
February sparked a pyrotechnic contraction. News of the road's $125 million in
liabilities shocked investors and stirred a stock exchange whose weaknesses had
already excited pointed comment. Not long before, *Bankers' Magazine* had
charged that American industrial corporations were often shoddily managed,
their securities "the worst gambling stocks ever listed."[15]

The Reading panic generated tight money and sales of 1.5 million shares
(close to an average week's total) in a sympathetically falling market on February 20. However, conditions seemingly reverted to normal soon afterward.
There were self-congratulatory assertions that quick recovery proved the essential soundness of the market;[16] nonetheless, evidence of uncertainty lingered.
For a month funds flowed from New York to the interior, where bankers had
reportedly come to share "the uneasiness which has been felt on Wall Street
for many weeks" and were strengthening their reserves in anticipation of a
contraction of credit.[17] It was in such inauspicious circumstances that on March
4, during a counterseasonal loss of money to the interior and amid widespread
anxiety, Grover Cleveland became president of the United States.

In a cold northwest wind, with snow melting to slush in Washington's gutters,
Cleveland offered his spare inaugural address and then took the oath of office.
His remarks emphasized at the outset the need for "a sound and stable currency" and concluded with promises to reduce the tariff. Events soon forced
his administration to wrestle with the problems of a declining treasury reserve
and faltering faith in the security of the gold standard.[18]

At the time of the inauguration Cleveland and his Secretary of the Treasury,
John Griffin Carlisle, believed that repeal of the 1890 silver law was necessary

to restore confidence in the dollar and protect the public credit. Even before assuming office the president had explored the possibility of a bond issue to augment the gold reserve. To avoid a struggle over the divisive silver issue before securing tariff reform, the administration persuaded banks to offer gold for the reserve in exchange for currency and circulated reassuring statements. These efforts secured $25 million in specie within two months, but after March 25 the reserve fell alarmingly. On April 20, Carlisle promised to redeem currency in gold as long as he had it "lawfully available for that purpose." Two days later the reserve fell below $100 million for the first time, and his reassurances seemed dangerously ambiguous. Fears lingered even after the president, a day later, released a statement to the Associated Press promising to continue to redeem even the 1890 notes in gold to uphold parity.[19]

On April 26, Carlisle tried unsuccessfully to arrange with New York bankers for a sale of $50 million in bonds to replenish the reserve. Meanwhile, hundreds of letters of advice arrived at the White House in response to news that the president would welcome suggestions from men in finance. The correspondence revealed the public's increasingly fearful mood. New York banker James Stillman, the president of the Burlington Railroad, and others urged quick action to protect the gold reserve and standard. Boston financier Henry Lee Higginson warned, "People are in a state to be thrown into a panic at any minute." The *Commercial and Financial Chronicle* editorialized that only repeal of the "absurd and vicious" Sherman law would restore confidence; other journals and spokesmen agreed.[20]

The first week in May, panic stalked the New York Stock Exchange. As trading opened, a selling wave shocked industrial securities. National Cordage Company was especially hard hit; its management had signaled difficulties by announcing an issue of bonds at par in the weak April market. On the evening of May 4, after several days of selling that forced declines in much of the industrial list, National Cordage announced that it was entering receivership; three brokerage firms had suspended trading earlier in the day. Early activity on Friday the fifth nearly demoralized the exchange, but conditions stabilized in the afternoon. Cordage common, which had sold at 75 in February and 49 ¾ on Wednesday, sank to 15 ½. General Electric common opened at 80, dropped to 70 in an hour, then to 58 ½, and closed at 70. American Sugar common ranged over 20 points; Cotton Oil, 9 ¼; National Lead, 10. The suspension of leading broker S. V. White heightened the alarm. Surveying the wreckage, the *New York Times* the next day reported:

To find a day to match yesterday's wild fluctuations in the less stable securities, Wall Street had to go back to the panic time of 1873. Even at that time greater jumps in quotations would have been hard to find.

On the Stock Exchange yesterday's session was fairly divided between spurts of the wildest excitement and lulls. . . . The floor might have passed for a morning in Bedlam.[21]

Prominent industrial stocks took most of the losses during the collapse and for a week thereafter. Soon, however, the entire market plunged into a steep decline that continued until mid-summer.

The May 5 stock market crash sent percussive waves of panic across the country. It became increasingly difficult to borrow against commercial paper: from a moderate opening, nominal rates in New York rose to average 7.12 percent in May, 10.33 in June, and 11.83 in July. Between February 4 and May 6, New York national banks reduced loans from $465 million to $425 million, but weakening securities prices and general trade cut the value of collateral, impelling a further curtailment of loans. Worsening conditions and shrinking credit provoked a crescendo of mercantile and banking failures and suspensions. As May ended, depositors for the first time succumbed to their distrust of banks and rushed to convert balances to cash. Interior banks, while reducing loans to strengthen their positions, besieged New York with demands for funds to satisfy the clamor of fearful depositors. By the end of June, withdrawals and gold outflows reflected both fear for the gold standard and payments for heavy merchandise imports, and had cut the money stock by 6 percent and deposits by 9 ½ percent; public holdings of currency were 6 percent greater. Financial spokesmen in the East emphasized anxiety over the gold standard as precipitating the panic, but the concentration of bank runs and failures in the South and West highlighted distrust of banks as well.[22]

Weaknesses in the banking system compounded deflationary pressures. National banks could place up to three-fifths of their reserves with larger institutions in central reserve cities—New York, Chicago, St. Louis—where they were not readily available in emergencies. When trouble threatened, each bank naturally looked to itself. The reserve centers, notably in New York, were subjected to a great demand for funds just when their own needs were urgent. Under such circumstances tight credit rippled through the banking system. Bank failures marked the progress of panic. In June, fifteen national banks failed; in July, twelve; and in August, seventeen more: their capital ranged from $50 thousand to $1 million. Country banks, especially in depressed wheat, cotton, and silver districts, bore the heaviest blows. By year's end 642 banks, including sixty-nine national banks, had succumbed. Their liabilities totaled $211 million.[23]

By early June the center of the financial storm had moved from New York to the Old Northwest and the Mississippi valley. Frantic calls for cash and waves of failure charted its advance. Interior demand summoned from New York shipments as high as $12.9 million in a single week. The drain on Eastern banks was described as "so enormous" in mid-June "that it produced a return wave of depression in the east by raising the [interest] rates, increasing fourfold the stringency and difficulty in borrowing money" and precipitating the first large bank failures in the East. The June 27 announcement that the coinage of silver was to be abandoned in India, a major consumer of monetary silver, caused profound shock. As silver prices fell, reducing the bullion value of silver dollars and making it more difficult to preserve parity, Eastern fears for the gold standard mounted. Demands for cash for mid-year payments heightened the pressure.[24]

On June 10 the banks of the New York Clearing House Association announced they would no longer settle their balances in specie; instead, they would exchange certificates secured by deposit of bills receivable, federal and state securities, treasury notes, and the like, with the trustees of the association. Using clearinghouse certificates, which paid 6 percent interest to their holders, was more expedient than selling securities or contracting loans to obtain funds for interbank transactions or to protect reserves, and it helped New York banks hold loan reductions from June through August to $22.3 million, although deposits fell $48.6 million. Before conditions eased, banking associations in Baltimore, Atlanta, New Orleans, and five other cities had taken similar action.[25]

Pressure on the reserve center banks subsided briefly as June ended. After a meeting of the Clearing House Association, a syndicate of New York's leading banks—the First National, Fourth National, Chase, Gallatin, and Corn Exchange—moved to relax credit. Within a few days $6 million was made available for trade on the stock exchange to force rates for call loans from the June 29 figure of 74 $7/16$ percent to 6 percent, and to ease commercial paper. An additional $10 million issue of clearinghouse certificates brought the total circulating between banks to more than $15 million. Interior calls for funds relaxed as panic ebbed. President Cleveland's June 30 call for a special session of Congress to deal with the emergency reassured anxious Eastern financial groups.[26]

After two weeks, a new wave of distrust struck Southern and Western banks. Half the banks in Denver closed. The drain on Eastern banks resumed, driving loans and deposits down; in mid-July the reserves of the New York clearinghouse banks fell below the legal requirement. Month's end brought the apex of panic. Amid renewed clamors for cash after the failure of the Erie railroad and one of the largest banks in Milwaukee, nominal rates for call loans in New York shot to 72 percent. In a selling wave, securities prices plummeted to lows for the year: National Lead was down from 52 $1/8$ in January to 18 $1/2$; United States Rubber, down from 46 $1/8$ to 25; Western Union, from 101 to 67 $1/8$; General Electric, from 36 $1/2$ to 12 $1/8$. An index of stock prices dropped from 46.9 to 34.8, more than half the loss occurring after the Cordage failure. The *New York Times* described the debacle:

With the morning papers bringing the news of the Erie receivership, Wall Street could not but look for a decline in prices yesterday. The result of the day's trading, though, was a slump which for the wide range it covered and the extent of the fall in quotations had been matched by nothing in this season of tight money and successful bear campaigns.

The weakness . . . developed from the opening of business. . . .

Prices began to drop, and they kept on dropping. There was a rush to sell, and apparently an almost utter lack of support for the market. Liquidation was heavy all day. . . .

Business on the Exchange reached a total of 460,000 shares, and there was far more excitement on the floor and in Wall Street offices than had been seen on other lively days in the course of the present movement in prices. Brokers' quarters were thronged from the opening to the close.[27]

At the nadir of the contraction, credit was so short in California that many farmers, unable to secure customary advances, could neither harvest nor ship their crops. Golden State agriculture was described as the most stricken in the nation, but equally appalling conditions obtained elsewhere. In the South, where depression and failure dated from 1891, many believed moving the cotton crop impossible. One South Carolina congressman reported that farmers who took loaded wagons to market in the morning could be seen returning home in the evening with their loads intact, because buyers had no money to pay for the cotton. Northwestern grain dealers and millers, including Charles A. Pillsbury of Minneapolis, purchased farmers' cereal with scrip.[28]

When their reserves fell below the legal requirement, New York's clearing-house banks decided to issue no further public statements until their certificates were retired. By the first week in August, continuing calls for currency and a reserve deficit of over $14 million had led the New York banks to announce that correspondents' drafts remitted in current business would not be paid in cash. The announcement of partial suspension of cash payments heightened pressure, forcing added restrictions. Some banks allowed withdrawals only after depositors submitted legal notice of intent; others limited withdrawals to favored customers, or froze deposits. Inaccessible deposits were discounted in gold and foreign exchange. Distrust and demand pushed currency to a premium on August 3; in New York gold coins were used for current transactions.

Depositors whose businesses enjoyed large cash receipts sold currency, thus cutting the flow to hard-pressed banks. Major purchasers of currency included firms hoping to meet payrolls, and interior banks attempting to enlarge cash holdings. Calm returned at the end of the month. City banks cut loans and restored reserves to legal levels; others sold certified checks drawn on themselves in currency denominations and purchased government bonds against which to issue additional notes. The banks drew strength from $40 million in gold imports for the month ending September 2. Gold exports had halted in June, although foreign exchange remained close to the export point. But the premium, expected to be temporary, and high interest rates encouraged borrowing sterling. A favorable merchandise balance of $21 million for July and August was probably an even more important influence on specie inflow, and the anticipated repeal of the 1890 silver law and low prices had stimulated foreign purchases of securities.[29]

As the financial tremors began to subside, Congress convened in special session on August 7 to deal solely with the financial situation. On the opening day, Congress received a presidential message urging quick repeal of the Silver Purchase Act to restore confidence in the dollar and ease pressure on the Treasury's gold reserve. The House acted on August 28, but a silverite filibuster delayed Senate approval until October 30. The bill was signed into law three days later, amid high hopes that repeal would effect a return of prosperity by restoring confidence.[30]

The anticipated improvement did not materialize; instead, it became increasingly apparent that the country was entering "a great depression in trade and manufactures" that promised to continue indefinitely.[31] As early as May, forty-five New England textile mills had announced a temporary halt in operations, beginning June 3, to induce more favorable prices. In mid-year, iron output tailed off sharply, and by July rail freight movement had begun to fall. Traffic to the World's Columbian Exposition (held in Chicago from May to October 30) was disappointing. Seasonally smoothed, August building-permit values were 50 percent below a year before. The number of new business incorporations was down 40 percent for the month; outside clearings, 30 percent; pig iron production, 22; stock prices, 20; an index of the physical volume of business, 19; railroad freight ton mileage, 6; and an index of wholesale prices, 5 percent. Job force, work time, and wage cuts were widespread: an index of factory employment was off 10 percent.[32]

The record of business failures for the year offered even starker evidence of the ruin issuing from months of financial panic in 1893. The iron industry suffered the worst year of its history. Before the end of June it counted thirty-two failures, including the Philadelphia and Reading Coal and Iron Company and the Pennsylvania Steel Company. Soon after, the Oliver Iron and Steel Company became the trade's first failure in the Pittsburgh area; other units throughout the country followed.[33]

The railroads suffered the heaviest blows. The Erie entered receivership five months after the Reading, on July 25. The Northern Pacific, weakened by a rate war with the Great Northern and saddled with a large floating debt incurred partly through overexpansion, followed on August 10. The Union Pacific went under on October 11; the Santa Fe on December 23; the New York & New England four days later. In all, 119 railroads succumbed in 1893. Together they operated 27,883 miles of line. Their stock outstanding totalled $836 million; their bonds, $1,160 million. As of June 30, 1894, 156 roads were in the hands of receivers. Twenty-eight firms accounted for 80 percent of the $2.5 billion capital and operated two-thirds of the thirty thousand miles of track involved. Fierce competition, declining traffic, credit restriction, and vast over-capitalization and fixed charges—only eighteen of the 156 had paid any dividends since 1880—told the story.[34]

By the end of the year, 15,242 failures, averaging $22,751 in liabilities, had been reported. Plagued by successive contractions of credit, many essentially sound firms, which would have survived under ordinary circumstances, failed. Liabilities totaled a staggering $357 million. The crisis of 1893 would not soon be forgotten.[35]

NOTES

1. Hoffmann, *Depression of the Nineties*, 186; table, 193; discussion, 157–97. See also Albert H. Imlah, "British Balance of Payments and Export of Capital, 1816–1913," *Economic History Review* 5, no. 2 (1952), 208–39; and, for a contemporary view, Worthington Chauncey Ford, "Foreign Exchange and the Movement of Gold, 1894–1895," *Yale Review* 4 (August 1895), 128–48.

2. *Historical Statistics, 1789–1945*, 339–41; Hoffman, "Depression," 152–57.

3. Friedman and Schwartz, *Monetary History*, 89–113.

4. Earnings early in 1893 were disappointing, especially in railroads. The current dollar value of the output of producers' durables had grown by 42.3 percent, from 1879 to 1889 and 4.3 percent from 1890 to 1892—consumer goods output had grown 31.1 and 6.4 percent in the same periods. The percentages suggest keen competition for a market that expanded slowly after 1890. *Commercial and Financial Chronicle* (February 25, 1893, and 1890–97); *Poor's Manual, 1900*, lix; Shaw, *Commodity Output*, 34–36; *Historical Statistics . . . to 1957*, 419–22; and Fels, *American Business Cycles*, 212–13.

5. The Treasury was permitted to pay no more than $1.29 for a fine ounce of silver. The authorized purchase nearly equaled domestic production. A synopsis of these events is in Faulkner, *Politics*, 94–118, 119–40. See also Barnes, *John G. Carlisle*, 222–27; Dewey, *Financial History*, 438–43; Margaret G. Myers, *A Financial History of the United States* (New York: Columbia University Press, 1970), 211–22; and David D. Hale, "The Panic of 1893," *Across the Board* 25 (January 1988), 24–32. On greenback issue, see Gretchen Ritter, *Goldbugs and Greenbacks: The Antimonopoly Tradition and the Politics of Finance in America*, (New York: Cambridge University Press, 1997).

6. *Statistical Abstract of the United States: 1898*, 37; *Statistical Abstract of the United States: 1900*, 27; *Historical Statistics . . . to 1957*, 712; U.S. Congress, House, *Report of the Secretary of the Treasury*, 56th Cong., 2d sess., 1900, House Document 8, cxvi–cxvii. Also Barnes, *John G. Carlisle*, 222; Faulkner, *Politics*, 94–118. Bond redemptions were $230 million during fiscal 1890–91 and $275 million by the end of the administration.

7. The Gold Reserve Act of 1882 authorized the issue of a new currency, gold certificates, but required suspension of its circulation whenever the reserve fell below $100 million. The Resumption Act of 1875—which provided for gold redemption of the inconvertible greenbacks, or United States notes, by January 2, 1879—allowed the sale of bonds, ultimately with a total face value of $95.5 million, to establish a redemption fund, and forbade the use of any part of the face value of the fund in current appropriations. Dewey, *Financial History*, 438–43.

8. Friedman and Schwartz, *Monetary History*, 104, 128–34. From 1890 to 1893 a $107 million fall in Treasury cash and silver purchases of $168 million should have increased federal monetary circulation by $275 million. Instead, circulation rose by $154 million; gold exports accounted for the difference.

9. Fels, *American Business Cycles*, 209–19.

10. Michael D. Harter, "Free Coinage, the Blight of Our Commerce," *Forum* 13 (May 1892), 281–84; William F. Vilas, "The Threat of the Present Coinage Law," ibid., 285–94; J. C. Hemphill, "Free Coinage and the Loss of Southern Statesmanship," ibid., 295–99; Louis Windmüller, "The Folly of the Silver Agitation," *Forum* 13 (August 1892),

718–24; George Fred Williams, "Imminent Anger from the Silver Purchase Act," *Forum* 14 (February 1893), 789–96.

The failure of the Brussels international bimetallic conference late in 1892 heightened conservatives' fears. *Commercial and Financial Chronicle* (February 25, 1893); "No Help from Europe," *Harper's Weekly* 34 (December 31, 1892), 1250.

11. The share of gold in New York Subtreasury clearinghouse settlements fell from about 80 percent to 50 percent in fiscal 1891–92 and to 5 percent in 1893; December 1890–December 1892, the portion of New York customs receipts remitted in gold fell from 90 percent to 5 percent. U.S. Congress, House, *Report of the Secretary of the Treasury*, 53d Cong., 3d sess., 1894, House Executive Document 2, 119, 121; U.S. Congress, House, *Report of the Secretary of the Treasury*, 56th Cong., 2d sess., 1900, House Document 8, cxiii–cxx; "Notes and Memoranda," *Quarterly Journal of Economics* 7 (July 1893), 494–95; Dewey, *Financial History*, 438–43; Myers, *Financial History*, 211–22.

Friedman and Schwartz, *Monetary History*, 128, argue that the Treasury might have minimized the monetary effect of silver purchases by stockpiling bullion acquisitions. Stockpiling was, however, unlikely to erase concerns over the adequacy of the Treasury reserve.

12. U.S. Congress, House, *Report of the Comptroller of the Currency*, 54th Cong., 2d sess., 1896, House Document 10, 591, 605; *Historical Statistics, 1789–1945*, 346, 349; Hoffmann, "Depression," 157–64.

13. Federal accounts exclusive of postal revenues and expenditures were in deficit early in 1893.

14. *Commercial and Financial Chronicle* (March 4, 1893).

15. Pierce, *Bankers' Magazine* 47 (January 1893), 495; *Commercial and Financial Chronicle* (January 28 and February 11, 1893, and January 6, 1894). Fels used the word "pyrotechnical" in *American Business Cycles*, 184. On the collapse of the Philadelphia and Reading Railroad see Whitten, *Emergence of Giant Enterprise*, 161–62; David O. Whitten, "Anthracite Coal," in *Extractives, Manufacturing, and Services: A Historiographical and Bibliographical Guide*, vol. 2, *Handbook of American Business History*, ed. David O. Whitten and Bess E. Whitten (Westport, CT: Greenwood Press, 1997), 112–14.

16. About 1.65 million shares were sold weekly in 1892, 1.58 million in 1893. The Reading Railroad was ruined. The collapse of an anthracite combination left the road with large inventories in a weak market. The Reading's attempt to gain control of New England trackage provoked financier J. P. Morgan, whose New Haven Railroad's territory the Reading was trying to invade, to force a denial of credit. Excepting coal inventories, the Reading's cash balance was $29,241, its current assets $13,346,324, and current liabilities, $18,477,828. *Commercial and Financial Chronicle* (February 18, 1893); *New York Times* (February 21, 1893); Campbell, *Reorganization of the American Railroad System*, 172–84.

17. *Wall Street Journal* (March 1, 1893). Hoffmann, "Depression," 152, asserts that funds flowed steadily to the interior in the first half of 1893, but Friedman and Schwartz, in *Monetary History*, 108–110, state that they did so only after May. Contemporary press reports, reinforced by New York bank losses of 6 percent ($30 million) in loans and 8 percent ($50 million) in net deposits, reveal a flow for a month after the Reading failure. U.S. Congress, National Monetary Commission, *Statistics for the United States, 1867–*

1909, 61st Cong., 2d sess., 1911, Senate Document 570, 101; *Commercial and Financial Chronicle* (March 11, 1893); *Chicago Daily Tribune* (February 26–March 28, 1893); *Wall Street Journal* (March 1, 1893); *Philadelphia Public Ledger* (February 25, 1893); *St. Louis Post-Dispatch* (February 19, 1893).

18. James Daniel Richardson, *A Compilation of the Messages and Papers of the Presidents, 1789–1902* (Washington, DC: Bureau of National Literature and Arts, 1897), 9: 389–93; *New York Times* (March 5, 1893).

19. Carlisle's statement, *Commercial and Financial Chronicle* (April 22, 1893); Cleveland's, Grover Cleveland, *The Letters of Grover Cleveland, 1850–1908*, ed. Allan Nevins (New York: Houghton Mifflin, 1933), 324.

20. Barnes, *John G. Carlisle*, 231, 250–60. See also *Commercial and Financial Chronicle* (April 22 and 29, 1893); *Chicago Daily Tribune* (April 16–22, 1893); *Cleveland Plain Dealer* (April 30–May 2, 1893); *Philadelphia Public Ledger* (April 1893); *Wall Street Journal* (March 6, 1893).

21. *New York Times* (May 6, 1893); *Commercial and Financial Chronicle* (May 6, 1893). For information on National Cordage Company see "Collapse of the National Cordage Company," *Public Opinion* 15 (May 20, 1893), 155–57; *Commercial and Financial Chronicle* (June 24, 1893); and White, *Recovery after 1893*, 1–11. In 1891–92 National Cordage had paid a 12 percent dividend on its preferred stock and 8 percent on its common stock; in January 1893 the firm had doubled its common to $20 million. In April National Cordage paid its usual dividend to maintain appearances, but the large floating debt forced the firm into receivership.

22. National Monetary Commission, *Statistics for the United States, 1867–1909*, 101; Sprague, *History of Crises under the National Banking System*, 153–67; *Historical Statistics, 1789–1945*, 346; Friedman and Schwartz, *Monetary History*, 108–11, 130–31.

23. U.S. Congress, House, *Report of the Comptroller of the Currency*, 54th Cong., 2d sess., 1896, House Document 10, 591–92, 605; U.S. Congress, House, *Annual Report of the Comptroller of the Currency*, 56th Cong., 2d sess., 1900, House Document 10, 495–99; *Commercial and Financial Chronicle* (January 11, 1896); editorial, "The Bank Failures," *Bankers' Magazine* 48 (July 1893), 1–5. Credit stringency was blamed for twenty-seven national bank failures; mismanagement and speculation accounted for most of the remainder.

24. Quote from Pierce, *Bankers' Magazine* 47 (July 1893), 5. *Commercial and Financial Chronicle* (June 10, 1893); *Cleveland Plain Dealer* (May 3, 1893); *St. Louis Post-Dispatch* (May 7, 1893); *Wall Street Journal* (May 9 and 23, 1893); *Chicago Daily Tribune* (May 22, 1893); National Monetary Commission, *Statistics for the United States, 1867–1909*, 101.

25. National Monetary Commission, *Statistics for the United States, 1867–1909*, 101; *Commercial and Financial Chronicle* (June 10–November 4, 1893); Alexander Dana Noyes, "The Banks and the Panic," *Political Science Quarterly* 9 (March 1894), 12–28; Albert Clark Stevens, "An Analysis of the Phenomena of the Panic in the United States in 1893," *Quarterly Journal of Economics* 8 (January 1894), 117–48. Certificates were used in New York until November; circulation peaked at $38.8 million. *Commercial and Financial Chronicle* (August 10 and 26, 1893). Redlich, *Molding of American Banking*, 158–65, begins his discussion of the evolution of the certificates with their introduction in New York during the panic of 1857. Also see Myers, *Financial History*, 189, 209, 246.

26. *New York Times* (June 30, 1893); *Commercial and Financial Chronicle* (July 1, 1893).

27. *New York Times* (July 26 and 27, 1893); *Commercial and Financial Chronicle* (July 22 and 29, 1893, January 6, 1894).

28. *New York Times* (July 25, 1893); Barnes, *John G. Carlisle*, 243–46; Woodward, *Origins of the New South*, 264–65. Bank failures in the South were no greater in 1893 than in 1891.

29. In New York the premium ranged from 0.25 to 4 percent over the month from August 3 to September 2. From August 1 to October 1, national bank deposits of bonds to secure note circulation rose from \$182,617,850 to \$209,407,100; circulation increased from \$163,221,294 to \$187,864,985. Bond deposits and circulation began to rise in July, when some banks began exchanging notes for Treasury gold. Friedman and Schwartz, *Monetary History*, 110–11; U.S. Congress, House, *Report of the Comptroller of the Currency*, 54th Cong., 2d sess., 1896, House Document 10, 524; Sprague, *History of Crises under the National Banking System*, 153–215; National Monetary Commission, *Statistics for the United States, 1867–1909*, 101.

30. Expectations for a repeal are stated in the *Boston Daily Advertiser* (November 6, 1893); *Chicago Daily Tribune* (November 1–9, 1893); *Cleveland Plain Dealer* (October 28–November 4, 1893); *Philadelphia Public Ledger* (September 11–December 1, 1893); *Wall Street Journal* (September 28, 1893); and *Commercial and Financial Chronicle* (October 28 and November 4, 1893).

31. *Cleveland Plain Dealer* (November 11, 1893); *Boston Daily Advertiser* (December 25, 1893); *Chicago Daily Tribune* (November 21, 1893); *San Francisco Chronicle* (October 2 and November 1, 1893); *Seattle Post-Intelligencer* (October 26, 1893).

32. *Commercial and Financial Chronicle* (May 27 and June 17, 1893); *Historical Statistics, 1789–1945*, 328–491; Moore, *Business Cycle Indicators*, passim.

33. Clark, *History of Manufactures*, 2:303.

34. *Poor's Manual, 1900*, lxxi–lxxii; U.S. Interstate Commerce Commission, *Eighth Report* (Washington, DC: Government Printing Office, 1894), 68–69. Railroad misman-agement was exemplified by Santa Fe officials, who deliberately falsified an earnings statement in 1893 to inspire unwarranted confidence in the road. *Commercial and Financial Chronicle* (April 11, 1893).

35. *Statistical Abstract of the United States: 1900*, 392–96; *Commercial and Financial Chronicle* (February–December 1893).

4

Hard Times: Profile of Depression, 1893–1897

The entire trouble is that people have no money to buy whisky.
—St. Louis distiller, 1897

The financial crises of 1893 accelerated the recession that was evident early in the year into a major contraction that spread throughout the economy. Investment, commerce, prices, employment, and wages remained depressed for several years. Changing circumstances and expectations, and a persistent federal deficit, subjected the Treasury gold reserve to intense pressure and generated sharp counterflows of gold. The Treasury was driven four times between 1894 and 1896 to resort to bond issues (eventually totalling $260 million) to obtain specie to augment the reserve. Meanwhile, restricted investment, income, and profits spelled low consumption, widespread suffering, and occasionally explosive labor and political struggles. An extensive but incomplete revival occurred in 1895. The Democratic nomination of William Jennings Bryan for the presidency on a free-silver platform the following year, amid an upsurge of silverite support, contributed to a second downturn peculiar to the United States; Europe, just beginning to emerge from depression, was unaffected. Only in mid-1897 did recovery begin in this country; full prosperity returned gradually over the ensuing year and more.

The final months of 1893 brought deceptive signs of the revival expected to accompany repeal of the Sherman Act. In November rising exports and trade (attending the harvest), rail freight ton-mileage, pig iron output, factory employment, and outside clearings all implied improvement. However, the gain was more apparent than real, largely a reaction to the severe contraction that had attended the panic. It was a season of crosscurrents, with some firms extending and others curtailing operations. New York bank deposits grew by 37 percent and reserves by 150 percent from their August lows, to $506.4 million and $197.9 million in December. In contrast, loans rose only 6.5 percent, to $417.6 million, despite low interest rates, and general trade was restrained, suggesting that the accumulation of funds was a sign of weak investment opportunities and caution rather than of economic recovery. Stock prices advanced but slightly, and trading was much less active than a year before. Moreover, although rail freight movement was large, earnings were low, and an index of the physical volume of business revealed persisting stagnation.[1]

The trough of the depression occurred in the first half of 1894. Trade was appallingly weak. The circumstances of the federal treasury contributed importantly to the situation. Almost fiscally independent while it had enjoyed a surplus, the government now, as a result of continuing deficits in the mid-1890s, ''lost its dominant position and became [financially] dependent on business'' to maintain its ability to pay in gold and, to a degree, to control fiscal policy.[2] The reserve was down to $65.5 million as February began. The sale that month of $50 million of 5 percent, ten-year bonds, at a premium price of 117.223 that reduced the actual yield to 3 percent, brought temporary moderation. However, two-fifths of the issue was paid for with specie obtained by redeeming greenbacks at the Treasury. The reserve consequently rose to a peak of only $107 million, on March 6, after which it fell rapidly.[3]

In August a request of the Secretary of the Treasury led New York banks to relieve the Treasury with deposits of $15 million in gold. Persistent deficits, however, required continued drafts against the reserve, necessitating a second issue of $50 million of bonds in November. December and January brought enormous greenback redemptions of $77 million, about half the sum going overseas as gold exports and much of the remainder being used to pay for the recent bond issues. The chief factor in heavy counterseasonal gold outflows was concern over the Treasury reserve. Greenback redemption forced the reserve down much more quickly than deficits dictated, and gold exports accounted for most of the reduction in January. Shipments occurred despite a favorable merchandise balance and lower short-term interest rates in London than in New York.[4]

To avert exhaustion of the gold reserve, which after shipments of $30 million during the preceding month was $45 million on February 1, 1895, the Treasury turned once more to an issue of bonds. Urgency demanded a private arrangement with a banking syndicate instead of another public sale. A contract of February 8 obliged the government to exchange $62 million in 4 percent, thirty-year bonds for 3.5 million ounces of gold worth $65 million. Responding to the Treasury's wish to forestall greenback redemption to obtain gold to pay for the securities, the syndicate agreed to acquire half the specie in Europe. Gold outflows and greenback redemption eased for several months, amid signs of increased confidence and economic revival.[5]

The year 1896 brought more crises for the Treasury reserve. The 1895 up-swing and attendant optimism were spent by December. President Cleveland's December 17 threat of unilateral American action to resolve the Anglo-Venezuelan dispute over the boundary between British Guiana and Venezuela had prompted a selling wave on the stock exchange, followed by three days of near panic and heavy sales of American shares in London and New York amid rumors of war. Moreover, a frightening increase of sympathy with the silver interests led Congress to reject administration proposals to protect the gold standard. Despite a favorable merchandise balance and a reduced federal deficit, greenback redemption to obtain specie for export rose sharply and eroded the Treasury reserve. In January the Treasury announced a public sale of $100 million in bonds to protect the reserve. That sale was a resounding success, netting over $111 million in February; the reserve rose to a satisfactory level, and specie drains subsided.

Political developments of the spring and summer of 1896, climaxing with the Democratic nomination of Bryan and his free-silver campaign, brought another Treasury crisis. When on July 23 the reserve dipped to $89.7 million, with renewed specie outflows and reports of hoarding, the Gallatin National and other leading New York, Philadelphia, and Chicago banks turned over more than $20 million in gold. Concerted action by New York banks kept the reserve from again falling below the safe minimum.[6]

Government efforts to defend the gold reserve were important during the depression of the 1890s. Bond sales demonstrated the administration's determination to secure specie sufficient to maintain gold payments, thus reducing speculative pressure on the dollar. Nonetheless, recurrent Treasury difficulties were at once a symptom and a cause of apprehension. Furthermore, administration measures had an important deflationary impact. Bond sales contributed to the severity and persistence of the depression by withdrawing money from circulation and enforcing the deflation dictated by European price movements and fears over silver inflation. Bond sales transmitted external pressure to the domestic stock of money and to prices and income; in tandem with gold exports, they held circulation about constant between 1892 and 1897, although needs were increasing.[7]

As the Treasury arranged the first bond issue, the country reached the nadir of depression. Indices of economic activity graphically depicted the contours and sweep of the "PROFOUND DULLNESS" and "EXTREME STAGNATION" that ruled at every hand. Seasonally smoothed, building permit values in February, 1894, were 48 percent below those of 1893. Outside clearings and the number of business incorporations were off 30 percent, and an index of the physical volume of business 23 percent. A wave of catastrophic strikes reinforced the general economic weakness and reversed springtime improvements in pig iron output and rail freight shipments. Although iron production rose 23 percent from January to April, it lost half the advance by July, when it was less than half the rate for a year earlier. In July, railroad gross earnings were down 26 percent, net earnings by 30 percent, and freight ton-mileage 24 percent, from May and June 1893.[8]

Changes in investment normally led and helped shape economic fluctuations, as varying profit expectations and returns on investment ramified throughout the economy. The record of the country's prime securities market, New York, was thus a signal index of conditions. New annual stock issues in New York fell 63 percent between 1892 and 1894, about $36.6 million. In 1896 they declined 1 percent from the preceding year's recovery peak of $77.1 million, and in 1897 some 30 percent to $53.3 million. In 1898 they edged back to $69.8 million, still about a third below 1892 levels, shooting up to $311.8 million only in 1899. Stock trading and prices moved comparably. Shares traded fell 43 percent in 1892–94, to just over forty-nine million; half the loss was restored in 1895. The ensuing year saw a new lapse, and in 1897 trading was still 10 percent below the 1892 total. Finally in 1898, sales leaped beyond pre-depression levels to 113 million shares. Prices fell 28 percent from the August 1892 high to the trough of the next August, sinking to a depression low in 1896, when they were 32 percent below the peak.

Bond issues had their own pattern. They fell only 20 percent from 1893 to 1894, to $139.3 million. The next year they rose by one-third, afterward settling by stages to $87.7 million in 1897. In 1898 they soared to a record $245.2 million. Stock and bond sales, 1892–94, reflected both a corporate resort to bonds to secure funds for reorganization and a rush from equities to bonds among investors, who had vivid memories of recent failures, low profits and dividends, and stagnation. In 1894 average bond prices fell less than 2 percent below 1893 levels, in contrast to a much greater decline in stock prices. Subsequently bond prices edged upward, except for a slight dip in 1896. The shift of money to the bond market, where many businessmen could not bid successfully for funds, probably made investment projects difficult to fund. Meanwhile diminished new issues and limited trading before 1898 testified forcefully to a low investment rate that was a severe drag on the economy.[9]

The record of railroad earnings and capital outlays, shown in Table 4.1, clarifies circumstances. Gross and net earnings rose into 1893, but an investment decline had set in the year before. The importance of investment in the roads as a major outlet for foreign and domestic savings meant that this development vitally affected the timing and amplitude of the depression. Gross earnings fell $145 million (net $50 million) in 1893–94. Then they advanced irregularly until 1898, when they finally exceeded the last peaks by 4 and 8 percent respectively. In the meantime, yearly gross capital expenditures fell 72 percent through 1897, with recovery beginning only in the next year. New track construction declined until in 1894 it was but half that for 1892, at 2,296 miles. It fell again the following year, to 1,989 miles, returned to the 1893 figures in 1898, and approached pre-panic levels a year later.

Purchases of rolling stock and steel rails varied similarly. Total cars in use increased by under 13 percent between 1894 and 1899. Freight car orders first

Table 4.1
Railroad Construction, Capital Expenditures, Freight, Earnings, 1891–1899

Year	Miles Built	Gross Capital Expenditures $000,000*	Freight (millions of ton-miles)	Gross Earnings $000,000	Net Earnings $000,000
1891	4,589	738	81,074	1,096.76	332.82
1892	4,579	720	99,241	1,171.41	357.65
1893	2,857	657	93,588	1,220.75	357.76
1894	2,296	568	80,335	1,073.36	305.39
1895	1,989	395	85,228	1,075.37	311.51
1896	2,069	223	95,328	1,150.17	339.22
1897	2,161	207	95,129	1,122.09	328.43
1898	2,199	262	114,139	1,247.33	387.42
1899	4,528	321	123,667	1,313.61	412.24

*1929 dollars.

Source: Rolling stock, revenue, rails, freight, Historical Statistics . . . to 1957, 416, 429, 434; construction, Varnum and Poor, Poor's Manual of Railroads, 1892–1901, ii–iii and passim in each volume cited; capital spending in 1929 dollars, Ulmer, Trends and Cycles, 60.

slumped in mid-1892, dipping by 75 percent in the next two years. Rallying in 1895, they dropped steeply for two years thereafter. From 1898 a slow rise reflected the general business revival. Output for 1898–99, 230,000 cars, exceeded that for the preceding five years by twenty thousand, illustrating the severity of cutbacks in the railroad industry. Quarterly orders for passenger cars fell from 230 in 1892 to eleven in 1894, and orders for locomotives fell from 205 in 1892 to less than twenty in 1894, remaining low through 1897 despite a partial recovery of locomotive orders to eighty in 1895. A 75 percent fall in orders for rails and a 25 percent fall in the quantity manufactured, which accounted for a fourth of rolled iron and steel output, figured prominently in a 25 percent drop in iron and steel production from 1892 to 1894.[10]

Charles Hoffmann has studied changes in producer-durable manufacture, drawn inferences for domestic consumption, and found clues to changes in manufacturers' investments, which shaped the depression. Figures show that investment for equipment (inventory and construction data were inadequate) began to ease late in 1892 but fell 1.8 percent in 1893 and 24 percent through 1894. A revival began in 1895 and continued into the next year, probably because of a lag between placement of orders and production to fill them. The advance carried output above the previous peak, then decline set in. Not until the end of the decade did manufacture of producer durables return to levels representing a resumption of prosperity.

Varying output of different groups of durables etched more sharply the contours of hard times. Ship and boat production, which began to falter in 1892, did not recover to prosperous levels until 1899. An estimated 18 percent fall in gross farm income because of price declines surpassing those for most categories of goods (and thus worsening the terms of trade for farmers with other sectors of the economy), suggested that the contraction must have sharply cut agricultural investment. Output figures for farm equipment and machinery corroborate this analysis: production of farm equipment began to drop in 1891; after a slight advance the next year, in 1894 it sank 27 percent below the 1890 peak. The next year brought a small improvement, followed by a loss in 1896 to the decennial low, 40 percent off the pre-depression total. The 1890 high was not surpassed until 1898. Seriously curtailed building construction helped restrict manufacture of carpenters' and mechanics' tools from 1893 to 1898. A substantial advance began a year later. In contrast, output of office and store furnishings and equipment, industrial equipment and machinery, and electrical apparatus suffered slighter declines and revived more quickly, pointing to less severe contraction in these sectors of the economy.

Building construction further illustrated the changing course of investment. Sketchy data suggest new building permit values reached a peak in some cities in 1890 and in others in 1892, then turned down. Recovery began early in some cities, but aggregate construction did not exceed former values until 1902–03. Not until 1905 did per capita construction resume pre-depression vigor. The value of new urban building permits fell between 35 and 39 percent from the peak to the 1894 trough. The next year nearly half the loss was made up, but in 1896 came a second trough, perhaps 30 percent below the initial high. Sharp crosscurrents masked a gradual rise through the turn of the century. In 1901, the dollar value of construction slightly surpassed that of 1892; in 1904–05 the per capita value exceeded earlier rates. The number of urban dwelling units started per year fell from some 381,000 in 1892 to 265,000 in 1894, rose to 309,000 in 1895, and then fell below 200,000 as the decade ended, but soared to 507,000, above the previous peak, in 1905. Domestic consumption of construction materials declined by about 20 percent between 1892 and 1894, improved slightly the next year, then abruptly dropped to the decennial trough in 1896, 30 percent below 1892 (1913 dollars). Construction materials consumption returned slowly and had exceeded the pre-panic peak by 1905. Reduced investment in building construction, a damaging drag on the economy, retarded recovery.[11]

The downturn in building construction and demand for consumer goods was accompanied by a decline in immigration. The flow of migrants varied with economic conditions on both sides of the Atlantic, usually lagging a year or so behind shifting circumstances in the United States. The 1893 economic contraction at least partially accounts for the 25 percent decline in new arrivals from

Table 4.2
Commodity Output Destined for Domestic Consumption, by Class, 1890–1900

(millions, 1913 dollars)

Year	Producer Durable	Consumer Durable	Consumer Semidurable	Consumer Nonfood Perishable	Food and Kindred Perishable
1890	641	654	1,260	658	2,485
1891	697	678	1,292	698	2,799
1892	734	731	1,355	732	2,914
1893	721	663	1,243	695	2,318
1894	557	593	1,207	692	3,129
1895	687	787	1,445	730	3,428
1896	787	744	1,410	710	3,441
1897	649	803	1,528	711	3,765
1898	692	782	1,521	773	3,808
1899	856	905	1,698	875	4,194
1900	995	854	1,690	895	4,219

Source: Shaw, Commodity Output, 70–77; Historical Statistics . . . to 1957, 419–21.

the 1892 total of 579,663, the even greater fall in 1894, and the drop to 258,636 in 1895. After a jump in 1896 in response to the commercial improvements of 1895, annual immigration sank to a decennial low of 230,000 for each of the next two years. The return to prosperity was slow; not until 1900 did the inflow of immigrants exceed the 1893 figure.[12]

Fluctuations in manufacture of different classes of consumer goods for domestic use, summarized in Table 4.2, illuminated hard times. Predictably, the decline in output of consumer durables, semidurables, nonfood, and food perishables was progressively less precipitous than that of producer durables. Between 1892 and 1894 the value of consumer durable goods produced fell by 18.8 percent; semidurables, by 11.0 percent; nonfood perishables, 5.6 percent; and food perishables, 3.1 percent (all 1913 dollars). Revival in the consumer goods sector began in 1895, paused for a year or two, then reached full recovery by 1899.

Among consumer durables, the most serious declines were recorded in the manufacture of musical instruments, pleasure craft, household furniture and floor coverings, silver jewelry, clocks and watches, and horse-drawn passenger vehicles. Carriage production waned through 1896 and remained low through the

end of the century. As late as 1899 it was below the 1892 high, reflecting perhaps the depths of agricultural depression, the growth of urban mass transit, and
increasing popularity of other forms of transportation in cities.[13] Production of
miscellaneous household furnishings (including mirrors and picture frames),
china utensils, monuments and tombstones, books, and ophthalmic articles and
artificial limbs fell briefly, then quickly approached former figures. The most
serious fall in output was in expensive luxury items, which could be sacrificed
without undue discomfort. However, reduced production of widely used goods
such as household furniture and floor coverings gives some reason to suspect
that depression struck seriously at the purchasing power and habits of lower-
middle and low-income groups.

The record for semidurables projects similar impressions. The value of dry
goods and notions produced fell by 15.3 percent between 1891 and 1894 (1913
dollars), temporarily increased in 1895, then lagged through the remainder of
the decade. The value of games, toys, and sporting goods fell by 11.2 percent
between 1893 and 1894, increased in 1895, and stabilized through 1900. The
value of clothes, personal furnishings, and household furnishings declined, returned to the previous peak in 1895, fell again in 1896, then began an increase
that reflected the regained prosperity of the next two years.

The output of widely used perishables fell by only 5 percent through 1893
and 5.6 points through 1894. However, manufacture of cigarettes and other
tobacco products dropped 14.6 percent through 1896 before it began a slow
return through the remainder of the decade. Production of distilled spirits declined 37 percent between 1893 and 1895, recovered partially the next year, fell
below 50 percent of the pre-depression maximum in 1896, and remained below
former per capita volume until 1903. Output of spirits for domestic consumption
fell 33 percent before prosperity returned. In 1897 a concerned St. Louis whole-
saler lamented the distilleries' plight, ''The entire trouble is that the people have
no money to buy whisky. The decrease has been going on the last three years
. . . the depression in whisky has been due to hard times.'' Publication of newspapers, magazines, and related products dropped by 15.5 percent between 1892
and 1894, then remained 9.2 percent below the 1892 volume as late as 1897,
recovering a year later. Production of drugs, toiletries and kindred items slumped
12.4 percent between 1892 and 1893, improved slightly in 1894, declined again
in 1896, and recovered fully in 1897.

There was perhaps no grimmer illustration of the impact of depression than
the fall in output of food and related products for domestic consumption by 3.1
percent from 1893 to 1894. Per capita production of canned corn, coffee, and
wines were off by 35, 17, and 40 percent, respectively. Production of nonfood
perishables in 1898 was 5 percent above that for 1892, durables 7 percent, and
semidurables 12.2 percent, but population had meanwhile risen 12 percent, leading to the sobering conclusion that many families had sustained sharply reduced
living standards. Adjusted for population growth, output of durables was estimated at but 70 percent, and of semidurables at 78 percent, of capacity in the

1894 trough. Nonfood perishables, still 4 percent below 1892 as late as 1897, may then have been at only 78 percent of capacity. Not until 1899 were earlier per capita levels of manufacture resumed.[14]

Savage unemployment and demoralizing wage reductions reflected the corrosive impact of depression at the 1894 trough and after. Most contemporary estimates of joblessness were for the winter of 1893–94, when exceptional distress attracted wide attention. Often of doubtful accuracy, they ranged upward from the estimate of Carlos C. Closson, Jr., in November 1893 of a half-million. In December, *Bradstreet's* proposed 0.8 million. The Colorado Bureau of Statistics computed the sum for January 1894 at 2.5 million. The Knights of Labor and American Federation of Labor asserted that there were three million out of work as the new year opened.[15]

Decennial national census figures on employment by occupation and industry, federal coal mine data, studies of building construction, and contemporary press accounts and state labor surveys allow a rough estimate of "the great number of idle, unemployed workers, the almost countless . . . men and women . . . suffering the pangs of hunger, the poignancy of distress and dependence" during the depression. A projection of Massachusetts's fairly reliable data puts the national fall of employment in manufacturing and steam and electric railroads from June 1893 to the succeeding winter at 16.7 percent, or 904,000. Based on building permit values and Bureau of Mines data for coal mining, and allowing for building construction, the total loss of time through unemployment in 1894 was perhaps 1.318 million man-years, a rate of 20 percent in the industries cited. Partial recovery in 1895 cut the loss to 15 percent, about one million man-years. After the downturn of 1896 the figure hovered between 1.2 million and 1.3 million, about 17 to 18 percent. It remained at 10 percent, or 750,000, as late as 1899, after improvement had been under way for years.

In forest industries, fisheries, trade, communications, agriculture, public service, and the professions, aggregate time loss through joblessness was lower than in the hard-hit sectors noted above. However, perhaps 17 to 19 percent of the urban work force, between 2.5 million and 2.7 million, was out of work during the winter of 1893–94. Recovery in 1895 increased employment, but the downturn of 1896 increased joblessness to an estimated 15 percent. Despite recovery after 1896, as much as 8 percent of the urban labor force was idle as late as 1899. As appalling as these figures are, they only hint at the extent of misery, shock, and loss of self-respect suffered in a society in which individual employment was the chief means of support and a symbol of personal dignity, integrity, and worth.[16]

Loss of work was the most important factor limiting the average annual earnings of labor during the depression, but reduced wages and hours compounded the force of hard times. As Table 4.3 shows, changed rates produced, between the 1892 peak and 1894 trough, a fall of 7.6 percent in the full time–equivalent average dollar earnings of nonfarm laborers. At the same time, reflecting time losses through unemployment as well as lower wage scales, estimated actual

Table 4.3
Average Nonfarm Earnings in the 1890s

Year	Full-time Equivalent	% Fall From Peak	Actual $ Earnings	% Fall From Peak	Cost of Living*	Real Earnings*	% Fall From Peak
1891	$560		522		79.0	$661	
1892	567		541		79.0	685	
1893	553	2.5	494	8.7	78.5	629	8.1
1894	524	7.6	429	22.7	76.5	561	18.1
1895	542	4.6	470	13.1	76.5	614	10.5
1896	537	5.3	448	17.2	78.5	571	16.5
1897	537	5.3	452	16.5	78.5	576	15.9
1898	542	4.6	462	14.6	78.5	589	14.0
1899	553	2.5	507	6.3	80.1	613	3.2
1900	563	0.7	521	3.7	81.8	637	7.0

*1910–1914 = 100.

Source: Stanley Lebergott, "Earnings of Nonfarm Employees in the U.S. 1890–1946," American Statistical Association, *Journal* 43 (March 1948), 74–93.

dollar and real earnings were off respectively 22.7 and 18.1 percent. Conditions worsened again after the 1895 upturn, and even in 1900, despite substantial recovery and advancing wages, unemployment held average real earnings 7 percent below the 1892 high.[17]

News of wage reductions was current as early as July 1893. On the 12th, Jones & Laughlin Steel published a new wage agreement authorizing cuts of up to 15 percent. On August 1 the giant Vermont Marble Company notified its twelve thousand operatives of a 15 percent curtailment effective in two weeks. The Chicago, Milwaukee & St. Paul and Chicago & Eastern Illinois railroads soon after reduced the salaries of officials and office staffs 10 percent, hinting that similar cuts impended for other workers. In autumn, as panic subsided, there were frequent reports that firms were resuming operations, but on reduced pay scales to minimize losses. Wage cuts joined with growing unemployment to set the stage for the terrible social and political upheavals of 1894. The privations of workingmen—gaunt, embittered but determined, and deeply troubled—strained the resources of government and charitable agencies and tore at the fabric of society.[18]

Wage movements varied with economic conditions during the depression. In general, and reinforcing inferences from changing patterns of consumption, the best-paid and best-organized workingmen suffered the smallest pay cuts. Average hourly earnings for industrial labor passed through two troughs, in 1894

Table 4.4
Principal Crops and Prices, 1891–1900

Year	Wheat 000 bu.	Price/ bu. $	Corn 000 bu.	Price/ bu. $	Cotton 000 lbs	Price/ lb. $	Tobacco 000 lbs.	Price/ lb. $
1891	677,543	.831	2,335,804	.398	9,035	.072	747,460	.082
1892	611,854	.624	1,897,412	.393	6,700	.083	756,845	.089
1893	505,795	.534	1,900,401	.361	7,493	.070	766,670	.079
1894	541,873	.489	1,615,016	.451	9,901	.046	766,870	.066
1895	542,119	.505	2,534,762	.252	7,162	.076	745,000	.068
1896	522,963	.721	2,671,048	.214	8,533	.067	760,035	.055
1897	606,202	.809	2,287,628	.260	10,899	.067	703,275	.074
1898	768,148	.579	2,351,323	.285	11,278	.057	909,090	.061
1899	658,534	.588	2,666,324	.298	9,535	.070	870,250	.071
1900	599,315	.621	2,661,978	.350	10,124	.092	851,980	.067

Source: Crop prices based on farmers' estimates as of December 1 of the season's average for each
   year, disregarding commissions and other charges. Corn yields for all purposes; wheat for grain
   only. *Yearbook of the Agriculture 1901*, 72–82; U.S. Congress, House, *Monthly Summary of
   Commerce and Finance of the United States 1901*, 56th Congress, 2d Sess., 1901, House
   Document 15, 1, 664–66; *Historical Statistics . . . to 1957*, 274, 297–98, 301–2, 389; and for
   the South, Woodward, *Origins of the New South*, 269–70 and passim.

and again in 1896, as did the economy, although scales for most other types of
labor reached single lows in the mid-decade. Losses for industrial, railroad, and
building trades employees were but 2 percent in current dollars. Scales for farm
labor dropped 6 to 7 percent, falling farthest in the South, where they were
already low. Low-skilled workers and bituminous coal miners endured declines
respectively of 14 and over 26 percent. Former rates were approximated in 1899
in most cases. As the index of wholesale prices fell 18 percent from February
1893 to May 1894, and the cost of living some 3.4–4 percent, some workingmen
fortunate enough to retain full-time employment in favored industries gained in
real income. For the greater number, the era held deepening distress.[19]

Hard times thrust grievous suffering upon farmers who depended on sales of
the staple crops of wheat, corn, cotton, or tobacco for their cash incomes. Table
4.4 shows that wheat prices in 1894, with output up 7 percent, averaged a cent
less than a year earlier, at just under $.50 a bushel. There was no improvement
until 1896. Meanwhile, William Allen White's *Emporia, Kansas Gazette* had
predicted editorially in August 1894 that because of rising prices and lower
transportation costs, "there will be no corn burned by Kansas farmers this
year."[20] However, crop failures that cut the corn harvest by one-sixth largely

offset the $.09 advance, to $.451. Bumper harvests in 1895 and 1896 slashed returns to $.252 and then a dismaying $.214 season average. An unsteady advance accompanied smaller production over the next three years. Not until 1900 did the crop value climb slightly past that of 1891; a short harvest in 1901 at last pushed the corn price to $.60 and the crop value 10 percent above the 1891 figure.

The 1894 cotton crop exceeded the previous record by almost a million bales. Yet prices fell two and a half cents in a year, to about half the 1892 rate. Planters received $33 million less than for the 1894 crop, which was but 57 percent as large. Fortunately, the next three years brought improvement. The coincidence of reviving foreign demand and prosperity with a record harvest in 1897 helped lift the pall of hard times.

Tobacco growers endured numbing depression well past the turn of the century. Virginia planters sold their 1894 harvest for less than half the return from any crop but one since 1880. Kentucky's producers suffered even more stunning losses. Tobacco prices and crop values both sank to troughs in 1896 about 38 percent below their 1892 peaks; recovery was complete only about a decade later.

Depression etched a similar record for oats, hogs, and cattle. Yearly average prices for hogs at Chicago plummeted from an 1893 high of $6.49 a hundredweight to $4.99 ⅜ in 1894 and $3.38 ½ two years later, thereafter struggling back to $5.02 ¾ in 1900. Agricultural prostration figured decisively in the shape, duration, and devastating social impact of the larger business contraction. Throughout the South tenancy and the lien system tightened their strangleholds, while in the West debt, foreclosure, and distress kept pace. In South and West alike farmers squinted across dusty years and sun-scorched fields, puzzling angrily over their misfortunes.[21]

Other indices reinforced the pattern of depression. Merchandise imports in 1894 were down 23 percent from the preceding year, helping produce a favorable net balance of payments. However, European depression held exports 14 percent below their last peak, and they dropped 7 percent more during the next year before beginning to improve in 1896 and rising to prosperous levels two years later.[22]

The cumulative picture depicted an economy operating perhaps 20 to 25 percent below capacity through 1894. Distress was evident in knots of idle men clustered murmuring around plant or store entrances, whiling away time at home, or tramping the countryside. It was apparent in the meager diets of sharecroppers and in foreclosures of farm mortgages. It was visible in restricted budgets and sluggish trade. It could be seen in strings of empty railroad cars and rusting sidings, in chimneys and stacks belching none of the clouds of smoke and soot that bespoke active enterprise but standing instead as gigantic sentinels outside silent factories, and in banked furnaces at iron and steel mills. Throughout the year the look of want was common in the land.

The bituminous coal strike that raged from April 21 into July, the catastrophic

American Railway Union boycott of Pullman cars that began on June 26, and other labor clashes, although mostly unsuccessful in a year of acute unemployment and low demand for labor, prolonged the trough of the depression. Triggering through their violence the use of militia and the army to protect property and restore order, the clashes hit the coal, iron, and especially the rail industry with particular force. Coal output and shipments suffered, contributing to a fall in iron production and an abrupt loss in railroad earnings—already low—to abyssal depths.[23] It was only during the last third of 1894 that signs of quickening investment, output, commerce, and reduced hardship began to appear.

The advance that began in the late summer and fall of 1894 and continued through the following year anticipated the similar recovery of 1933–37 in being incomplete and falling within a longer period of depression. The largely self-generated improvement had multiple roots. The persistent hope—often nothing more than autosuggestion or optimistic fancy unsupported by concrete evidence, and occasionally inspired by partisan motives—that business was improving and that better times were ahead was an important spark. It was especially so after the February 1895 bond issue, when signs at hand suggested growing activity. The pessimism that encouraged gold hoarding at year's beginning was displaced by an optimism that floated new securities issues and attracted foreign capital. Increased investment to finance output to replenish depleted inventories, supply the wants of a growing population, and finance corporate reorganization paced advancing commerce. Important added impetus was found in accelerated building construction, which took advantage of easy money and growing needs as well as of rents, which had fallen less than prices. Other stimuli were the improved international trading position of the country resulting from lower prices, and a return of strikers to work.[24]

Further momentum for expansion derived from the remarkable growth of new industries apparently untouched by depression because their markets had not been saturated when panic struck: electric street railways, electric light and power, mining (the metallic and mineral output of which was one of the foundations of a mechanizing and industrializing economy), telephone service, and general manufacturing. Electric street railways boomed during the depression, spreading weblike throughout cities and even into modest towns with immodest ambitions. Over the decade the value of realty and equipment belonging to electric railways rose 330 percent, or $2,456 billion (1929 dollars). Electric light and power property values gained 470 percent, $663 million. Decennial increases for telephone and mining companies, 173 percent or $772 million and 95 percent or $792 million, were also impressive.

Property worth in general manufacturing advanced 65 percent, $3.838 billion. Annual sales of the bicycle industry concurrently shot from a few millions to $30 million a year through 1898. In contrast, agricultural property values rose only 33 percent, steam railroads 34 percent. Behind figures representing such disparate rates of growth lay compelling developments. Rapid increases elsewhere helped take up the slack resulting from a declining growth rate of steam railroads. More important, they hastened the process transforming the economy from an overreliance on agriculture and international earnings secured through the sale of farm produce, with attaching disadvantages, to a primary reliance on industry and sales of manufactures. In both respects the outlines of a new pattern of economic life emerged.[25]

Investment, building construction, and the iron and steel industries showed the most conspicuous improvement in the revival of 1895. New issues of stocks doubled those of 1894, and sales consistently surpassed levels for that year. Producer durables consumption surged to erase three-fourths of the total loss since 1892. Annual residential construction rose perhaps 15 percent during the upswing. From July to August 1894, monthly pig iron production rose 140,000 tons, some 25 percent. It advanced that much more by the end of the year and reached record rates of over 900,000 tons monthly, just under three times the preceding year's trough, at the end of 1895, while unsold stocks declined. Monthly rail freight ton-mileage mounted 20 percent to a peak in November, pausing, and then reaching a new high in January–February, 1896.[26] Optimistic reports of the progress of industry and trade stirred anticipation of greater gains. The *New York Times* in August 1895, recording resumptions by hundreds of firms, an addition of "not less than 200,000" to employment, and pay raises and longer hours for a million workingmen, predicted a return to full prosperity.[27]

The recovery was incomplete and unsatisfactory. Although Europe was also emerging from depression, British prices continued to fall until 1896, reducing the market for the more expensive American goods and attracting money from America for imports, investment, and tourist expenditures. American merchandise exports fell in 1895 to $300 million, 2 percent of GNP, below the pre-depression peak. Declining American exports dampened the nation's recovery.[28]

American agriculture continued to suffer the consequences of reduced foreign purchases of surpluses. Wheat yields, prices, and exports in 1895 were about the same as in 1894. A 45 percent fall in prices just about offset a slightly larger rise in corn output. Cotton and tobacco markets showed little improvement. Before scattered signs of recovery in 1896, low farm prices spelled restricted agricultural investment and consumption, and poor railroad earnings. Farmers had to produce, sell, and ship more just to maintain income.

Declining railroad construction and capital outlays, and a weak employment recovery restricted the 1895 economic revival. Railroad capital expenditures fell that year, although consumption rose slightly, probably through requirements for corporate reorganization.[29] Total employment was about the same as 1894, but the labor force was larger, and joblessness averaged 10 percent for the year. Other indices of business, including outside clearings and rail freight movement, also failed to meet or pass previous peaks before beginning to decline. Agricultural surpluses, restricted demand, and foreign influences like the British price movement prompted price declines that continued to a trough in 1897 and made circumstances difficult for producers and sellers.

By late 1895 it was apparent that expansion was nearly spent. Monthly indicators began to turn down as early as June, when the value of urban building permits faded. Wholesale prices, New York bank loans and deposits, and factory employment stopped moving up in June, July, and August; common stock prices in September; shares traded in New York, outside clearings, the number of business incorporations, and imports in October. In November pig iron output and railroad gross earnings levelled. Of the major monthly series only rail freight shipments improved into 1896. Foreign demand for American securities had begun to slow in the third quarter. Inventories of pig iron began accumulating in December, despite the rapid development of new uses for iron and steel.[30] Small exports, low railroad earnings, and a demoralized agricultural sector meant more bad times; prosperity was unlikely until these sectors revived. Recognition of a stillborn recovery starved buoyancy and fed caution and pessimism. Seasonally adjusted, commercial paper in New York rose 33 percent from September's average of 3.17 percent to 4.23 in October. A continued rise in short-term interest rates through year's end, and a fall in New York bank loans and deposits of 6 and 10 percent from September through November, reflected spreading uncertainty.[31]

Events during and after December 1895 helped transform what might have been a pause into a severe downturn. Unsettled political affairs in Europe and the collapse of speculations in South African mining shares, occurring when American securities trading was weakening, sparked repatriation of American shares and renewed drains on the treasury and specie outflows. Financial stringency was only momentary in Europe, but reawakened fears for the dollar joined with profit taking here and abroad to produce continued sales of stocks and bonds, and gold shipments. At the beginning of December the reserve was $79.3 million, and falling.

On the seventeenth another crisis flared. As noted above, President Cleveland, rebuffed in efforts to persuade Britain to accept arbitration of a boundary dispute between Venezuela and British Guiana, sent an explosive message to Congress. Using the Monroe Doctrine to justify intervention to avert a settlement extending British influence, he sought authority to determine and uphold the boundary unilaterally. Prompt congressional approval followed. The message incited an international crisis that seemed to take the country to the brink of war.[32] The public erupted in a patriotic frenzy, and jingoism flared. The *Washington Post, New York Sun*, and *Louisville Courier-Journal* explored the possibility of hostilities. Republican Senators Henry Cabot Lodge of Massachusetts and William Eaton Chandler of New Hampshire loudly advertised their patriotism, placing themselves in the unfamiliar company of Western silverite solons, who advocated war with Britain as a means of freeing the country from the control of an alleged international bankers' conspiracy. Impeccably respectable and conservative individuals and organizations joined dissatisfied Democratic newspapers, Anglophobes, and fuzzy-minded opponents of the "gold conspiracy" to support the president. New York's Union League Club, composed of 1,800 of the city's most prominent business leaders, rallied behind the administration, as did the president of Chase Manhattan National Bank, Russell Sage, and Chauncy Mitchell Depew, president of the New York Central Railroad.

Most businessmen believed that war was improbable, although the possibility could not be disregarded.[33] The *New York Times* predicted that Britain would accept a just award. A deeply disturbed *Commercial and Financial Chronicle*, however, deplored Cleveland's message and its effect on Anglo-American relations as "in every way unfortunate" and denied the applicability of the Monroe Doctrine.[34]

In any case, however unlikely war seemed, the crisis provoked a minor panic and large sales of American securities—fifty thousand shares in London the day after Cleveland's speech—at home and abroad. Pressure on the market grew intense, credit tight, and prices unstable as selling mounted. Wild rumors of impending huge gold shipments, threatening the Treasury reserve further, added to alarm. On Friday, December 20, the market succumbed to panic. Some 750,000 shares, more than twice the daily average for the year, changed hands as investors rushed to unload. Nominal rates for call money soared to 90 percent, stock prices fell by as much as 10 percent, and several financial houses caught by surprise had to suspend. At the height of the emergency a number of prominent bankers met and devised plans to restore order.

Frederick D. Tappan, president of the Gallatin National Bank and a key figure in efforts to combat panic in 1893, took the lead with representatives of the Merchants' National Bank and the Union, Atlantic, and Central Trust companies. It was decided to refrain for the time being from action to support securities values, and to force foreign investors who intended to do so to liquidate at the least remunerative prices. However, the Central Trust Company moved at once to ease credit, making $1.5 million available at 4 to 5 percent. It was not until Monday, though, when the banks' action was publicized, that money rates relaxed. Saturday's gold exports were $7,132,644. Losses for the week were up to fifteen points for Rock Island, fourteen for St. Paul, and ten each for Kansas & Texas, Denver & Rio Grande, and Southern Railway preferred. American Sugar common was off eleven points; American Tobacco, six; American Leather preferred, nine; and Tennessee Coal and Iron, eight.[35]

Gold exports arising from a weak market and panic drained the Treasury reserve and speeded contraction by intensifying fear over the security of the gold standard. A presidential plea on December 20, when alarm was spreading, for currency reform to restore confidence in the dollar and the Treasury fell on deaf ears. Senate silverites approved a free coinage bill, and House Republicans sought partisan advantage by passing a revised tariff that proposed to protect the reserve by raising duties and thus federal receipts. Thwarted on Capital Hill, in February 1896 the administration turned for the last time to a bond issue to obtain specie.[36]

The Venezuela crisis passed early in 1896, when Britain and Venezuela accepted a draft arbitration treaty as the basis for ending their dispute. Meanwhile the February bond issue eased monetary fears and the disposition to hoard or export gold. Short-term interest rates in New York fell 30 percent from January through April; commercial paper still averaged a high 4.75 percent. New York bank loans and deposits began an unsteady and gradual expansion at the beginning of February. However, political disturbances soon arose in another quarter, as congressional sympathy for the rebellion that had begun in Cuba in 1895 swept to the fore. The Senate at the end of February, and the House on April 6, approved a concurrent resolution calling for recognition of Cuban belligerency. Administration and Senate opposition prevented action on more radical proposals, including resolutions favoring American intervention on behalf of the rebels. Contemporary reports indicate that some businessmen took alarm at discussion of such steps, which seemed to promise political instability or even war, with their disturbing dislocations of trade.[37]

Had there been no further disruptive developments in 1896, business might have begun to recover in late spring or summer. To be sure, securities values and trading, building construction, business incorporations, outside clearings, rail freight movement, pig iron manufacture, factory employment, wholesale prices, and an index of the physical volume of business continued (seasonally smoothed) on an irregular downward trend. However, panic had passed. European recovery was well advanced, furnishing a ready market for growing American exports. Spring brought signs of a seasonal growth of trade, exciting expressions of "confidence that times are permanently improved and improving." With harvest yet to come, hopes were high for a return of prosperity in the near future.[38] Such hopes proved empty.

The presidential contest of 1896 (treated below), stretching from late spring through early November, intervened decisively to cause a continued and severe decline of business unshared in Europe. In spring, silver inflationists captured one state party convention after another and secured declarations for free coinage or bimetallism. Even Ohio Republicans failed to endorse a gold standard unequivocally. The Republican nomination in mid-June of former Ohio governor William McKinley for the presidency on a high tariff and gold standard platform offered a temporary measure of reassurance. But a week later, on June 24, proponents of a gold standard suffered a shattering blow when New York Democrats wavered from financial orthodoxy and announced for international bimetallism. The Democratic national convention that began in Chicago on July 7 was an even more bitter reverse. Silverites, in command from the beginning, stampeded for the inclusion of a platform plank endorsing free coinage. Then, as the *Commercial and Financial Chronicle* reported in a masterpiece of understatement, William Jennings Bryan of Nebraska, "who captured the convention by one of his speeches"—his July 8 "cross of gold" oration—was overwhelmingly nominated.[39] Ominously, dissident silver Republicans and the People's Party, meeting simultaneously in St. Louis soon after, embraced the Democratic candidate. With the subsequent secession of a rump of gold Democrats, who at Indianapolis in September selected a separate slate, the stage was set for the electoral battle of the century.

By May the possibility that silverites would capture one of the major political parties, and perhaps the presidency, was sufficiently alarming to provoke a renewal of greenback redemption at the Treasury to secure gold for hoarding or export. Redemptions, May–July, were $47.6 million, and exports $37.9 million despite a favorable merchandise balance. Short-term interest rates in New York had remained abnormally high since autumn, but they began to rise again in May before crop-moving time. As the election neared, commercial paper in New York rose from a monthly average of 4.82 percent in May to 7.40 in October. New York bank loans declined from $479.5 million in July to $442.1 million in November, a loss of 8 percent, and deposits shrank thirteen points. Milton Friedman has argued cogently in his *Monetary History of the United States* that if Bryan had been expected to win, currency redemption and specie exports would probably have exhausted the reserve and forced the country off the gold standard. As it happened, uncertainty and tight credit meant hardship for many businessmen. Loans were extremely difficult to negotiate at whatever rate.

On July 21, representatives of New York's chief banks and financial houses met in J. P. Morgan's office to plan measures to reduce gold outflows and protect the Treasury. It was agreed to furnish foreign exchange bills drawn on London in whatever quantities were needed to meet domestic requirements for remittances to Europe, until cotton and grain shipments after harvest earned enough exchange to meet the demand. The Gallatin National Bank and other New York, Chicago, and Philadelphia financial institutions deposited specie in the Treasury to increase its gold holdings to a safe level. Quick action broke the movement to hoard gold until the eve of the election, when large-scale hoarding resumed. Specie briefly commanded a premium of about 1 percent. Call funds in New York on October 29 reached 100 percent, and on the 30th, 127 percent.[40]

Falling investment joined other prominent financial symptoms of the uncertainty that was plunging the country into recession. It was very difficult to raise funds through new issues of stocks and bonds. Equity issues on the New York exchange slipped slightly below the 1895 total and remained 23 percent under the 1892 peak; bond issues were down 12 percent from the previous year. Trading in New York dropped abruptly in May. It continued low, save for a spurt in November, through the year's end. In May too, prices spun into a decline to the decennial trough three months later. Seasonally smoothed, building permit values fell through October. Railroad capital expenditures continued to wane, and it may be inferred that orders for producer durables, led by industrial machinery and equipment, fell off sharply. The 1895 revival carried consumption of industrial machinery and equipment in 1896 to 37.4 percent above the 1892 figure, measured in 1913 dollars, but a year later it was 13 percent below the pre-depression peak.

Meanwhile, tight money and slackening trade forced a serious wave of failures, which peaked during the politically troubled second half of the year. In March, high fixed charges and low income forced the Baltimore & Ohio Railroad into receivership. In the same month one of the largest textile manufacturers in Texas succumbed. A speculative collapse toppled the Diamond Match Company in Chicago on August 4, resulting in a temporary closure of the Chicago stock exchange to avert a general demoralization of trading. Summer also saw the New England textile industry, which through reduced costs had largely escaped the disasters of the past three years, suffer serious reverses as markets wilted.[41] Total failures for the year were second only to those of 1893, at 15,088. Aggregate liabilities of suspended firms were $226,096,834, an average of $14,245. In the third quarter 3,757 concerns with liabilities of $73,285,349 (and average liabilities of $19,507) went under. Altogether 144 banks of all types, with assets of about $50 million, fell, many because of inability to make collections on loans that would in easier times have been sound.[42] Outside clearings, wholesale prices, and factory employment also struck lows in the third quarter, slumping through August. Rail freight shipments eased through September. Pig iron output and merchandise imports fell for an additional month. Bank loans, deposits, and reserves drifted downward until mid-November. Thus despite a feeble popular response to Bryan's August 12 Madison Square Garden speech launching his Eastern campaign, and despite a growing conviction that McKinley would probably win the election, industrial and commercial activity declined well into autumn.

There were very few encouraging signs before the balloting. Bank support enabled the gold reserve, despite a brief interval of hoarding and near panic just before the election, to rise after July. Growing crop exports, perhaps with some aid from high interest rates and possibly, according to some contemporary reports, with added help from British fears that the sale of securities would enhance Bryan's chances of victory by further depressing conditions, produced a large inflow of gold in September and October.[43] Finally, early in November, when frightened employers were intensifying efforts to coerce workers to vote Republican and as monetary stringency was becoming acute in New York, anticipation of a McKinley victory provoked a frantic spurt of speculation in securities.[44]

McKinley's decisive 7,104,244–6,505,835 success in the voting removed most of the political sources of business uncertainty. The gold standard and treasury now seemed secure. The Republicans had promised an upward revision of tariff to grant American industry added protection. There could be no doubt that the financial policies of the new administration would favor business. There remained only two major obstacles to a return of prosperity. These were overcome in the next few years with the gradual appearance of economic stimuli exciting a revival of commerce, and the replacement of pessimism and apprehension with optimism and confident expectations.

NOTES

1. Many papers wishfully reported improvement toward the end of 1893, often tailoring reports to fit their political positions. See *Atlanta Constitution* (September 12, October 15, and November 17, 1893); *Boston Daily Advertiser* (September 26 and November 6, 1893); *Chicago Daily Tribune* (November 6, 13, 1893); *Cleveland Plain Dealer* (October 28, 31, and November 11, 1893); *Emporia (Kansas) Gazette* (November 18, 1893); *Philadelphia Public Ledger* (October 21 and November 18, 1893); *Raleigh (North Carolina) News & Observer* (October 12 and 31, 1893); *St. Louis Post-Dispatch* (November 4 and 5, 1893); *Seattle Post-Intelligencer* (September 16, October 21, and November 21, 1893); *Wall Street Journal* (October 30, 1893).

For railroad earnings see the *Commercial and Financial Chronicle* (February 24, 1894, January 6 and February 20, 1896, and January 11, 1897); for New York bank data, National Monetary Commission, *Statistics for the United States, 1867–1909*, 101–102; and for monthly series, *Historical Statistics, 1789–1945*, 329; and Moore, *Business Cycle Indicators*, 2:15.1, 130 and passim.

2. Barnes, *John G. Carlisle*, 226; also Esther Rogoff Taus, *Central Banking Functions of the United States Treasury, 1789–1941* (New York: Columbia University Press, 1943), 85–96.

3. U.S. Congress, House, *Report of the Secretary of the Treasury*, 56th Cong., 2d sess., 1900, House Document 8, cxvii–cxviii; *Commercial and Financial Chronicle* (November 17, 1894); Nevins, *Grover Cleveland*, 598–99; Barnes, *John G. Carlisle*, 307–17.

4. The November issue, in 5 percent, ten-year bonds, drew several hundred bids totalling $178 million. The Treasury accepted the high bid of 117.077, offered by a syndicate organized by J. P. Morgan. The bid brought in $57,665,000 of gold while cutting the real interest rate of the issue to 2.878 percent.

Each syndicate member took at least $100,000 of bonds. Drexel, Morgan & Company took $3,350,000; Harvey Fisk & Sons and the First National Bank of New York each took twice that amount. The city banks also pledged not to aid bond buyers who intended to pay for their securities with specie obtained by redeeming greenbacks, but redemptions in November and December exceeded gold exports by nearly $30 million.

See U.S. Congress, House, *Report of the Secretary of the Treasury*, 56th Cong., 2d sess., 1900, House Document 8, cxvii–cxviii; *Commercial and Financial Chronicle* (November 17, December 1, 8, and 22, 1894, and January 5, 1895); Barnes, *John G. Carlisle*, 354–60; Nevins, *Grover Cleveland*, 532–33; Noyes, *Forty Years of American Finance*, 231.

5. *Commercial and Financial Chronicle* (February 9, September 28, January–February, 1895). The bonds sold at 104.499, yielding 3 ¾ percent. Later the syndicate (or syndicates, for there were two, one in Europe and one in America), marketed the securities at 112 ½. Enthusiastic buyers drove the price to 119, then 123.

6. U.S. Congress, House, *Report of the Secretary of the Treasury*, 56th Cong., 2d sess., 1900, House Document 8, cxvii–cxviii; *New York Times* (December 12–23, 1895); *Commercial and Financial Chronicle* (December 28, 1895; and February 15–June 1896); "Business and Finance," *Public Opinion* 19 (December 26, 1895), 862; Noyes, *Forty Years of American Finance*, 251–54.

7. Friedman and Schwartz, *Monetary History*, 111–13, 128–34. Contemporary business opinion attested to the reassuring effect of reduced gold drains after bond sales; *Cleveland Plain Dealer* (February 8, 1896); *St. Louis Post-Dispatch* (February 17, 1895); *Wall Street Journal* (February 11, 1895); *Commercial and Financial Chronicle* (February, November 1894, January 5, 1895, January 4, 1896, January 2, 1897); and Noyes, *Forty Years of American Finance*, 242–43.

8. Headlines, *Chicago Daily Tribune* (December 11, 1893); *Philadelphia Public Ledger* (February 24, 1894). For monthly series, Evans, *Business Incorporations*, 80; *Commercial and Financial Chronicle* (January 6, 1894–January 12, 1901), and *Eleventh Census of the United States: 1890, Population*, 1:xxiv–xxxiv.

9. Securities issues and trading, *Commercial and Financial Chronicle* (January 8, 1898, 13, 1900, and first January number 1894–1901); Alfred A. Cowles III and Associates, *Common Stock Indexes, 1871–1937* (Bloomington, IN: Principia Press, 1938), 41–42, 62–63, 66, 454; *Historical Statistics . . . to 1957*, 656, 657; Hoffmann, "Depression," 139–41 and *Depression of the Nineties*, 92–98, 113–16, 119, 234–36.

10. Rolling stock, revenue, rails, freight, *Historical Statistics . . . to 1957*, 416, 429, 434; construction, *Poor's Manual, 1892–1901*, ii–iii and passim in each volume cited; capital spending in 1929 dollars, Ulmer, *Trends and Cycles*, 60; Hoffmann, "Depression," 140–42. Large capital consumption for reorganization and operation contributed to negative net expenditures, 1895–99.

11. For building see *Historical Statistics . . . to 1957*, 376, 383, 393; Clarence D. Long, Jr., *Building Cycles and the Theory of Investment* (Princeton, NJ: Princeton University Press, 1940), 213–33; Riggleman, "Building Cycles," 174–83; Hoffmann, "Depression," 128.

12. U.S. Congress, Senate, *Reports of the Immigration Commission*, 61st Cong., 3d sess., 1911, Senate Document 756, "Statistical Review of Immigration, 1820–1910," "Distribution of Immigrants, 1850–1900," 11–12; *Historical Statistics . . . to 1957*, 48–51, 57.

13. Whitten, *Emergence of Giant Enterprise*, 35–56; Spiro G. Patton, "Local and Suburban Transit," in *Extractives, Manufacturing, and Services: A Historiographical and Bibliographical Guide*, vol. 2, *Handbook of American Business History*, ed. David O. Whitten and Bess E. Whitten (Westport, CT: Greenwood Press, 1997), 357–74.

14. Quoted in *St. Louis Post-Dispatch* (January 22, 1897); Shaw, *Commodity Output*, 30–64 (current dollars), 70–77 (1913 dollars); *Historical Statistics . . . to 1957*, 419–21; and for an able discussion, Hoffmann, "Depression," 148–49.

15. Hoffmann, *Depression of the Nineties*, 97–110; Carlos C. Closson, Jr., "The Unemployed in American Cities," *Quarterly Journal of Economics* 8 (January, April 1894), 168–217, 257–60, 453–77; *Proceedings of the General Assembly of the Knights of Labor*, Seventeenth Regular Session, 1893 (Philadelphia: Journal of the Knights of Labor, 1893), 11; *Report of Proceedings of the American Federation of Labor, 1893* (Bloomington, IN: American Federation of Labor, 1893), 12–23.

16. Quote, Samuel Gompers, *A.F.L. Proceedings, 1893*, 12. Estimates for manufacturing and railroads, Paul Howard Douglas, *Real Wages in the United States, 1890–1926* (Boston: Houghton Mifflin Company, 1934), 454–60. Building construction and coal mining totals were figured from decennial census and Bureau of Mines data in ibid., 454, 455; Riggleman, "Building Cycles," 180; and *Historical Statistics . . . to 1957*, 383. A framework for discussion, as well as the fullest treatment, appears in Hoffmann, *Depression of the Nineties*, 97–110; Alvin Harvey Hansen, "Industrial Class Alignments

in the United States," *Quarterly Publications of the American Statistical Association* 17 (December 1920), 417–22.

17. Stanley Lebergott, "Earnings of Nonfarm Employees in the U.S. 1890–1946," American Statistical Association, *Journal* 43 (March 1948), 74–93, provided the basis for Table 4.3 and the accompanying discussion. Lebergott's estimates were adjustments from Douglas, *Real Wages*, adding data for trade, finance, and construction workers' incomes to those of the groups that Douglas treated. Lebergott set the percentage of time lost through unemployment of nonfarm workers in 1894 at 18.1; in 1895 at 13.3; 1896, 16.6; 1897, 15.8; 1898, 14.8; 1899, 8.4; and in 1900 at 7.5.

18. *New York Times* (July 13–August 1 and October 3–December 31, 1893).

19. The average workweek changed little. Pay for coal miners hit bottom as late as 1898. For cost of living and wages see Lebergott, "Earnings," 74–93; for wages, Douglas, *Real Wages*, 390–94 and passim; *Historical Statistics . . . to 1957*, 91; for farm labor also Shannon, *Farmer's Last Frontier*, 364.

20. *Emporia (Kansas) Gazette* (August 21, 1894).

21. Crop prices are based on farmers' estimates as of December 1 of the season's average for each year, disregarding commissions and other charges. Corn yields for all purposes; wheat for grain only. See *Yearbook of the Department of Agriculture 1901*, 72–82; U.S. Congress, House, *Monthly Summary of Commerce and Finance of the United States 1901*, 56th Cong., 2d sess., 1901, House Document 15, 1, 664–66; *Historical Statistics . . . to 1957*, 274, 297–98, 301–2, 389; and for the South, Vann Woodward, *Origins of the New South*, 269–70 and passim.

22. *Historical Statistics . . . to 1957*, 562.

23. The strikes are discussed below. The earnings of the Chicago & Eastern Illinois Railroad in the first week of July were $8,244, against $93,643 for the same period in 1893. St. Paul gross receipts were down from $646,410 to $312,317, those of the Wabash from $270,101 to $45,267, and the Grand Trunk from $75,003 to $6,555. Gross earnings for all roads, June–July, were off about 20 percent from 1893, net receipts respectively 28 and 19 percent. *Commercial and Financial Chronicle* (August 11, 1894, January 5, 1895, and February 20, 1896).

24. *Seattle Post-Intelligencer* (November 10 and 13, 1894); also *Atlanta Constitution* (June 11, 1894); *(Boise) Idaho Daily Statesman* (April 6, 1895, and May 22, 1896); *Chicago Daily Tribune* (September 3 and December 24, 1894); *Cleveland Plain Dealer* (January 23 and September 5, 1894, and April 6, 1896); *San Francisco Chronicle* (June 9, 1894; March 2, 1895; and February 29 and September 26, 1896); *Wall Street Journal* (September 5 and 6, 1894, and February 11, 1895). On the recovery see Fels, *American Business Cycles*, 184–200.

25. Hoffmann, *Depression of the Nineties*, 75–78, offers a provocative treatment of the economic transformation of the 1890s. See also Simon Smith Kuznets, *National Product since 1869* (New York: National Bureau of Economic Research, 1946), 231. In 1929 dollars, agricultural and steam railroad property values increased respectively by $2.489 billion and $929 million in the 1890s.

26. Pig iron inventories and monthly rail earnings respectively, *Commercial and Financial Chronicle* (January 6, 1894; January 11, 1896; February 24, 1894; February 20, 1896); also *Historical Statistics . . . to 1957*, 332, 329; and note 1, above.

27. *New York Times* (August 5, 1895).

28. Fels, *American Business Cycles*, 193–200; Friedman and Schwartz, *Monetary His-*

tory, 111; Mitchell and Deane, *British Historical Statistics*, 472–73; *Historical Statistics ... to 1957*, 143, 562.

29. Ulmer, *Trends and Cycles*, 60; Shaw, *Commodity Output*, 56.

30. For pig iron stocks, *Commercial and Financial Chronicle* (August 1894–December 1895); Spiro G. Patton, "Blast Furnances and Steel Mills," in *Manufacturing: A Historiographical and Bibliographical Guide*, ed. Whitten and Whitten, 239–62; Ann Harper Fender, "Iron and Steel Foundries," in *Extractives, Manufacturing, and Services*, ed. Whitten and Whitten, 287–310.

31. Monthly series cited above, note 1; see also Hoffmann, *Depression of the Nineties*, 79–88; Fels, *American Business Cycles*, 193; Noyes, *Forty Years of American Finance*, 242–43.

32. For foreign conditions, Thorp, *Business Annals*, 171; for Venezuela, Richardson, *Messages and Papers of the Presidents*, 9:655–58; *Commercial and Financial Chronicle* (December 1895–January 1896); Nevins, *Grover Cleveland*, 629–48; La Feber, *New Empire*, 242–83.

33. *Bradstreet's* reached this conclusion after surveying business opinion in twenty-three cities. See "Business and Finance," *Public Opinion* 19 (December 26, 1895), 862.

34. "The Anglo-Venezuelan Boundary Dispute," *Public Opinion* 19 (December 26, 1895), 838–44, sampled press opinion. See also *New York Times* (December 18, 1895); Nevins, *Grover Cleveland*, 641; and for the quote, *Commercial and Financial Chronicle* (December 21, 1895).

35. *New York Times* (December 18–23, 1895); *Commercial and Financial Chronicle* (December 21, 28, 1895); "Business and Finance," *Public Opinion* 19 (December 26, 1895), 862.

36. Cleveland's message in Richardson, *Messages and Papers of the Presidents*, 9: 659–60. Also pertinent, *New York Times* (December 21, 1895–February 10, 1896); *Commercial and Financial Chronicle* (December 1895–February 15, 1896, June 1896); Barnes, *John G. Carlisle*, 412–16; Nevins, *Grover Cleveland*, 636–38; Noyes, *Forty Years of American Finance*, 251–54; and Fels, *American Business Cycles*, 200–203.

37. Cuba discussed below; U.S. Congress, *Congressional Record*, 54th Cong., 1st sess. (Washington, DC: Government Printing Office, 1896), 28:3, 541; for a sample of business fears, *Commercial and Financial Chronicle* (February–April 1896).

38. See *Raleigh (North Carolina) News & Observer* (January 1, 1896); *Commercial and Financial Chronicle* (March 21, 1896); *(Salt Lake City) Deseret Weekly* (May 2, 1896); *Chicago Daily Tribune* (February 8, 1896); *Cleveland Plain Dealer* (April 4, 1896); *Philadelphia Public Ledger* (May 19, 1896); *St. Louis Post-Dispatch* (February 2 and May 10, 1896); *Commercial and Financial Chronicle* (January 2, 1894); *(Boise) Idaho Daily Statesman* (December 28, 1895); and note 1, above.

39. *Commercial and Financial Chronicle* (January 2, 1897).

40. Friedman and Schwartz, *Monetary History*, 128–34. Also U.S. Congress, National Monetary Commission, *Statistics for the United States, 1867–1909*, 61st Cong., 2d sess., 1911, Senate Document 570, 104; *Commercial and Financial Chronicle* (July 18–25 and November 7, 1896); *New York Times*, July–November 7, 1896); Noyes, *Forty Years of American Finance*, 254; and for added evaluations of the significance of the money question in 1896, "Editorial Comment," *Bankers' Magazine* 52 (June 1896), 703–7; and Fels, *American Business Cycles*, 203.

41. Fall River, Massachusetts, textile mills, for example, paid annual dividends, 1893–95, of 8, 5.25, and 8 percent. Clark, *History of Manufactures*, 3:184; *Commercial and*

Financial Chronicle (March 28 and August 8, 1896); *Cyclopedic Review of Current History* 6 (October 1–December 31, 1896), 866–67.

42. *Statistical Abstract of the United States: 1897*, 349–53; U.S. Congress, House, *Annual Report of the Comptroller of the Currency, 1895*, 54th Cong., 2d sess., House Document 10, 676, 721.

43. U.S. Congress, 61st Cong., 2d sess., Senate Document 570, 104; *Commercial and Financial Chronicle* (January 9, 1897; January 8, 1898; and January 13, 1900).

44. *Commercial and Financial Chronicle* (October 24–November 7, 1896, and January 2, 1897).

5

Recovery: A New Economic Order

The second trough of the depression fell in the weeks preceding the 1896 election. However, shortly before the balloting the growing promise of a McKinley triumph encouraged confident predictions, especially among Grand Old Party stalwarts, that the outcome of the struggle would "sweep away the last vestige of the clouds which have hovered so long over the business horizon." Signs pointed "to an immediate revival of business all over the country." "After four years of gnawing industrial distress, of commercial hemorrhage . . . [the United States was] about to have good times again." The press released optimistic statements from businessmen who saw economic revival in harness with an anticipated Republican victory.[1]

The buoyant securities trading that began on November 2, the day before voters went to the polls, continued into the post-election period. Stock prices on the New York exchange jumped two to eight points on the day after McKinley's election, and speculation remained active for some time following. Moreover a rush of resumptions followed the election, as if to make the predictions come true. Within three weeks, over seven hundred firms were reported to have resumed or expanded operations. Estimates of increased employment ranged up to a perhaps extravagant hundred thousand for the week succeeding the election.[2] Seasonally smoothed, monthly outside clearings rose 6 percent over November and December, and the number of business incorporations increased about ten points.

Pig iron output rose from 540,000 to 620,000 tons a month, while inventories fell. Iron production remained below the year's average, but the advance was impressive nevertheless. Building permit values grew by 18 percent from October's low to year's end. Increased exports and scattered price advances reflected upward pressure, growing partly from advancing prosperity in Europe. Merchandise exports for fiscal 1896, $1,048 million, were 23 percent above 1895, and in the fiscal year ending June 30, 1897, they rose about 8 percent, more to $1,136 million. In both instances the country enjoyed a favorable net balance of payments. Prices rose most markedly for drugs, chemicals, and wheat. Reduced harvests in France, British India, European Russia, and South America, combined with a barely increased yield in the United States to increase the average yearly wheat price by a full twenty cents to $0.721. In September wheat on the New York produce exchange reached the highest figure in several years, $1.06 ¾.[3]

Improvement was not recovery. December brought a rush of business failures in delayed reaction to the summer's contraction. An index of the physical volume of business continued to rise at about 1 or 2 percent a month, but trade was restrained. In January outside clearings fell back to November's level, where they remained until June. Merchandise exports levelled in the last quarter of 1896 and relaxed during the first half of the next year. Rail freight ton-mileage fell a fraction of a point in December, then crept up during the next four months. Factory employment behaved comparably. Monthly business incorporations slumped into July 1897. In December the wholesale price index began a decline that took it to a post–Civil War low in June 1897. The growth in pig iron output slowed, and competition destroyed several pools in iron and steel. An eighteen-month-old combine of wire nail makers disintegrated in December. Pools of steel rail and beam makers followed suit in February and May.[4] Before the end of November 1896 observers knew that the effect of the election on business, despite some expansion of trade, was psychological. The mood had improved, a gain in itself, but as one editor observed, if "confidence is a good thing . . . possession is better." Performance was short of promise.[5]

Although excess capacity created by the deep contraction of 1896 was probably the drag that prolonged stagnation into 1897, limited investment opportunities must be considered. Building construction remained weak through the end of the decade, undoubtedly because immigration declined through 1898. Railroad capital expenditures in 1897 sank to their decennial low, $207 million, down from $738 million in 1891, and the industry's prospects were not bright. In the absence of alternatives to take up the slack in railroad and building construction, the outlook for ancillary industries and the iron and steel trades was cloudy. Electric street railways and interurbans, electric light and power, telephone, and other comparatively new industries with bright futures were growing rapidly, but they were not yet strong enough to stir a general business revival. And there was little inducement to invest. Domestic consumption of producer durables declined 12 percent from 1896 to 1897.

Securities trading in New York slumped after November's election spurt, with prices and monthly share sales waning through most of the next spring. Foreign investors hesitated to send funds to the United States, because of uncertainty about the gold standard in the absence of comprehensive currency reform and because of the dismal state of American business. New issues of stocks and bonds in New York in 1897 were off 30 and 52 percent from their 1895 and 1894 levels. Under the circumstances, although average monthly rates for commercial paper in New York fell from 7.40 percent in October to 3.72 percent in January and eased into spring, idle funds accumulated rapidly in the city banks. Just before the election, loans had slightly exceeded net deposits. During the next five months loans increased by about 15 percent and deposits by twice as much; reserves rose even faster.[6]

Other developments added to the disappointing end of 1896 and persisted into the following spring. Congressional consideration of Pennsylvania Senator James Donald Cameron's resolution recognizing Cuban independence provided a temporarily alarming legislative counterpoint to the adverse weather that accompanied the arrival of winter. The stock market broke when the Foreign Relations Committee reported the resolution favorably on December 18; it was soon tabled, however, and the flurry subsided.[7] Spring brought a special session of Congress to revise the tariff. The only apparent effect on business was a short-lived jump in imports to avoid the new duties.

Newspapers reported, unconvincingly, that uneasiness among businessmen over the outcome of tariff discussions had discouraged trade, but the evidence pointed to general confidence that a new law satisfactory to enterprise would result.[8] Earlier, a price break from twenty-five to seventeen dollars per ton following the February collapse of the steel rail pool had seemed to add to the disheartening prospect. But it turned out to be one of the few heartening developments in a gloomy season. Low rates prompted enormous orders that in a short time nearly equalled the 1896 product of 1.1 million tons of Bessemer rails. The disturbingly low prices, moreover, enabled domestic manufacturers to launch a successful invasion of overseas markets. Among the new orders were several from England. However, despite the receipt of encouraging orders, output in the iron and steel industry remained nearly unchanged for many months. General trade too failed to show much improvement until late spring.[9]

On March 4, 1897, William McKinley became president of the United States. In his inaugural address he praised the American people for their fortitude and courage in the face of depression. Moving quickly to fulfill campaign and platform pledges to revise the tariff, he summoned Congress into special session on March 15 to enact a bill protecting more fully the country's industry and increasing the government's revenues through higher duties. McKinley's proposals and his announced determination to work ''to restore the prosperity of former years . . . [and] aid its return by friendly legislation'' cheered business interests, as had his earlier appointment of Lyman J. Gage, the well-known and conservative head of the First National Bank of Chicago, as Secretary of the Treasury.[10]

Congress deliberated over the Republican tariff bill from March 15 to July 24, when it finally became law. In the meantime the president, hoping to conciliate moderate silverites and find some permanent place for silver in the nation's monetary system, dispatched a three-member commission to Europe to explore the possibility of an international bimetallic agreement. After several fruitless months in various European capitals the delegates returned empty-handed to the United States. Their failure persuaded the chief executive that an international bimetallic accord was not attainable. He moved subsequently to firm support of a single gold standard. From spring 1897 onward, the administration began also to mature proposals for currency and banking reform, to eliminate an additional source of contemporary financial difficulty.

While the new Republican administration was getting under way, a restoration of prosperity began. The process moved gradually to completion during the next two or three years, as time was required to repair the psychological and material damages inflicted by five years of depression. In June 1897, New York securities trading and prices registered their first important advances. Sales nearly doubled, rising three million shares to a total of 6,436,000. Investment and speculation electrified in July and reached feverish heights in the next two months. September's sales of 13,142,000 shares exceeded by 13 percent the figure for the active market of February 1892. Revival surged forward in 1898, attended by rising expectations and buoyant trading.

Output of producer durables for domestic use, railroad capital expenditures, and new stock issues in New York all remained below former peaks. Yet they rose respectively 7, 27, and 30 percent in 1898, accelerating the widespread expansion of business and anticipating much greater gains the next year. In 1898 new bond issues in New York leaped 180 percent to a record $245.2 million. Behind more active investment, rail freight traffic had been creeping upward since December, although the first big jump did not occur until May. July's shipments actually surpassed the previous record of June 1893. December's traffic was greater than that of June 1893, seasonally adjusted, by 750 million ton-miles, or 9 percent, and there was a growth of 11 percent again by the end of 1898. Gross and net earnings increased in proportion, rising respectively 10 and 15 percent in 1898. Growing revenues permitted the year's expansion of capital expenditures, the first since 1891. Repair and replacement of long-neglected equipment were speeded. As previously shown, locomotive and car purchases in 1898 surpassed those of the expansive year of 1895, and a year later they were above the 1893 peak.

An index of the physical volume of business advanced strongly from May 1897 onward. Outside clearings began to score important gains in June and that month wholesale prices sagged to their lowest point since the Civil War, when they were 21 percent less than in February 1893. In July they moved up a modest 0.5 percent, heralding the end of a generation of deflation and the advent of an era of rising prices. In August monthly pig iron output bounded ahead by 7 percent, inaugurating a growth that exceeded 20 percent through December, when production reached a record 950,000 tons monthly. An index of factory employment also began to reflect quickening activity in August. Meanwhile, the liabilities of business failures, save for a brief jump in April, fell off sharply during the first half of 1897 and remained moderate through the year's end. Completing the picture of a stirring commerce, the monthly number of business incorporations began a recovery in August.[11]

Before mid-year, however, the barely perceptible stirrings of trade failed to dispel lingering dissatisfaction over the very limited nature of the recovery that followed the election. Democrats sarcastically asked where was the vaunted prosperity of which, in the late campaign, Republicans had billed McKinley the advance agent. Even where a modest springtime improvement of affairs was conceded, it was often deprecated as "disappointing."[12] In June and July, however, the mood improved as expanding industry and trade encouraged a renewal of optimism. The progress of confidence was measured in announcements that there were "BETTER TIMES COMING" and that the "recuperative powers of business . . . will partially compensate for the long delay" in the return of prosperity.[13] Glowing accounts of expanding business were by August driving doubters into hiding, as the nation seemed at last to be escaping from the wilderness of depression in which it had wandered for five years.

Confidence was important to recovery, although it was itself a product of the growth it helped fuel. Even before the hesitancy of spring yielded to a more positive outlook in summer, there were many who believed that business, having sunk to a "bedrock" level, must soon improve.[14] Others were aware that inventories had been greatly depleted, which must before long stimulate greater output to satisfy the demands of even a restricted market.[15] A mixture of wishful thinking and native optimism, these attitudes and the conditions on which they rested helped account for the mercurial shift of mood that greeted the beginnings of recovery.

The most important stimulus to revival in 1897 was the coincidence of disastrously short wheat harvests abroad with a bumper crop in America. As shown in Table 5.1, yields were much reduced in European Russia, Austria-Hungary, France, South America, and British India, while the United States enjoyed its finest harvest since 1892. Pacific Coast newspapers printed accounts of starvation in India even before the arrival of spring, although the world wheat situation was not clear before June.[16] In addition, it was said that the world visible supply of cotton was down by 1.4 million bales from the preceding year, while domestic crop prospects were good.[17] It was widely recalled that the coincidence of failures overseas with a large American wheat crop had lifted the country out of depression in the 1870s. Thus brightening prospects for American agriculture,

Table 5.1
Estimated World Wheat Crop, 1891–1899

(millions of bushels)

Year	Austria-Hungary	European Russia	British India	South America	France	United States	World
1891	180	254	257	53	219	612/*678*	2,432
1892	202	338	207	56	311	516/*611*	2,482
1893	212	462	269	82	278	396/*506*	2,563
1894	201	418	253	105	343	460/*542*	2,672
1895	196	377	234	85	339	467/*542*	2,553
1896	206	366	206	58	340	428/*523*	2,506
1897	127	286	191	40	247	530/*606*	2,234
1898	189	408	260	67	364	675/*768*	2,942
1899	204	394	237	125	364	547/*655*	2,768

Source: U.S. Department of Agriculture, *Yearbook of . . . 1895* (Washington, DC: Government Printing Office, 1896), 529–30; U.S. Department of *Agriculture, Yearbook of . . . 1900* (Washington, DC: Government Printing Office, 1901), 763–64. Reliability of contemporary estimates was sufficient only to indicate general trends; *Historical Statistics . . . to 1957*, 297, for corrected figures (in *italics*).

especially for wheat farmers, as the season advanced became a major spark for increasingly buoyant expectations and business.[18]

The harvest fulfilled the hopes that early reports had aroused, generating a broad expansion of trade and investment, attended by growing optimism. Rising foreign demand for American wheat and the lively speculation in grain futures that it stimulated sent wheat prices to their highest level in years. The average price paid farmers during the year was $0.809, a $0.088 gain over 1896 and $0.304 over 1895. In New York in August the option on September wheat reached $1.07. During the next two months wheat options in the financial center seldom fell below one dollar.[19] The harvest and better return of the year brought an important increase in purchasing power for wheat farmers, even after shipping, storage, and other charges were paid. Had the entire crop been marketed during 1897, the gain over 1896 would have amounted to approximately $110 million, about 30 percent. A cool spring and then a widespread epidemic of yellow fever in summer and fall delayed the cotton harvest. When the crop was picked, the result was further cheer and economic expansion. The revival of business overseas and at home, with reduced inventories and inadequate foreign output, brought ready markets. Prices held steady on an increase in output of

2,366,000 bales, to a record 10,899,000. The farm value of the 1897 crop was $85 million, or 30 percent, greater than that of 1896. Although a short harvest, which just about offset resultant price advances, prevented corn growers from sharing in the good fortune of wheat and cotton planters, American agriculture was at last beginning to grope its way back to prosperity. A year later manufacture of farm machinery and equipment for domestic use leaped by half, to more than $90 million in 1913 dollars, twice the 1896 rate, implying the first big increase in agricultural investment since 1890 as a register of improving farm conditions.

The record for farm exports after the harvest of 1897 spoke eloquently of the role of foreign demand for American crops in inducing business recovery. Increased shipments abroad of agricultural products were the decisive agent in a pronounced growth of merchandise exports. In fiscal 1898 and 1899 the movement overseas of American goods rose by about $225 million, perhaps 2 percent of gross national product, over the year ending June 30, 1897. Enlarged wheat shipments that totaled $130 million more than the annual rate for fiscal 1897 accounted for more than half the increase. Cotton shipments had recovered by $40 million, to $230 million annually, a year earlier. Remaining at high levels, they helped sustain the vigorous flow of produce. Moreover, European prosperity and demand supported a strong movement of wheat and cotton through the end of the decade, acting as a continuing stimulus to business.[20]

Although agriculture took the lead in inspiring recovery in 1897, rising exports of manufactures also contributed. Between 1890 and 1900 the share of agricultural goods, including raw cotton, in American merchandise exports fell from about two-thirds to about one-half. The declining relative importance of farm produce spoke vividly of the transformation shaping an industrial society. The country was moving away from an excessive reliance on exports of agricultural surpluses and the unstable world markets in which they sold, for its international earnings and domestic prosperity, toward greater dependence on the sale of more valuable manufactures in firmer, less uncontrollably competitive markets abroad. Falling costs and necessary economies during the depression helped encourage a steady growth, except for a brief lapse in fiscal 1898 when crop shipments leaped ahead, in the share of manufactures among all merchandise exports. Iron and steel mill products, if still a small fraction of total exports, underwent a spectacular development that symbolized the trend for manufactures in general. Goaded by hard times and favored by location, the mills of Birmingham, Alabama, were so efficiently and inexpensively operated by 1896 that they were underselling British firms in the industrial Midlands of the United Kingdom itself. Alabama pig iron reached England for as little as $7.50 a ton. In fiscal 1897–98 some three hundred thousand tons were sent to foreign markets. During the same period exports of American iron and steel mill products showed their first sharp rise, nearly doubling to $5 million in 1896, jumping to $11 million a year later, and almost doubling twice again by 1900. The decade contained a remarkable turnabout in the place of iron and steel in the country's foreign trade. As recently as 1890 exports (with machinery) and imports of iron and steel products were $23 million and $42 million respectively; in 1900 they were $117 million and $20 million. By that time nonfood finished manufactures constituted 24 percent of all American merchandise exports, against two-thirds as much when the depression began. Concurrently iron and steel mill products and machinery gained as a share of such exports from 19 to 35 percent.[21]

Besides generating economic expansion, the increased exports of the late nineties testified to a profound change that the hard times spelled for the country's balance of payments. As early as the fiscal year ending June 30, 1894, the business contraction, by forcing a severe cut in imports and in the price of domestic manufactures, allowed a favorable net balance of payments to replace the adverse outcome characteristic of recent years. Larger imports accompanying the partial revival of the following year temporarily reversed the trend. However the scales subsequently tipped back toward the United States, decisively in and after 1897 as a prosperous Europe made rising purchases of American goods. Led by farm products, the nation's record merchandise shipments during the last third of calendar 1897 and the ensuing years, seasonally adjusted, approached and then consistently exceeded $100 million per month. Monthly imports, meanwhile, ran at $50 million to $60 million. In fiscal 1897 the merchandise balance was favorable by $333 million, and in 1898, as recovery proceeded, by a staggering $651 million. These developments summoned large net inflows of gold, amounting to $100 million in fiscal 1898 and half as much the following year. The troubles of the Treasury during the mid nineties seemed increasingly remote as the glittering stream flowed in to augment the currents of investment and commerce.

Discerning contemporaries were aware of the immediate significance of the shifting international trade position of the country in prompting recovery, and they took pride in its larger importance as evidence of growing commercial power. In April 1897 the American consul at Birmingham, England, reported growing British fears of the vigor of the iron and steel industry on the American side of the Atlantic. A November 20 speech by the Austrian foreign minister, Count Agenor Goluchowski, attracted wide attention in the American press. The minister proclaimed in Vienna that the nations of Europe were locked in commercial war with the United States and "must fight shoulder to shoulder against the common danger . . . with all the means at their disposal." The *New York Journal of Commerce* in reply praised the count's perceptivity but concluded that European opposition must prove fruitless in view of America's insuperable advantages in resources, technology, and productivity. The *Iron Age* commented more modestly in December that there were indications that "the commercial supremacy of the English nation" was slowly moving to the United States.[22]

Joining with European recovery, a fortuitous agricultural coincidence, and enlarged exports as a major agent of economic expansion in 1897 was a rapid increase of world and domestic gold output. As early as 1895 the *New York Times* had editorialized that increasing returns from mines would make the free

Table 5.2
U.S. Stock of Currency: U.S. and World Gold Output, 1891–1899

($ on June 30 of each year; output millions $ or fine oz.)

Year	Total Currency	In Treasury	Outside Treasury	Gold $	U.S. Gold Prod. $	World Gold Prod. Oz.	World Gold Prod. $
1891	$1,605	$173	$1,433	$587	$33.18	6.320	$130.65
1892	1,676	147	1,528	597	33.00	7.094	146.65
1893	1,658	138	1,520	519	35.96	7.619	157.49
1894	1,711	142	1,569	547	39.50	8.764	181.18
1895	1,718	215	1,602	547	46.61	9.641	199.30
1896	1,688	288	1,398	502	53.19	9.784	202.25
1897	1,785	261	1,524	591	57.36	11.420	238.81
1898	1,953	231	1,722	754	64.46	13.878	286.88
1899	2,079	273	1,806	860	71.05	14.838	306.72

Source: Statistical Abstract of the United States, 1899, 51; Statistical Abstract of the United States, 1900, 37–42.

coinage of silver unnecessary as a means of generating higher prices. American output of the yellow metal was growing rapidly. In South Africa, mines discovered in 1886 promised much more and would probably lead the world in a year. As early as 1894 the Witwatersrand had approximated the production of the United States, and its output was up 50 percent in a twelvemonth.[23] Soon after, in the summer of 1896, the first claims were located on the Klondike River in the Yukon. The arrival of the steamer *Portland* in Seattle in July 1897 with sixty-eight men aboard with $700,000 in gold foretold even greater mining returns and precipitated a rush to the Yukon, in a season when crop prospects had already evoked a brisk expansion of hopes and trade.[24] Colorado discoveries of the past few years and improvements in mining and refining techniques, notably the development of the cyanide process, further accelerated the rate of rise of gold output.

As shown in Table 5.2, world gold production grew steadily through the 1890s. The United States, however, failed to benefit monetarily from increased output before McKinley's election and improved conditions the following year, its stock of monetary gold falling to lows in the downturns of 1893 and 1896. Subsequently, restored European prosperity and low American prices, the coincidence of crop failures abroad with huge harvests at home, and the elimination (by McKinley's election) of fears for the maintenance of the gold standard permitted a shift in the net balance of payments that brought record gold inflows. Renewed confidence in the security of the gold standard was of fundamental importance. During the preceding five years apprehension had figured vitally in prompting large speculative specie movements—discouraging inflows, provoking drains, and threatening massive flights. These movements had acted to curb the expansion of the country's money stock and thus to sustain the erratic deflationary drift of prices that had characterized the past generation. From mid-1897 through 1914, however, the country's holdings of monetary gold grew rapidly, 27 percent through 1898 alone, and the share of the world's monetary gold held in the United States increased from 14 to 25 percent. Concurrently, the 7 percent yearly rise in the gold stock illustrated in the table accounted for most of the growth of public hand-to-hand currency holdings after 1897 and in turn loomed large in a 7 ½ point average annual increase of the money stock. The swift monetary expansion played an essential part in reversing the previous deflationary price tendency and permitting the United States to participate in a worldwide price increase after 1897. Through 1914 wholesale prices advanced about 2 percent a year, helping to stimulate more sanguine expectations, investment, and commerce.[25]

Among the prominent engines of economic revival were the tariff of 1897 and the competitive efficiency pressed on American enterprise by the depression. The increased duties of the Dingley Tariff assured home markets to domestic entrepreneurs just as consumers became able to make purchases they had deferred during hard times. Merchandise imports remained low after recovery got under way, and expanding business made investment in protected industries increasingly attractive. Many obsolescent or marginal firms had closed. These purges and suspensions were a more complex matter, entailing both the elimination of inadequate competitors and important changes for the economy as well.

Liquidation accompanying contraction involved outright failures, extensive reorganizations, and, especially when capital became abundant with the return of prosperity, an acceleration of business combination that propelled investment bankers to ever greater power. The puissance of the banking community was intensified during the depression when the federal government was forced repeatedly to rely on it to protect the Treasury. Nowhere, perhaps, was it more sharply shown than in the reorganization of the railroad industry. The collapse, in forcing "an unprecedented number of railroad failures," required the reconstruction of huge, crippled roads and at the same time "laid the foundations for the movement towards the consolidation of railroad properties to the exclusion of competition." Under the lead of bankers who controlled the resources requisite for the task, the reorganizations conformed more or less to a common pattern.

Securities bearing fixed charges were converted in part to contingent obligations, as preferred stock with non-cumulative charges, to bring fixed charges into line with earning capacity. Capital structure was simplified, but capitalization was rarely reduced. Holders of new junior securities demanded and received compensation in the form of additional common or preferred stock. Reorganization thus frequently exacerbated, rather than solved, the underlying problem of overcapitalization. Moreover, because fixed charges were pegged to earning ability, there was little hope for a return on common stock. Reorganization cost the roads dearly: Kuhn, Loeb & Company received $5 million for underwriting the reconstitution of the Union Pacific. Furthermore, bankers commonly perpetuated their control of the roads to protect their investments and curb speculative management practices, by establishing voting trusts. Also, they established communities of interest with other roads, looking to regional groupings to replace the old pattern of ruinous competition. They failed, however, to provide for any marked improvement of service.[26]

J. P. Morgan played the leading role in the drama of railroad reorganization. Under his watchful eye tottering individual properties were welded into wide systems, ailing branch lines were abandoned, and competition minimized. The depression allowed his ambitions and talents free play. His greatest achievements of the era were the creation of the Southern Railway and the rehabilitation of the Erie, Northern Pacific, and Reading railroads, bringing them all into the orbit of his control. The first of these was chartered in February 1894, a nine-thousand-mile system built on the ruins of the old Richmond & West Point Terminal Railway and Warehouse Company. By June 1899 the creation owned fifty-eight lesser roads and operated thirteen more under agreement. In November 1895 Morgan revamped the Erie, and the Reading followed in 1896–98. Concomitantly Morgan joined hands with James Jerome Hill of the Great Northern to reconstruct the Northern Pacific (1896). The two men also had an important part in the reorganization of the Baltimore & Ohio in 1898. Joining Morgan and Hill as a leader in the industry was Edward H. Harriman, who won control of the Union Pacific in its reorganization in October 1895. Other important ventures included the reconstitution of the Santa Fé, in March 1895, and the St. Louis & San Francisco the following year.[27]

Combination proceeded apace elsewhere. Collapsing prices moved Colorado silver producers to agree in June 1893 to suspend mining. Angry mine operators in other Western states soon followed suit. Two years later, manufacturers controlling 80 percent of the country's sales formed the American Glass Company. Anthracite shippers joined in 1896 to combat a demoralization of their trade. In 1897, beleaguered textile producers in the South, and in Fall River and New Bedford, Massachusetts, agreed to limit output. The cordage and whisky trusts underwent several reformations. The elimination of some and the reorganization of other weak banks advanced financial concentration.[28] Withered prices, wrote the principal historian of American manufacturing, "steadily" forced "out of production the smaller and less advantageously situated" iron mills. In the six years following 1892, the number of nominally active furnaces shrank from 569 to 420, and of these, fifty were not expected to operate again. The remainder, however, could outproduce the total number active in 1892, illustrating the progress of concentration.

Meanwhile, pools formed and rapidly dissolved in bar iron, wire nails, steel billets and beams, Bessemer steel, and elsewhere, at length giving way to other, less fragile forms of combination. New York, Pennsylvania, and Ohio steel castings makers merged in 1894. Concurrently, John D. Rockefeller took advantage of low prices to buy vast ore deposits in the Mesabi Range of Minnesota at a fraction of their value. In 1896 he leased them to Andrew Carnegie, who was also active in the region, for a $0.25 per ton royalty and guaranteed shipment from mine to mill via a Rockefeller railroad and Rockefeller ore ships. The arrangement helped cement the Scottish ironmaster's position as the industry's leader. In 1899 Carnegie reorganized his firm and joined it with the Frick Coke Company. He thereby gained control of five major mills, several coke plants, the Oliver Mining Company, and a railroad linking its Pittsburgh facilities with Lake Erie.[29]

Except in the crucially important and devastated railroad industry, where reorganization often urged corporate combination, depression temporarily retarded outright merger while spurring other efforts to escape competition. Weak commerce underlay a continuing flow of funds from country banks to New York City into the latter years of the decade. Outside bank clearings averaged but $73 million per day as late as 1898. They rose to $91.5 million the following year, 30 percent above the 1892 peak. Although rising expectations outpaced recovery, the growing availability of loan funds in New York made it practicable to finance ever-larger business entities. The striking expansion of manufacturing that was transforming the economy and enlarging trade drew growing investment. A depression-reinforced will to control markets and prices, and continuing reorganization of firms buffeted by bad times further drove combination. The Supreme Court in 1895 had rendered the national legal climate favorable, ruling that the Sherman Antitrust Act forbade only combination in restraint of trade, not of manufacturing. Following the 1888–89 lead of New Jersey, several states had eased the formation of holding companies by permitting them to be chartered under general incorporation laws rather than requiring special legislation. Speculators, entrepreneurs eager to control prices and output in different lines of business, and others joined to form in the three years after 1897, as an early writer recorded, "almost twice as many combinations," (149) as in the preceding eleven years, capitalized at $3.78 billion. In three years, he wrote, the number of giant combinations spurted from twenty to 185; more recent scholarship has shown this figure to be too low.

The merger movement that overtook American industry between 1895 and 1904 was of unrivaled proportions. While combinations occurred in every major mining and manufacturing industry, they were concentrated in only a few: bituminous coal, primary metals, petroleum products, food products, transportation equipment, chemicals, fabricated metal products, and machinery. Picking up from a yearly pace of five in 1895 and 1896 to ten in 1897, the total reached twenty-six in 1898 and 106 in 1899. It settled to between forty-two and fifty-three during each of the following three years, before dropping to fifteen in 1903 and nine in 1904. Altogether, 319 consolidations took place, involving $6.3 billion of capital. More than a third of the new combinations were monopolistic in intent. The new industrial landscape saw 319 firms controlling 40 percent of all manufacturing assets in the United States. In each of fifty industries, a single firm generated 60 percent or more of output. Of the firms dominating American enterprise at the middle of the twentieth century, twenty came into being between 1895 and 1904. Among them were United States Steel, American Tobacco, International Harvester, DuPont, Corn Products, Anaconda, and American Smelting and Refining. DuPont, General Electric, American Tobacco, Westinghouse, and Pullman were among sixteen companies that accounted for at least 85 percent of the product in their businesses. Another measure of the extent of combinations, 86 percent of which involved holding companies while only 14 percent involved outright acquisition, lay in the number of firms absorbed each year into these giant entities. The yearly average was 301 between 1898 and 1902, with 1,028 firms disappearing through consolidation in 1899 alone. Combines had come to dominate manufacturing. Investment bankers meanwhile had achieved new heights of power through participation in the planning, financing, and control of the new industrial behemoths.[30]

Adversity and aspiration had stirred farmers toward cooperation and association long before panic erupted in 1893. During the preceding decade the spreading Farmers' Alliance movement spawned hundreds of cooperative stores, mills, gins, buying and selling exchanges, and tobacco warehouses in the South, and talk of a state-built railroad from the northern plains to the Gulf of Mexico to end agrarian dependence on discriminatory trunk lines to the East. The Alliance's Dallas Cotton Exchange in two years saved members costs of $3 million in marketing 1.3 million bales, inspiring imitations in several cities and at the state level in Florida, Georgia, and Mississippi. The financial storms of the '90s doomed most such efforts, already declining because of inept management, small resources, and the opposition of business. Planters then turned, with no greater success, to crop limitation as a remedy for depressed prices. Meetings in Jackson, Mississippi, and New Orleans in January and April 1895, and in Memphis the next year failed to achieve a system of acreage limitation through county planters' referenda, the creation of a Cotton Congress, or state and local administrative machinery.[31] Grain producers also made little headway in establishing cooperative elevators in the Midwest before the turn of the century. While achieving limited gains in political cooperation to regulate trusts and railroads or to influence monetary policy, farmers failed to bring agricultural output under national control. Individualism and sheer numbers meant that the choice of what and how much to grow, except in the cases of favored special crops, had to remain with millions of independent farmers. Renewed prosperity brought relief in 1897. The longer-term solution, however, lay with the national government, which alone possessed the means to meet the prime needs of farmers—credit and the regulation of output—until in the late twentieth century the character of American agriculture itself changed radically through a process of consolidation similar to that which had transformed industrial organization at the turn of the century.

Some farm groups did cooperate or combine effectively, participating thereby in the economic transformation occurring in the depression era. Benefiting from limited numbers and from specialization, dairymen expanded and multiplied the cooperative creameries that had begun to appear in the Civil War era. Minnesota had none in 1890, but 450 of a national total of 650 in 1900. Wisconsin and the Dakotas registered impressive gains. California deciduous fruit growers in 1892 formed the Santa Clara County Fruit Exchange to battle high commission-house charges and low prices. Their success and that of other such groups in giving "a strength and stability to the market which it had never before known," despite severe depression the following year, invited copies. California raisin and wine producers, orchardists near Boise, Idaho, northern Ohio vintners, and others fashioned new combinations. Associated owners of sun-drenched foothill orange groves in Redlands united in 1895 with groups in Claremont, Riverside, and elsewhere as the Southern California Fruit Exchange. (It evolved into the California Fruit Exchange, with the famed Sunkist label.) Meanwhile, drought and depression compelled determined central plains farmers to new adaptations. Numbers forsook the familiar pattern of cash grain-farming and corn culture for irrigation, dry farming, new crop strains such as Turkey Red wheat, grain sorghum, and a livestock regime.[32]

The depression of the 1890s was the product of complex forces at work in a changing economy. Panic, growing out of anxiety over the ability of the Treasury to maintain the established standard of gold payments and the growth of inflationist pressures, interacted in 1893 with foreign depression, weak investment opportunities reflected in a slowing rate of railroad growth and building construction, agricultural distress, and falling prices resulting in large part from the failure of monetary circulation to rise apace with aggregate demand to transform recession into a sharp, sustained contraction of business. Monetary and political disturbances united with other factors to delay recovery for some five years, precipitating a second downturn in 1896. In 1897, the removal of fears for the dollar and gold standard with the defeat of Bryan and free silver in the previous year's election, European revival, a bumper crop in America coinciding with bad crops abroad, growing world gold production, the elimination of obsolescent and marginal firms, improved exports of industrial products, and a more favorable tariff combined to regain prosperity and sanguine expectations. Recovery, however, was not complete before 1899 and 1900.[33]

One of the most severe contractions in the history of the United States, the depression of the 1890s slashed through the middle of a decade of profound economic change. The economy that emerged from the depression differed profoundly from that of 1893. Consolidation and the influence of investment bankers were more advanced. The nation's international trade position was more advantageous: huge merchandise exports assured a favorable net balance of payments despite large tourist expenditures abroad, foreign investments in the United States, and a continued reliance on foreign shipping to carry most of America's overseas commerce. Moreover, new industries were rapidly moving to ascendancy, and manufactures were coming to replace farm produce as the staple products and exports of the country. The era revealed the outlines of an emerging industrial-urban economic order that portended great changes for the United States. Consideration of the social, intellectual, and political consequences of the contraction, and the changes in public policy that it elicited, brings the emerging order into sharper focus.

NOTES

1. Quotes respectively from the *Seattle Post-Intelligencer* (November 4, 1896); *San Francisco Chronicle* (November 4, 1897); *Philadelphia Public Ledger* (November 6, 1896). For a sample of business interviews see *Chicago Daily Tribune* (November 5, 1896). Optimistic statements were common over the next three weeks, as for some days before the election.

2. *New York Times* (November 9, 1896).

3. For world wheat output see Table 5.1. For 1896 developments, *Commercial and Financial Chronicle* (July–October 1896); Hoffmann, *Depression of the Nineties*, 82; for Europe, Thorp, *Business Annals*, 79–81 and passim. Monthly indices cited are in *Historical Statistics, 1789–1945*, 329; and Moore, *Business Cycle Indicators*, 2, ser. 15.1, 130, and passim.

4. Monthly series, note 3, above; also *Commercial and Financial Chronicle* (November 21, 1896; January 2 and February 13, 1897); Clark, *History of Manufactures*, 3: 87–96.

5. *Cleveland Plain Dealer* (November 22, 1896). William Allen White's *Emporia (Kansas) Gazette* (December 24, 1896) replied to such Democratic critics of developments after McKinley's victory by observing that things would have been much worse had Bryan won the presidency. Rather than slipping into despondency or criticism, White asserted, "The thing to do is to get up and dust."

6. Fels, *American Business Cycles*, 204–8. See also *Commercial and Financial Chronicle*, first January number, 1894–1901, for securities trading and issues; U.S. Congress, National Monetary Commission, *Statistics for the United States, 1867–1909*, 61st Cong., 2d sess., 1911, Senate Document 570, 104.

7. *Congressional Record*, 54 Cong., 2d sess. (1896), 29:39, 326, 1118, 1151, and 1612. Administration and moderate congressional opposition prevented action on Cameron's resolution after the Christmas holiday. Illustrative of business reaction: *Commercial and Financial Chronicle* (December 26, 1896; February 27, 1897); *New York Times* (December 19, 1896–February 27, 1897). See also Fels, *American Business Cycles*, 205.

8. *San Francisco Chronicle* (March 8 and April 12, 1897); *St. Louis Post-Dispatch* (April 11, 1897); *Cleveland Plain Dealer* (May 17, 1897), 27; *(Boise) Idaho Daily States-*

man (April 3, 1897); *Commercial and Financial Chronicle* (March–July 1897 and January 1, 1898).

9. *Commercial and Financial Chronicle* (February 20, 1897); Clark, *History of Manufactures*, 3:87–89.

10. James Daniel Richardson, *A Supplement to a Compilation of the Messages and Papers of the Presidents, 1789–1902*, comp. George Raywood Devitt (Washington, DC: Published by Authority of Bureau of National Literature and Art, 1904), 10.

11. Shaw, *Commodity Output*, 52–64, 75–77; Edwin Frickey, *Production in the United States, 1860–1914* (Cambridge, MA: Harvard University Press, 1947), 15; *Historical Statistics . . . to 1957*, 297.

12. See for example *Cleveland Plain Dealer* (May 1, 17, 27, and June 7, 1897); *Raleigh (North Carolina) News & Observer* (May 4, 25, and June 2, 1897); *St. Louis Post-Dispatch* (May 25, 27, 30, June 6 and 12, 1897).

13. *Wall Street Journal* (June 24, 1897); *(Boise) Idaho Daily Statesman* (June 20, 1897). Also *San Francisco Chronicle* (June 15, 1897); *Seattle Post-Intelligencer* (April 10, 1897); *Philadelphia Public Ledger* (June 7, 1897); *Chicago Daily Tribune* (July 5, 1897); *Raleigh (North Carolina) News & Observer* (June 17, 1897); *St. Louis Post-Dispatch* (July 4, 1897); *New York Times* (July 2, August 12, 16, September 2, and October 24, 1897).

14. *(Boise) Idaho Daily Statesman* (May 26, 1897).

15. Visible unsold stocks of pig iron held nearly steady from February through July 1897, when they began to fall abruptly despite a rapid increase in output. Scattered inventory data on pig iron and other staples appeared in *Commercial and Financial Chronicle* throughout 1897 and 1898.

16. *Seattle Post-Intelligencer* (March 20, 1897).

17. *Wall Street Journal* (April 30, 1897).

18. For crops and rising expectations, *New York Times* (April 26, July 2, September 2, November 7 and 14, 1897); *Commercial and Financial Chronicle* (July 17 and August 28, 1897); *(Salt Lake City) Deseret Weekly* (August 7, 1897); *Wall Street Journal* (April 21, 30, and May 22, 1897); *Cleveland Plain Dealer* (July 17, 1897); also sources cited in note 13, above.

19. *Commercial and Financial Chronicle* (August–December 1897).

20. For crop exports, *Historical Statistics . . . to 1957*, ser. U 74–79:546; harvest and prices, ser. K 265–71, 302–303:297, 301. For output of farm equipment, in 1913 dollars, Shaw, *Commodity Output*, 75–77.

21. Export statistics, *Historical Statistics . . . to 1957*, especially series U 61, 65, 66, 91, 92, 107, 544–48. For extended discussion, Hoffman, *Depression of the Nineties*, 157–91; and White, *Recovery after 1893*, 82–90. For Birmingham steel see W. David Lewis, *Sloss Furnaces and the Rise of the Birmingham District: An Industrial Epic* (Tuscaloosa: University of Alabama Press, 1994).

22. *Kansas City Star, New York Evening Post* (November 22, 23, and 24, 1897); *New York Journal of Commerce & Commercial Bulletin* (November 24, 1897); *Iron Age*, 61 (December 23, 1897); quoted in White, *Recovery after 1893*, 87–88. Also Worthington Chauncy Ford, "The Turning of the Tide," *North American Review*, 161 (August 1895), 187–95; and La Feber, *New Empire*, 377–78. Balance of payments data estimated by Matthew Simon in *Historical Statistics . . . to 1957*, 557, 562; monthly series, note 3, above.

23. *New York Times* (January 3, 1895).

24. *Seattle Post-Intelligencer* (July 15–18, 1897); *Appleton's Annual Cyclopedia and Register of Important Events for the Year 1897*, Third Series, 2 (New York: D. Appleton, 1898), 443–45.

25. Friedman and Schwartz, *Monetary History*, 130–36; and Fels, *American Business Cycles*, 208.

26. Peter Tufano, "Business Failure, Judicial Intervention, and Financial Innovation: Restructuring U.S. Railroads in the Nineteenth Century," *Business History Review* 71 (Spring 1997), 1–40; Campbell, *Reorganization of the American Railroad System*, 319–42.

27. Campbell, *Reorganization of the American Railroad System*, 145–255; *Poor's Manual*, 1900, lxxix, 136, and passim; Noyes, *Forty Years of American Finance*, 276–79; Fels, *American Business Cycles*, 208; and Tufano, "Business Failure," 1–40. The Union Trust Company of New York took a leading part in the reorganization of the Santa Fé, and a banking syndicate directed that of the "Frisco."

28. *Wall Street Journal* (June 27 and July 1, 1893); *Philadelphia Public Ledger; St. Louis Post-Dispatch* (June 30 and July 1, 1893); *Commercial and Financial Chronicle* (February 1 and June 27, 1896, January 23 and February 13, 1897, and January 1, 1898); Clark, *History of Manufactures*, 3:241–42, 261.

29. *Commercial and Financial Chronicle* (February 11, 1893, and September 11, 1897); *New York Times* (April 3 and 4, 1894, and December 9, 1895); Charles E. Edgerton, "The Wire-Nail Association of 1895–96," in William Zebina Ripley, ed., *Trusts, Pools, and Combinations*, rev. ed. (Boston: Ginn, 1916), 46–47; Joseph Allan Nevins, *John D. Rockefeller: The Heroic Age of American Enterprise* (New York: Scribner's, 1940), 2:365–402; Clark, *History of Manufactures*, 3:29, 43–44, 87–89, 92–96, and 220–49. By 1898, many large steel companies were building furnaces to supply their own needs for pig iron.

30. Quotation, Eliot Jones, *The Trust Problem in the United States* (New York: Macmillan, 1929), 40, also 28–45. *U.S. v. E. C. Knight Company*, 156 U.S. 1 (1895). Also John Moody, *The Truth about the Trusts* (New York: Moody, 1904), 453; Redlich, *Molding of American Banking*, 359–97; Ralph L. Nelson, *Merger Movements in American Industry, 1895–1916* (Princeton, NJ: Princeton University Press, 1959), 71–105, 139–69; Naomi R. Lamoreaux, *The Great Merger Movement in American Business, 1895–1904* (New York: Cambridge University Press, 1985); Hoffmann, *Depression*, 34–37; Stuart Bruchey, *Enterprise: The Dynamic Economy of a Free People* (Cambridge, MA: Harvard University Press, 1990), 340–44. Robert Higgs, *The Transformation of the American Economy, 1865–1914* (New York: Wiley, 1971), 18–49 and 123–24, does not stress the depression but provides a concise, statistically based and theoretically informed review of economic transformation in America, 1865–1914.

31. Hicks, *Populist Revolt*, 56. Current views, Lawrence Goodwyn, *Democratic Promise: The Populist Movement in America* (New York: Oxford University Press, 1976); Barnes, *Farmers in Rebellion: The Rise and Fall of the Southern Farmers' Alliance and the People's Party in Texas*; Ostler, *Prairie Populism: The Fate of Agrarian Radicalism in Kansas, Nebraska, and Iowa, 1880–1892*; and Robert C. McMath, Jr., *American Populism: A Social History, 1877–1888* (New York: Hill and Wang, 1993).

32. Quotation, Edward F. Adams, "Cooperation among Farmers," *Forum*, 20 (November 1895), 364–76. See also Joseph B. Kenkel, *The Cooperative Elevator Movement* (Washington, DC: Catholic University of America, 1922), 13–23; Edmund Mitchell, "Co-operation and the Agricultural Depression," *Westminster Review*, 142 (September

1894), 241–49; *San Francisco Chronicle* (February 25, June 13, 20, and 25, 1894); *Boise (Idaho) Daily Statesman* (September 26, October 7, 10, 1893, and July 25, 1895); *Cleveland Plain Dealer* (February 16 and March 1, 1894); Rahno Mabel McCurdy, *The History of the California Fruit Growers' Exchange* (Los Angeles: G. Rice & Sons, 1925).

33. Hoffmann, "Depression," 137–38; Ross Eckler, "A Measure of the Severity of Depression, 1873–1932," *Review of Economics and Statistics*, 15 (May 15, 1933), 75–81; Arthur F. Burns and Wesley Clair Mitchell, *Measuring Business Cycles* (New York: National Bureau of Economic Research, 1946), 403, 475–79, and passim; Moore, *Business Cycle Indicators*, 1:45–105, and passim.

6

Social Repercussions

Twelve Italian families ... starving ... about to be dispossessed.
—*New York Times*, February 1, 1894

The business contraction of the 1890s washed over American life like a swirling tsunami over an exposed coastline. Everything that was exposed and vulnerable felt its effects. The pattern and pace of life changed. Problems such as unemployment, poverty, vagrancy, and labor relations swept to unprecedented urgency. Social tensions, including nativistic and jingoistic impulses, sharpened in an atmosphere of "strain" that broke "men down by scores."[1]

Depression buffeted even the most intimate aspects of life. Joblessness, fear of layoffs, reduced or uncertain income, empty dinner pails, and poor economic prospects forced many young couples to prolong courtship and defer marriage. The national marriage rate reflected differing conditions. In 1892 it stood at 9.2 per thousand. It fell slightly in 1893, then sharply to 8.6 (7 percent) the following year. After partial recovery in the next two years, it relapsed to 8.4 in 1897. Returning prosperity, renewing hope for the future, encouraged a return to former levels by the turn of the century.[2] The rates of matrimony varied from city to city, no doubt in reply to differing local circumstances. Marriages actually grew slightly in number in New York (all boroughs), 1893–94, although the rate fell slightly. The number was off 2 percent in Boston, as much as 11 to 13 percent in Cook County (Chicago), Cincinnati, and Pittsburgh.

The same hard circumstances that curbed the marriage rate led couples to defer adding children to their families, temporarily hastening the downward movement of the national birthrate. Lagging a year behind cyclical business peaks and troughs, births fell lowest in 1895, rose the next year, and edged down again in 1897. In 1895 the number of births was off more than 3 percent in New York (all boroughs), from 4 to 5 percent in Indianapolis, Philadelphia, and Pittsburgh, and up to 13 to 16 percent in Baltimore and Cincinnati. Reduced marriage and birth rates contributed to reduced demand for such things as new housing, furniture, and household furnishings, reinforcing the commercial stagnation from which they grew.

The bitter vintage of personal tragedy spilled far beyond frustrated romance. The suicide rate did not depend on business conditions. But there were bankrupted businessmen, defeated debtors, despairing jobseekers, broken farmers, and others who lost all hope and took their own lives. The *San Francisco Chronicle* in March 1895 reported the suicide in Denver of an unemployed man allegedly blacklisted for joining the American Railway Union's great strike of the preceding year.[3] The commercial crisis did not affect death rates in a dozen leading cities. These edged unsteadily downward throughout the 1890s, reflecting improving care and hygiene despite the prevalence of hardship.[4] The statistical record of starvation and malnutrition-related diseases is too sketchy to permit generalization. The human record, in contrast, was frighteningly more clear. Hunger gnawed at the strength and health of the rural and urban poor during the depression, leaving a legacy of emaciation, bent bones, sunken-eyed and listless figures, and at times, particularly during the bitter winter of 1893–94, death. December brought news that three impoverished immigrants had starved to death in Pittsburgh.[5] The *New York Times* two months later cited the discovery in a Long Island City tenement house of "twelve Italian families, numbering fifty persons . . . in a starving condition . . . without food and coal, and . . . about to be dispossessed by their landlord."[6] These extreme cases— such reports surfaced occasionally even amid prosperity—witnessed vividly to the grimness of conditions in a land of plenty. So did accounts of eviction and dispossession that filled newspapers. A single court in New York City heard 150 cases in March 1894 alone.[7] At least one paper, attempting to aid a campaign to raise funds for a relief effort, appealed to Victorian morality with a sensational account of an innocent young woman driven by want to prostitution.[8]

Distress and simmering anger at times drove people to break the law. Ashen-faced, ragged, jobless workingmen as a last resort hurled stones through store windows, hoping to be arrested and sheltered in jail.[9] A Cheyenne, Wyoming, court at the end of 1893 sentenced six Nebraska farmers for rustling and butchering cattle to feed their hunger-stricken families.[10] Fearful propertied people shielded themselves behind stricter law enforcement as well as charitable giving to deal with the alarming mass of jobless and homeless persons. Arrests for vagrancy rose sharply in many cities. They advanced by 15 percent in Cincinnati during 1893–94, 27 in Philadelphia, 29 in the borough of Manhattan, and as much as 40 in Baltimore, which was notorious for its harsh treatment of transients. In contrast, they fell in Chicago, Pittsburgh, and Boston, which acted more compassionately. Vagrancy bookings fell off the next year, probably as a result of improving trade and employment. Afterward, the pattern was less clear. Fiercely contested labor conflicts arising from layoffs, wage reductions, and employer determination to crush unions were largely responsible for a rise in arrests for riot in some major cities. Peaks coincided with such struggles as the 1894 railroad strike and a streetcarmen's violent dispute in Philadelphia two years later. Some newspapers hostile to the gold standard charged during the election campaign of 1896 that the depression, for which they blamed ruinous conservative monetary policies, had pushed so many people to desperation that a massive crime wave had erupted. The actual record indicated otherwise. Deeply rooted and habitual constraints on behavior held firm even during the acutely depressed mid-1890s.[11]

The experience of a dozen urban areas suggests that bad times did not immediately affect school enrollments or attendance. In the near term, these depended mainly on legal requirements and custom. Not until the end of the decade, when children born during the depression reached school age, was there much evidence of an impact on enrollment.[12]

Colleges and universities suffered more. The difference probably reflected several facts. Their students bore much larger direct personal costs than primary and secondary pupils; they paid with discretionary income and enrolled at their option, not driven by legal mandates. Registrations rose unsteadily at the University of North Carolina until 1896, when they fell 7 percent. Pausing only briefly after the panic, they rose at the University of Wisconsin. However, rigid economies pared the faculty almost 20 percent over the period 1895–97. Stagnant trade drew blame for a 4 percent loss of students at Michigan, 1893–94, as well as for a slowdown in the construction of new campus buildings. The student population at Stanford fell 5 percent through 1895, exceeding former levels only as the decade ended. Although confident that ''nothing [could] hold back the growth of the university,'' Stanford sociologist Edward A. Ross in the fall of 1893 admitted in a letter to his friend Lester Frank Ward, ''We have now about 875 students registered. We should have had a thousand but for the financial crisis.''

Higher education enrollments began to grow as before only with the return of prosperity at the end of the century. Until then, the depression's negative impacts on enrollment, tuition and endowment income, and state appropriations forced remedies that were often painful. The territorial University of Arizona released three professors in 1894, leaving one colleague to staff three combined departments while enduring a 15 percent cut in salary. The chancellor was to serve without pay that year. The University of California slashed its spending by nearly 10 percent in 1893 and 1894, and cut back further two years later. Harvard blamed the release of a half-dozen faculty members in 1894 on falling income from its endowment.[13]

Vastly more pressing than academic adversities were industrial unemployment, reduced incomes, and related troubles, which after the crash cast hundreds of thousands of factory, field, and mercantile hands out of work and ravaged others with cuts in hours of work or in pay rates. Unexampled "poverty, gaunt hunger, physical and mental anguish, brooding despair" beginning in autumn 1893 summoned unprecedented relief efforts.[14] Patriotism for a time found a convenient ally in the difficulty of finding work. The number of volunteers for the armed services surged, although legal quotas strictly limited opportunities to enlist.[15] Confronted with unemployment on a previously unimaginable scale, many turned for hope to the deep-rooted belief that the needy could find new opportunities by turning to labor or to farming in the underdeveloped or vacant lands of the South and West.[16]

Agrarian actualities mocked the hope. Ease of entry had permitted multitudes to join in the spread of farming to raw new areas in the prosperous 1880s. In the 1890s, ease of failure, which ruthlessly adjusted output to markets, slowed migration to less-developed regions and even forced disheartened marginal farmers to abandon their barely tamed acres and already weathered homes. Nebraska had added six hundred thousand inhabitants in the 1880s; in the 1890s it added 3,600. In varying degrees the rest of the trans-Mississippi West also met with reduced population growth during the 1890s. Large areas of western Kansas, Nebraska, the Dakotas, and eastern Colorado, withered by drought as well as commercial prostration, lost population. Homestead entries dropped unevenly from 55,113 in 1892 to 33,250 in 1897 before beginning to recover. The total of all original entries for public lands behaved comparably. Perceptive contemporary writers realized that a lack of money to move or to buy land, inexperience, ignorance of farming, and poor social and economic prospects all discouraged emigration of the jobless from cities, particularly when trade was stagnant. The belief that open lands promised opportunity persisted nonetheless. Its allure was as touching as the contention, advanced a hundred years later in debates about welfare reform, and despite overwhelming evidence to the contrary, that the country boasted a uniquely mobile society founded on limitless prospects equally open to all who would work.[17]

If the possibility of making a new home on vacant land turned out to be a chimera, that of becoming a homeless transient was all too real. Vagrancy had been rare in the United States before industrialization and urbanization were very far advanced. When industrial unemployment first became serious, in the depression of the 1870s, it became a major, and for propertied persons a menacing, condition. The return of hard times twenty years later, when a much larger segment of the workforce was subject to layoffs, made it even more so. Unnumbered men, faces covered with stubble, found themselves without jobs, incomes, or the ability to pay for food or shelter. Belongings in battered valises or in bandanas dangling from sticks set across their shoulders, many who did not hunker down beneath bridges or in abandoned buildings took to the road or hitched rides on freight trains, bound for rumored work, or for nowhere in particular. Often they banded together for protection or companionship. The propertied groups who dominated local government, failing to distinguish be-

tween itinerant job seekers and longtime hoboes, saw in the growing mass of
tramps a dangerously rootless, shiftless, potentially violent population. One result was the passage of harsh vagrancy laws, designed to speed the departure of
tramps lest they become public charges or worse.[18]

The mid-1890s were filled with reports of hobo migrations to cities or rural
areas said to have work. San Francisco, Chicago, and Baltimore (for a time)
attracted large numbers. Many job seekers became migratory farm workers, following the harvests in various parts of the country. Occasionally they stirred
local populations to panic, as in August 1895, when anxious North Dakotans
prepared for the anticipated arrival of a "horde of tramps."

As early as autumn 1893 there were reports of hobo organizations, complete
with semi-military rules, elected officers, and agreements to share provisions.
Often companies of from fifty to three hundred men attempted to compel free
railroad transportation. By December Californians were circulating tales of train
thefts. Some railroads agreed to carry vagabonds free; most rail managers resisted, using force to expel tramps from trains and sometimes sidetracking trains
carrying large numbers of them to remote areas.[19]

The industrial army movement of 1894 replied sensationally to unemployment. A leader emerged in Jacob Sechler Coxey, a visionary, wealthy quarry
owner from Masillon, Ohio. A Populist and former Greenbacker, Coxey adapted
an earlier scheme to the needs of the moment. His grandiose plan offered jobs,
monetary inflation, public works, and a support level for wages and hours. Congress was to authorize state and local governments to deposit in the Treasury
up to $500 million of non-interest-bearing bonds as security for a like amount
of new fiat currency to be paid for them in exchange. The money was then to
be spent on public works. The projects were to employ all willing American
citizens at $1.50 per eight-hour day, thus encouraging wages and hours to sta-
bilize at these figures. At the suggestion of Carl Brown, a dreamy California
labor agitator whom he had met at the 1893 Populist convention in Chicago,
Coxey decided early in the spring to lead a march of the unemployed to Washington to petition for the enactment of his program. On March 19, sympathetic
Kansas Populist Senator William Alfred Peffer introduced a bill incorporating
Coxey's proposals. Soon after, on Easter Sunday, the Ohioan set out with the
announcement that he would arrive in the capital in May at the head of a force
of hundred thousand marchers needing work.

Coxey's announcement set in motion perhaps forty tattered armies of the
unemployed. Jack London estimated that these numbered possibly five to ten
thousand of the forty to sixty thousand tramps in the country. Six hundred
followed Lewis C. Fry out of Los Angeles on March 15, only to be stranded at
a remote Texas desert siding by a hostile Southern Pacific Railroad. Charles T.
Kelly led the largest corps. After expulsion from Oakland, California, his command in a series of misadventures dwindled to a third of its original 1,500 men
before straggling into Washington on July 12. William Hogan's army comman-
deered a train and set out on a spectacular three-hundred-mile chase across

Montana before surrendering to federal troops. Agrarians in the South and West and some segments of the working class sympathized with the Coxeyites and their "pacific, although irregular methods." The governors of Oregon, Kansas, Colorado, and Texas all expressed support for this generally orderly and well disciplined movement. Texas's chief executive even compelled the Southern Pacific to carry Fry's band on eastward. The more conservative East was cooler, even hostile.

The movement itself ended in failure. Long before the last of the armies reached Washington, Coxey himself had met a pathetic fate. While former Freedmen's Bureau head General Oliver Otis Howard, as a key singer in a panicky conservative chorus, likened the Coxeyites to the Marseilles regiment advancing on Paris in 1792, congressional stand-patters beat down numerous attempts of agrarian radicals to appoint a delegation to welcome the approaching industrials. Coxey and about five hundred footsore men arrived on April 30. The next day he attempted to speak from the Capitol steps; mounted policemen chased him and two others across the grounds for walking on the grass. When the friendly crowd that had gathered to hear the reformer showed anger at his arrest, police brutally dispersed it. Coxey was later fined. Remnants of his force, with additions from other corps, remained in the vicinity of Washington until troops evicted them at the end of July. Conservatives in and out of Congress sighed in relief at the forcible removal of these "idle, useless dregs of humanity." The movement illustrated the extent to which the depression drove men to hopeless causes, presaged similar quests in the Great Depression of the 1930s, and augured an expanded role for government in addressing business downturns. The suppression of the armies expressed the imperviousness of the interests controlling the economy and the government to the claims of humanity in times of economic crisis.[20]

After the industrial armies melted away beneath the pressure of police and military action, the country's labor unions were left almost alone to offer organized defense of the America's wage earners. The Knights of Labor all but vanished before the decade was over. Decline had begun in 1886 when defeat in a rail strike and public suspicion of complicity in the notorious anarchist riots at Chicago's Haymarket Square in connection with an eight-hour-day rally brought wholesale desertions. Within four years, membership had fallen from over seven hundred thousand to about one hundred thousand. Because defections were greatest among urban supporters, small-town and rural adherents gained influence.

Panic in 1893 hit the Knights of Labor very hard. Declining, divided, its treasury depleted as dues receipts fell with membership, it was unable to pay unemployment benefits to members, who continued to drift away. That year agrarian and radical political activists ousted Grand Master Workman Terence Victor Powderly, replacing him with Iowa farm journalist James R. Sovereign. The new chieftain at once weakened the order's appeal to laborers concerned mainly with regaining wage and work losses. He emphasized instead partisan farmer-labor political action. In 1894 he declared that the Knights aimed not "so much . . . to adjust the relationship between employer and employee as to adjust natural resources and producing facilities to the common interests of the whole people . . . abolishing the wage system and . . . [establishing] a cooperative industrial system." Two years later its officers called on the body to expend its last energy in the political crusade to defeat "the money power and the corporations" believed to be oppressing the country under Cleveland and the McKinley ticket that hoped to succeed him.[21]

A struggle with the American Federation of Labor complicated the decline of the Knights of Labor. Merger talks, attempted several times before the panic, resumed in 1894 and 1895. Leaders of the American Federation of Labor traced the decline of the Knights of Labor to grandiose mass unionism (one union for all workers regardless of skill or employment) and so insisted on organization by trades to capitalize on common interests and skills. Federation leaders stubbornly spurned Knights of Labor proposals to allow simultaneous membership in craft unions and the local general assemblies uniting both skilled and unskilled toilers of which the knights were composed. When discussions collapsed, destructive rivalry followed. The leaders of the Knights were unable to stem the decline, and membership fell from 73,600 in 1893 to 54,000 in 1897. In 1896 the order returned to the secrecy with which it had begun in 1869, but it was too late to recapture the spirit of a secret fraternal association embracing all laboring groups. Some local general assemblies persisted well into the twentieth century. But the return to secrecy prefigured in the end not renewal but oblivion. The American Federation of Labor was left without a serious rival. The demise of the Knights may have ended the last serious prospect for a European type of class consciousness to drive organized labor in the United States.[22]

Several factors enabled the American Federation of Labor to become the first major labor body in American history to weather a depression largely unscathed and to emerge as the cornerstone of the country's modern labor movement. Pragmatic, pot-bellied president Samuel Gompers assigned the survival of affiliated unions primarily to their following his advice to levy dues high enough to allow payment of substantial benefits to needy members, thus holding their loyalty even in bad times. Business declines struck the federation's skilled members less severely than the unskilled mass of workers. Able leadership and a structure of tightly knit unions whose efforts added to the competitive advantages of members played a key role in survival and growth. An emphasis on the material interests of labor, rather than on ambitious political programs to reshape society, maintained a clear focus. The A.F.L. joined the consumer mentality that was coming to dominate the country. The federation declined during the depression in only two years, when membership fell from 275,000 in 1894 to 265,000 in 1896. When business began to improve the following year, it entered a period of rapid expansion. In 1897 the A.F.L. issued eight new national charters—

unions of bicycle workers, paper makers, and steam engineers, among others—adding 180,000 followers overall.[23]

As early as the summer of 1893 Gompers replied vigorously to failing business. In keeping with business unionism—unions operated carefully in the manner of a well-run business—Gompers called for and presided over a union conference on unemployment in New York on August 20. Participants resolved that New York Governor Roswell P. Flower should summon a special session of the legislature to provide relief. Gompers soon after spoke at a meeting in Madison Square Garden designed to intensify pressure for public action. He stirred his audience to cheers with his vivid description of the misery of the jobless and a militant call for emergency public works jobs.[24]

Gompers returned to the theme in his annual report for the year, presented at the American Federation of Labor's annual convention: "Since August we have been in the greatest industrial depression this country has ever experienced." Considering the "almost countless thousands" who were without work, he claimed that "human ingenuity has rendered it easier to produce all that mankind may . . . desire and [that men] are thereby made the sinless victims"; therefore he condemned America's as a "societary system based on injustice and cruelty." He ended with a plea for a more humane social order. The convention responded with resolutions approving Coxey's public works plan, the free coinage of silver, direct popular legislation, and the support by individual A.F.L. members of political candidates who favored the eight-hour day. Indignation at the suffering of the jobless also won approval of resolutions asserting a right to employment, branding as "inhuman and destructive of the liberties of the human race" a society that denied men a chance to labor and then treated them as felons for being unemployed, and calling on government to furnish work when private enterprise could not.[25]

Political activism linked partly with socialist penetration of the A.F.L. in 1893 contributed to the radicalism of the year's resolutions. Even after the radical tide ebbed, events shocked the federation to action. In 1894 it condemned the use of a federal court injunction and federal troops to crush the Pullman strike, directing its executive committee to frame a bill restricting the application of the law of contempt in cases involving disobedience of restraining orders by strikers. It later called for a national voluntary arbitration law.[26] It also reluctantly embraced a position that Gompers had argued with growing urgency since 1891: unlimited immigration, amid continuing depression, threatened to deny jobs to Americans. For three years, until business began to improve in 1897, the federation repudiated its commitment to the ideal of America as a haven for oppressed foreigners. Instead, it advocated restrictive laws to stabilize the labor force and spread existing work among American citizens.[27]

Aware of the riskiness of striking against wage and time cuts amid rising unemployment after the crash of 1893, labor hesitated as to the best means of defense. Fresh memories of crushing defeats the year before of strikes by miners at Coeur d'Alene, Idaho, switchmen at Buffalo, and iron workers at Homestead, Pennsylvania, called for caution.[28] In the mid-1890s the more politically oriented leadership and rural membership of the Knights of Labor practically rejected the strike as a weapon. Elsewhere, adversity provoked renewed militancy, expressed in a surge of industrial unionism and the outbreak of a series of ferocious conflicts.

There was no significant increase in strike activity in 1893. Workers generally accepted retrenchment as an unpleasant necessity. Yet several Western metallic mining unions joined to form the Western Federation of Miners, which had a tempestuous history. And at the height of the panic on June 20 a handful of experienced labor activists meeting in Chicago organized the American Railway Union, thereby launching the era's most ambitious experiment in industrial unionism.[29]

The following year desperation touched off industrial warfare greater even than that of 1886. Nearly seven hundred thousand men joined in 1,400 disputes, with direct financial losses to capital and labor estimated at almost $56 million. Improving business in 1895 brought struggles involving about three hundred thousand persons. The number of strikers fell by nearly half as business worsened the next year. With the beginning of commercial recovery in 1897, 332,570 workers went out, mostly for higher pay. Lockouts affected at least 7,751 more. Conditions began to calm soon afterward. Over 60 percent of the strikes in 1894, when commerce was at its nadir, failed. In 1897, with business improving, more than half succeeded. This limited success, with the concentration of union strength in the skilled trades, helped maintain the wages of organized labor at a substantially higher level than those of nonunion workers throughout the era.[30]

The first of 1894's major conflicts flared in February, when five hundred members of the Western Federation of Miners began a 130-day strike for an eight-hour day at Cripple Creek, Colorado. The state's Populist governor sent in the militia to avert a massacre of strikers by special deputies hired by the mine owners, before the effort collapsed. Strife among the miners' shanties on the high, wind-swept slopes of Pike's Peak preceded a much greater struggle in the nation's coal fields in the spring.[31]

The $100 million soft coal industry offered an exaggerated version of the difficult adjustments accompanying industrialization and depression. Rapid expansion during the 1880s with the opening of Southern and Midwestern fields had thwarted consolidation and had left the industry fragmented and unstable. Operators geared capacity to peak demand yet lived in uncertainty, unable to predict future needs or bear expensive storage costs, and subject to the whims of the weather as well as of a market that magnified fluctuations in railroad and manufacturing business. Unable to divert capital easily to other enterprises, mine owners found adjustments affecting labor, whose wages were most of the cost of producing coal, the only practical way to rationalize the industry. Thus they periodically turned to wage agreements, to equalize competitive conditions among the coal producing regions and maintain a stable price structure.

Miners were a volatile, frequently bitter party to wage pacts. Even in good times life was bleak and hard in coal camps. At best, miners could expect seven to eight months of work a year. One miner in twelve died underground, one in three suffered injury. Real income remained stable but fell from 10 to over 30 percent short of that of manufacturing labor over the years 1889 to 1893. The gap was wider in 1894, for while manufacturers laid off hands, mine operators spread wages more thinly. Unionization attempts were frequent and discouraging. The creation of a strong union depended partly on winning strikes, and conditions in the coal industry did not favor victory. Even so, labor strife was epidemic in the coal fields, hitting nearly every mine during the 1890s. Three-fourths of the strikes were over wages, and only a fifth succeeded. In depression the strike mechanism was almost automatic, invariably coming into play when some operator announced an unbearable pay cut so as to gain a competitive advantage. The general strike was the only means of policing the industry once price and wage arrangements broke down. Thus coal towns and mine management, which had no room to concede more since it had increased the wage share of coal prices from half to over two-thirds as prices fell from 68 to 34 cents a ton between 1883 and 1894, sympathized with general strikes, at least until violence erupted.

When in the spring of 1894 the New York and Cleveland Gas Coal Company, to win a competitive edge, broke a delicate marketing agreement, it demoralized the industry. The United Mine Workers began a general strike in the bituminous coal fields on April 21, two weeks after thousands of coke workers at Connelsville, Pennsylvania, had quit work. Some 170,000 men joined the stoppage, closing nearly every mine in Colorado, West Virginia, Pennsylvania, Alabama, and the Midwest. Strikers enjoyed public favor until truculent miners—largely of southern and eastern European immigrant background, who tended to view strikes as warfare—embraced violence. Before labor surrendered in June, the governors of most of the affected states had, sometimes regretfully and as a last resort, followed a familiar course in deploying militia to protect mine property or strikebreakers against threatened attack, or to suppress rebellious miners.[32]

The strike failed, and United Mine Workers membership plummeted from eighty to twenty thousand, and the real wages of coal miners shrank 10 percent from 1894 to 1897. As the coal fields calmed in June, St. Louis carpenters and Gogebic County, Michigan, iron miners went out for higher pay. Before year's end, packing house workers had struck in Omaha, silk weavers in Paterson, New Jersey, shirt makers in New York, miners in New Mexico, and textile workers in New Bedford, Massachusetts. The last entailed a lockout of twenty-five thousand textile hands at Fall River, Massachusetts, as well. Finally, late in the year, riots greeted attempts of English shippers to use black screwmen—men who loaded bales of cotton onto riverboats—on the wharves of New Orleans.[33]

The depression ignited the most incendiary episode yet in American labor relations—the fierce rail strike of 1894, an eruption that burned as intensely as a refiner's fire, clarifying in the process ingredients of a transforming economy and society. The contest pitted antagonists of unprecedented size: the American Railway Union and the managers of two dozen major railroads. Like no other walkout, it highlighted competing effects of industrialization and mirrored the discontents that flowed from the growing dependence of an urbanizing work force on a market economy subject to cyclic fluctuations. It vividly revealed the capacity of ever larger concentrations of business power to provoke labor to reply in kind. The American Railway Union's experiment in industrial unionism failed. Its brief, meteoric rise and fall foretold things to come in a nation assuming its twentieth-century pattern of social and economic relationships.

Five men long active in railroad labor circles formed the American Railway Union in Chicago in June, 1893. Most important among the founders was Eugene Victor Debs, the magnetic and humanely idealistic editor of the *Journal of the Brotherhood of Locomotive Firemen*. The new organization was to be an industrial union open to all classes of railroad labor, unlike the four craft-based railroad brotherhoods. Despite the hostility of the brotherhoods, the A.R.U. drew widening support from the mass of unskilled rail workers. By the end of 1893 it had penetrated several major lines and won nearly all of the unskilled employees of the Union Pacific, Santa Fé, and Rio Grande systems. Quick victories the following spring in wage disputes with the Union Pacific and the Great Northern magnified its appeal. In June, 1894, 465 lodges claimed perhaps 150,000 members. Then, with a zeal that only partially offset a lack of cohesion and experienced leadership, it collided with the country's greatest combination of railroads.

The confrontation began as a local dispute at the model company town of Pullman, Illinois, outside of Chicago. Admitted because the few miles of siding at the factory technically qualified them as railway workers, four thousand of the Pullman Palace Car Company's 5,500 local manufacturing hands had joined the A.R.U. Depression had reduced work and brought wage cuts of 20 percent or more, although the firm had refused a reduction of rents for housing in Pullman—required residence for Pullman employees, with rents some 20 percent higher than those in nearby neighborhoods. Extreme hardship resulted. One operative, after deducting his rent, netted only seven cents for two weeks' work. Other problems, including misunderstanding over the dismissal of members of a union grievance committee, precipitated a unanimous decision to walk out on May 11.

The strike was a month old and clearly doomed without outside help when on June 12 four hundred delegates gathered at Uhlich's Hall in Chicago for the first A.R.U. national convention. A plea on the sixteenth by representatives of the strikers led to an investigation. A request that the company arbitrate followed. Last came an ultimatum to the company to accept arbitration by June 26 or face a nationwide refusal of members to handle Pullman cars on trains. Union president Debs had feared a boycott as too risky at a time when high unemployment offered a large supply of potential strikebreakers. But, as one pro-business journal put it, the "stubborn and insolent refusal of the company to arbitrate," on grounds that management alone had the right to set company policy, forced the union to act or concede.[34]

Strict orders against violence and obstruction of mail trains, which was illegal, accompanied the beginning of the embargo. The work stoppage spread slowly, but in two days 4,000 Illinois Central men were out. As the number of strikers grew to fifty thousand on June 30, and ultimately to 125,000, there were reports of an attempt to derail the crack Diamond Special outside of Chicago, mob interference with trains, and spiked switches.

Meanwhile the General Managers' Association became involved in the conflict. Linking twenty-four important Chicago roads with forty thousand miles of track, 220,000 employees, and two billion dollars of capital, the eight-year-old combine moved to assist the Pullman company and crush the union, which now loomed as a serious challenge to the power of management. It ordered Pullman cars attached to all trains; men who refused to handle them were to be fired. Boycotters promptly struck the roads. Enemies blamed the A.R.U. for an interruption of mail service and to win public and government support circulated rumors of threatened violence. Still, it appeared briefly that the tie-up would succeed. Rail traffic from Chicago west was virtually stopped. The city's stockyards were emptying. Business was preparing to cut back. On July 2, the Association conceded a stalemate. But public alarm was mounting as the struggle, set in the context of Coxeyism and widespread labor strife, assumed an increasingly revolutionary aspect. Hostile newspapers contributed to increasing panic. The *Chicago Daily Tribune* on June 30 inaccurately shrieked, "MOB IS IN CONTROL." The *New York Times* on July 9 questioned Debs's sanity. Long before that the entire Chicago police force had been called to duty, although there was some doubt that it was equal to the task. A maze of rails criss-crossed the city, and the police commissioner was making contradictory statements.[35]

Even as the boycott was beginning, United States Attorney General Richard Olney, a railroad lawyer who hoped to destroy the A.R.U., initiated federal intervention. On June 28 he instructed U.S. marshals to assure the passage of the mails, procuring warrants and special deputies as needed. On receipt of notice that mobs in Chicago were obstructing the mails, Olney, with the president's approval, authorized on the thirtieth the appointment in Chicago of large numbers of deputy marshals to maintain order and protect rail property. He also sought an injunction against the boycott, to prevent interference with the mails and protect rail property. The Chicago circuit court of Judges Peter Grosscup and William A. Woods, no friends of labor, issued the requested order on July 2. Debs necessarily ignored it: its terms were so sweeping as practically to forbid communication between union officials and members. On the same day a mob that had for some time occupied the Rock Island line's Blue Island yards defied a marshal's order to disperse, blocking trains and overturning cars before calm was restored. The marshal, with the agreement of Grosscup and other federal officials in Chicago, requested troops. On July 4, the administration sent several companies of army regulars into the city from nearby Fort Sheridan. Governor John Peter Altgeld, who sympathized with the union, protested the use of federal forces without application from the state, insisting that local authorities could maintain order. On the sixth, disorder obliged him to send in the militia. Before peace returned, six thousand regulars and five thousand special deputies had served with the militia and Chicago's three thousand police.

The arrival of troops sparked violent episodes on July 5 and 6. Raging fires consumed many of the buildings of the 1893 World's Fair, and hundreds of freight cars and other rail property worth $340,000 were destroyed. The next day the military provided escorts for trains and began clearing actions. On July 8 President Cleveland ordered the strikers in Illinois to scatter to their homes within twenty-four hours or be treated as public enemies. On the ninth he extended the order to Utah, New Mexico, California, Washington, Wyoming, and North Dakota. Soldiers cleared the Santa Fé, Union Pacific, and Northern Pacific main lines. A dozen states called up or considered using militia before the boycott ended.[36]

Military force, the injunction, and the use of strikebreakers from the East had defeated the union. On July 10 officers arrested Debs and others on criminal charges under the Sherman Antitrust Act of 1890 for conspiring to restrain interstate commerce and for obstructing the mails. Quickly released on bail, Debs at a July 12 meeting with the A.F.L. executive committee and local union leaders asked support for a general sympathy strike in Chicago. With papers trumpeting of the boycott, "THE END IS AT HAND," Gompers prudently declined, refusing also to bear a message to the managers' association seeking terms. The mayor of Chicago, himself a former Pullman employee, delivered the message, which was worded to imply a truce rather than surrender, and requested that strikers be allowed to return to work without prejudice. The managers' group, victory in their grasp, dismissed it. On the seventeenth Debs voluntarily surrendered to the Chicago circuit court, which planned to cite him for contempt, for violating the injunction. By month's end rail traffic was moving normally. A special A.R.U. convention in August instructed locals to act as they pleased. The "boycott never officially ended, but simply dissolved." Despite Debs's assertion that "IT IS NOT DEFEAT" but a "tocsin," warning of the growing power of labor, the failure destroyed the A.R.U.[37] The railroads blacklisted large numbers of strikers. The Pullman works reopened in mid-August. The government dropped criminal charges against Debs, but in December a federal court found him guilty of contempt and sentenced him to six months in prison, and the Supreme Court upheld the judgment.[38] Depression, the power of capital, and unfriendly government had combined to crush labor's most ambitious reply to industrialization. But the persistence of the same conditions that had given birth to the A.R.U. was bound, in time, to stir further and increasingly successful attempts at unionization.

Despite vivid memories of the bitter reverses of the previous year, improving commerce in 1895 led labor into a new wave of strikes. Again the use of troops against unions was common, as in connection with a violent and unsuccessful trolley strike in Brooklyn in January. March brought renewed troubles between black and white screwmen on the docks of New Orleans. Later the coal fields erupted, as sixty thousand miners in and near the Ohio Valley fought, with some measure of success, for higher pay.

After a decline amid worsening business in 1896, industrial strife flared up with the economic improvement that began afterward. In 1897 labor trouble hit most lines of enterprise to some degree. The threat of ferocious new wage cuts, as the rupture of marketing agreements again demoralized the bituminous coal industry, provoked the U.M.W. to go out on July 4. The contest quickly involved 150,000 men throughout most of the key coal-producing states. It raged for two months. Finally on September 15 the men returned to the pits, having won about half of their initial demand. The partial victory thereafter enabled the union to enroll most Midwestern coal miners and become an effective force. In fact, the 1897 wage agreement made the U.M.W. the de facto stabilizing force in the industry. Returning prosperity was also a potent ally in many of the year's other conflicts, helping labor win a good part of its objectives.[39]

A final serious expression of the wrenching social impact of hard times lay in an ominous growth of anti-foreign sentiment, jingoism, and ethnic tensions. Here as elsewhere, the 1890s were like the 1990s: newcomers faced fierce competition for a paucity of jobs, sought charity when out of work, and participated conspicuously in strikes and radical movements, making themselves easy targets for citizens placing blame for social problems. Deteriorating conditions in mushrooming urban ghettoes and corrupt bosses in misgoverned cities sharpened negative popular impressions of immigrants. Stereotyped views that magnified ethnic and other differences, as the primary sources of immigration shifted from Western to Southern and Eastern Europe during the late nineteenth century, invited native-born Americans to blame new arrivals for the evils besetting a society in fearful transition. In ways that seem eerily familiar a century later, this volatile mix ignited in an incendiary increase of nativism during the trying years that followed panic in 1893.

Where local conditions encouraged, as where immigrants were numerous or competed directly with citizens for scarce jobs, spontaneous demonstrations of workingmen's anger sometimes paralleled the growth of organized labor's opposition to immigration. The anti-Oriental vitriol that had scarred the Far West in the commercial crises of the 1870s and '80s flowed again. In August 1893, riotous unemployed farm laborers in Fresno, California, chanting "The Chinese must go," forced the dismissal of local "mongolians" to make room for themselves. Outbursts spread as far south as Riverside, San Bernardino, and Mentone. Hop pickers near Butterville, Oregon, soon after drove out Chinese rivals. There were other incidents as well. The theme of job competition colored 1893 congressional debates over an amendment to Chinese-exclusion legislation. Labor also renewed pressure that had bent several states in the late 1880s to reserve jobs on public works projects for citizens. New York and Pennsylvania did so in 1894 and 1895, the latter later discriminating against alien miners as well, although such actions were rare.[40]

Many businessmen agreed with a writer in the *Iron Age*, April 6, 1895, that the country was "not yet by any means independent" of its need for immigrant labor. The belief that America was the land of opportunity, and traditions of cosmopolitanism and democracy restrained the growth of nativism among businessmen and others. Acute unemployment and the feared radicalism of foreign-born workingmen in time encouraged the spread of restrictionist sentiment among businessmen, however. Ordinarily such opinions were individual, rather than organized, and they reflected the growing general popularity of restrictionism.[41]

A slowly dawning awareness that by 1890 immigrants were coming mainly from Southern and Eastern Europe added a racist note to the America's deepening anti-foreign mood. Aristocratic Senator Henry Cabot Lodge of Massachusetts, one of the first to charge that racial inferiority of the so-called new immigration threatened to reduce "the general quality of our citizenship," became the foremost restrictionist on such grounds. Although its membership was confined to a small group of prominent New England intellectuals, the formation of the Immigration Restriction League in Boston shortly after the panic of 1893 brought into a being a potent propaganda vehicle. Soon hundreds of newspapers were publishing I.R.L. releases, and its lobbying won important congressional support.

The progress of restrictionism, and Republican control of Congress, at length permitted passage of Lodge's bill requiring a literacy test for immigrants, in February 1897. By then even the West and South, which had traditionally welcomed immigration as a source of population needed for development, had been won over. In one key House vote the entire trans-Mississippi western delegation and thirty-nine Southerners were in the majority of 193 favoring restriction, although Southerners also numbered twenty-four of the minority of thirty-seven opposing it. The victory was short lived; returning prosperity soon eased anti-foreign spirit. Republicans found that immigrant votes had provided McKinley's margin of victory in a half dozen midwestern states. Immigrant and foreign opposition mounted. Thus the Senate sustained Cleveland's veto of the bill as contrary to American tradition and hypocritical. Not until nearly two decades had passed did public opinion again favor restriction.[42]

Contemporary strains also fueled anti-Semitism. Current conceptions of the Jew were in many ways sympathetic. Yet they contained stereotypes that frustration easily translated into virulent hostility, especially after the turn of the century. Jews often seemed strange, because of their immigrant background and distinctive customs; mercenary, because of their commercial bent; and mysterious, because of perceptions of their historic mission, singular survival as a people, and cosmopolitanism. Angry Southern farmers sometimes lashed out at Jewish supply merchants and landlords as imagined oppressors. The worst year was 1893. Night riders in southern Mississippi burned dozens of farm houses belonging to Jewish landlords. Threats drove numbers of Jewish businessmen from Louisiana. In Northern cities there were also insults and occasional violent outbreaks.

The political ascendancy of the silver issue in mid-decade struck a more sinister note. A few agrarian radicals found in the current Jewish stereotypes, the Shylock image, the fame of certain Jewish financiers—such as the English Rothschilds—and the growth of a threatening commercial civilization of which Jewish merchants seemed an advance guard the key to understanding contemporary economic distress. All of these things could be construed as showing hard times were the result of an international conspiracy of Jewish bankers who aimed to use the gold standard to gain world domination. Minnesota Populist Ignatius Donnelly's novel, *Caesar's Column*, one of the period's most popular books, was the most famous statement of the view. At times agrarian politicians echoed the charge. Some few Eastern conservatives, of whom Henry Adams was an example, succumbed to prejudice, too, adding urban anti-Semitic feeling. The attitudes toward Jews that were maturing in the 1890s contained a frightening potential for harm. Overt anti-Semitism remained relatively rare, however. The depression was probably more important for fixing the stereotypes and frustrations from which it later grew than for inciting immediate outbursts.[43]

Anxiety expressed itself much more sensationally in a flare-up of anti-Catholicism. American prelates offered repeated assurances of loyalty to national institutions. However, the multiplication of Catholic churches and the expanding influence of Irish Catholic politicians—especially with the 1892 Democratic election sweep—aroused profound uneasiness. Ad hoc committees and fraternal and lobbying bodies, such as the 160,000-member Junior Order of United American Mechanics, had long sustained the cause of militant Protestantism in post–Civil War America. But a secret organization hardly a half-dozen years old when panic struck, the American Protective Association (A.P.A.), quickly emerged as the leader. New direction in the person of William J. Traynor, a gifted publicist and organizer, provided part of the spark; depression furnished the rest. The A.P.A. claimed only seventy thousand members, mostly in the Midwest, when the crisis began. Within a year a vigorous recruiting campaign and claims that a "popish plot" to Catholicize America lay behind it had won perhaps five hundred thousand adherents. Support centered in the area between Nebraska and Pennsylvania.

Frightening reports laid bank runs to papal agents bent on destroying the economy. Others said that Rome was behind the dumping of hordes of ignorant immigrants in America, to demoralize the labor market. Traynor's newspaper published a bogus encyclical attributed to Pope Leo XIII, which absolved Catholics of allegiance to the United States in preparation for a massacre of Protestants scheduled for September 1893. Other writers embellished the story with lurid reports of as many as seven hundred thousand Catholic soldiers drilling secretly in American cities to ready themselves for revolution. Popish agitators allegedly provoked the era's terrifying labor strikes. Midwesterners whose

neighborhoods boasted scarcely a single Catholic were reported arming in fear.
By 1894, the A.P.A. was a feared political force in the Midwest. Thereafter it
rapidly declined, rent by internal dissension. The secularization of society, which
made anti-Catholicism less relevant than formerly, contributed to the decline. A
lack of ethnic and anti-foreign content also limited its appeal, as did Democratic
charges, often true, that its leadership was making it an instrument of the Republican Party.[44]

The aggressive psychology of jingoism joined the defensive reaction of nativism as a rallying point for people who found in contemporary troubles reason
to doubt the safety of American institutions. The jingoists hoped to prove national virility through compensatory adventurism beyond the country's borders.
The nativists aimed to do so by purging foreign influences thought to be the
causes of domestic discord and difficulties. The bellicosity that in 1891 greeted
news that two American sailors had been killed in a saloon brawl in Valparaiso,
Chile, and that Italy had protested the lynching of eleven Italian immigrants in
New Orleans was a prelude to greater outbursts later on. Cleveland's 1895 message about the Venezuelan boundary dispute stirred a frenzied popular bellig-
erence. The outbreak of revolution in Cuba earlier that year began a series of
incidents that, with some significant shifts of popular opinion and economic
values, eventually led to war with Spain. There is no reason to disagree with
the judgment of the leading student of the problem that to an important degree
these outbursts "flowed from the same domestic frustrations that generated nativism."[45]

For Southern blacks the depression was a period of confusion in race relations.
On the one hand the caste system that had grown after emancipation now hard-
ened. Deep-rooted prejudice and a chasm of discrimination divided the races.
African Americans also suffered from the same pressures that bore so heavily
on immigrants. Strife between black and white screwmen in New Orleans was
symptomatic. So was a January 14, 1894, Little Rock dispatch reporting that
jobless whites at Black Rock were preparing to drive dark mill workers from
town and force the employment of whites alone. Lynching rose to an appalling
peak. About 1890 as the South neared the nadir of years of agricultural depression, the number of blacks lynched per year rose above the number of whites
subjected to that brutality. Thereafter the crime became increasingly racial and
Southern, tendencies that continued into the next century. In 1892 there was a
high of 235 lynchings, 156 of them of African Americans, and many of them
indescribably savage. Despite a gradual decline, frenzied mobs claimed the lives
of 107 as late as 1899.[46]

On the other hand political conditions during the mid-1890s seemed briefly
to offer an alternative to a pervasive system of legally imposed racial segregation. Some debt-ridden, impoverished members of the Farmers' Alliances and
People's Party in several Southern states adopted daring tactics in their battle
against state Democratic machines dominated by conservative industrial and
planter interests. While unwilling to offer social equality to blacks, they agreed

with Georgia Populist Tom Watson's attempt at a political alliance of poor whites and blacks to achieve common goals. Contending that "the accident of color can make no difference in the interests of farmers, croppers, and laborers," he bid strongly for a biracial coalition. When he raised a force of two thousand to protect a sympathetic African American speaker in the 1892 state campaign, he became a hero to Peach State blacks. In North Carolina, a Populist-Republican combination, with African-American support, won the legislature in 1894. It moved promptly to increase black voting and office holding and retained a shaky grip on power for four years. Agrarians attempted cooperation in Alabama, covertly in Mississippi, and elsewhere. The consequences of success for future race relations could have been very great.

The fragile experiment in racial cooperation aborted. Even as Watson moved to protect dark supporters in 1892, Negrophobic election violence took at least fifteen lives. There were also riots in North Carolina and Virginia that year, precursors of worse ahead. Conservatives abandoned any pretense at paternalism toward African Americans and used racist appeals to arouse whites against the spectre of black rule if the Populists should win. At the same time they deployed the votes of compliant black-belt African Americans and manipulated the returns to defeat their opponents. Other blacks could not break habitual voting patterns, and still others, as in Kansas, pursued their own interests rather than making common cause with poor whites on economic issues.

In bitterness and frustration, unsuccessful agrarians began to turn against their former allies. Defeat in the election of 1896 and the later return of prosperity destroyed Populism. Sullenly, poor white farmers continued to revert to old prejudices. Memories of recent racist political appeals were a powerful incentive to do so. The failure of blacks to deliver promised votes added its weight. The belief that honest elections and real reform were impossible as long as African-American voters could be manipulated provided further fuel. The rise of a new, radical racism completed the circle. Conservative Southern propertied interests capitalized on these impulses to forge a new political balance, uniting whites over the prostrate blacks. At the end of the decade came constitutional conventions in Southern states disfranchising blacks and opening the way for passage of laws mandating far-reaching racial segregation. The brief hope for an improvement in race relations through political cooperation had evaporated. Tenuous at best, because it attempted to unite blacks and the most Negrophobic elements in Southern society, poor rural whites, its failure was one of the most significant and ultimately tragic legacies of the commercial crisis of the 1890s. Long years passed before black and white began to move together again.[47]

NOTES

1. Quote from Henry Adams to Elizabeth Cameron, September 15, 1893, *Letters of Henry Adams*, 2:32.

2. *Historical Statistics, 1789–1945*, 41, 49; *Historical Statistics . . . to 1957*, 21. In-

terestingly Marilyn Irvin Holt, *Linoleum, Better Babies and the Modern Farm Woman, 1880–1930* (Albuquerque: University of New Mexico Press, 1995), says nothing of the impact of depression in the 1890s. See also Michael L. Goldberg, *An Army of Women: Gender and Politics in Gilded Age Kansas* (Baltimore, MD: Johns Hopkins University Press, 1997), and Marion Knox Barthelme, *Women in the Texas Populist Movement: Letters to the Southern Mercury* (College Station: Texas A&M University Press, 1997).

3. *San Francisco Chronicle* (March 8, 1895). See also *San Francisco Chronicle* (May 19 and November 9, 1893); *Boston Daily Advertiser* (August 11, 1893); *Emporia (Kansas) Gazette* (December 28, 1893); *Cleveland Plain Dealer* (October 25, 1893); *St. Louis Post-Dispatch* (December 22, 1893); *Wall Street Journal* (January 17, 1896).

4. National births, *Historical Statistics . . . to 1957*, 18, 23; local data from a sample of incomplete records in annual health office reports, variously titled, from Baltimore, Boston, Chicago, Cincinnati, Columbus, Indianapolis, New York, Philadelphia, Pittsburgh, and St. Louis, 1890–1900; and Emerson Haven and Harriet E. Hughes, *Population, Births, Notifiable Diseases and Deaths Assembled for New York City, New York, 1866–1938* (New York: Columbia University, n.d.).

5. *St. Louis Post-Dispatch* (December 24, 1893); Susan L. Smith, *Sick and Tired of Being Sick and Tired: Black Women's Health Activism in the United States, 1890–1950* (Philadelphia: University of Pennsylvania Press, 1995).

6. *New York Times* (February 1, 1894).

7. Ibid. (March 31, 1894).

8. *St. Louis Post-Dispatch* (January 11, 1894).

9. For example, *Seattle Post-Intelligencer* (October 24, 1894) and *(Salt Lake City) Deseret Weekly* (December 29, 1894).

10. *St. Louis Post-Dispatch* (December 8, 1893).

11. Ibid. (September 20, 1896); *Cleveland Plain Dealer* (October 27, 1896). Discussion above draws on annual police reports for Baltimore, Boston, Chicago, Cincinnati, Indianapolis, New York, Philadelphia, and Pittsburgh, 1890–1900. Erratic law enforcement, compounded by incomplete and sometimes inconsistent local records, makes an interpretation of crime during the depression a difficult task.

12. Annual school reports, variously titled, for Baltimore, Boston, Cincinnati, New York, Philadelphia, Pittsburgh, Providence, Salt Lake City, Los Angeles, St. Louis, and Chicago.

13. Quoted in Richard Stern, ed., "The Ward-Ross Correspondence, 1891–1896," *American Sociological Review* 3 (June 1938), 362–401. Also records of Princeton and Stanford universities, the universities of North Carolina (Chapel Hill) and California; Michigan, *The President's Report to the Board of Regents . . . 1891–1899* (Ann Arbor: University of Michigan Press, 1891–1899); for Arizona, *Appleton's Annual Cyclopedia, 1894*, 24; *San Francisco Chronicle* (January 5 and May 2, 1894); and U.S. Bureau of Education, *Report of the Commissioner of Education on the Years 1893–94—1898–99* (Washington, DC: Government Printing Office, 1896–1900).

14. Junius Henri Browne, "Succor for the Unemployed," *Harper's Weekly* 38 (January 6, 1894), 10.

15. *St. Louis Post-Dispatch* (October 29 and November 27, 1893); *San Francisco Chronicle* (February 25, 1894). Armed services strength rose by 4,700, about 9 percent, during 1893–94: *Historical Statistics . . . to 1957*, 736.

16. J. S. Rankin, "Come West with Your Unemployed," *Outlook* 49 (January 20, 1894), 154; *(Boise) Idaho Daily Statesman* (August 22, 1893); *St. Louis Post-Dispatch*

(January 4, 1894); *(Salt Lake City) Deseret Weekly* (March 10, 1894); *Atlanta Constitution* (May 12, 1894); Walter A. Wyckhoff, *The Workers: An Experiment in Reality* (New York: Charles Scribner's Sons, 1898), 2:298.

17. For perspective, Billington, *America's Frontier Heritage*, 30–47, 292–93; also Fite, *Farmers' Frontier*, 110–11, 131; Fred Albert Shannon, "The Homestead Law and the Labor Surplus," *American Historical Review* 41 (January 1936), 637–51, and *Farmer's Last Frontier*, 356–59. Population and land data are summarized in *Historical Statistics . . . to 1957*, 12–13, 236–37.

18. Twenty years later F. C. Mills took to the rails during another depression. His observations of life among the traveling unemployed are revealing for 1914 as well as for the depression two decades earlier. Gregory R. Woirol, *In the Floating Army: F. C. Mills on Itinerant Life in California, 1914* (Champaign: University of Illinois Press, 1992).

19. *Appleton's Annual Cyclopedia, 1895*, 267. Also *New York Times* (August 18–21, 1893; January 30, 1895; and August 18, 1896); Closson, Jr., "The Unemployed in American Cities," 206–15. The standard account: Donald LeCrone McMurry, *Coxey's Army: A Study of the Industrial Army Movement of 1894* (Boston: Little, Brown, 1924), 14 and passim, supplanted by Carlos A. Schwantes, *Coxey's Army: An American Odyssey* (Lincoln: University of Nebraska Press, 1985).

20. William Thomas Stead, "Coxeyism: A Character Sketch," *Review of Reviews* 10 (July 1894), 56; Thomas Byrnes, "The Menace of Coxeyism," *North American Review* 158 (June 1894), 697; Oliver Otis Howard, "The Menace of Coxeyism," ibid., 687–96; Jack London, "Hoboes That Pass in the Night," *Cosmopolitan* 44 (December 1907), 190–97; McMurry, *Coxey's Army*; Schwantes, *Coxey's Army*.

21. *Proceedings of the General Assembly of the Knights of Labor . . . 1893*, 69; *1894*, 6–9; *1896*, 10, 56–57, and 94–96; John Rogers Commons, et al., *The History of Labour in the United States* (New York: Macmillan, 1918–1935), 4:482–95. For incisive new examinations of the Knights and the ways in which cultural influences affected their history, see Kim Voss, *The Making of American Exceptionalism: The Knights of Labor and Class Formation in the Nineteenth Century* (Ithaca, NY: Cornell University Press, 1993); and Robert E. Weir, *Beyond Labor's Veil: The Culture of the Knights of Labor* (University Park: Pennsylvania State University Press, 1996).

22. *Proceedings of the General Assembly of the Knights of Labor . . . 1893*, 1–12; *1894*, 17; *1895*, 15; *1896*, 32, 114; *1897*, 19–25; *A.F.L. Proceedings, 1894*, 82, 84; *1895*, 70; *1896*, 75; *1897*, 55; "Mistaken—Perhaps Honestly—Let Us Unite," *American Federationist* 1 (January 1895), 257–58; "A Last But Contemptible Act," ibid., 3 (December 1896), 217–18. For a subtle treatment of the interplay between events and the culture of the Knights of Labor see Weir, *Beyond Labor's Veil* and Voss, *American Exceptionalism*.

23. *A.F.L. Proceedings, 1893*, 12; *1895*, 85; *1896*, 15–16; Commons, *History of Labour*, 501; Leo Wolman, *The Growth of American Unions, 1880–1923* (New York: National Bureau of Economic Research, 1924), 15–21, 32.

24. Bernard Mandel, *Samuel Gompers: A Biography* (Yellow Springs, Ohio: Antioch Press, 1963), 123–24.

25. *A.F.L. Proceedings, 1893*, 11–12, 47–48, 62, 72–75; *1896*, 57–60. In 1896, when free silver became a partisan issue, the federation resolved that previous monetary declarations were nonpartisan, so as to preserve the appearance of political neutrality that its leaders advocated.

26. *A.F.L. Proceedings, 1894*, 28–34, 48, 52; and Chapter 9, below.

27. *A.F.L. Proceedings, 1895,* 61–63; *1896,* 22–26, 81–82; *1897,* 56; "Labor, to the President," *American Federationist* 4 (December 1897), 236–38. In autumn 1897, the A.F.L.'s leaders conferred with President McKinley about immigration restriction. Mandel, *Gompers,* 174–98.

28. David P. Demarest, Jr., *"The River Ran Red": Homestead 1892* (Pittsburgh: University of Pittsburgh Press, 1992); Paul Krause, *The Battle for Homestead, 1880–1892: Politics, Culture, and Steel* (Pittsburgh: University of Pittsburgh Press, 1992).

29. *Appleton's Annual Cyclopedia, 1893,* 288–93; *1894,* 762; New York, *The Christian Advocate* (November 2, 1893); *New York Times* (December 31, 1893); Commons, *History of Labour,* 2:499–501.

30. U.S. Congress, House, *Sixteenth Annual Report of the Commissioner of Labor. 1901. Strikes and Lockouts,* 57th Cong., 1st sess., 1901, Doc. 18, 1–41, 340–43, 429–52, 674–77, and passim; *Historical Statistics . . . to 1957,* 99; for a comparison of union and nonunion wages see Douglas, *Real Wages,* 73–108; Albert Rees, *Real Wages in Manufacturing, 1890–1914* (Princeton, NJ: Princeton University Press, 1961), 20, 59–60, and passim.

31. The Cripple Creek mines were the last major gold discoveries in Colorado. The El Paso Lode was discovered by Robert Womack in October 1890, and Winfield Stratton, an itinerant carpenter, filed a claim for the Independence Mine in 1893. The Cripple Creek mines produced $125 million in gold by 1901. Charles K. Hyde, "Metal Mining," in *Extractives, Manufacturing, and Services: A Historiographical and Bibliographical Guide,* vol. 2, *Handbook of American Business History,* ed. David O. Whitten and Bess E. Whitten (Westport, CT: Greenwood Press, 1997), 67–90.

32. Richard Jensen, *The Winning of the Midwest: Social and Political Conflict, 1888–1896* (Chicago: University of Chicago Press, 1971), 250–68; Robert David Ward and William Warren, *Labor Revolt in Alabama: The Great Strike of 1894* (University: University of Alabama Press, 1965); David Nelson, *Farm and Factory: Workers in the Midwest, 1880–1990* (Bloomington: Indiana University Press, 1995), 31, 44–45.

33. *Appleton's Annual Cyclopedia, 1894,* passim, under entries for each state and territory; *Commercial and Financial Chronicle* (August 25 and October 20, 1894).

34. *Boston Daily Advertiser* (July 12, 1894).

35. For background, Almont Lindsey, *The Pullman Strike* (Chicago: University of Chicago Press, 1942), 239–332; Stanley Buder's brilliant revision, *Pullman: An Experiment in Industrial Order and Community Planning, 1880–1930* (New York: Oxford University Press, 1967), 139; and Ray Ginger, *The Bending Cross: A Biography of Eugene Victor Debs* (New Brunswick, NJ: Rutgers University Press, 1949), 88. On Debs also see J. Robert Constantine, *Gentle Rebel: Letters of Eugene V. Debs* (Urbana: University of Illinois Press, 1995), and Nick Salvatore, *Eugene V. Debs: Citizen and Socialist* (Urbana: University of Illinois Press, 1982). For a revisionist view of labor conflict at Haymarket Square, Homestead, and Pullman see Charles W. Baird, "Labor Law Reform: Lessons from History," *Government Union Review* 12, no. 1 (Winter 1991), 22–55.

36. Richardson, *Messages and Papers of the Presidents,* 9:499–501.

37. *Boston Daily Advertiser* (July 12, 1894); Buder, *Pullman,* 187; and a Debs editorial in the A.R.U. newspaper, *Chicago Railway Times* (August 15, 1894).

38. Federal action, sources cited above and Nevins, *Grover Cleveland,* 613–24; Mandel, *Gompers,* 128–29; U.S. Congress, Senate, *Report on the Chicago Strike of June–July, 1894, by the United States Strike Commission,* 53d Cong., 3d sess., 1894, S. Exe. Doc. 7; and Chapter 9, below.

39. *Appleton's Annual Cyclopedia, 1895*, 263–69; *1896*, 427–28, 543; *1897*, 265–71, 296–306; and *A.F.L. Proceedings, 1895*, 13; *1896*, 29; *1897*, 30–32. See also *Commercial and Financial Chronicle* (January 4, 1896, July 10 and September 18, 1897).

40. *San Francisco Chronicle* (August 15, 1893); and J. Thomas Scharf, "The Farce of the Chinese Exclusion Laws," *North American Review* 146 (December 1898), 85–97. Also *San Francisco Chronicle* (August 23–September 6, 1893); *Seattle Post-Intelligencer* (September 3 and 5, 1893); *Congressional Record*, 53d Cong., 1st sess. (1893), 25:2420 (re H.R. 3687); and John Higham, *Strangers in the Land: Patterns of American Nativism, 1860–1925* (New York: Athenaeum, 1963), 35–73.

41. Morrell Heald, "Business Attitudes toward European Immigration, 1890–1900," *Journal of Economic History* 13 (Summer 1953), 291–304.

42. Henry Cabot Lodge, "The Census and Immigrations," *Century Magazine* 46 (September 1893), 737–39; John Chetwood, "Immigration, Hard Times, and the Veto," *Arena* 18 (December 1897), 788–801; Sidney George Fisher, "Has Immigration Increased Population?" *Popular Science Monthly* 47 (December 1895 and January 1896), 244–55, 412; *Congressional Record*, 54th Cong., 1st (1896) and 2d (1897) sess., 28: 2817, 29:372; Rowland T. Berthoff, "Southern Attitudes toward Immigration, 1865–1914," *Journal of Southern History* 39 (August 1951), 328–60; Higham, *Strangers*, 63–74, 87–105.

43. Ignatius Donnelly, *Caesar's Column: A Story of the Twentieth Century* (Chicago: F. J. Schulte, 1891); Oscar Handlin, "American Views of the Jew at the Opening of the Twentieth Century," American Jewish Historical Society *Publications* 40 (June 1951), 323–44; Hofstadter, *Age of Reform*, 77–81. John Higham, "Anti-Semitism in the Gilded Age—A Reinterpretation," *Mississippi Valley Historical Review* 43 (March 1957), 559–78, and *Strangers*, 92–94; Vann Woodward, *Origins of the New South*, 188.

44. Donald L. Kinzer, *An Episode in Anti-Catholicism: The American Protective Association* (Seattle: University of Washington Press, 1964); Higham, *Strangers*, 77–87.

45. Nativistic fears of foreign radicalism, papists, and financial power were transformed into jingoistic hostility toward the countries from which threats seemed to emanate. See Higham, *Strangers*, 75, 74–77; Richard Hofstadter, *The Paranoid Style in American Politics* (New York: Vintage Books, 1967), 145–62, and *Age of Reform*, 71–93.

46. *(Boise) Idaho Daily Statesman* (January 17, 1894). Lynchings, 1880–1892, numbered at least 3,337; 2,585 (77 percent) of the victims were black. *Historical Statistics . . . to 1957*, 218; James Elbert Cutler, *Lynch Law: An Investigation into the History of Lynching in the United States* (New York: Longmans, Green, 1905), 155–92; and for a powerful reflection, Joel Williamson, "Wounds, Not Scars: Lynching, the National Conscience, and the American Historian," *Journal of American History* 83 (March 1997), 1221–53, referees' comments, 1254–72.

47. Thomas E. Watson, "The Negro Question in the South," *Arena* 6 (October 1892), 254–368, and C. Vann Woodward, *The Strange Career of Jim Crow*, 4th ed. (New York: Oxford University Press, 1974). Sheldon Hackney, *Populism to Progressivism in Alabama* (Princeton, NJ: Princeton University Press, 1969), and William H. Chafe, "The Negro and Populism: A Kansas Case Study," *Journal of Southern History* 34 (August 1968), were among important challenges to Vann Woodward. See also Joel Williamson, *The Crucible of Race: Black-White Relations in the American South since Emancipation* (New York: Oxford University Press, 1984), 180–233; George M. Frederickson, *The Black Image in the White Mind: The Debate on Afro-American Character and Destiny,*

1817–1914 (New York: Harper & Row, 1971), 256 and passim; Dewey W. Grantham, *The South in Modern America: A Region at Odds* (New York: HarperCollins, 1994), 11–22; John Cell, *The Highest Stage of White Supremacy: The Origins of Segregation in South Africa and the American South* (New York: Cambridge University Press, 1982). David Thelen, ''Introduction,'' in ''Perspectives: *The Strange Career of Jim Crow,*'' *Journal of American History* 75 (December 1988), 841; Howard Rabinowitz, ''More Than the Woodward Thesis: Assessing *The Strange Career of Jim Crow,*'' ibid., 842–56; and C. Vann Woodward, ''*Strange Career* Critics: Long May They Persevere,'' ibid., 857–68.

7

Contemporary Reactions: Issues and Opinion

> RESOLVED, *That the right to work is the right to life.*
> —American Federation of Labor, 1893

"Men died like flies under the strain, and Boston grew suddenly old, haggard, and thin," wrote Henry Adams of the panic of 1893.[1] Contemporary commercial and social stress were potent intellectual influences. The collapse and its chief social effects stimulated important changes in the loose body of attitudes that constituted the country's individualistic social and economic credo.

The ferocity of the financial storm that raged for three months following the collapse in May of the National Cordage Company stirred deep alarm. But severe as it was, the 1893 crash prompted only a gradual realization that it marked the onset of a major depression. One commentator wrote, "It is a fact not sufficiently considered that the influence of Wall Street is essentially local and special. The constant tendency is to magnify it and make it appear to be a vital part of the business system of the country, when in reality it is a thing to be lightly considered. There is no reason for alarm in an excited stock market because it does not touch the interests upon which our prosperity truly depends. . . . Ours is a large and prosperous country, and its financial welfare is beyond the reach of transient and superficial circumstances."[2] Only in mid-autumn did most of the press at last reluctantly admit that the United States had entered a period of depression, of a "PROFOUND DULLNESS" of business, or even "unexampled depression."[3]

With recognition that a major business downturn had begun came a grudging

sense that recovery must be gradual. Experience, and the country's tradition of
administrative minimalism, suggested that it would take years to heal wounds
as grievous as those of the summer of 1893.[4] Even so, a note of optimism
survived. The national faith in inevitable progress appeared to be intact. Partisan
politicians nourished hope with promises of a speedy business recovery under
their tutelage.[5] Wishful thinking played a role. So did the news media and the
rest of the business community, which probably felt an institutional duty to try
to talk the country back into prosperity.

Most persons—reflecting the reigning economic faith of the time—interpreted
the panic, and business cycles as well, in terms of a single cause or set of causes.
A widely shared belief that "depressions . . . were periods of penance for economic sins, and recovery was expected as soon as the rituals of liquidation and
reorganization could be performed," reinforced this simplistic approach. Business fluctuations were "natural events" that recurred from time to time, much
as ocean tides flowed and ebbed.[6] For the most part the sins that brought on
hard times did so by destroying confidence.[7] The way to restore prosperity was
to purge the sources of worry, practice rigid personal and business economy,
and permit deflation and liquidation to progress without interference. These last
eliminated "rottenness," unsound firms, and inflated speculative values. Once
placed on a basis of new, sound values, business was poised to expand, restoring
prosperity. There was security in these simple ideas that promised automatic, if
gradual, recovery and stirred additional hope during the 1890s.

Government, in such a scheme of things, had only a small role to perform.
Businessmen, like others, were only too willing to accept favors. In doing so
they referred selectively to current economic canons to defend their actions. The
conventions of the time generally permitted public measures only to counter
such incorrect government policies as were believed to have caused a contraction. Otherwise, government steps interfered with the operation of the natural
laws that controlled business, thus impeding economic growth. Of these laws
the most vital was the Social Darwinist rule of "the survival of the fittest."[8]
This was "inexorable and merciless" in its agency and assured civilization's
progress if not violated by government caprice. Cherishing such notions, at least
in the abstract, businessmen and perhaps most of the public sighed in relief
when legislative sessions closed and so ended for a time the threat of statutory
interference with business.[9]

The severity of the depression in time provoked sharp challenges to the notion
of a self-regulating economy. Increasing numbers of people endorsed government intervention to restore prosperity. Geographic, partisan, economic, and
other influences, and rising tension between old and new views, made coherent
action difficult. Several groups drew on an old inflationist tradition and proclaimed money the culprit, especially after the November 1893 repeal of the
Sherman silver purchase law failed to restart business. Prominent among these
were farmers (corn, wheat, and cotton growers were chronically plagued with
surpluses and low prices), many industrial workers, Western silver miners, and

even a few intellectuals such as Henry and Brooks Adams.[10] They argued that the country's circulating medium was inadequate and growing less quickly than the population—deflation.

Deflation, bitter personal experience taught, meant falling prices and personal income as needs outstripped the currency supply. Confidence yielded to the realization that enterprises fail in the face of falling prices—who will buy this year if prices are to be lower next year? One editor alleged, "The fact is that the present depression is caused by low prices. . . . Business is stagnant; there is no profit in what is done." The country resounded to charges that a bankers' conspiracy was at the bottom of things. The crisis of 1893 was the latest manifestation of a scheme of financial monopolists whose immediate aim was to compel repeal of the 1890 silver law. Their long-term goal was to force use of the yellow metal whose supply they selfishly and absolutely controlled as the basis of the monetary system.[11]

It was popularly believed that only unlimited coinage of silver could restore prosperity. Silver's abundance, intrinsic value, and historic use as money made it an ideal medium. It would be much safer than the fiat currency that the Greenbackers had formerly, and the Populists currently, proposed. When William Hope Harvey's *Coin's Financial School* appeared in 1894 it immediately became a rallying point for the silver legions. "His book purported to be a series of class discussions in which the teacher effectively demolished all the arguments of students opposed to free coinage of silver. Since he gave actual names to the students—Professor James Laurence Laughlin of the University of Chicago, Marshall Field the merchant, and the like—many readers believed that the debates had really taken place." Despite cleverly titled rebuttals like *Coin's Financial Fool*, Harvey's arguments swayed masses of American readers. It was but a step more for William Jennings Bryan to electrify the depression-swelled inflationist horde and come within an ace of the presidency on his condemnation of a cross of gold.[12]

Silverite claims stirred alarm and contempt in the Northeast and Midwest, particularly among business and middle-class groups.[13] Financier Henry Clews assigned the uncertainty precipitating the panic to dangerously inflated securities prices resulting from overspeculation. *The Commercial and Financial Chronicle* identified poor railroad earnings in 1892 as an added source of uneasiness. It was well known that 1892 had not been a good agricultural year. Cornell University professor J. W. Jenks saw the panic as merely the latest phase of a period of depression dating back twenty years. Others observed that European recession after the 1890 Baring suspension had curtailed foreign investment here.[14] Economist Albert Clark Stevens published a balanced examination of political, industrial, wage, price, agricultural, and other factors contributing to the downturn.[15] But the prevailing view blamed the contraction on "apprehension as to the maintenance of gold payments by the United States," originating in a rapid fall of the Treasury gold reserve, coinage of overvalued silver dollars, and the deepening threat that silverites might soon win free coinage. Repeal of the offensive 1890 silver law and an end to the coinage of silver dollars were essential to restore confidence.[16]

The debate over the causes and best means of ending the depression renewed after repeal of the Sherman Silver Purchase Act failed to spark recovery. Monetary explanations remained most common, but in time popular analyses began to shift. Samuel Gompers put the most important rival view succinctly in his 1896 presidential report to the A.F.L. Drawing on ideas current for several years, he charged that "industrial crises and stagnation results [*sic*] from many causes, but particularly from the lack of opportunity of the workers to consume more largely of the product of their labor." Wage cuts meant "a lesser consumption of these products, thus rending the labor of other workers unnecessary and throwing them out of employment. The crisis becomes intensified and prolonged." He proposed raising wages, which by stimulating larger consumption would stir an improvement of business.[17]

Similar ideas gained favor among businessmen as growing numbers of them agreed with the diagnosis of James M. Swank, General Manager of the American Iron and Steel Association: "The principal cause of the depression . . . [lies] in the capacity of the country to produce much more . . . [than it can] consume." Excess production had provoked demoralizing competition, helping bring on panic in 1893. He believed that a higher tariff was needed to restore prices and profits.[18]

Manufacturers and tradesmen increasingly inclined to other action, too. In an 1895 article Worthington Chauncy Ford illustrated the drift of opinion. He wrote that restricted crop exports, despite prevailing low prices, taught that America's relatively costly agriculture could not compete in world markets and must thus concentrate on home consumption. But rising exports of manufactures and the growing share of manufactures in exports showed that at new lower prices American industry could compete abroad. Foreign sales of manufactures could prove a major factor in restoring prosperity. Ford foresaw that Latin American and Asian markets would be particularly important. Chase Bank president Henry W. Cannon placed the need for financial reform foremost. He echoed Ford, though, writing, "It is necessary . . . [in order] to restore complete prosperity . . . [to] compete in the markets of the world."[19]

Views such as these prompted formation of the National Association of Manufacturers at a January 1895 meeting of industrialists in Cincinnati. Governor William McKinley of Ohio was the featured speaker. He drew a standing ovation with the words, "we want our own markets for our products . . . and . . . foreign markets for our surplus products." The N.A.M. adopted a program calling for tariff protection for American industry, and an aggressive national effort to expand exports. Months later the Atlanta Cotton States Exposition and the contemporaneous formation of numerous commercial bodies, such as the Philadelphia Commercial Museum, rested on the same impulses. The expanding interest in foreign markets bore importantly on foreign policy. It was a potent source of the surging expansionism that ended the century.[20]

Writers Frederick Jackson Turner, Josiah Strong, and Alfred Thayer Mahan enlarged popular expansionist opinion by heightening a feeling of social crisis. In July 1893 Turner read to a Chicago convention of historians his momentous essay on the significance of the frontier in American history. His paper articulated a sense of profound change that his countrymen widely shared. It also implied a diagnosis of the country's predicament. He wrote that the existence of a body of free land, and its exploitation, explained the development of America and such key national traits as opportunity, social mobility, and democracy. But the frontier had vanished by 1890, closing "the first period of American history." In 1896 Turner added that the energies of expansionism were fundamental and would probably seek new outlets through foreign policy.[21]

Meanwhile, others were asking whether new lands or markets might revive prosperity and ease class strife by replacing the opportunity that had vanished with the frontier. Josiah Strong, a Congregational minister, added a spiritual dimension to the discussion. In a series of popular volumes beginning with *Our Country* he spun out an alluring imperial theme. After its own religious conversion was complete, the American West could sponsor worldwide missionary action. Doing so would make the West the seat of a new empire. It would fulfill the civilizing mission and assure the predominance of the Anglo Saxon race. It would win access to foreign markets needed to replace prospects lost with the frontier. In accomplishing these things it would avert an imminent revolutionary class struggle in the United States.[22]

Navy captain Mahan added a strategic note. Viewing the seas as highways, he saw naval power as the key to national safety and prosperity. Territorial empire was unnecessary. Overseas naval bases were sufficient to control vital ocean shipping lanes and assure access to markets. Assigning depression largely to overproduction, he looked to foreign markets for relief. He wrote in 1897, "States having a good seaboard will find it [advantageous to] seek prosperity and extension by way of the sea and of commerce, rather than in attempts to unsettle . . . political arrangements."

Turner's writings reached Theodore Roosevelt and Woodrow Wilson, Strong's, hundreds of thousands, and Mahan's impressed Roosevelt, John Hay, Henry Cabot Lodge, Brooks Adams, and Cleveland's Secretary of the Navy, Hilary A. Herbert, to name but a few. Together they were a powerful expansionist influence.[23]

Meanwhile, Democratic efforts to fulfill 1892 campaign promises to reduce the tariff had directed attention to the connection between import duties and the crash. The tariff was the main issue during the 1894 congressional canvass, which occurred soon after passage of that year's Democratic Wilson-Gorman tariff. Republican speakers on the eve of balloting charged that "utter uncertainty . . . appalling doubt" about future duties has caused the crisis. Worried businessmen had retrenched in anticipation of competition from a flood of cheap foreign goods, faced credit restriction, then succumbed to panic.[24] Democrats replied in kind. They contended that the 1890 McKinley Act, imposing duties so high as to exclude imports, had cut Treasury receipts just as Benjamin Harrison's administration was embarking on a spending spree. The gold reserve then began its alarming fall. Meanwhile, American manufacturers had hurt themselves by greedily pricing their goods above the world market. Such arguments were wasted; depression-inspired discontent produced a GOP tidal wage presaging that of 1896.[25]

Severe though it was, the crisis led few Americans to reject capitalism. A few syndico-anarchist speakers briefly found more receptive audiences. Occasionally, desperate jobless workingmen in New York, Cleveland, and elsewhere participated in riots attributed to anarchist leadership. There were infrequent reports of malevolent Red plots to assassinate prominent public figures. Even these greatly magnified any actual danger. The country held no more than a few hundred anarchists, most of them recent immigrants from Europe.[26]

Socialism held a somewhat greater appeal. Hard times stirred a handful of frankly Marxist attacks upon the unjust operation of what one writer termed the country's "dying" competitive economy, with its uncontrollable cyclical fluctuations.[27] The most influential contemporary plea for socialism was Henry Demarest Lloyd's *Wealth against Commonwealth* (1894). But not even this angry expose of corporate consolidation and greed, with its ringing call for a democratic-collectivism, won many converts.[28]

Some Americans, robbed of their faith in capitalism by hardship and poverty, appraised alternative economic philosophies. The Marxian Socialist Labor Party (S.L.P.) won hundreds of recruits, and its local units multiplied from 113 to 200 between 1892 and 1896—its presidential vote rose from 21,512 to 37,275. Collectivists won a number of local and state legislative contests in Massachusetts, their first notable success at the polls. In the years 1893 to 1895, under fiery Daniel De Leon, the S.L.P. threatened to exploit discontent and make serious inroads into the labor movement. Of greater importance, hard times saw an energetic new leader, Eugene Debs, rise to prominence. Dispirited by the failures of the American Railway Union and Bryan's 1896 bid for the presidency, Debs rejected capitalism for socialism and formed the Social Democratic Party, quickly forging it into the nation's leading socialist body.[29]

Socialists remained a minuscule, marginal population during the nineties, as most Americans remained firmly committed to economic individualism and held little sympathy even for the Populists, decrying their calls for nationalizing the rail and communications systems as foolish, paternalistic, and socialistic.[30] The agrarians for their part regarded government ownership as a way to broaden individual opportunity within a capitalist framework and eliminate corporate oppression.

While eliciting scant sympathy for socialism, hard times softened resistance to government intervention in the economy. Continued agrarian radical support for the Populist Subtreasury plan is a compelling case in point. Proposed in 1889, the design called for the government to stabilize crop markets and boost farm prices with loans to farmers, and warehouses to store the harvest.[31]

Economic hardship severely strained debtor-creditor relations. Distressed laborers and farmers in about two dozen mostly Western and Southern states turned to a remedy commonly sought when money was tight. They won passage of a rash of new or more liberal mechanics' lien, stay, and execution laws. These typically increased protections for wage earners and debtors. North Dakota's foreclosure statute exempted from dispossession for debt homesteads to the high value of five thousand dollars.

The period's conservative judiciary often struck down measures designed to help debtors.[32] The wide variation in debtors-aid legislation and the absence of a uniform national bankruptcy statute often made it difficult for creditors to collect from insolvents or defaulters. Congress had begun to consider a new bankruptcy law in 1892. The arrival of panic, "when failures are frequent," brought general recognition of the "necessity of a good bankruptcy law."[33] Despite clear constitutional authority to act and a clear need, Congress was unable to pass a new law until 1898. Democratic and Western and Southern agrarian opposition to a provision—even if necessary to secure a settlement or prevent fraud—empowering creditors to force debtors into bankruptcy proceedings delayed approval.[34]

The era's staggering business failures also aroused profound concern. Abuses often accompanied failures. Frequently corporate officers evaded creditors or stockholders by arranging for friendly courts to appoint them as receivers of the very firms they had mismanaged. The February 1893 Reading receivership involved this stratagem, which is still familiar. There were many more such instances.[35] A loud cry for corrective action resulted. The *Wall Street Journal* joined in the chorus, declaring, "Now is a good time to bring about reform."[36] There were also calls for passage of laws requiring publication of the names of corporate shareholders, to make management more responsive to investors, creditors, and the public.[37] Implementation of these demands awaited the next century.

Popular hostility toward big business surged during the depression. The self-interested political activities of powerful businessmen contributed. The contrast between the affluence of giant enterprise and the condition of the needy added fuel. Repeated instances of alleged corporate greed and disregard for the commonweal stirred greater anger. Layoffs and the era's bitterly fought, mostly unsuccessful strikes also contributed. Angry speakers charged that big business was "organized in greed" to prey on a helpless public.[38] The prologue to Lloyd's *Wealth against Commonwealth* lent tornadic expression to popular anger: "Nature is rich; but . . . man, the heir of nature, is poor. The world, enriched by thousands of generations of toilers and thinkers, has reached a fertility which can give every human being a plenty undreamed of even in the Utopias." But "the 'cornerers,' the syndicates, trusts . . . , with the cry of 'overproduction,'— too much of everything" intervened. They greedily held "back the riches of the earth, sea, and sky . . . [declaring] that there is too much light and warmth" and regulating "the consumption by the people of the necessities of life."[39]

Nevertheless, most critics preferred regulation to more radical antitrust measures. Leaders of the Grange, Farmers' National Congress, and Southern Farmers' Alliance knew that if properly managed, big business offered important economies. Samuel Gompers believed that labor unions were a natural counterpart of industrial combination and feared that misguided public action could easily be bent to "deprive labor" of the benefits of organization.[40]

Commercial prostration stirred rising anger at specific corporate abuses. Tax evasion, rate increases amid depression, callous refusal to obey public officials, and high-handed manipulation of municipal and state governments provoked spirited battles. These raged, for example, in Ashland, Superior, Milwaukee, and elsewhere in Wisconsin. It soon became clear that quasi-public utilities such as franchised electric, trolley, telephone, and water companies could not be bent to local community wishes. In response a statewide reform movement emerged that aimed to subject business and local authorities to state regulatory powers. After repeated failure to secure effective regulatory authority, reformers often turned to public ownership as an alternative.[41] A mix of socialist influence and aggravated social tensions led the A.F.L. in 1893 almost to endorse government ownership of enterprises that were by nature monopolistic, such as railroads and communications.[42] Reform-minded economist Richard Theodore Ely boldly called for public operation of all natural monopolies. This step would end unfair rates and prices, waste, and needless duplication of services or equipment. It would also stabilize growth of these enterprises, limiting the evil effects of cyclical business fluctuations.[43]

Railroads lay at the heart of social aggravation with big business. They attracted deep popular enmity fed by years of rate and service discrimination designed to maximize profits at the expense of farmers and businesses too small to strike favorable deals, practices condoned by a railroad-friendly judiciary little restrained by the Interstate Commerce Act. Revelations of mismanagement accompanying the failure of 119 railroads—one-sixth of the nation's overbuilt mileage—in 1893 exacerbated public anger. Outrage grew still more with the creation of vast new systems, such as the Southern. A hostile chorus demanded closer regulation, augmenting the demands of agrarian and labor radicals for nationalization. Progressives suggested the creation of a National Transportation Board to wield broad powers of control.[44] Some even urged that the railroads be made free public highways, open to anyone who wished to operate trains on them.[45] As hostility rose, one conservative editor worried that "the time may come when the demand shall become general upon the government to take the management of at least one of the principal roads in its strong hands [as a disciplinary yardstick]."[46]

Ruinous competition and disastrous earnings in 1894 led railroad management to redouble efforts (which antedated the panic) to detain congressional approval for pooling traffic revenues. Obliging lawmakers introduced several bills and debated them into the next year. Important Eastern commercial interests and the Interstate Commerce Commission lent support to the proposal. Opponents, including Western and Southern agrarian and mercantile shippers, resisted fiercely. They argued that the plan threatened to create "the most gigantic monopoly ever proposed or conceived of." In the end they prevailed. Comparable negative public reaction defeated a renewed attempt to legalize pooling after the Supreme Court's 1897 Trans-Missouri Freight Association ruling that the Interstate Commerce Act forbade it.[47]

Pooling was a thorny issue. Competing railroads (and other interstate competitors like meat packers and refiners) found in pooling agreements relief from the destructive struggle for markets—destructive because each firm tried to undercut the others in a battle for market share that drove prices below cost. Pooling or market-sharing plans allowed each participant a portion of the market and a price above average cost. Consumers hated pools, because such agreements brought an end to low prices—consumers, after all, are rarely concerned with the long-run stability of an industry or the firms constituting it. Furthermore, a successful pool could price like a monopoly, and there is little American consumers fear more than monopolies. (This is because of the persistent and widespread misunderstanding of monopoly pricing, that is, the belief that a monopoly can charge whatever price it wants regardless of demand. In fact, a profit-maximizing monopoly is restricted by the demand for its good or service, and while it will certainly seek the profit-maximizing price, that price is not whatever the firm wants to charge.)

A legislator who supports legalized pooling commits political suicide; yet without legal support a pool has little chance of survival, because participants have an incentive to cheat. At the pool-established price each participant prefers to sell more and increase profits. Because there is no way to enforce effectively the pooling agreement and because members anticipate or observe cheating among other members and non-members, each responds by violating the agreement. The most direct means of enforcing a pooling agreement is to sue violators in court, but the judiciary refused to hear the cases on grounds that pooling agreements are not legally binding. Legislators faced the choice between angering their constituents by passing laws making pooling argeements legally binding and therefore sending prices higher, or sidestepping the issue and forcing competitors to find other ways of managing excessive supply offered by overbuilt industries. In most industries the result was continued overbuilding and eventually bankruptcies as shakeouts reduced the number of competitors and left society to pay the social costs of overexpanded rail lines and factories. Industries like interstate meat packing that found ways to enforce pooling provoked a deep-seated antipathy among consumers that lingers a century after the depression of 1894.[48]

Catastrophic bank failures in 1893 combined with a growing concern with the financial system to focus attention on the country's money and banking systems. More than a dozen states, including Alabama, New Hampshire, California, and Tennessee, legislated to strengthen their banks. Interest focused, though, on the national banks and currency. Public officials, including the pres-

ident, Secretary of the Treasury, and comptroller of the currency, vied with
individuals and with conferences of financiers in offering analyses of the defects
in the financial system and legislative schemes for its improvement. However,
intense popular passion over the money question blocked agreement on any
reform before the century's end.[49]

Crushing unemployment, most devastating in the winter of 1893–94 and serious throughout the decade, brought unprecedented relief measures. The severity of joblessness illuminated the paucity of reliable statistical information
creating a demand for timely and accurate social and economic statistics. A state
bureau of labor statistics to collect and analyze employment data first appeared
in Massachusetts in 1869, and twenty-four other states had followed the Bay
State's lead by 1890. Economic difficulties of the 1890s generated growing
support for expanding the scale and scope of state bureaus of collection and
analysis of employment indicators, and spurred interest that would culminate in
the establishment of the National Bureau of Economic Research on the eve of
the Great Depression of the twentieth century.

The concern over unemployment and poverty that the spread of labor strife
and industrial slums had aroused in recent years widened rapidly during the
depression. Hard times put a new, keen edge on the debate over unemployment
and poverty, producing two major interpretations: traditional and innovative. In
the traditional argument Calvinist and Social Darwinist dogma justified destitution as the wages of personal failings. It followed from human frailty that
poverty was ineradicable. But, hope was not dead; the American experience
suggested that escape from destitution was possible. One of the most interesting
popular responses to joblessness and associated poverty appeared in the guise
of various self-help efforts. The work ethic undergirded these, as it did the
country's entire approach to relief. One Midwestern editor put it succinctly:
"The opportunity to labor is what is wanted." Among self-help efforts, community gardens were attempted in Boston, New York, Brooklyn, Buffalo, Philadelphia, Pittsburgh, Chicago, St. Louis, Omaha, Denver, Seattle, and even
smaller places like Reading, Steubenville, Galesburg, and Winona. Labor ex-
changes were established in several cities, including Cleveland, trading goods
and services among their members. Others turned to cooperative stores. Dakota,
Iowa, and Minnesota farmers tried to build farmers' railroads. Finally, numbers
found in planned communities a hope for escape from poverty. Of these the
Colorado Cooperative Colony, which became Nucla, Colorado, was perhaps the
best known. The eventual return of prosperity, the collision of idealism with
pragmatism, and inadequate capital ended these ventures. From one perspective,
they were a triumph of individual initiative. From another they demonstrated
the imperviousness of Americans to whatever lessons the depression might have
to teach. Received truth triumphed over the conditions of industrial life, dogma
over fact, as is still the case.[50]

The innovative interpretation suggested that new conditions discredited old
convictions. For the first time social workers and clergymen weathered extensive

contact with the unemployed. Many of them discovered that relief needs exceeded the capacities of public almshouses and private charities. They also learned that many of the jobless were in dire straits through no fault of their own. Finding that misfortune struck the "competent no less than the incompetent, the industrious as well as the slothful," they redoubled efforts to meet unexampled needs for charity.

The scale of joblessness and limited means of regular charities produced in the 1890s a first, reluctant provision of work relief outside of almshouses. Even here old prejudices died hard. Officials separated the temporarily jobless from the chronically idle. Opinion held that aid should remain under local control and be granted only when applicants proved themselves willing to work. Josephine Shaw Lowell, a leading welfare professional, offered a guiding principle at an 1894 conference. Work relief, she warned, should be reserved for the victims of hard times, not paupers. To "be a benefit" and not reduce recipients to permanent dependence it "must . . . be *continuous, hard, and underpaid.*" In words strangely redolent of those of the welfare reformers of the 1990s she cautioned that not even the worthy poor should receive aid so generous as to discourage their seeking ordinary work. Most folks still wanted to discourage vagrancy, a major current problem, by corporal punishment if need be. But many in time relented. These followed the recommendation of an 1895 Fond du Lac, Wisconsin, conference on vagrancy. Tramps should be treated as victims of circumstances and given shelter and woodlot jobs, rather than arrested as criminals.[51]

There were other responses to unemployment. Some states—New York, Montana, Nebraska—and many cities established free public employment agencies. Several states tightened regulations governing privately owned employment services.[52] Economist John R. Commons urged cities to replace the contract system for public works with municipal day labor to spread work over the winter season, when private construction firms were often idle.[53] Finally, a desire to spread existing work among more laborers greatly increased pressure for passage of a general eight-hour law.[54]

Hard times discredited the distinction between the worthy and the vicious poor. Plans for extensive, even national, aid to the needy came from every side. No less a skeptic about government action than Samuel Gompers as early as August 1893 urged "that the [New York] City, State, and General Government relieve the distress of the unemployed by beginning great public improvements," including waterway and highway projects.[55] The A.F.L. in convention four months later "RESOLVED, That the right to work is the right to life, that to deny the one is to destroy the other. That when the private employer cannot or will not give work the municipality, state, or nation must."[56]

The 1894 odyssey of Jacob Coxey from Masillon, Ohio, to the District of Columbia jail by way of the Capitol lawn revealed the popularity of these views. Conservative opinion dismissed the industrial army movement as ridiculous— at least until reports of train seizures and the approach of a few corps to Washington spread alarm. Coxey's good roads and non-interest-bearing bond schemes had the air of a "burlesque" of sound economics that portended "class legislation," paternalism, or socialism.[57] Many continued to attribute poverty to vice. A few even claimed that depression had elicited *too much* charity![58] Even so, Coxey's and similar projects attracted broad sympathy. After the A.F.L. endorsed Coxey's program in December 1893, Gompers, who was outraged at the plight of the jobless, tried repeatedly to gain a congressional hearing for the scheme. Meanwhile, Hazen S. Pingree, mayor of Detroit, who advocated an ambitious program of municipal relief, adopted a heightened social concern that made him an important precursor of twentieth-century urban Progressive reform. Swelling support for public action led young economist Thorstein Veblen to observe that a large minority of Americans were abandoning unbridled economic individualism for the maxim that "society owes every honest man a living." The motto "life, liberty, and the pursuit of happiness" was coming to mean "life, liberty, and the means of happiness."[59]

The incendiary strikes of the mid-1890s heated contemporary controversy over labor relations to the combustion point. Religious as well as secular circles heatedly discussed the labor question no less than other issues raised or made more acute by the crash. During the previous few decades individual clerics and middle-class parishioners in the dominant Protestant bodies had begun to direct attention toward applying Christian ethics to the most serious problems of industrialization. Labor relations, the distribution of wealth, and the spread of slums led among these. This Social Gospel impulse had won growing sympathy but had not yet captured the major religious groups when depression struck. The crisis affected the churches variously. It sped the moment when some were willing to grapple, nationally, with thorny social issues. It also harshly tested the progressive humanitarianism of many proponents of the Social Gospel.

Traditional Protestant individualism remained strong. It shaped denunciations in the church press of anarchism, Coxeyism, socialism, and Populist efforts to "defraud creditors" by forcing the unlimited coinage of debased silver money. The Pullman boycott provoked fearful condemnation. With other labor clashes it may have moved some adherents of Social Christianity to retreat to more conservative attitudes. The *New York Churchman*, often friendly toward organized labor in calmer times, branded the Pullman boycott as "monstrous" and preposterous, berated industrial unionism and "solidarity of labor," and promoted in its place the tried and true organization by trade and craft.[60] Many conservatives continued to rationalize poverty through that enduring misinterpretation of the scriptural maxim, "For the poor always ye have with you."[61]

Yet events shook the churches, and religious opinion. Effects on membership were not clear, but falling offerings forced widespread retrenchment. Such notable Christian reformers as Richard T. Ely, John R. Commons, Washington Gladden, George D. Herron, and William Dwight Porter Bliss expanded their efforts. Ely and Commons in 1893 formed the American Institute of Christian Sociology, one of several such groups. Social Gospel analyses of conditions became more complex and diverse during the decade. Many church folk gained a larger view of their social responsibilities. Prodded by progressive clergymen, they expanded parish social services to include soup kitchens, rescue missions, and the like. They also embraced a deeper civic consciousness, now directing the moral zeal of the old anti-vice crusades to the goal of social as well as individual regeneration. National denominational meetings, some for the first time, considered social and economic problems while they were immediate and controversial.

Southern Baptists in convention consistently stressed other-worldly concerns. In contrast, the Bishops' Address at the 1896 quadrennial Methodist General Conference called forcefully for the removal of "all unjust distribution of property." Action was imperative: "Classes are arrayed against each other. . . . A ripple has come to our shores from the far off tidal wave of the French Revolution, declaring that all property is theft." A year before, Washington Gladden had reported to the Congregational General Conference that class strife could be abated only by freeing the Gospel to work its healing power, declaring, "If our Gospel means anything it means that no man can prosper by despoiling his fellows." The growing appeal of such views and the spread of church relief and social activity measured the widening sway of Social Christianity in reply to problems of industrial life made more serious by bad times.[62]

Considering popular opinion and labor issues more broadly, business, the urban middle class, and conservative rural folk held to deep-rooted, traditional attitudes. They largely agreed that the "whole question of strikes . . . just as . . . [that] of the right to work, the right to do business, to own property, . . . to manage it, and the right as a person to make contracts" rested on "the doctrine of individual rights." When these rights were protected, strikes posed no great danger. Strikers made mistakes, however, when they insisted on "the right to keep other men from working" or combined "for the purpose of destroying property" or of taking "vengeance in case they cannot accomplish their purpose in a peaceful way."[63] Strikers who employed violence or tried to interrupt business violated the property rights of management. Likewise, efforts to prevent strikebreakers from taking their places violated the rights of others to contract freely for jobs.

Such attitudes, fortified by fearful reports of violence, went far to explain the horror that gripped most of the public during the Pullman strike. The plight of the Pullman employees at first stirred broad sympathy. This eroded as violence spread. The American Railway Union's action came to be branded as "reckless, wicked," "deplorable," or even "REVOLUTION."[64] A minority was threatening the welfare of a helpless people by paralyzing business. Thus the use of the army to prevent an interruption of mail shipments won general assent. The same held for the use of troops to restore rail traffic, under the guise of a legitimate exercise of federal authority over interstate commerce. The president won approval, even applause, for employing military force to quell disorders growing out of the strike. Theodore Roosevelt, who later threatened to use soldiers to achieve a different result in a labor controversy, privately described Cleveland's handling of the Chicago violence as "excellent."[65]

Conversely, labor troubles stirred a growing number of Americans, probably at length a majority, to recognize a serious need for reform. Concern extended to many social groups. Businessmen and chambers of commerce condemned George Pullman. The Wisconsin Women's Suffrage Association in 1894 for the first time expressed support for labor unions. Two years later the state Women's Christian Temperance Union addressed the labor problem, explaining that industrial conditions rather than character defects alone dragged women to vice. There was a gathering consensus favoring passage of a national law providing for voluntary arbitration of labor disputes falling within the sphere of federal authority.[66] The special commission that President Cleveland created to investigate the Pullman strike proposed requiring compulsory arbitration of railway labor contests that ordinary negotiations could not resolve. Moreover, rail unions ought to be recognized, and yellow dog contracts—employment-prerequisite agreements that the employee would forsake unionism—in the industry abolished. The press generally argued that even these sweeping recommendations be given serious consideration.[67] Following a battle that dragged on for more than three years, the strong pressures for reform growing out of the labor strife of the mid-1890s resulted in passage of a voluntary railway arbitration act, in 1898.

Other reform proposals fared less well. After the Pullman strike the A.F.L.'s *American Federationist* called for government ownership of the railroads.[68] Controversy raged over the use of court injunctions to quell strikes. Labor, agrarian radicals, urban progressives, and the 1896 Democratic platform condemned the practice, but a conservative Congress refused to outlaw it.[69] Profit sharing was put forth as the solution to future labor troubles.[70] Social observers held that the failure of the Pullman struggle had discredited the strike as a weapon and that labor must find some new means of fighting its battles.[71] Finally, looking toward the twentieth century and back to the Knights of Labor, a few labor spokesmen proposed that all workingmen join one giant union; only so organized could they overcome the forces arrayed against them.[72] Samuel Gompers disagreed.[73]

Calls for change fell on deaf ears among the conservative business, middle-class, and rural Americans who opposed any extension of the power of labor, or of government to the same end. Instead, conservatives favored new restrictions on unions and unionism, extension of the Sherman Antitrust Act to include unions;[74] reactionaries advised placing rail workers under contract to make them liable to legal penalty if they struck or quit before the expiration of their service obligation.[75]

Second only to the Great Depression of the 1930s in severity and duration, the depression of the 1890s buffeted a more agrarian, self-sufficient population than did its twentieth-century counterpart. Moreover, the world was less receptive to Marxism than it was after 1917. The last depression of the nineteenth century profoundly affected popular attitudes in the United States, yet old beliefs retained great appeal. Few rejected economic individualism. Familiar notions of the inexorability and nature of business cycles maintained wide currency. Where changes were apparent, they suggested a tentative groping for solutions and adjustments in response to problems accompanying industrialization and urbanization—problems that depression aggravated. Contemporaries assigned blame to money and banking, excess industrial capacity, and a paucity of foreign markets—views reflected in federal monetary, diplomatic, and industrial policy in the twentieth century.

The popular view of poverty as a vice, the sole responsibility of the individual, was modified to allow that social and economic conditions, circumstances, could force unemployment and poverty on the most moral men and women. Distinctions between virtuous and vicious poor blurred and lost relevance; the community assumed greater responsibility for jobs and sustenance when private enterprise faltered.

Hard times intensified social sensitivity to a wide range of problems accompanying industrialization by making them more severe. Those whom depression struck hardest, as well as much of the general public and major Protestant churches, grew in civic consciousness about currency and banking reform, regulation of business in the public interest, and labor relations. Although nineteenth-century liberalism and the tradition of administrative minimalism that it favored remained viable, public opinion began to swing toward the governmental activism and interventionism associated with modern, industrial societies, erecting in the process the intellectual foundation for the reform impulse that was to be called Progressivism in twentieth-century America. Most important of all, these opposed tendencies in thought set the boundaries within which Americans for the next century debated the most vital questions of their shared experience. The depression was a reminder of business slumps, commonweal above avarice, and principle above principal.

NOTES

1. Henry Adams, *The Education of Henry Adams* (New York: Random House, 1931), 338; Lee Benson, "An Approach to the Scientific Study of Past Public Opinion," *Public Opinion Quarterly* 31 (Winter 1967–68), 522–67, for theory; Rezneck, "Unemployment," 324–45, for contemporary popular attitudes. An edited form of this chapter appeared in *Mid-America* 47 (July 1965), 155–75. This version is published with the permission at *Mid-America*.

2. *St. Louis Globe-Democrat* (May 6, 1893); *Commercial and Financial Chronicle* (May 6–September, 1893); *Cleveland Plain Dealer* (May 14 and July 15, 1893); *Philadelphia Public Ledger* (July 3 and September 11, 1893); *Chicago Daily Tribune* (May 8 and September 3–9, 1893); and *San Francisco Chronicle* (May 6 and July 14, 1893).

3. *Wall Street Journal* (October 30, 1893); *Chicago Daily Tribune* (December 11, 1893); *Boston Daily Advertiser* (December 25, 1893).

4. *Philadelphia Public Ledger* (July 22, 1893); *Chicago Daily Tribune* (November

11, 1893); *Seattle Post-Intelligencer* (September 4, 1893); *Boston Daily Advertiser* (January 1, 1894).

5. Discussed in chapters 7, 8, and 9.

6. Thomas Childs Cochran and William Miller, *The Age of Enterprise: A Social History of Industrial America* (New York: Macmillan, 1942), 137; *Raleigh (North Carolina) News & Observer* (August 17, 1893); *Wall Street Journal* (July 8, 1893); *St. Louis Post-Dispatch* (May 21, 1893); *Chicago Railway Times* (January 1, 1894); *Seattle Post-Intelligencer* (March 28, 1895); Henry Clews, *Fifty Years on Wall Street* (New York: Irving Publishing, 1908), 157–59.

7. Fels, *American Business Cycles*, 206–10 and passim; Kirkland, *Industry Comes of Age*, 8–12; *Commercial and Financial Chronicle* (May 6, 1893); *Philadelphia Public Ledger* (July 22, 1893); *Atlanta Constitution* (January 1, 1893); *San Francisco Chronicle* (July 5, 1893); *Boston Daily Advertiser* (January 1, 1894).

8. *Commercial and Financial Chronicle* (May 13 and September 2, 1893); *St. Louis Post-Dispatch* (July 23, 1893); *Boston Daily Advertiser* (January 1, 1894); *Emporia (Kansas) Gazette* (February 5, 1894); *San Francisco Chronicle* (February 2, 1894); *Philadelphia Public Ledger* (February 4, 1895); Edward Atkinson, "The Benefits of Hard Times," *Forum* 20 (September 1895), 79–90.

9. *(Salt Lake City) Deseret Weekly* (December 31, 1893); *Emporia (Kansas) Gazette* (February 5, 1894); *Wall Street Journal* (July 6, 1894); *Chicago Daily Tribune* (August 14–18, 1894); *Philadelphia Public Ledger* (January 5, 1895); Edward Kemball, et al., "The Business Revival," *North American Review*, 49 (November 1894), 613. For professional economic thought, largely disregarded here, Joseph Harry Dorfman, *The Economic Mind in American Civilization* (New York: Viking, 1949), 3:215–305; Paul Barnett, *Business Cycle Theory in the United States, 1860–1900* (Chicago: University of Chicago Press, 1941).

10. Adams, *Education of Henry Adams*, 335–44; Arthur F. Beringause, *Brooks Adams: A Biography* (New York: Knopf, 1955), 109.

11. *San Francisco Chronicle* (July 5, 1893); *(Boise) Idaho Daily Statesman* (February 25, 1896).

12. William Hope Harvey, *Coin's Financial School* (Chicago: Coin Publishing Company, 1894), 3; Horace White, *Coin's Financial Fool* (New York: J. S. Ogilvie, 1895); Myers, *Financial History*, 218–19, ch. 9; Glyn Davies, *A History of Money from Ancient Times to the Present Day* (Cardiff: University of Wales Press, 1994), 492–97; *San Francisco Chronicle* (July 16, 1893); *(Boise) Idaho Daily Statesman* (December 10, 1893); *Raleigh (North Carolina) News & Observer* (November 11, 1893); *Chicago Railway Times* (July 1, 1895).

13. White, *Coin's Financial Fool*; J. Laurence Laughlin, *Facts about Money* (Chicago: E. A. Weeks, 1895); Willard Fisher, " 'Coin' and His Critics," *Quarterly Journal of Economics* 10 (January 1896), 187–208; Jeanette P. Nichols, "Bryan's Benefactor: Coin Harvey and His World," *Ohio Historical Quarterly* 47 (October 1958), 299–325.

14. Clews, *Fifty Years*, 948; "Railroad Prosperity and General Welfare," *Quotation Supplement of the Commercial and Financial Chronicle* (May 26, 1894), 1–2; Pierce, H. A., *Bankers' Magazine* 47 (January 1893), 490–96; Rezneck, "Unemployment," 324.

15. Stevens, "Analysis of the Phenomena of the Panic," 117–48.

16. *New York Times* (September 10 and April 12, 1893); *Commercial and Financial Chronicle* (May 6, 1893); *Philadelphia Public Ledger* (February 25, July 22, and December 23, 1893); *Wall Street Journal* (October 30, 1893); *Chicago Daily Tribune* (May

5, 1893); *Boston Daily Advertiser* (August 2, 1893); *Seattle Post-Intelligencer* (September 10, 1893); Pierce, *Bankers' Magazine* 47 (September 1893), 180–87.

17. *A.F.L. Proceedings, 1896*, 18–19.

18. *Commercial and Financial Chronicle* (May 13, 1893).

19. J. Sterling Morton, et al., "The Financial Muddle," *North American Review* 160 (February 1895), 151.

20. Albert Kleckner Steigerwalt, *The National Association of Manufacturers, 1895–1914: A Study in Business Leadership*, Michigan Business Studies 16 (no. 2, Ann Arbor: Bureau of Business Research, Graduate School of Business Administration, University of Michigan, 1964), 32. Also Ford, "Turning of the Tide," 187–95; Charles Stewart Smith and Francis B. Thurber, "What Will Bring Prosperity?" *North American Review* 164 (April 1897), 428–30; *New York Evening Post* (May 11, 1893); *Atlanta Constitution* (June 28, 1894).

21. "The Significance of the Frontier in American History," *Annual Report of the American Historical Association, 1893* (Washington, DC: Government Printing Office, 1894), 199–227; and "The Problem of the West," *Atlantic Monthly* 78 (September 1896), 287–97.

22. Josiah Strong, *Our Country: Its Possible Future and Its Present Crisis* (New York: Baker & Taylor, 1885); *The New Era; or, the Coming Kingdom* (New York: Baker & Taylor, 1893); *Expansion under New World Conditions* (New York: Baker & Taylor, 1900).

23. Alfred Thayer Mahan, *The Influence of Sea Power upon History, 1660–1783* (Boston: Little, Brown, 1890), and *The Interest of America in Sea Power, Present and Future* (New York: Little, Brown, 1885); also Pierce, *Bankers' Magazine* 48 (February 1894), 563–67; Billington, *America's Frontier Heritage*, 1–22; La Feber, *New Empire*, 62–196; and Ralph Dewar Bald, Jr., "The Development of Expansionist Sentiment in the United States, 1885–1895, As Reflected in Periodical Literature" (Ph.D. diss.: University of Pittsburgh, 1953).

24. *San Francisco Chronicle* (October 14, 1894); *Boston Daily Advertiser* (August 16, 1894); *(Boise) Idaho Daily Statesman* (September–October 1894); *Chicago Daily Tribune* (June 9–November 11, 1894). The protectionist, Democratic *Philadelphia Public Ledger* (August 14, 1894) agreed.

25. *St. Louis Post-Dispatch* (August 17 and October 7, 1894); *Raleigh (North Carolina) News & Observer* (October 17, 1894); *Cleveland Plain Dealer* (December 18, 1893 and October 16, 1894).

26. *New York Times* (August 18–20, 1893); *Cleveland Plain Dealer* (May 1–6, 1894); *Boston Daily Advertiser* (February 21, 1894).

27. James Gowdy Clark, "The Coming Industrial Order," *Arena* 40 (January 1895), 239–40; also *Chicago Railway Times* (June 15, 1894).

28. Henry Demarest Lloyd, *Wealth against Commonwealth* (New York: Harper & Brothers, 1894).

29. Howard H. Quint, *The Forging of American Socialism: Origins of the Modern Movement* (Columbia: University of South Carolina Press, 1953), 144–64, 173–74, 225–38, 289–318, 324–25; Commons, *History of Labour* 2:509–14; *A.F.L. Proceedings, 1893–1896*.

30. *Boise (Idaho) Daily Statesman* (February 25, 1894); *St. Louis Post-Dispatch* (May 8, 1893); *Seattle Post-Intelligencer* (January 4, 1893); *Raleigh (North Carolina) News & Observer* (October 12, 1894).

31. Hicks, *Populist Revolt*; and Woodward, *Origins of the New South*, 188–204, 269–70, and passim still offer the soundest interpretations of agrarian radicalism. More recent works, underestimating the depression's influence, have taught more about the issues foremost in their writers' times than about Populism.

32. U.S. Commissioner of Labor, *Second Annual Report: Labor Laws of the United States*, 2d ed. (Washington, DC: Government Printing Office, 1896); Rezneck, "Unemployment," 342–43; *Appleton's Annual Cyclopedia, 1893–1897*.

33. *Raleigh (North Carolina) News & Observer* (December 14, 1894); *Chicago Daily Tribune* (October 24, 1893); *Boston Daily Advertiser* (December 11, 1893); *San Francisco Chronicle* (November 6, 1893); *Cleveland Plain Dealer* (April 26, 1897); Jay Linn Torrey, "The Torrey Bankrupt Bill," *Forum* 23 (March 1897), 42–49; Arthur George Sedgewick, "Bankruptcy in the United States," *Nation* 45 (December 1897), 135–43.

34. Charles Warren, *Bankruptcy in American History* (Cambridge, MA: Harvard University Press, 1935), 135–43.

35. *Commercial and Financial Chronicle* (February 18 and 25, 1893); *New York Times* (February 21, 1893).

36. *Wall Street Journal* (December 30, 1893); *St. Louis Post-Dispatch* (March 14, 1893); *Seattle Post-Intelligencer* (December 14, 1893); *Atlanta Constitution* (May 9, 1894); Henry Wollman, "The Bane of Friendly Receiverships," *North American Review* 157 (March 1897), 250–51.

37. *Wall Street Journal* (December 11, 1893); V. H. Lockwood, "How to Reform Business Corporations," *North American Review* 164 (March 1897), 294–304.

38. *Cleveland Plain Dealer* (December 29, 1894); *Emporia (Kansas) Gazette* and *Raleigh (North Carolina) News & Observer* (July 18, 1894); *St. Louis Post-Dispatch* (May 17, 1894); *Chicago Daily Tribune* (December 4, 1895); Albion Winegar Tourgee, "The Anti-Trust Campaign," *North American Review* 157 (July 1893), 30–41; "The Question of the Trusts," *Public Opinion* 21 (December 10, 1896), 757–59.

39. Lloyd, *Wealth against Commonwealth*, 1.

40. Dorfman, *Economic Mind*, 3:217, 216–18, 250; *Commercial and Financial Chronicle* (July 31, 1897); *Wall Street Journal* (December 17, 1894); Arthur George Sedgewick, "Pools, Trusts, and Combinations," *Nation* 65 (December 16, 1897), 471–72; Lloyd Stephens Bryce, "The Trusts and the Workingman," *North American Review* 159 (June 1897), 719–31; A. B. Salom, "Truth and the Trusts," *Scientific American* 76 (June 5, 1897), 362.

41. *St. Louis Post-Dispatch* (January 20, 1893); *Philadelphia Public Ledger* (February 6, 1894); *San Francisco Chronicle* (July 22, 1894); *Seattle Post-Intelligencer* (July 22, 1897). For Wisconsin, David F. Thelen, *The New Citizenship: Origins of Progressivism, 1885–1900* (New York: Columbia University Press, 1972), 130–312.

42. *A.F.L. Proceedings, 1893*, 31–41; *1894*, 36–42; *1895*, 65–69; Commons, *History of Labour*, 2, 509–13.

43. Richard Theodore Ely, "Natural Monopolies and the Workingman: A Programme of Social Reform," *North American Review* 147 (March 1894), 294–303.

44. Carroll Davidson Wright, "Steps toward Government Control of Railroads," *Forum* 18 (February 1895), 704–13; Henry J. Fletcher, "The Railway War," *Atlantic Monthly* 74 (October 1894), 534–41; "A National Transportation Department," *Atlantic Monthly* 76 (July 1895), 119–26; *(Boise) Idaho Daily Statesman* (December 7, 1894); *St. Louis Post-Dispatch* (June 2, 1894); *San Francisco Chronicle* (October 9, 1893).

45. Carl J. Buell, "A Partial Solution to the Railway Problem," *Arena* 12 (May 1895), 321–22.

46. *(Salt Lake City) Deseret Weekly* (July 6, 1894).

47. *Congressional Record*, 53d Cong., 3d sess. (1895), 27:1149; also 2d sess. (1894), 26:3055; 55th Cong., 1st sess. (1897), 30:462, 471, and passim; U.S. Interstate Commerce Commission, *Eighth Annual Report, 1895, Ninth Annual Report, 1896, Tenth Annual Report, 1897*, and *Eleventh Annual Report, 1898*; Gabriel Kolko, *Railroads and Regulation, 1877–1916* (Princeton, NJ: Princeton University Press, 1965), 74–80. See also Robert F. Himmelberg, *The Rise of Big Business and the Beginnings of Antitrust and Railroad Regulation, 1870–1900* (New York: Garland, 1994).

Opinion, *New York Times* (December 12, 1894); *Philadelphia Public Ledger* (September 25, 1895); *Wall Street Journal* (March 23, 1897); *Washington Post* (March 23, 1897); *Raleigh (North Carolina) News & Observer* (March 23, 1897); *San Francisco Chronicle* (March 27, 1897); *St. Louis Post-Dispatch* (March 27, 1897); *Emporia (Kansas) Gazette* (April 1, 1897); *Commercial and Financial Chronicle* (May 20, 1897); Lloyd Stephens Brice and James J. Wait, "The Railway Problem," *North American Review* 164 (March 1897), 327–48.

48. Chandler, *Visible Hand*, 79–185; Porter, *Rise of Big Business*; Whitten, *Emergence of Giant Enterprise*; Lloyd D. Mercer, "Railroad Transportation," in *Extractives, Manufacturing, and Services: A Historiographical and Bibliographical Guide*, vol. 2, *Handbook of American Business History*, ed. David O. Whitten and Bess E. Whitten (Westport, CT: Greenwood Press, 1997), 313–53.

49. *Appleton's Annual Cyclopedia, 1893–97*, under entries for the states.

50. H. Roger Grant, *Self Help in the 1890s Depression* (Ames: Iowa State University Press, 1983), 15.

51. Robert H. Bremner, *From the Depths: The Discovery of Poverty in the United States* (New York: New York University Press, 1956), 14; Josephine Shaw Lowell, "Methods of Relief for the Unemployed," *Forum* 16 (February 1894), 660; *San Francisco Chronicle* (December 21, 1893); *Raleigh (North Carolina) News & Observer* (December 28, 1893); *Boston Daily Advertiser* (November 17, 1893); *Philadelphia Public Ledger* (February 15, 1894); *Chicago Daily Tribune* (April 1, 1894); E. R. L. Gould, "How Baltimore Banished the Tramps and Helped the Idle," *Forum* 19 (June 1894), 487–504; Washington Gladden, "Relief Work—Its Principles and Methods," *Review of Reviews* 9 (January 1894), 38–40; C. S. Denny, "The Whipping Post for Tramps," *Century Magazine*, new series, 27 (April 1895), 794; W. M. Hutt, "The Tramp and the Reform School," *Century Magazine* 26 (December 1894), 311; Thelen, *Citizenship*, 57–62, 113–24.

52. U.S. Congress, House, *Bulletin of the Department of Labor No. 15*, 55th Cong., 2d sess. (1898), House Document No. 206, 385, 457, 994–1000.

53. John R. Commons, "The Day and Contract Systems of Municipal Works," *Yale Review* 5 (February 1897), 428–45.

54. Charles Beardsley, Jr., "The Effect of an Eight Hours' Day on Wages and the Unemployed," *Quarterly Journal of Economics* 9 (July 1895), 450–59; *A.F.L. Proceedings, 1895*, 61–63; *1896*, 22–26, 81–82; and *1897*, 56.

55. *New York Times* (August 21, 1893); Mandel, *Gompers*, 121–25.

56. *A.F.L. Proceedings, 1893*, 37; *Chicago Railway Times* (January 1, 1894).

57. *Atlanta Constitution* (May 3, 1894); *Raleigh (North Carolina) News & Observer* (April 29, 1894); *St. Louis Post-Dispatch* (March 26, 1894); *Cleveland Plain Dealer*

(March 10–May 3, 1894); *Commercial and Financial Chronicle* (April 28, 1894); *Chicago Daily Tribune* (March 17–May 2, 1894); *Boston Daily Advertiser* (March 19–April 25, 1894); David MacGregor Means, "The Dangerous Absurdity of State Aid," *Forum* 17 (May 1894), 296; Rollo Ogden, "Vagabonds' Disease: Coxey's Army," *Nation* 58 (April 12, 1894), 266; Howard, "Menace of Coxeyism," 687–96.

58. Edwin Lawrence Godkin, "What to Do with the Unemployed," *Nation* 57 (December 28, 1893), 401–2; Rollo Ogden, "The Real Problem of the Unemployed," ibid., 59 (July 5, 1894), 6; *(New York) Churchman* (August 2, September 16, and December 23, 1893); *(New York) Christian Advocate* (August 3, 1893); *New York Times* (June 12 and December 31, 1893).

Defenders of laissez faire in the 1890s opposed relief for the jobless and supported government repression of strikes, thereby profoundly weakening the humane tolerance of nineteenth-century liberalism. See Sproat, *Best Man*, 237–42.

59. Thorstein Veblen, "The Army of the Commonweal," *Journal of Political Economy* 2 (June 1894), 456–61. Also Melvin G. Holli, *Reform in Detroit: Hazen S. Pingree and Urban Politics* (New York: Oxford University Press, 1969), 56–73.

60. Henry Farnham May, *Protestant Churches and Industrial America* (New York: Harper & Brothers, 1949), 235–39, 109, 106–20, 267–70; *(New York) Churchman* (December 16, 1893, and July 7, 1894); *Outlook* (July 14, 1894); *(New York) Independent* (April–May 1893 and 1893–1897); *(Salt Lake City) Deseret Weekly* (March 31 and May 26, 1894, and 1893–1897).

61. *(New York) Churchman* (May 5, 1894); *(New York) Christian Advocate* (August 3, 1893 and January–March, 1894).

62. *Journal of the 22d General Conference of the Methodist Episcopal Church* (New York: Eaton & Mains, 1896), 59, 58; *Minutes of the Ninth Session of the National Council of the Congregational Churches* (Boston: Congregational Sunday School and Publishing Society, 1896), 149.

63. *Cleveland Plain Dealer* (June 14, 1894).

64. *Philadelphia Public Ledger* (July 16, 1894); *Seattle Post-Intelligencer* (July 6, 1894); *Cleveland Plain Dealer* (July 8 and August 23, 1894); *Chicago Daily Tribune* (July 10, 1894); *(Boise) Idaho Daily Statesman* (July 8–August 12, 1894); *Emporia (Kansas) Gazette* (July 11, 1894); *Boston Daily Advertiser* (July 12, 1894); *St. Louis Post-Dispatch* (July 12, 1894); *New York Times* (July 9, 1894).

65. Letter to Anna Roosevelt (July 22, 1894) in Theodore Roosevelt, *Letters of Theodore Roosevelt*, ed. Elting E. Morison et al. (Cambridge, MA: Harvard University Press, 1951–1954), 1:391. Public opinion: *Chicago Daily Tribune* (June 27, 1894); *Philadelphia Public Ledger* (July 4, 1894); *Boston Daily Advertiser* (July 12–13, 1894); General Nelson A. Miles, "The Lesson of the Recent Strikes," *North American Review* 149 (August 1894), 186; *San Francisco Chronicle* (May 29, 1894); *(Boise) Idaho Daily Statesman* (May 29, 1894); *St. Louis Post-Dispatch* (May 27, 1895).

66. *Chicago Daily Tribune* (July 8, 1894); *Boston Daily Advertiser* (July 14, 1894); *Raleigh (North Carolina) News & Observer* (July 11, 1894); *(Salt Lake City) Deseret Weekly* (July 7, 1894); *Emporia (Kansas) Gazette* (July 9, 1894); *Seattle Post-Intelligencer* (May 3, 1895); Thelen, *Citizenship*, 74, 94–98, for Wisconsin.

67. *Report on the Chicago Strike*, xlvi–liv; *St. Louis Post-Dispatch* (November 11, 1894); *Philadelphia Public Ledger* (November 11, 1894); *Seattle Post-Intelligencer* (November 11, 1894); *San Francisco Chronicle* (November 11, 1894); "Editorial Summary," *Public Opinion* 17 (November 22, 1894), 120–27.

68. "Don't," "Pullman," "The Strike and Its Lesson," *American Federationist* 1 (August 1894), 120–127.

69. *St. Louis Post-Dispatch* (July 15, 1896); *Washington Post* (November 20, 1895); "The Debs Case," *American Federationist* 2 (June 1895), 48; *A.F.L. Proceedings, 1894,* 52; *1895,* 50; *1896,* 13–14.

70. Nelson O. Nelson, "Organized Labor," *New England Magazine* 13 (November 1895), 338–45.

71. *(Salt Lake City) Deseret Weekly* (July 21, 1894); *A.F.L. Proceedings, 1896,* 20; *1897,* 30–32; *Proceedings of the General Assembly of the Knights of Labor, 1896,* 9– 12; Commons, *History of Labour,* 2, 499–500, 519–20.

72. John Swinton, *A Momentous Question: The Respective Attitudes of Capital and Labor* (Philadelphia: Keller, 1895); Stockton Bates, "How to Prevent Strikes and Lock- outs," *North American Review* 160 (March 1895), 171–74.

73. *A.F.L. Proceedings, 1893,* 12; *1895,* 85; Commons, *History of Labour,* 2, 501.

74. Congress explicitly exempted labor unions from antitrust prosecution in the Clay- ton Antitrust Act of 1914. For a comprehensive review of antitrust in the United States see Theodore P. Kovaleff, ed., *The Antitrust Impulse: An Economic, Historical, and Legal Analysis,* Columbia University Seminar Series (Armonk, NY: M. E. Sharpe, 1994).

75. *Seattle Post-Intelligencer* (March 29, 1893); *San Francisco Chronicle* (June 18, 1894); *Cleveland Plain Dealer* (July 19, 1894); *Chicago Daily Tribune* (July 15, 1894).

8

Economic Crisis and Culture

The silver shoes have wonderful powers.... They can carry you to any place in the world.

—L. Frank Baum, 1900

Shock waves from the Depression of 1894 washed over American culture, even to the December 1894 meeting of the American Historical Association, where the president in his annual address documented the pervasive sense of crisis and despondency and cast doubt on faith in human perfectibility. Worse, he argued, the science of history that so many sought must inspire grave stresses if it were achieved. If it discovered that the future held a return to an epoch of religious faith like the Middle Ages, then science itself faced rejection. If it learned that progress was to continue through a cycle of communism, propertied interests would be stirred to hostility and repression. If it proved that the present evils of the world, huge armaments, vast accumulations of capital, advancing materialism, and declining arts were to continue, then despair and disorder would displace hope for a better human condition.[1]

Shortly before, a University of Chicago economist had entered the world of practical affairs. He declared publicly, "If the railroads would expect their men to be law-abiding, they must be law-abiding. Let their open violation of the interstate [commerce] law testify as to their past in this regard." A character in a novel set in the business downturn mused, "Yes, it's 'hard times,' a time of psychological depression and distrust." An obscure poet cried, "Work shut down, the workers tramping,/Vainly looking for a job." Commercial blight penetrated national scholarship, art, and letters. Its impact, while varied, followed the pattern of society, popular opinion, and politics.[2]

Americans of the early 1890s knew a simpler material, mental, and moral world than would their counterparts of the 1990s. They neither consumed nor amused themselves to death and would have found the claims of 1990s post-modernists and deconstructionists absurd. They were confident that authors knew what they meant when they wrote, and they believed that readers, sharing a common vocabulary with writers, could interpret without recourse to a rhetorical philosopher's stone or arcane literary theory. Those who thought about such matters recognized that no genuine discourse is possible absent such an understanding. The notion that literature and art are mechanisms of class hegemony would have stirred amazement.

Physical, natural, and social science promised continuing human progress for Americans as the 1890s opened. Settled moral principles scarcely invited argument. The functions of nonfiction were to inform and instruct, of belles lettres and the fine arts to create beauty, and of popular culture to entertain. Fruitful exploration of the impact of depression on American culture must proceed from these beginning points, and from the premise that authors were as good as their word, in lieu of compelling evidence to the contrary.[3]

The growing appeal of scholarly social observers Frederick Jackson Turner, Josiah Strong, and Alfred Thayer Mahan reflected the impact of the business depression on public opinion. The experience of the nation during the 1890s, with its first great industrial collapse, engaged intellectuals' attention. Professional interest and sharply increased public demand for informed opinion gave scholars, particularly in the new social sciences, an expanded and prominent role in discussions of current issues.

Popular requests spurred the University of Wisconsin to add to its extension-course offerings in the social sciences. Invitations brought scholars to new audiences: business organizations, women's clubs, and ministerial associations, all moved by depression conditions to investigate social problems. Informed scholars appeared before political and labor groups, and they met with educators eager to replace formalism and rote memorization with practical training to improve the prospects of the poor for employment. The demand for informed discourse stimulated the founding of such issues-oriented bodies as the Economics Club of the University of Chicago, which spun off dozens of branches in the Midwest.

The political and theoretical observations of academics appeared in popular and professional publications. James Laurence Laughlin, Francis Amasa Walker, Frank William Taussig, and John Bates Clark propounded orthodox, conservative economic views. Opposing them were reformers Richard T. Ely, John R. Commons, Edward Bemis, the acerbic but soft-spoken Thorstein Veblen, and sociologist Edward Alsworth Ross. The contentions of some social scientists that society was exchanging competition for cooperation stirred public opinion and prepared Americans for reform.

The business crisis left its mark in the development of some notable scholars.

His early writings and an unpublished memoir suggest that Vernon Louis Parrington was among them. While teaching at the College of Emporia, Kansas, during the 1890s he acquired some of the Populistic fervor that later shaped his classic *Main Currents in American Thought* (1927–1930). Future historian Charles Austin Beard moved from a humane but complacent family and intellectual background to a bracing experience at Indiana's DePauw University. Depression and its labor and political struggles "deeply affected" him, as they did many of his generation. An 1896 visit (after his freshman year) to Chicago, "the Midwest's most potent evidence that the Industrial Revolution had descended on America," was pivotal. Young Beard saw firsthand the startling condition of the working class. He felt the full force of reform thought and politics. He visited with John R. Commons, and he heard Bryan and Altgeld speak. His faith in the conventions of Hoosier Republicanism shaken, he set out on a reformist path that he followed for the rest of his life.[4]

In contrast, it was doubtful that hard times very much affected the thinking of intellectuals who had matured earlier. The most striking exceptions were Henry and Brooks Adams. The traumatic impact of the crisis on their views was possibly without parallel. In 1892 Brooks had predicted a revolutionary struggle between the haves and the have-nots. With the arrival of panic and social upheaval Henry exclaimed, "We are all ruined." Events, among them the near loss of the family fortune, shattered the brothers' fundamental beliefs about class and politics. Both turned to free silver as a means of combating the plutocratic forces they thought were oppressing society.[5]

Brooks completed *The Law of Civilization and Decay* (1896) under the shadow of depression and dark forebodings about the country's future. In it he proposed a law that controlled society's evolution from barbarism to civilization. Barbaric societies, he believed, possessed decentralized, rural economies. Their spirit was vigorous and imaginative. Martial rulers sustained them, by generating and conquering the requisite energy, or capital. In time these processes produced an accumulation of surplus wealth. The conquest or production of wealth and the physical extension of a society, Adams continued, caused a proportionate increase in social movement, or velocity. This in turn brought a comparable centralization. As development progressed, a spiritual stage succeeded. Fear and imagination now encouraged martial piety and a rule of religious classes, under which expansion and the amassing of capital continued. A degree of commercial concentration occurred.

The third phase of civilization's course Adams termed "materialistic." Massive consolidation—of institutions, wealth, political power—took place. Greed and economic man, epitomized by the banker, held sway. Consumption outran production of energy. All-powerful bankers replaced expansion and currency elasticity with currency contraction. The resulting deflation enlarged their wealth by increasing the value of the money supply that they controlled. Contraction meanwhile oppressed debtors. It ground down with critical force on the producing classes, of which "bold, energetic, audacious" merchant adventurers were the highest type. Economic stagnation and fierce class antagonism resulted. Social decay, the withering of imagination and the arts, and the disappearance of fear and martial qualities accompanied the rise of economic man. Social disintegration, Adams mused, continued until a fresh infusion of barbarian vigor renewed imagination and expansionism. However crude, even quaint, this attempt to construct a theory of social evolution founded on history and an emerging science of energy, its meaning was clear enough. Banker dominion and a gold standard portended an end of national growth and progress. Decline and class warfare over the distribution of wealth loomed ahead.

After the defeat of Bryan and free coinage in 1896, Adams searched for a way to exempt the United States from the decay that his law demanded. He held no hope that power could be wrested from the bankers, who had acquired unchallenged power with Bryan's failure. New energy must therefore come from some external source. The loss of the frontier as a "boundless field for the expansion" of America implied a solution. Relief must be found in two sources. The one was centralization, to achieve maximum national efficiency. The other was discovery of an imaginative martial leader (who turned out to be Theodore Roosevelt) to lead a program of overseas economic expansion through which to obtain new sources of energy, or wealth. Postulating that world empires attached to centers of exchange, Adams by 1898 had identified a solution. Commercial predominance in a backward and vulnerable Asia would make an energized United States the economic bridge between the Orient and the Occident, and thus the world's premier power. These notions won considerable publicity, joining others in the swelling stream of expansionist thought.[6]

Meanwhile, the participation of academics in debates on current issues added seriously to the tensions straining the country. Their outspokenness provoked several controversies involving invasions of academic freedom. In the previous few decades scholars, with those in the new social sciences in the lead, had debated public questions. At the same time growing industrial fortunes had permitted a new scale of philanthropic giving to colleges and universities and an accompanying growth of business influence over them. In 1860, 48 percent of the trustees of twenty-five leading private and state institutions of higher education were businessmen, lawyers, or bankers. The figure jumped to 64 percent by 1900, with the influence of clerics falling correspondingly. Implications of the change of the guard in higher education boardrooms crystalized during the depression when President E. Benjamin Andrews of Brown University was asked to withhold his advocacy of free silver, and when local gas trust officials and supporters forced the dismissal of Edward Bemis from the University of Chicago in 1895—he had attacked the trust and spoken in support of the Pullman strikers.

Maturing during the troubled nineties, John R. Commons, a protégé of Richard T. Ely, hungered to apply the logic of rational economic theory to social problems. His keen awareness of the deflationary drag on the national economy in the years since the Civil War led him to support Bryan's free silver cause as a second-best alternative to the elastic currency the economy needed.[7] Heterodox views expressed in his *The Distribution of Wealth* (1893) and his other writings and speeches drew press criticism that forced him from his post in economics and social science at Indiana University, to accept an appointment in sociology at Syracuse. He exposed the roles of monopoly, legal privileges, and personal rights as determinants of the distribution of wealth. Bitingly assigning most great fortunes to monopoly and privilege, he contended that the fundamental personal right was "the right to life." If the state fully guaranteed it, it must both preserve domestic order and grant each individual "a share of the social product equal to his minimum of subsistence."

Provision of this minimum of subsistence was for Commons a compelling government responsibility. Technological change and industrial depression, "caused by overproduction," were the chief sources of unemployment. Trusts were organized to curb output and thereby combat depression. But in limiting operations they actually added to joblessness. The state should therefore aid the jobless. It should provide employment bureaus and tax incentives to encourage the productive development of land and resources held idle for speculative gain.[8]

Because Wisconsin's superintendent of public instruction and its conservative press found Ely's alleged support of strikes and union boycotts intolerable, they plotted his purge from the state university in 1894, a year before Commons's departure from Indiana. Ely denied the charges vigorously. He won staunch backing from prominent scholars and the sympathy of the university's president and trustees. The effort to oust him backfired and ended with a declaration of academic freedom.

J. Allen Smith was less fortunate. He supported liberal monetary views and William Jennings Bryan in 1896, and the year after he paid the price. Charles G. Dawes, Republican partisan and commanding member of the board of trustees, forced his dismissal from Marietta College's faculty. He went on to find that conservatives were not alone in intolerance. Soon after losing his job he was offered an appointment at the University of Missouri. He declined the invitation, his moral scruples offended when he learned that Missouri's Populist president planned to fire a gold-standard professor in order to make a place for him. Subsequently, he accepted an offer from the University of Washington's president, also a Populist.

Meanwhile Populist regents at Kansas Agricultural College in 1894 engaged sympathetic economist Thomas Elmer Will, to assure "unprejudiced" examination of "the principles maintained by advocates of land nationalization, public control of utilities, and reform of the . . . monetary system." Two years later a radical state administration purged the faculty. It made Will president and encouraged recruitment of a reform-minded staff. Republicans after regaining control of the state government replied in kind, in 1899. They ousted Will and his allies, replacing them with instructors devoted to conservative principles.[9]

These were the most celebrated and visible contemporary assaults on academic freedom that occurred while commercial blight strangled the country.

There were many more—most unreported, because the professor or teacher involved did not command national attention—as political whirlwinds swept state governments and the emotion-charged political and economic issues agitated academic governing boards and sometimes moved professors to controversial statements. Memories of these attacks persisted well beyond the return of prosperity. In the twentieth century they were part of the context from which, with the addition of new eruptions of strife, grew a powerful movement to protect academic freedom. The tenure system that grew from the ashes of academic destruction in the late nineteenth century protected most American teachers and professors through the harsh years of World War I, the Great Depression, World War II, the McCarthy era, the civil rights movement, and the Vietnam War.

A return to the days when powerful politicians could punish their academic opposition is never more than a ballot away. The tenure system has been under determined attack from its inception, and conservative politicians rank its destruction high on their list of targets, perhaps immediately behind eradication of the welfare system.[10]

The intersection of the business crisis with the arts is a useful lens through which to view contemporary art and culture. Barely a trace of the business crisis was evident in either serious theatre or popular stage performances, aside from those for small, eclectic audiences. Commercial motives dominated the stage. Producers found safety in proven and popular plays by European writers. They rarely offered works from the pens of domestic playwrights. Not that it mattered: native dramatists held tightly to accepted conventions, rarely injecting current political or social topics into their works. The function of the serious stage was to entertain, profitably. It catered to an audience largely immune to, and uninterested in, the effects of bad times. This fact itself spoke eloquently of the widening cultural chasm separating the well off from the masses.[11]

Poetry displayed comparable traits; most serious writers neglected social questions in verse. William Dean Howells was a conspicuous exception. In 1894 he asked, "Are We a Plutocracy?" and answered, "Yes." The next year he offered "Society." There is no evidence that polite society paid heed, and the poem never came to the attention of impolite society. If Americans examined social issues in verse they read poems forthrightly crafted to support labor, socialist, and Populist causes. Here again the gap between the privileged and the unprivileged and, of course the grip of received wisdom, found expression. Contemporary radical verse satisfies few of the esthetic demands of today's reader. It does, however, offer glimpses into the culture and mental world of the discontented.

"The Lay of the Unemployed," which appeared in 1894, grieved in part, "Starving little children crying; Hear the poor wife sob/Hear the clink of golden millions/Growing larger every day." Readers of the *American Federationist* learned in verse of "The Pullman Strike and Its Lesson." Populists wondered, "Why should the farmer delve and ditch/ . . . The Government can make 'em rich." The era even delivered up a handful of volumes of radical rhyme. The socialist *Wind Harp Songs* was published in 1895. *Carmina Noctis and Other Poems* followed three years later. These musings reflect the power of an emerging consumer ethos, the durability of the old producer ethic, and the scant trace of genuine class consciousness beyond the thin socialist ranks. Lack of work, suppression of strikes, poverty, hunger, and farmers' distress brought specific complaints in verse, but rarely attacks on the industrial system itself.[12]

The business downturn left no trace in either serious or popular music. Newly arrived as a characteristic musical entertainment, operettas vied with revues for command of the popular musical stage. Frothy productions such as "A Trip to Chinatown," "Rob Roy," and "The Geisha" were stage hits. The audiences for symphonic music and opera were still farther removed from the influence of the crisis. "When the Roll Is Called Up Yonder," "Sidewalks of New York," "Sweet Rosie O'Grady," "After the Ball," and similar tunes amply represented popular parlor songs. They fairly overflowed with forced cheerfulness, mawkish sentimentality, "commonplace emotions and . . . platitudes of social intercourse." Just scraps, such as "Down on Poverty Row" in 1895 and "The Tramp's Dream" three years later, injected a possibly timely, but still heavily sentimental, note.[13]

In contrast to its complete lack of effect on art songs and its scant impact on mainstream popular lyrics, the depression of the 1890s, like all American depressions, left a sharp musical imprint in the folk idiom. Its legacy included a number of Populist, labor, and hobo songs, some still familiar. Among them were "The People's Party Song" and "A Hayseed Like Me." The latter began:

> I once was a tool of oppression
> As green as a sucker could be
> And monopolies banded together
> To beat a poor bum like me.

The industrial army movement inspired "The National Grass Plot." Set to the melody of the national anthem, it sardonically celebrated the heroism of Washington's police "with their buttons of brass," whose arrest of Coxey protected the victoriously waving Capitol grass.

The Pullman struggle produced the bitter "Pullman Strike" and "A.R.U.":

> Been on the hammer since ninety-four
> Last job I had was on the Lake Shore
> Lost my office in the A.R.U.
> And I won't get it back till nineteen-two
> And I'm still on the hog train flagging my meals
> Riding the brake beams close to the wheels.

Hoboes added "Hallelujah, I'm a Bum" and the classic "Big Rock Candy Mountain" to the chorus of discontent. In its unexpurgated original form the last was a far cry from the version popularized in the twentieth century. It told how a tramp's extravagant description of the joys of vagabondage, with its cigarette trees, soda water fountains, and lemonade springs, lured a Hoosier lad to the hobo life and, probably, to sexual exploitation. Measurably closer to the popular pulse, protest songs left a more indelible mark than angry verse. They contained more vivid hints, too, of a society that desperation was dividing deeply and that was becoming increasingly aware that this was so.[14]

The visual arts displayed tendencies resembling those in poetry, music, and scholarship. Academism, rural genre, portraiture, landscape, personal experience, classicism, rare hints at experimentalism, and the infrequent introspection of an Albert Pinkham Ryder defined their limits. The thematic possibilities of an industrial society lay unexploited in serious visual art until after the turn of the century.[15]

The impact of bad times on the visual arts is best reflected in illustration and editorial cartoons. Thomas Nast had popularized the editorial cartoon in the preceding two decades. In the nineties, cartoons with a political message were beginning to spread from magazines to newspapers. Contemporary events provided subject matter for cartoons and many illustrations. Editorial policy, partisanship, and target audiences determined the tenor of the treatment.

Thus of anarchist displays in New York in August 1893, the conservative Democratic weekly *Puck* published a cartoon captioned "NO RIOTERS NEED APPLY." It pictured a contented workingman and his family seated around a heavily laden dinner table beneath a portrait of a benevolent George Washington. The honest wage earner was speaking to a sinister anarchist agitator. His dismayed words: "Help you destroy law and order?—not much—and your stories that we are all starving are all false." Early in the following year *Life*, a mildly progressive and equally genteel Republican magazine, timorously acknowledged the gulf between the prosperous and the poor in an illustration entitled "LENT." Later, it offered a gently humorous pictorial comment on the sufferings of the victims of financial reverses.

Coxey's industrial army movement pushed *Life* to sarcastic criticism. One panel depicted Dame Columbia standing in the Capitol speaking to a crowd of tramps who surrounded her. To them she remarked, "THE PRECIOUS TRAMPSY-WAMPSIES SHALL BE TAKEN CARE OF, YES THEY SHALL; AND THEY SHALL STEAL TRAINS, AND HAVE LOTS OF PAPER MONEY, AND NOT WORK NOR LET ANYBODY ELSE WORK EITHER, THE DARLINGS." Illustrations in *Coin's Financial School* typified the replies of the discontented. Conspicuous was the famed drawing of a malevolent octopus, labeled "Rothschild" for the great English banking family. Seated in London, the sea creature was extending its tentacles to the far corners of the earth in order to draw in wealth.[16]

The dark reflection of hard times in the cultural mirror of the 1890s pales in comparison with twentieth-century works like Pablo Picasso's "Guernica," the power of Diego Rivera's murals, the haunting photographic images captured in the 1930s for the Farm Security Administration, the horrors of the Holocaust exhibited in every art form; television, newspaper, and magazine coverage of bloody conflict in Vietnam, Iraq, Ireland, Bosnia, and the African states; and myriad other engagements of art with social circumstances—the violent lyrics of rap music sired by the inner cities in late-twentieth-century industrial America—make the cultural responses to the deprivations of the 1890s depression look tame. Media attacks of the 1890s are timid in comparison to editorial cartoons and illustrations directed at President William Clinton's alleged sexual peccadilloes, cartoons lending credence to claims of reactionary politicians that so-called "welfare queens" found in unemployment and public assistance an effortless road to unearned wealth, and drawings skewering public officials for real and imagined offenses. Nonetheless, when set in the context of middle and upper-class Victorian values in the 1890s, contemporary editorial cartoons take on a different color. They are direct, at times biting, and they challenge prevailing sentimentality. The pressure at the limits of propriety suggests that the times were desperate indeed.

In the realm of fiction the depression left a clearer mark. During the last quarter of the nineteenth century several influences inspired a growing if minor current of fiction that used salient social and economic developments thematically or examined them critically. Rapid social change and wrenching dislocations associated with industrialization led among these. Labor strife and the spread of urban slums were particularly important. The panic of 1893 and the following train of events offered grist with which writers milled a growing output of this stream of fiction. Christian ideals informed the treatment of social questions in the hundred or so novels that were the principal literary expression of the Social Gospel in the fifty years after 1865. The fictional quest for Utopia was familiar long before the publication in 1888 of Edward Bellamy's enormously popular *Looking Backward*. The success of his work stimulated a host of imitations as writers and publishers rushed to capitalize on a tantalizing market whose scale they had not previously imagined. These genres were subsumed in a broader literary response to industrialization, the economic novel.

It would be overly generous to characterize most of this fiction as belles lettres, or even, to use a less imposing term, imaginative literature. Its literary merit and importance were slight. Characterization, plot, and story line were often weak, even nonexistent. In the place of these writers often substituted the fictional equivalent of what a later generation would term "talking heads." Authors filled page after page with conversation rather than action. They used this conversation between their characters didactically, as heavy, blunt instruments with which to beat their ideas into their readers.

Characters in economic novels were generally of the same middle to upper-class backgrounds as their authors and readers. Writers had little direct experience with lower-class folk who might have served as models. Ordinarily they expressed liberal, not radical, ideas. They usually urged social reform through moral regeneration of the individuals making up society or through democratic collective action, not violence. Their analyses of conditions and prescriptions for a better future were often naive or simplistic, by the standards of later generations. Their works sometimes expressed the fears of conservative writers. Their work as a body bore no resemblance to the proletarian fiction, and much of the naturalistic writing, that came to the fore after 1900. Despite these very real limitations, the small but swelling stream of economic novels was a notable feature of American letters. Perhaps three hundred such works found their way into print between 1870 and 1900.

It was scarcely surprising that the radicalism surging across an anguished nation in 1894 found expression in fiction. Social turmoil, Coxeyism, strikes, and political upheaval provided plenty of raw material. Publication of *Wealth against Commonwealth*, John Swinton's *A Momentous Question* (labor), and Henry Champernowne's *The Boss* (exposing municipal corruption) added to this stock. In 1894 at least eight utopian novels appeared. Among them were Solomon Schindler's *Young West*, William Nathaniel Harben's *The Land of the Changing Sun*, and S. Byron Welcome's fantastic *From Earth's Center: A Polar Gateway Message*. Welcome's work described a Utopia located in the bowels of the earth.

William Dean Howells's *A Traveler from Altruria* was a mature expression of the socialism of one of the country's foremost writers, who here employed the depression to add an air of timeliness to his skillful critique of capitalism. Much better crafted than most of the works in the genre, *Traveler* nevertheless employed a familiar device to relay its message. Extended—perhaps interminable—conversation between the chief characters contrasted conditions in the United States with those in Altruria. Howells referred tellingly to economic distress and to the narrowing of opportunity resulting from the close of the frontier. His dialogue exposed the shallowness of the pursuit of material success and mourned a changing society and the breakdown of old middle-class virtues.

Hamlin Garland joined in the literary assault on the evil effects of capitalism. Even before the panic he was a friend of Howells, Populism, and of Henry George's scheme to tax the unearned increment that market pressures added to land values so as to assure cheap land and opportunity for the masses. During the distressed mid-1890s he added to his mordant stories of the Middle Border pointed advice to writers and other artists. A close reading of this advice shows that it was not particularly radical. What seemed to be and undoubtedly was a heartfelt call for reform was tightly bound to the same self-interest that fueled capitalism. Garland complained that writers "as artists . . . are addressing only a handful of the great democracy . . . a minority that does not grow." Worse, "Times are hard and growing harder. There is no expansion, no widening of your field or my field; it is . . . narrowing. The whole country is like a factory town when the engines are on hold." He claimed further that the "whole social order must undergo change before American art will become the jubilant and perfectly wholesome art it should be." He reminded his readers, revealingly, that art did not depend on support of the few but on that "of the many. Its fate" was "tied to that of the working man. . . . [Artists] too . . . must become reformers,'' then; they ''must stand for equal rights with all that the fearless leaders of the present-day thought have made the phrase mean.'' Publishers in 1894 printed two dozen or more novels dealing with socioeconomic questions. During the depression the total was about a hundred, a third of that for 1870–1900.[17]

Contemporary conditions affected the small body of economic fiction in several ways. While the form of the writing remained unchanged, increasingly urgent problems of labor relations, slums, unemployment, and agrarian distress provided context, content, incident, and occasionally themes that added to pressures for reform. Representing a movement born in agricultural depression, Populist writers penned most of the reform novels. Their output peaked twice, first in the early nineties; after a gradual decline it rose a second time with the impassioned 1896 election campaign. Several titles are representative: James B. Goode lashed out at the Cleveland administration in his brief tale *The Modern Banker*, silverite Frederick Upham Adams chronicled an imaginary and peaceful revolution to socialism in *President John Smith*, George Rivers legitimized the agrarian movement with *Captain Shays: A Populist of 1786*, and Bert J. Wellman's *The Legal Revolution of 1902* aimed to rally the followers of William Jennings Bryan after his electoral defeat.

The Reverend Charles Sheldon drew on deep religious convictions and an intimate knowledge of industrial conditions in Topeka, Kansas, to fashion an enormously popular tale, *In His Steps*, which appeared in 1897. The story, simple and direct, tells how social ills fall away one after another as growing numbers of people responded to a challenge to model their lives after that of Jesus. Although it sold more than eight million copies there is no counting how many lives it transformed. Even so, its popularity witnessed to the wide interest in applying Christian ethics to social problems.

A tramp is the protagonist in Elbert Hubbard's *No Enemy*. On the other side were works such as Charles King's story, ''A Tame Surrender.'' King's protagonist is an army officer, his narrative a flimsy fictional vehicle for a virulent attack on the Pullman strikers. He trivializes the motives of the workers by portraying a strike leader as a mere aspirant for social position and the unionists as a rabble. In contrast the troops sent to crush the Chicago disorders win the highest praise. They are ''superb in their . . . indifference to absolute outrage.'' For ''hours, for days, they coolly held that misguided, drink-crazed, demagogue-excited mob at bay.'' They heroically cleared the railways and ''turbulent districts, until the fury of the populace wore itself out against the rock of their iron discipline, and one after another the strikers slunk off to their holes, unharmed by even one avenging bullet.''[18]

Only a handful of writers dealt directly with the depression. Those who did treated it as a symptom rather than an unavoidable companion of industrialization. Carolyn Walch's *Doctor Sphinx* is an insipid romance set against a background of financial panic and deepening paralysis of trade. It offers occasional diatribes against Cleveland's financial policies, speculators, free silver, and striking unions—which it blames for the crisis with a fine disregard for fact and coherence. The most that can be said for these references is that they help, a little, to relieve the tedium of the narrative.

Robert Herrick's *The Web of Life* and Hervey White's *Differences*, both published at the end of the decade, are almost alone in their ability to capture the despair and discontent that the business crisis generated. *The Web of Life* is an uninspired but well-told account of an idealistic young Chicago physician who rebels unsuccessfully against the society that produces, then suppresses, the Pullman strike. With his common-law wife he rejects materialistic aspirations. The couple become recluses, taking up shelter in an abandoned building on the grounds of the 1893 Chicago World's Fair. His mate's suicide is shattering; her death and the incendiary events of 1894 in Chicago force him to reflect deeply on the meaning of life. He comes to see that a web of mutual responsibility links all of humanity. The story's ending fits its readers' morality reassuringly. Free of an ethically inconvenient relationship, the hero wins respectability and means by wedding the daughter of a prosperous merchant. He takes up a suburban practice and with his new wife he ministers to the needy.

Differences is more compelling. Its heroine is from a social background congruent with the audience White targetted. She is a well-to-do young woman who joins a Chicago settlement house. There she experiences her first truly human contact with working-class people. In time she abandons her aristocratic and patronizing attitudes toward the poor, coming to believe that all persons are equal and none have the right to live off the labor of others. She also recognizes that many people are poor through no fault of their own. In an improbable ending, she gives up her inheritance and social position, becomes a teacher, and marries a working-class widower with two children. *Differences* in the end dares to break out of the standard formula that requires the heroine marry within her social class. It portends even greater change in its sympathetic descriptions of the poor and the jobless as they suffer through bad times. In these respects it is a forerunner of John Steinbeck's novel about a later depression, *The Grapes of Wrath*.[19]

The most interesting literary legacy of the distressed 1890s seems at first an unlikely choice. It is a children's story that becomes something more when coupled with the experiences of its author, Lyman Frank Baum. Baum had been born into a wealthy family near Syracuse, New York, in 1856. In 1887 he moved his wife and two children to Aberdeen, South Dakota, where grim rural realities were replacing with agrarian radicalism a romantic and benign view of nature. Baum edited Aberdeen's weekly newspaper until it failed in 1891, when he relocated to Chicago. There, although not a political activist, he marched in campaign "parades for William Jennings Bryan and sympathize[d] with the laboring classes."

At the decade's end, after one rejection, he found an outlet for a small volume that he had written. George M. Hill, a minor Chicago house, published *The Wonderful Wizard of Oz* in 1900. As nearly everyone knows, it is the story of young Dorothy and her adventures after a tornado whirls her and her dog Toto, trapped inside their house, from Kansas to the magical land of Oz. A long series of adventures intervenes before Dorothy and Toto return home to Kansas, Aunt Em, and Uncle Henry.

The story is a remarkable parable of Populists and their America. Dorothy represents the American people: her attempts to return home, their struggles for justice. The tornado drops her house into the Land of the Munchkins, tiny people whom the Wicked Witch of the East has treated as slaves—the Munchkins are labor, the wicked witch Eastern money power. Symbolically, Dorothy's house falls on the witch and kills her, showing American labor the way to freedom. The Good Witch of the North embodies progressive Northern voters. Appearing soon after Dorothy's arrival, she explains that the way home depends on the help of the Wizard of Oz, who resides in the Emerald City.

The way to Oz? Take the yellow brick road—gold—in magical silver slippers—keep gold and silver at parity in a bimetallic monetary system. On the dangerous road Dorothy makes three friends, a scarecrow, a tin woodsman, and a cowardly lion. The first, supposedly brainless but in fact quite clever, stands for farmers. The second, like industrial workers, is powerless by himself, unable even to oil his own joints; he thinks himself heartless though in fact he is sensitive. The third roars fiercely but fears combat; nonetheless, he is brave when he needs to be—William Jennings Bryan. The wizard, like presidents of the United States who deceive the American people, is a fraud who has duped the people of Oz, by having them wear green glasses, into believing the city is wondrous. He tells Dorothy that he will help her return to Kansas if she destroys the Wicked Witch of the West—land and mortgage monopolists.

Upon destroying the witch Dorothy returns to the Emerald City to find that Oz is not a wizard at all: "I'm really a very good man; but I'm a very bad wizard, I must admit." Happily, she can return home without his help. The Good Witch of the South—reform-minded Southern voters—informs her that all along she has possessed the means of returning home. " 'The silver shoes,' said the good witch, 'have wonderful powers. . . . They can carry you to any place in the world in three steps.' " Dorothy returns with the help of the silver slippers. Baum's message was clear. A coalition of Northern and Southern Progressive voters could employ bimetallism to bring America home, restoring it as the land of liberty and opportunity.[20]

The impact of depression on scholarship, letters, and arts was uneven. Its direction, however, was unmistakable. It sharply challenged the customary optimism of intellectuals as well as the public, despite the continued allure of old beliefs. Current utopian, socialist, and Christian reform fiction were parts of a larger literary response to industrialization. In stimulating reform impulses, hard times encouraged their representation in literature. This representation occurred as incidental thematic reference to labor strife, business conditions, sometimes financial and commercial stagnation. It also propelled the plots of reformist fiction. It was a minor current that grew appreciably during the desperate nineties. In contrast, bad times only slightly affected belles lettres, the visual arts, and the performing arts, with the revealing exception of music in the folk tradition.

There were several reasons for the lumpy texture of the impact of the crisis. The arts and high culture remained insulated from ordinary life. They depended mainly on artistic norms and the personal experiences and associations of their practitioners for inspiration. Most artists, writers, and intellectuals came from the upper and middle-classes. Social background and personal experience often constrained them even where the practical need to reach an upper or middle class audience did not. The recency of industrialization was also a limiting factor. Serious criticism of the emerging industrial and urban order was a new phenomenon even outside the realms of arts, letters, and scholarship. Moreover, criticism carried risks, as a number of academics and others discovered.

The United States had yet to experience the buoyant determination of early twentieth-century reformers. The hopes of those who saw the World War I as a crusade to make the world safe for democracy could not stir until after the outbreak of that terrible conflagration. The Bolshevik revolution and the wave of radicalism it inspired lay in the future. Intellectuals had yet to feel the disillusionment and alienation that overtook many of them a generation later, in the 1920s. Besides, there were barely hints of a Marxian stimulus in the realms of arts and letters, as elsewhere. Only a handful, mostly recent European immigrants and an infinitesimal group of intellectuals, had so far found cause to spurn capitalism and embrace Marxist dogma. Finally, the "average American socialists" before the Great War "still more than most other Americans tended to regard art as a kind of ornamental gilding on the practical realities of everyday life." It had for them no "significant interaction with social problems."

The outlines of the academic, artistic, and literary repercussions of depression revealed a society in transition and self-redefinition. Circumstances hastened scholarly examination of the emerging industrial order. They invited exploration of its artistic and literary possibilities. So far this exploration was in its very early stages. Many of the currents set in motion or speeded in the troubled nineties swelled to great prominence in the next century. The growing social concern already apparent was to be central to the work of an increasingly influential group of progressive academics. Among these were Commons, Bemis, Veblen, Ely, Turner, Beard, Parrington, Ross, and others after about 1900. The flowering of a social art awaited further experience with industrial life and particularly the shock of the Great Depression of the 1930s. Nevertheless, by the end of the 1890s the main outlines of a literary response to industrialism were becoming clear.[21] Together, these developments were further evidence of the ways in which the Progressivism of the new century was rooted in the business crisis of the 1890s.[22]

NOTES

1. Henry Adams, "The Tendency of History," *Annual Report of the American Historical Association, 1894* (Washington, DC: Government Printing Office, 1895), 21, 17–23.

2. Edward Bemis as quoted in Richard Hofstadter and Walter P. Metzger, *The Development of Academic Freedom in the United States* (New York: Columbia University Press, 1955), 427; Robert Herrick, *The Web of Life* (New York: Macmillan, 1900), 136; Sumner Claflin, "The Lay of the Unemployed," from *Coming Nation* (July 20, 1894) as quoted in Quint, *Forging of American Socialism*, 186.

3. For an arresting discussion of the implications of deconstructionism and related post-modernisms, see Gertrude Himmelfarb, "Revolution in the Library," *The American Scholar* 66 (Spring 1997), 197–204.

4. Richard Hofstadter, *The Progressive Historians: Turner, Beard, Parrington* (New York: Alfred A. Knopf, 1968), 167; Vernon Louis Parrington, *Main Currents in American Thought* (New York, 1927–1930); Dorfman, *Economic Mind*, 3:215–305; Benjamin O. Rader, *The Academic Mind and Reform: The Influence of Richard T. Ely in American Life* (Lexington: University of Kentucky Press, 1966); Thelen, *Citizenship*, 62–130.

5. Henry Adams to Charles Milnes Gaskell, July 30, 1893, *Letters of Henry Adams*, 1:30.

6. Brooks Adams, *The Law of Civilization and Decay* (New York: Macmillan, 1896), 303; and "The Spanish War and the Equilibrium of the World," *Forum* 25 (August 1898), 641–51; La Feber, *New Empire*, 80–86; Thornton Anderson, *Brooks Adams: Constructive Conservative* (Ithaca, NY: Cornell University Press, 1951), 1–71.

7. The National Bank Act, passed on February 25, 1863, provided for national charters for qualified banks. The national banks were permitted to deposit federal bonds with the comptroller of the currency in return for 90 percent of their value in national banknotes, thereby establishing a market for bonds. Although the system established the first uniform national paper currency, it also created an inelastic currency that expanded when the economy was contracting and contracted when the economy was expanding. An expanding economy drove interest rates up and bond prices down. (Because bonds pay a fixed return, if the market rate of interest rises the market value of bonds must fall until their yield equals the going rate.) To avoid capital losses banks returned their national banknotes to the comptroller to redeem and sell their bonds. An increased supply of bonds on the market drove bond prices down further still, and interest rates rose. When the economy was in most need of money the supply contracted—in economic terms, it was inelastic, unresponsive to the needs of commerce.

To encourage state banks to surrender their state charters for national commissions the 1863 act provided for a tax on state banknotes beginning in 1866, charging 10 percent of face value annually. State banks declined from 1,466 in 1863 to 349 in 1865. By 1865 there were 1,601 national banks, with $171 million in notes. They were allowed no branches and were prohibited from investing in real estate. State banks staged a return late in the century, when checks were substituted for notes.

8. John R. Commons, *The Distribution of Wealth* (New York: Macmillan, 1893), 66, 84; "The Right to Work," *Arena* 21 (February 1899), 131–42; Dorfman, *Economic Mind*, 3:276–94.

"When sociology was separated from political economy in university teaching, charity was transferred to sociology. I never could reconcile myself to this separation. I taught 'sociology' at Syracuse University and got out a book in 1895 on machine politics, which was to be cured, I thought, by proportional representation. I ended four years at Syracuse with a series of articles on 'A Sociological View of Sovereignty.' A critic surprised me by naming the articles An Economic View of Sovereignty. It became for me eventually Institutional Economics.'' John R. Commons, *Myself* (Madison: University of Wisconsin Press, 1963, reprint of 1934 edition), 43–44. Commons went to Syracuse in 1895 to interview for a new chair in sociology. ''When I went to Syracuse in the spring of 1895, to interview with Chancellor Day, I thought I would tell the whole truth. I told him I was a socialist, a single-taxer, a free-silverite, a greenbacker, a municipal-ownerist, a member of the Congregational Church. He answered to the effect: I do not care what you are if you are not an 'obnoxious socialist.' That settled it. I mistakenly thought I was not of the obnoxious kind'' (pp. 52–53). Commons's mistake became evident in 1899, when the university discontinued the chair.

9. Hofstadter and Metzger, *Academic Freedom*, 420–42; Rader, *Academic Mind*, 135–36; Dorfman, *Economic Mind*, 276–94; Abigail A. Van Slyck, *Free to All: Carnegie Libraries & American Culture, 1890–1920* (Chicago: University of Chicago Press, 1995).

10. James Buchanan ''Buck'' Duke endowed Trinity College in Durham, North Carolina. Trinity professors had publicly attacked his exploitation of tobacco farmers during the days of the American Tobacco Trust. ''Duke promised the trustees a huge bequest if they would transform the school into Duke University. The faculty bridled at the idea but in the end the trustees accepted.'' Robert Sobel, *They Satisfy: The Cigarette in American Life* (New York: Anchor, 1978), 60.

11. *New York Times* (January 21, 1894); Montrose J. Moses, ''The Drama, 1860–1918,'' in William Peterfield Trent et al., *The Cambridge History of American Literature* (New York: G. P. Putnam's Sons, 1917–1921), 4:266–98; Willard Thorp, ''American Writers on the Left,'' bibliographical and other selections in Donald Drew Egbert and Stow Persons, eds., *Socialism in American Life* (Princeton, NJ: Princeton University Press, 1952), 601–20.

12. Sumner Claflin, in *Coming Nation* (July 20, 1894), in Quint, *Forging of American Socialism*, 186; T. C. Walsh, in *American Federationist* 1 (November 1894), 200; *Greensboro Patriot* (July 27, 1892); Hicks, *Populist Revolt*, 248; William Lloyd, *Wind Harp Songs* (Buffalo: Peter Paul, 1895); James Allman, *Carmina Noctis and Other Poems* (New York: W. Hammer, 1898); William Dean Howells in *North American Review* 158 (February 1894), 185–96, and *Harper's Magazine* 90 (March 1895), 630; Egbert and Persons, *Socialism*, 2:489.

13. Joseph Walker McSpadden, *Light Opera and Musical Comedy* (New York: Thomas Y. Crowell, 1936); David Ewen, *Complete Book of American Musical Theatre* (New York: Henry Holt, 1958); Sigmund Spaeth, *A History of Popular Music in America* (New York: Random House, 1948), 252–95.

14. John Greenway, *American Folksongs of Protest* (Philadelphia: University of Pennsylvania Press, 1953), lyrics and titles quoted respectively on 60, 63, 56, 57, 198–201, 204.

15. Oliver W. Larkin, *Art and Life in America* (New York: Rinehart, 1949), 235–67; Daniel Mendelowitz, *A History of American Art* (New York: Holt, Rinehart & Winston, 1960), 416–90; Bremner, *From the Depths*, 108–20.

16. William Murrell [James Guy Fisher], *A History of American Graphic Humor* (New York: Macmillan, 1938), 2:106–41; *Puck* 34 (September 6, 1893), cover; *Life* 23 (Feb-

ruary 22, 1894), 120–21, 24 (July 12, 1894), 26–27, 23 (May 10, 1894), 306–307; Harvey, *Coin's Financial School*, 124.

17. Hamlin Garland, "The Land Question and Its Relation to Art and Literature," *Arena* 9 (January 1894), 174, and *Crumbling Idols* (Gainesville, FL: Scholars' Facsimiles & Reprints, 1957), i–viii; William Dean Howells, *A Traveler from Altruria* (New York: Harper & Brothers, 1894); and Edwin H. Cady, *The Realist at War: The Mature Years 1885–1920 of William Dean Howells* (Syracuse, NY: Syracuse University Press, 1958), 139–204; Solomon Schindler, *Young West: A Sequel to Edward Bellamy's Celebrated Novel, Looking Backward* (Boston: Ticknor, 1894); William Nathaniel Harben, *The Land of the Changing Sun* (New York: Merriam, 1894); S. Byron Welcome, *From Earth's Center: A Polar Gateway Message* (Chicago: Charles H. Kerr, 1894).

18. Charles Monroe Sheldon, *In His Steps: "What Would Jesus Do?"* (Chicago: Advance, 1897); Elbert Hubbard, *No Enemy (But Himself): The Story of a Gentleman Tramp* (New York: G. P. Putnam's Sons, 1894); Charles King, "A Tame Surrender. A Story of the Chicago Strike," *Lippincott's Monthly Magazine* 4 (March 1895), 376.

19. Carolyn C. Walch, *Dr. Sphinx: A Novel* (New York: F. Tennyson Neely, 1896); Herrick, *Web of Life*; Hervey White, *Differences* (Boston: Small, Maynard, 1899). Also W. T. Nicholls, "The Strike at Barton's," *Lippincott's Monthly Magazine* 9 (October 1897), 545–61; Robert Barr, *The Victors* (New York: Frederick A. Stokes, 1901); Louise Betts Edwards, "Step Brothers to Dives," *Harper's New Monthly Magazine* 89 (August 1894), 436–40; J. W. Sullivan, *So the World Goes* (Chicago: Charles H. Kerr, 1897).

20. Lyman Frank Baum, *The Wonderful Wizard of Oz* (Chicago: George M. Hill, 1900), quotes from New York, Barnes & Nobel Edition, 1994, 153; Henry Littlefield, "The Wizard of Oz: Parable on Populism," *American Quarterly* 16 (Spring 1964), 47–58; Martin Gardiner and Russell P. Nye, *The Wizard of Oz and Who He Was* (East Lansing: Michigan State University Press, 1957); and Jensen, *Winning of the Midwest*, 282–83.

21. Donald Drew Egbert, "Socialism and American Art," in Egbert and Persons, *Socialism* 1 (1952), 705, 650–751; John Ireland Howe Bauer, *New Art in America: Fifty Painters of the Twentieth Century* (New York: Praeger, 1957); Larkin, *Art and Life*, 235–367; Lisle Abbot Rose, "A Bibliographical Survey of Economic and Political Writings, 1865–1900," *American Literature* 15 (January 1944), 381–410; Walter Fuller Taylor, *The Economic Novel in America* (Chapel Hill: University of North Carolina Press, 1942).

22. See Walter Benn Michaels, *The Gold Standard and the Logic of Naturalism: American Literature at the Turn of the Century* (Berkeley: University of California Press, 1987).

9

Depression Politics

Demand work. If they do not give you work demand bread. If they deny you both, take bread. It is your sacred right!
                                              —Emma Goldman, August 1893

The political fireworks of the mid-1890s were ignited by business depression, fueled by economic, social, and intellectual puissance, and prolonged by despair. Powerful forces clashed: stagnation lent new urgency to long-festering agrarian unrest; unemployment, reduced pay, and the deportment of corporate giants mingled with unpopular government policies to provoke urban discontent; reform zealots, questing for a more humane industrial system, added a note of stubborn, sometimes impractical idealism; a wee minority, mostly recent European immigrants, advanced the claims of a newer radicalism in the forms of collectivist anarchism and Marxian socialism.

To the transitory but pregnant efforts of a handful of radicals striving to end a capitalist order were added the culmination of a generation of agrarian insurgency, in the brief and meteoric career of the People's Party, and a major realignment of American politics. For twenty years before the mid-nineties the country's two major parties had been poised in near equilibrium, despite the strident diversions of a succession of third parties. Republicans generally controlled the Senate, while Democrats organized eight of ten Houses. Democrats gained thin pluralities in all presidential contests, save 1880, but won the White House only in 1884 and 1892. Only in 1889–91 and 1893–95 did the same party control both the legislative and executive branches. Yet by 1896 depression had helped the Republicans break the stalemate and become a majority party that predominated for a generation.[1] The Democrats were consigned to wander in the wilderness. As Populist power declined, a reinvigorated socialism appeared under the leadership of Eugene V. Debs.

Although anarchist exertions produced little sound and less motion, they bore fruit in at least one instance: the jobless on Manhattan's East Side, angry at the failure of state officials to act on the requests of labor leaders for relief work, gathered in August 1893 in uneasy assemblies to hear anarchist Emma Goldman speak. Riots followed her advice to "demand work. If they do not give you work demand bread. If they deny you both, take bread. It is your sacred right!" After a trip to Philadelphia for additional speeches she was arrested, tried, and imprisoned for her incendiary statements in New York. Meanwhile the volatile mood and acute distress of New York's unemployed spurred Samuel Gompers to press for emergency public works jobs.[2]

Hard times strengthed socialists at the polls and eased them into labor unions. Daniel De Leon, the guiding voice of the Socialist Labor Party, hoped to transform unions into agents for the political mobilization of the industrial proletariat. Working through the United Hebrew Trades of New York, which had become dominant in the city's District Assembly 49 of the Knights of Labor, De Leon made his move in 1893. He arranged for socialists to support Populist James R. Sovereign in his successful bid to displace Terence V. Powderly as Grand Master Workman at the Knights of Labor national convention. In return Sovereign was to name a De Leon protégé as editor of the Knights' *Journal*. Sovereign reneged and battled De Leon for control of the order. The credentials committee at the 1895 convention awarded Sovereign's faction a slight majority; delegates representing thirteen thousand socialist unionists seceded.[3]

In the meantime a rising tide of radicalism had all but engulfed the A.F.L. The 1893 call by New York labor organizations for public employment for the jobless was symptomatic of a spirit abroad among unionists as far away as northern California. Gompers, participating in summer meetings, called for emergency relief work, and his angry remarks at the year's A.F.L. convention in Chicago evidenced further the spirit of labor. His "graphic indictment of the causes which brought about the present depression" was "heartily" approved, and sentiment for political action was very high. A year earlier the federation had endorsed the demands of the People's Party for the initiative, referendum, and public ownership of telecommunications. Now it added resolutions favoring Coxey's public works plan, the free coinage of silver, and a formal effort to effect political cooperation between farmer and labor organizations. Peter James Maguire of the carpenters' union forcefully advocated an alliance with the Populists. Thomas Morgan, a Chicago socialist elected that year as secretary of the machinists' international, offered a comprehensive, eleven-point political program that included a controversial call for collective ownership of the means of production. The delegates narrowly accepted the scheme. They proceeded by overwhelming vote, 2,244 to 67, to refer it to constituent unions for consideration. Final federation action was to be taken at the 1894 convention.

When the 1894 conclave began on December 10 in Denver, it appeared that a majority of the federation's rank and file favored the platform. Seventy-seven delegates had instructions to vote for it, seventeen of thirty nationals and a solid majority of locals and city state centrals were sympathetic, and three nationals had approved the collective ownership plank. Yet while conceding that labor faced a "need for practical legislation" because of continued business paralysis "resulting from the incompetency of our modern captains of industry," the federation's head planned to scuttle the political program. Distrustful of political action and socialism as divisive influences, he had in 1893 refrained from voting on the motion asking that member unions consider the scheme favorably. Afterward, with Adolph Strasser of the cigar makers' union and others, he had moved into more open opposition. Now, employing a wide variety of parliamentary tactics, Gompers and company beat down the political design after several days of heated debate by a vote of 1,173 to 735. Vengeful socialists joined with other opponents to elect United Mine Workers head John McBride president, but socialism had been dealt a decisive defeat. Gompers returned to power a year later, retaining it for decades.[4]

Repulsed in the Knights of Labor and faced with the A.F.L.'s. rejection of political activism, Daniel De Leon launched a new socialist labor movement to organize the great body of unskilled workingmen. The Socialist Trade and Labor Alliance was founded in December 1895. It soon embraced about fifteen thousand members, drawn from the United Hebrew Trades, the seceded District Assembly 49 of the Knights, and the collectivist Central Labor Federation of New York, Brooklyn, and Newark. Factionalism, a preoccupation with ultimate political goals that failed to attract laborers more interested in immediate economic objectives, and the opposition of even socialist A.F.L. leaders (who branded the S.T.L.A. a divisive exercise in dual unionism), destroyed the new body in a few years.[5]

Eugene Debs stood as a galvanic new socialist leader forged on the anvil of the Pullman strike, and by jailhouse discourse with Thomas Morgan and Victor Berger. His hopes for a reformed capitalism went down with William Jennings Bryan in 1896. In the January 1, 1897, A.R.U. *Chicago Railway Times* Debs proclaimed: "The issue is Socialism versus Capitalism. I am for Socialism because I am for humanity." The following June the few officers in attendance at the national convention reorganized the A.R.U. into the Social Democracy of America (S.D.A.). They agreed to launch a cooperative colony in a Western state as a springboard to socializing the state and nation. At Debs' insistence they added a political platform that included calls for the nationalization of mineral resources, railroads and communications, and trust-dominated industries, and public works to employ the jobless. The following year a battle for control of the S.D.A. was won by utopians, and political activists split off into the Social

Democratic Party. Disaffected Socialist Labor Party sections in Chicago, St. Louis, San Francisco, Philadelphia, and Milwaukee were quickly drawn to the new party, as were independent groups in Texas and Iowa. Debs's magnetism, as he traveled about the country to lecture or speak in behalf of striking unions, won other adherents. Undoubtedly memories of unemployment, the ruthless suppression of strikes, and distress during the depressed nineties contributed their share. By 1900 Debs's party, though it claimed but 4,356 members in 226 branches in twenty-five states, was firmly established. A dozen years later Debs polled nearly a million votes in presidential balloting.[6]

The flames of agrarian political revolt, raging through the cotton states and the Great Plains, dwarfed the antics of the socialist minority. Generated in a volatile mixture of declining prices, rising debt, foreclosures, delinquent-tax sales, and commercialization of farming, it defied statistical description. When financial panic hit the cities in 1893 rural Americans had already struggled with a quarter-century of depression. Wheat was being fed to cattle as far east as Ohio, because elevator prices did not warrant hauling it to town for sale. A bumper corn crop in 1895 fetched as little as eleven cents a bushel at remote local markets and only twice as much in Chicago. At such prices it was burned for fuel or dumped on the ground. Californians were advised to feed grapes to livestock.[7]

Flooding and drought compounded agrarian grief. In 1893 drought ravaged Kansas. A year later grasshoppers mangled sun-burnt fields from Kansas and eastern Colorado to the Dakotas, and hot winds scorched two-thirds of Nebraska's counties. In the South the boll weevil began an inexorable march of destruction in 1892. For three years running, through 1893, the Mississippi burst its levees and flooded vast delta areas; a raging hurricane inundated the Sea Islands rice plantations in the third year. A winter later, a hard freeze blasted the Florida citrus groves. Summer heat in 1895 scorched the hill country cotton lands of Louisiana, Mississippi, Arkansas, and Texas, also halving Louisiana's rice output from two years before. Adversity bore down on farmers, bringing tales of terrible hardship. In February, 1895 a battered prairie schooner creaked eastward into Keokuk, Iowa, in minus-twenty-five-degree cold. The son of its owners alighted and asked for relief; he was wearing only gunny sacking for shoes. People remaining in blizzard-blown plains homes suffered even more.[8]

The agrarian movement, with roots in the depressed, difficult quarter-century after the Civil War, grew from a local Texas group founded in the 1870s to apprehend rustlers. It was still small when C. W. Macune became its leader in 1886 and energized it. Within five years the Farmers' Alliance and Industrial Union, or Southern Alliance, straddled the South and boasted three million members. In 1880 Milton George, editor of the Chicago weekly *Chicago Western Rural*, founded in Cook County, Illinois, the society that became the National (Northern) Farmers' Alliance. By the end of the decade it claimed a million members in the Mississippi Valley. The Colored National Farmers' Alliance and

Industrial Union, formed at the insistence of George's group in 1886, professed a million adherents.

The alliances, which stressed social activity and agricultural improvement, sparked the prominent contemporary cooperative movement. More important, they elaborated a series of legislative demands that inevitably drew them into pressure politics and finally third-party action. In 1890 they scored impressively. Forty-four congressmen, three senators, and majorities in several state legislatures, mostly in the South, won office with their support. Independent farmer parties materialized in the Midwest, and when anticipated legislation was slow in materializing, sentiment grew for the organization of a national third party.

A series of 1891–92 meetings at Cincinnati and St. Louis resulted in a call for a national nominating convention of a newly formed People's Party to meet in Omaha in July of 1892. The call shattered the Alliances, because it collided with traditional party loyalties; also, in the South there were fears that independent action might restore to Negroes (as had sometimes been true during Reconstruction) a pivotal position between divided whites. Even so, the Democratic nomination of Cleveland in June led many Southerners to bolt to the new standard. At Omaha 1,400 delegates approved a platform epitomizing the agrarian demands of the past decades. Despite a Jeffersonian-Jacksonian rhetoric that extolled traditional virtues and spoke darkly of a sinister conspiracy of financial interests to impoverish the producing classes, the platform called for the humanization rather than the rejection of industrialism and commercial agriculture. Collective means were to be employed toward individualistic and democratic ends—the extension of prosperity, economic opportunity, and political rights to the people. The platform stressed money, transportation, and land— fiat government currency and unlimited coinage of silver to replace banknotes, a money supply equal to fifty dollars per capita (to revive prices and industry);[9] postal savings banks, graduated income tax, federal ownership of railroads and telecommunications; laws against land monopolies and alien ownership; an eight-hour day, immigration restriction, popular election of senators, a single-term presidency, and the initiative and referendum. James B. Weaver of Iowa and James G. Field of Virginia were selected to carry the party banner.[10]

The Democrats swept the congressional and presidential races, but Populists were not without successes, winning statehouses in Kansas, Colorado, and North Dakota, and perhaps fifty statewide and fifteen hundred state legislative and county posts. Moreover, the Populists captured eight congressional seats, including five of Kansas's seven through fusion with Democrats, and sympathetic independents held two more seats. Local influence meant many more friendly, if non-Populist, representatives. Senate strength was up by two, to five. Weaver drew a million votes to carry five states—Kansas, North Dakota, Idaho, Nevada, and Colorado. His twenty-two electoral votes were the first granted a minor candidate since the Civil War. The showing of the new party was good enough to alarm Republicans and Democrats; nonetheless, it fell short of anticipations.

An agrarian party, it won only two farm states. Its Western vote, achieved through fusion with Democrats, was for silver, not the Omaha demands. The Democrats retained the South, where they were taking up agrarian proposals (although Weaver ran second to Cleveland in several instances). East of Iowa the Northern Populist vote was negligible.[11]

The events of the ensuing two years added oil to the flames of political revolt. Panic, depression, and the policies of the Cleveland administration antagonized growing numbers of voters. Cleveland's ruthless use of pressure and patronage to force repeal of the purchase clause of the Sherman silver law on October 30, 1893, and the excited congressional discussion preceding repeal drew attention to the money issue as perhaps nothing else could. The vote on the measure revealed a sectional spread of silverite sentiment: fifteen of eighteen Democratic senatorial votes against repeal were from the South—Missouri Representative Richard Parks Bland, long a leading silver spokesman, warned Democratic supporters of the administration that "we will never offer you another compromise. . . . You can go your way and we will go ours." Cleveland, with the passage of repeal, was set on a course that must hopelessly divide his party and inhibit constructive monetary legislation for the remainder of his term. The president expected repeal to fuel economic recovery by inciting business confidence in the Treasury's ability to maintain gold payments. Cleveland clung to his expectations long after any hope for them faded. In February 1894 the first of four federal bond issues to replenish the Treasury gold reserve was launched. In March the president vetoed a widely supported bill to coin the silver seignorage (the government revenue realized from the manufacture of coins), a perhaps politically suicidal move after a generation of falling prices and the exhortation of inflationists arousing the antagonism of a growing mass of agrarian voters.

Angry voters vented their rage at the Democrats in the off-year elections of 1893. Republicanism waxed, especially in industrial states hard hit by business reverses. The GOP won eight states that in 1892 had been divided between the parties, its plurality greater by 340,000. William McKinley smashed his way to a second term as Ohio's governor. Running as the "Advance Agent of Prosperity" and blaming panic on business fears of Democratic designs to cut the tariff, he won a plurality of eighty thousand and added 4.9 percent to the share of the state vote that his party had won the previous year. Local issues permitted capture of the New Jersey legislature. In New York, where depression apparently became a decisive political factor only a year later, factionalism cost the Democrats control of the legislature and an upcoming state constitutional convention, on only a slight vote-shift.[12]

As the 1894 congressional elections approached, Republican and former Speaker Thomas Brackett Reed remarked presciently, "The Democratic mortality will be so great next fall that their dead will be buried in trenches and marked 'unknown' "—adding later, "till the supply of trenches runs out."[13] Everywhere gloomy omens multiplied as if to verify in advance the axiom that no party in power ever survived bad times.

The Democratic split was wider than ever. In the South, Democratic Governor Benjamin Ryan Tillman of South Carolina vied with Georgia Populist Tom Watson in venomous attacks on the president. Nebraska Democrat Bryan campaigned for a Senate seat on free silver and denunciations of Cleveland. From Florida to the high plains, open-air meetings rang to fervent Populist oratory. The Republicans unmuzzled their heavy artillery. Having long claimed that tariff reductions would injure American business, they found the conjunction of economic prostration and an unpopular Democratic tariff made to order. Former President Harrison and Tom Reed spoke widely in the Midwest and East. William McKinley, the leading contender for the 1896 Republican presidential nomination since his Ohio victory, spoke 371 times in sixteen states from Maine to Nebraska, and twenty-three times in a single day as his train crossed the Beef State. In contrast to the essentially negative administration program of repeal, protection of the Treasury reserve, and tariff reduction, Republicans offered an apparently dynamic and positive alternative in proposals to enact a protective tariff to revive industry and put men to work. Insistently they repeated the theme of which McKinley was the personal symbol—in Reed's words to a Chicago audience, "all periods of prosperity have been periods of protection."[14]

The defeat pointed toward a political realignment of unprecedented scope. Such Democratic luminaries as Ways and Means Chairman William L. Wilson, Illinois's William McKendree Springer, Indiana's William Steele Holman, and Missouri's Bland were ousted from the House. Senator David B. Hill was crushed in the New York gubernatorial race. Twenty-four states returned no Democratic congressmen, six others but one each. The party lost 113 seats in the House, keeping 105, while Republicans added 117, for 244. Dissatisfaction gave the Populists nearly 1,500,000 votes, a 42 percent increase. However, the People's Party lost power, winning at the state level only in North Carolina, through fusion with Tarheel Republicans. All of the states that had supported Weaver in 1892 were now Republican, and three fusionists joined only four admitted Populists—three of them from North Carolina—in the House. The Democrats kept technical control of the Senate, but only with help from four Populists and two sympathizers.

In the states from Pennsylvania northeastward, Republicans added forty-four House seats, including six from New Jersey in the party's first sweep of the state's eight, for a total of ninety-two. Democrats held but seven seats in the Northeast, four of them in the Tammany Hall district of New York City and one in Boston's Irish center. In the old Northwest, Wisconsin and Illinois returned to the party of Lincoln. Democratic House strength fell from forty-two to three (two in Ohio and one in Illinois) as Republicans captured thirty-nine new seats for a total of seventy-five. Republicans dominated the Midwest north of Arkansas, electing forty-four representatives to four Democrats, one Populist, and one fusionist. The GOP was as successful from the Rockies west, where silver Republicans drove opponents from the field. Even the border states of Delaware, Maryland, West Virginia, and Missouri swung over. The party won

Delaware's sole House seat, all four of West Virginia's, three of Maryland's six, eleven of Missouri's fifteen, five of Kentucky's eleven, and four of Tennessee's ten. Silver Democrats secured conspicuous triumphs at the expense of administration men in the South.

Contemporaries described press analyses as "positively bewildering," but an examination of local voter behavior clarifies the significance of the results. To an unusual degree national issues relating to the depression pervaded the campaign. Voters chose the GOP and its program over a range of alternatives that included Populism, the Socialist Labor Party, and others, although fringe movements registered new support. Rural areas north of the Mason and Dixon line tended to slide gradually to Republicanism, cities to turn abruptly. Longtime Democratic strongholds in city tenement districts, where working populations were especially liable to pay cuts and unemployment in bad times, shifted *en bloc*. Germans and old stock Democrats in Buffalo and Queens County (Brooklyn), New York, had begun to desert in 1893. In 1894 the party's statewide vote share was off five points. There were sharp losses in all thirty assembly districts in New York City, with appreciable falls in East European Jewish, Polish, Italian, and even Irish Catholic neighborhoods. Citywide the party lost 14.3 percent, and there were declines of 9 percent in Queens, 12.8 in Rensselaer (Troy), and 8.2 in Albany counties, with corresponding Republican gains. In New Jersey the GOP added solid advances in the industrial centers of Paterson, Passaic, Camden, and Elizabeth to the previous year's increases in rural areas. An unusually high midterm turnout in Connecticut gave Republicans gains in all of the counties, 159 of 168 towns, and 7.5 percent more of the vote than in 1893, with comparable Democratic losses. A similar pattern held elsewhere.

Samuel T. McSeveney has argued convincingly that in a strong two-party system the Republicans were the logical beneficiaries of discontent, particularly as they seemed to offer a positive alternative to the administration's policy. Through the tariff, long a familiar issue, they were able to focus discontent arising from hard times on the Democrats and to offer an attractive analysis of economic conditions and a prescription for a restoration of prosperity. They now occupied an excellent salient from which to conquer the presidency in 1896. At the same time, Populists could take heart in their enlarged popular vote. If they could find the right issue to channel voter dissatisfaction, there was even reason to hope that they could replace the severely shocked Democratic party. Moreover, northern Democratic setbacks strengthened the position of Southern and Western agrarians and silverites, who hoped to seize power in the party. A hostile congress was thus only one feature of the dismal scene facing the hapless administration.[15]

Not the least of the election's results was that through his prominent campaign role William McKinley added important momentum to his drive for the next Republican presidential nomination. Soon after the voting, Cleveland industrialist Marcus Alonzo Hanna, the governor's friend for a half dozen years, retired from business to manage his campaign. The two men were a superlative team.

Both were economic nationalists, although Hanna had a larger vision of national welfare. Hanna's unswervingly loyal service, warmth, and managerial skill complemented his friend's correctness and political acumen.

Tom Reed and Senator Shelby Moore Cullom of Illinois were among several favorite-son candidates advanced by a group of primarily Eastern party bosses (that included Nelson Aldrich of Rhode Island, New York's Thomas Collier Platt, and Matthew Stanley Quay of Pennsylvania) to defeat McKinley. But by the time the party's national convention opened on June 16, 1896, at St. Louis, the Ohioan's skill and popularity, together with the splendid organization that Hanna had created and lubricated with $100,000 of his personal fortune, had routed the opposition.

The only exciting moments at St. Louis came on the third and final day of the conclave. Republican strategists had initially anticipated a campaign built around the tariff and prosperity, with a straddle on the silver issue. Depression had demonstrated the appeal of the tariff argument. Moreover, the party's record was consistent on protection, but not on silver. Many Republicans, McKinley included, had favored the Bland-Allison and Sherman acts but then later supported repeal. The Republican House after convening in December 1895 rushed through a protectionist tariff to dramatize the issue, only to see the measure fail in the Senate. Henry Moore Teller of Colorado led a handful of protectionist silver Republicans in preventing action, warning that they would accept no bill without a free coinage amendment.

While still hoping to run on the tariff, McKinley and Hanna recognized that they must mollify Eastern conservatives alarmed at the growth of inflationist agitation and the governor's inconsistency on silver. Hanna travelled to St. Louis before the convention with a confidential draft money plank favoring gold. In ensuing platform negotiations he shrewdly appeared to yield to Eastern claims for an unequivocal declaration for gold, thus augmenting support for McKinley. As reported on June 18 the platform was a masterly harmonizing document. Most of it was devoted to a condemnation of Democratic policies that had "precipitated panic, blighted industry and trade with prolonged depression," and to a call for protection to revive the home market and for reciprocal trade agreements to secure an overseas "outlet for our surplus" production. However, it contained a ringing paragraph urging maintenance of "the existing gold standard" and opposing the free coinage of silver except "by international agreement," which was recognized as unlikely. Teller presented a minority report offering a free coinage substitute monetary plank. With its rejection he announced his withdrawal from the party, and the platform was resoundingly adopted. Ohio's forty-six votes fittingly gave McKinley the nomination on the first ballot.[16]

The defection of a silver minority at the Republican convention was only a minor skirmish in a conflict disrupting American politics. As early as 1889 a conference of bimetallists at St. Louis had organized a lobby, the American Bimetallic League. Civil War veteran General Adoniram J. Warner, a Marion,

Ohio, businessman, directed its affairs and soon made its Washington office a center of activity. Just weeks before Cleveland's second inauguration a League gathering agreed to invite representatives of all the country's industrial and labor groups to future meetings, to unite the silver forces. As the 1893 special congressional session neared, Western mining districts—Denver, Reno, and Ketchum, Idaho—erupted with demonstrations for silver. The League called a special meeting for August 1 and 2 at Chicago to organize pressure against repeal of the Sherman Silver Purchase Act. When the eight hundred delegates assembled, their numbers enabled Western and Southern agrarians to obtain special positions. Nebraska's young congressman Bryan secured a place on the resolutions committee. Populist national chairman Herman E. Taubeneck, whose party hoped to seize command of the silver movement, became a member of the League executive committee. Only with difficulty did the League preserve its nonpartisan character at the meeting, which adopted a series of resolutions for the free coinage of silver. An October gathering yielded new calls for free coinage, while the special session of Congress brought hints of silverite efforts to capture the Democratic party. Bland, Bryan, and others joined Nevada's Senator William Morris Stewart, moreover, in inflationist speeches that aroused multitudes in the South and West.[17]

Events of the succeeding years kept silver at the center of attention. By 1894 a great debate was raging. The appearance of *Coin's Financial School* in June— total sales were estimated at 650,000 to a million, and the Democratic National Committee distributed 125,000 copies in the campaign of 1896—stirred hundreds of thousands. The white metal's appeal spread, and silver speakers were in great demand as the fall elections neared. Nebraska Democrats indicated fealty to Bryan in June when they approved his free coinage platform and a program to convert the state party wholly to silver. Elsewhere the silver chorus grew more raucous. A final spur to the festering agitation was the February 1895 Treasury bond sale to a banking syndicate; it aroused furious criticism. On February 22 a group of leading bimetallists met in Washington to lay plans for an American Bimetallic Party.

In the spring of 1895 President Cleveland moved to stem the silver surge within his party, concentrating on the South—the West was already lost. Recalling that its slavery stand had cast the Democrats from power for a generation, he feared the consequences of embracing a silver heresy. He hoped that a loyal South could hold back the inflationist forces. The president opened correspondence with such sound-money men as Senator Donelson Caffery of Louisiana and Governor Charles Triplett O'Ferrall of Virginia, and arranged for distribution of a sound-money speech by Tennessee Representative Josiah Patterson. In April he drafted the first of a series of public letters upholding "our traditional [party] doctrine of sound and safe currency." In May members of the cabinet and Comptroller of the Currency James Herron Eckels accepted speaking engagements to defend administration monetary views. Carlisle toured the border states, talking forcefully at Covington, Louisville, Bowling Green, and most importantly to seven hundred Southerners at a Memphis sound-money convention on May 23. In October Cleveland and his cabinet journeyed to the Atlanta Cotton States Exposition, where he decried sectional and selfish interests in politics to an audience of fifty thousand. Meanwhile, sound-money gatherings were encouraged in several cities.[18]

Such efforts were fruitless at a time when Ben Tillman was telling angry Southern farmers, "Send me to Washington, and I'll tickle Cleveland's fat ribs with my pitchfork," Tom Watson was exhorting Georgians for silver, and Bryan was acting as the arch-evangelist of the silver gospel in numerous speeches and a widespread correspondence that gave him increasing fame. Shortly before Carlisle's tour, representatives from seventeen states and territories assembled for a silver convention at the Mormon Tabernacle in Salt Lake City. Carlisle was hanged in effigy in New Orleans on May 26 for his Memphis speech. A Des Moines Democratic conclave declared for free coinage on June 6. In mid-June Bryan shared the spotlight with Altgeld when an Illinois Democratic gathering at Springfield announced for silver. Three days later the Nebraskan spoke to a thousand silver Democrats at a Memphis meeting held to reply to Carlisle's recent speech. Within weeks groups of Texas, Mississippi, and Missouri Democrats endorsed free coinage.[19]

Silver Democrats, at an August meeting in Washington, formed a committee, including Senators James Kimbrough Jones of Arkansas, North Carolina's Thomas Jordan Jarvis, Florida's Wilkinson Call, Virginia's John Warwick Daniel, and Tennessee Representative Isham Green Harris, to superintend strategy and the organization of silver clubs to wrest control of the party from the administration. The following January, silverites forced the choice of Chicago over New York for the party's national convention. Days later, on February 22, a silver convention in Washington replaced the old organizations with a new educational arm, the American Bimetallic Union, and a party, the American Silver Organization (Party). The silver party was to hold its national convention in St. Louis on July 22. Factional leaders later agreed that if the silver Republicans bolted, they too would meet in St. Louis on July 22. An attempt would be made to nominate Teller at the Democratic convention. If the Chicago conclave chose a free coinage candidate, the silver groups would join behind him.

With the encouragement of Bryan, who favored a coordinated strategy yet hoped through a conversion to silver to keep the Democracy from slipping to minority status in the South and West, the People's Party national committee also consented to a July 22 St. Louis meeting. The decision was a calculated gamble. James B. Weaver had written Bryan that the party had "had quite enough" of defeat on the Omaha platform. If the major parties held for gold, Populist leaders hoped to assume leadership of the silver movement and unite all dissidents to win power. It remained to be seen, though, whether the party would control silver or silver the party.[20]

In spring 1896 the contest for delegates to the Democratic national convention reached its height. Last-minute administration efforts that included a presidential appeal for party loyalty to conservative financial principles won only limited successes in Michigan, Wisconsin, and a handful of Eastern states. From the opening of May, gold men suffered two defeats for each victory, as one state convention after another declared for free coinage. When the national assembly opened on July 7, Republican acceptance of the money issue had offered a natural opening for silverites intending to fight the campaign on the question. A belligerent free coinage majority rejected Senator Hill as temporary chairman in favor of Senator Daniel, 556 to 349.

The next day, with approval of a credentials committee decision seating silver men from Nebraska, Michigan, and enlarged territorial delegations, inflationists secured the two-thirds vote needed to nominate. Bryan triumphantly led his company to its place and joined the resolutions committee to work on the platform. When submitted on July 9 the document defined the money question as "paramount to all others," condemned "monometallism which has locked fast the prosperity of an industrial people in the paralysis of hard times," and demanded free coinage. It denounced the sale of Treasury bonds in peacetime, the issue of currency by national banks, federal interference in local affairs, trusts, and the use of injunctions to suppress strikes. Among others were calls for immigration restriction and a revenue tariff. Bryan planned the debate on the platform and awarded himself the final speech. He was convinced that the situation pointed to his own nomination, as the most available candidate. He believed that Teller's membership in the Republican Party until only a short time ago disbarred the latter, while age and other disabilities disqualified Bland, Iowa's Horace Boies, and the remaining contenders.

When his moment to speak arrived Bryan bounded athletically to the stage, then paused dramatically. Sure that the time had passed for a systematic review of the case for silver, he offered an emotional appeal instead. His words cast a spell that became hypnotic; crying, "You shall not press upon the brow of labor this crown of thorns, you shall not crucify mankind upon a cross of gold," he gestured as if to press the thorns upon his own head and then spread his arms as if crucified, finally letting them fall slowly to his sides. Bedlam followed his stunning peroration. By a two-thirds vote the platform was approved and a motion commending the president's courageous service rejected. The next day, while administration men sat in bitter silence, the delegates nominated Bryan on the fifth ballot and chose Arthur M. Sewall, a Bath, Maine, shipbuilder and silverite banker, as his running mate. Eastern conservatives were thunderstruck. Cleveland's intimates muttered darkly of treachery. The *New York Times* termed the convention's decisions "wild and disordered." Theodore Roosevelt with characteristic intemperance branded the proceedings a "Witches Sabbath."[21]

Even before leaving the Windy City, conservative Democrats agreed on a statement repudiating the Chicago decisions and calling for a new convention. It was published July 14 over the signatures of Illinois Senator John McAuley Palmer, Comptroller Eckels, and others. The Reform Club of New York lent important Eastern support to the movement, which eventuated in a convention of "National Democrats" in Indianapolis on September 2. Delegates from forty-one states and three territories nominated Palmer and General Simon Bolivar Buckner of Kentucky. A brief platform praised the Cleveland administration and a gold standard, and it condemned efforts to interfere with the Supreme Court. Cleveland, whose views were well known, remained discreetly quiet, as did most of the cabinet. However, he purged silverites from the civil service, while Olney as early as July 15 had openly attacked the Chicago ticket. The new party had no hope of winning; Palmer in his final speech actually advised, "I will not consider it any great fault if you decide . . . to cast your ballot for William McKinley." Its purpose was to preserve some semblance of a conservative Democratic organization and enable partisans to oppose Bryan and aid McKinley without having to vote Republican. The rupture of the Democratic Party was complete.[22]

The Prohibition Party split over free coinage. The Silver Party and silver Republicans acquiesced in the Chicago slate, the latter hesitantly. The Populists faced a cruel dilemma. They had staked their hopes on riding the silver tide to success. Now, to accept the Democratic ticket was to risk party suicide, but not to do so was to split the reform vote and defeat the progressive cause. To placate Southern delegates who threatened to bolt unless the party chose a separate slate on the Omaha platform, it was decided to reverse the usual order and select a vice presidential candidate—anti-fusionist Tom Watson—before making the presidential choice. Bryan replied to inquiries that he repudiated any nomination rejecting Sewall. On the convention's last day pragmatism triumphed. Weaver nominated Bryan, and three-fourths of the delegates backed him. The Nebraska orator thus became the nominee of the majority Democrats, the Silver Party, the Silver Republicans, and the Populists.[23]

Bryan undertook an unprecedented personal campaign. On August 8 he set out for New York, the beginning of four trips totalling eighteen thousand miles. He ranged from Tennessee and the Carolinas to New England, concentrating on the crucial Ohio Valley and middle border—the East was lost, the South and West safe. By election day he had spoken six hundred times to an estimated five million people, offering as many as thirty-six addresses in a single day. His message was consistently agrarian and silverite. In New York City he denounced a system that forced the farmer to "sell at wholesale and buy at retail," contending that a prosperous agriculture was the only basis of national prosperity. The surest way to "destroy the market" for manufactures was to embrace a deflationary policy that lowered "the price of the farmer's crops" and thus his purchasing power. The remedy was free coinage, to increase prices and purchasing power.[24]

Bryan's aggressive effort had such impact that GOP strategists advanced their campaign from a planned September opening to July. McKinley, believing that departure from a pledge not to take the stump would indicate weakness and a lack of dignity, hit on bringing the people to his Canton home as a means of reaching them. By November 2,750,000 in three hundred delegations from thirty states had made the pilgrimage, to hear carefully planned speeches. Hanna's national committee through persuasion and assessments raised $3.5 million for the campaign. A Chicago headquarters coordinated 1,400 speakers, supervised the distribution of 125–200 million copies of 275 tracts in eleven languages, and fed material to newspapers reaching five million people weekly. Except for the *New York World*, leading Eastern papers unanimously favored McKinley. Prominent clergy lashed out at Bryan, whose platform was said to be "made in hell."

The GOP message reached masses of voters through such publications as the *Chicago Prairie Farmer*, and even the *Algona (Iowa) Upper Des Moines*. Mc-Kinley skillfully tied sound money to protection and prosperity. He said that free coinage, through the bullion value of silver dollars, meant dollars worth fifty-three cents. Cheap dollars in turn were an inflationary threat to savings and income. Confidence and business would fall, cutting labor's earnings at the expense of the narrow agrarian and sectional interests that the Democratic program represented. Low farm prices were laid to overproduction. Sound money was essential for the confidence that prosperity required. Protection would benefit all by stimulating expanded manufacturing and employment for a secure home market, thereby raising the purchasing power of the farmers' urban consumers. After September, when it was believed that such points had dulled Bryan's appeal, McKinley stressed protection even more.[25]

On September 1 Vermont returned the largest Republican plurality in twenty-four years. Maine followed two weeks later. The stock market rallied, but redoubled Democratic exertions precipitated near panic among conservatives in the final weeks of the contest. When the votes were tallied the outcome was not a GOP landslide, but the party had won its first decisive victory since 1872. McKinley polled 7,102,246 votes to 6,492,559 for Bryan, including 217,000 cast for Bryan-Watson electors. McKinley, the first candidate to draw a popular majority since 1876, had won a huge victory, by stalemate standards. Bryan later showed that a shift of 19,436 votes in California, Oregon, Kentucky, Indiana, North Dakota, and West Virginia would have reversed the 271–176 decision in the electoral college, but such a transfer would still have left McKinley a popular margin of 570,000.[26]

Many Democratic partisans tried, as have some later historians, to lay the defeat to Republican fraud, vote buying, and intimidation and coercion of voters. Altgeld claimed that Illinois had been stolen. There were instances in which businessmen inflicted GOP speakers on employees, insisted that they participate in McKinley demonstrations, or worse. Insurance agents offered farmers mortgage extensions on liberal terms if Bryan was defeated. Orders for goods were placed contingent on Republican victory. Significantly the Republican *Idaho Daily Statesman* in a November 1 editorial referring to orders for iron admitted, "The laborers know if Bryan should be elected those orders would never be filled." Loyal William Allen White conceded that "labor as a class was persuaded to the point of coercion'' that a Democratic success would shatter business confidence and plunge the country into deeper depression.[27]

Yet conspiratorial explanations ignored too much. Bryan was an uncommonly strong candidate. He outpolled all previous victors. He carried five Western states that had favored Harrison in 1892—Nebraska, South Dakota, Wyoming, Montana, and Washington—and four that had chosen Weaver—Kansas, Colorado, Idaho, and Nevada. He recaptured straying Democrats to repair many of 1894's Midwestern congressional losses. Republicans lost forty House seats, keeping 204 to the opposition's 153. Yet Bryan lost, and decisively. McKinley's great margin, 140,000 in Illinois alone, makes explanations based on theft implausible. He missed carrying South Dakota and Wyoming by only a few hundred votes and the agrarian strongholds of Kansas and Nebraska by less than fifteen thousand each. He came within nineteen thousand each in Virginia, North Carolina, and Tennessee, which he might have won if blacks had been allowed to vote freely. State legislative successes enabled the GOP to add four Senate seats, for a total of forty-seven. Bryan's party lost five, keeping thirty-four, and Populists and others gained one, for seven. The election was a critical turning point, completing a basic alteration of the political balance under way since 1893. Popular interest was at record levels, up to 80 percent of the eligibles voted in parts of New England. Shifts of 1893–94 gave way to exceptional transfers in 1896, when masses of voters became Republicans, forging a new party alignment that lasted for a generation.

Bryan's candidacy polarized voting; it won for the Democrats twenty-two Southern and Western farming and mining states and lost twenty-three others to McKinley. The Ohioan ran best where his party had gained most since 1893, in the populous, urban-industrial, and older farming states from the Northeast into Iowa and North Dakota. McKinley also won California, Oregon, and the border states of Maryland, West Virginia, and Kentucky, where 5,114 National Democratic votes probably furnished his lead of 281. He won over two-thirds of the New England vote, erasing Cleveland's 1892 margin of five thousand in Connecticut with an advantage of fifty-four thousand. He swept the three Middle Atlantic states, where Cleveland had lost only Pennsylvania, by 657,000. McKinley replaced Cleveland's fifty-six electoral votes and twenty-one thousand plurality in the Old Northwest with a thumping 350,000-vote lead. Bryan could have the rest of the country.

Of the forty-five states, thirty-two contained eighty-two cities of forty-five thousand or more; McKinley took twenty states with sixty-five cities, leaving Bryan twelve with seventeen cities. He carried sixty-nine cities, including seven in Bryan states, while his rival won only Troy, Los Angeles, and Fort Wayne in the GOP states. Capturing only three of the states without sizeable cities, McKinley left ten to Bryan. Nationally Bryan secured 48.3 percent of the rural vote and only 40.6 percent in urban areas. Only in New England and the Rocky Mountain mining states was his urban share greater than in the country, with

33.5 to 24.5 and 87.1 to 80.1 points respectively. In the Middle Atlantic region Bryan's city and country support was about even, at a low 37 percent of the total; in the thirteen East North Central states it was 42.5 and 44.6 points respectively. In the agricultural South and West, which he carried, rural support exceeded urban.

Local statistics elaborated the pattern. Despite urban-rural differences in New England, the gross movement in both city and countryside favored Lincoln's party. Republicans strengthened their grip on Connecticut's eleven largest cities, adding 9 percent to their share of the state vote and 12.7 percent in rural areas. McKinley's share in New York was 6 percent over 1894, at 57 points. Bryan carried twenty of thirty-five New York City assembly districts, doing best in Irish and native laboring areas on the lower east and west sides. However, he lost at least 5.7 percentage points in each district and suffered continued labor defections, with notable losses among Germans and Jews. Midtown middle-class areas were solidly Republican and, with the GOP share of the city vote up 11.7 percent to 50.7, the metropolis for the first time since 1848 repudiated the Democratic nominee. While the greatest state losses occurred in the seven metropolitan counties, as in 1893–94, and his upstate performance varied with local economic conditions, Bryan was soundly beaten upstate.

In New Jersey the Republican vote share was up 7.4 points. The party took all major cities and the congressional and legislative races. German wards came over wholesale, and even some Irish wards in Elizabeth. Rural areas continued the GOP trend that had begun in 1893. In New England the magnitude of Democratic desertion was revealed by a 35.8-point rise in the Republican vote, while the total was only 3 percent above 1892. In Chicago, as in Eastern cities, Democratic support fell sharply in immigrant and native working class, as well as middle-class, neighborhoods. More successful in Irish and Polish districts, the party met serious losses in Italian, German, and Scandinavian areas. That immigrant and native labor moved together and with the middle classes suggested that the ethno-cultural factors and questions that commonly governed local voter party attachment had yielded to economic issues growing out of the depression. The march of workers into the Grand Old Party tended to reduce class differences between the major parties, although the Republicans remained somewhat more middle and upper class than the Democrats.[28]

Voter discontent with depression and the Democratic response to it best explains McKinley's triumph. Economic conditions strengthened Republican loyalty and made the GOP, the opposition pole in the country's two-party alignment, a natural magnet for disaffected Democrats. Republican wealth and overwhelming press support, especially in the East, enabled the party to saturate the country with propaganda. McKinley's well-known friendship for labor was probably helpful. His deft handling of the prosperity issue undoubtedly played an important role also. In the first major depression since the nation had become substantially urban and industrial, the protectionist argument was a potent device to define the common ideological ground among the diverse groups constituting the GOP, encouraging concerted voter action.

Carl Degler and others have shown that McKinley's management of ideology enhanced the party's image and attracted urbanites concerned with jobs and increased income. The GOP appeared to offer a dynamic, nationalist policy of change and government encouragement of economic growth, at a time when Democrats were stigmatized with business collapse, Cleveland's narrow conception of government's role, and then in 1896 with an agrarian outlook and financial and tariff policies unattractive to city dwellers. In short, Republican protectionist proposals to revive industrial, thus national, prosperity were more in tune with the perceptions of an increasingly urban population than was Bryan's program.[29]

The role of farm prices in shaping the election is ambiguous. New sources of gold and advancing wheat prices in the fall of 1896 did not restore prosperity. Much of the wheat crop had been moved before prices improved, while gains were confined largely to major marketing centers. Scattered evidence suggests that local prices for agricultural staples trended downward, or at best steadied, that autumn. However, it is possible that products such as butter and eggs loomed larger than cereal or fiber staples as week-to-week sources of cash for farmers. In this connection the movement of butter and egg prices in some Midwestern local markets could have been an important influence. Gilbert Fite has shown that in Algona, Iowa, butter sold for one cent less in October than in January, but four cents, or 25 percent, more than in June. Eggs varied from sixteen cents a dozen to eight cents, rebounding 75 percent to fourteen cents in October. Some other Midwestern local markets showed similar tendencies. Such developments, with press publicity for wheat price gains that tradition linked to farm prosperity, may have created an impression of improving conditions that in turn tempered the agrarian discontent that was the basis of Bryan's appeal. At the same time, press reports of continued silver price declines while wheat prices rose may have discredited the Nebraskan's inflationary argument and lent credence to the view that a vote for the "Advance Agent of Prosperity" was the surest means of ending depression.[30]

The role of the People's Party in 1896 further illuminates Bryan's failure. The election was the high-water mark of agrarian protest. Although complicated fusion arrangements make it impossible to separate and count the Populist vote, Watson's twenty-seven electoral votes clearly exceeded Weaver's 1892 total. Twenty-five congressmen (five were fusionists), six Populist senators, and six more silver Republicans or independents were chosen.[31] Moreover, fusion had enabled the party to hold its organization intact through the campaign, although blurring its identity.

Such artificial symptoms of vitality were deceptive. Populism had a narrow base. In the South it was strongest in counties with concentrations of small white farmers struggling with liens, depressed cotton prices, tenancy, and marginal

land. Mining interests devoted to free silver rather than Populism were conspicuous and often unreliable sources of support in the far West. In the Midwest
Populist strength lay in a tier of counties running from central Kansas through
the Dakotas into northwestern Minnesota. Corn and wheat growers in this area
faced special problems that made them, native or foreign born, prone to radicalism. Many had begun farming during the abnormally wet years of the previous decade, frequently planting corn or other crops suited to familiar humid
eastern areas. Often they had started with less than five hundred dollars of
capital, taking mortgages to obtain funds to pay for their land or supplies. Not
uncommonly annual cash incomes were under three hundred dollars. Elevator
and railroad discriminations, an undiversified agriculture that rendered them particularly dependent on a single cash crop, difficulties and crop failures attending
adaption to a region with unreliable precipitation, inadequate understanding of
the conditions of commercial farming, and price declines accompanying depression all multiplied to affect catastrophically income and ability to meet
debts. Subsistence farmers who hung on in the West and better-established practitioners of a more diversified agriculture to the East, who enjoyed more regular
rainfall as well, were much less vulnerable. Hence they were less likely to
respond to proposals concerning money, land, and transportation that Populists
articulated to meet their problems.[32]

Comparable limitations impeded efforts to forge an effective farmer-labor
coalition. It appeared briefly that growing agrarian and labor unrest favored
concerted action. In 1893 the Wisconsin State Federation of Labor approved the
Omaha platform, endorsing the People's Party itself a year later. The state Populist convention reciprocated by adopting the A.F.L.'s proposed political program along with the Omaha demands. Workingmen in several cities, with
Milwaukee, New York, and St. Paul socialists, were drawn into the People's
Party. Twenty percent of the German laborers in Milwaukee voted Populist in
1894, as did substantial numbers in Racine, La Crosse, Sheboygan, and elsewhere. A series of conferences of labor, reform, and Populist leaders at Springfield, Illinois, suggested cooperation. A tumultuous July gathering there
resolved, after a ringing speech from Henry Demarest Lloyd, to support the
Populist state ticket and a national farmer-labor alliance. It also grafted to the
Omaha demands most of the A.F.L. political scheme, including a compromise
modification of a plank seeking "collective ownership by the people of all such
means of production and distribution as the people elect." The November *American Federationist* illustrated waxing trade union radicalism with a report that
three hundred unionists were candidates for public office. When the year's Republican tidal wave swamped all but a half dozen of them, Gompers was vin-
dicated in his belief that organized labor was too immature to risk direct political
action, and he prepared to defeat the political program at the federation's 1984
convention. After the 1894 elections factionalism drove Populists, reformers,
and labor apart. The Populists remained interested in united action but turned
increasingly to free silver, which had limited appeal to labor, as the issue with

which to win power. In 1896 many local unions supported Bryan despite the opposition of A.F.L. leaders to direct action. However, masses of workingmen spurned agrarianism and free coinage to elect McKinley and protectionism.[33]

Bryan probably persuaded as many voters as he could have, but that was not enough. Bryan's strength, and the victory of McKinley and his program, were significant measures of the continuing hold of traditional values. Both men honored customary national ideals, including personal, political, and property rights, although the electorate in choosing among a range of options extending beyond socialism probably regarded McKinley as the better representative of accepted principles, as well as better attuned to contemporary needs. The return of prosperity beginning soon after the election, seeming to validate Republican claims and prove Democratic incompetence, confirmed the new political balance struck in the depression. Fusion had seriously compromised the identity of the People's Party, despite heroic efforts to protect it. The end of farm distress, destroying the party's reason for existence, was the coup de grâce. Populism was for all practical purposes dead by the election of 1898, as was a wide spectrum of dissent generated by hard times. The political consequences of the economic crisis, nonetheless, lingered on. The Republican Party, elevated to predominance by a coalition of new agrarian recruits and urban workingmen with its older middle-class and Northern rural centers of support, retained power (with a single interruption) for a generation. The long shadow of distress possibly helped Debs during the next few years to arouse sympathy among hundreds of thousands for his proposals for a democratic socialism. And memories of depression-inspired issues and reform proposals entailing changes and extensions of government functions leavened American thought and action well into the twentieth century, serving as an agenda for social adjustment to the exigencies of industrial life.[34]

NOTES

1. Hollingsworth, *Whirligig of Politics*, 28–31; H. Wayne Morgan, *From Hayes to McKinley: National Party Politics, 1877–1896* (Syracuse, NY: Syracuse University Press, 1969); Lee Benson, "An Approach to the Scientific Study of Past Public Opinion," *Public Opinion Quarterly* 31 (Winter 1967–68), 522–67; Samuel P. Hayes, "The Social Analysis of American Political History, 1880–1920," *Political Science Quarterly* 80 (September 1965), 384–88; and "Political Parties and the Community-Social Continuum," in William Nisbet Chambers and Walter Dean Burnham, eds., *The American Party Systems* (New York: Oxford University Press, 1967), 157–62.

2. Emma Goldman, *Living My Life* (New York: Alfred A. Knopf, 1931), 1:121–62 and passim; *New York Times* (August 18–21, 1893); "Movement of the Unemployed," *Public Opinion* 15 (August 26, 1893), 499–500; Eunice Marie Schuster, *Native American Anarchism: A Study of American Left Wing Individualism* (Northampton, MA: Smith College, 1931), 158–70; George Woodcock, *Anarchism: A History of Libertarian Ideas and Movements* (Cleveland: World, 1962), 453–67; and Mandel, *Gompers*, 123–34.

3. *Proceedings of the General Assembly of the Knights of Labor, Seventeenth–Nine-*

teenth Regular Sessions, 1893–95; Washington Post (November 11–23, 1895); Terence V. Powderly, *The Path I Trod* (New York: Columbia University Press, 1940), 365; Commons, *History of Labour*, 2:519 and passim; Nathan Fine, *Farmer and Labor Parties in the United States, 1828–1928* (New York: Rand School of Social Sciences, 1928), 146; David Herreshoff, *American Disciples of Marx: From the Age of Jackson to the Progressive Era* (Detroit: Wayne State University Press, 1967), 120–23 and passim; Quint, *Forging of American Socialism*, 153–57.

4. *A.F.L. Proceedings, 1893*, 42; *1894*, 10–11; and *1893–95*, passim; Mandel, *Gompers*, 149–55; Louis S. Reed, *The Labor Philosophy of Samuel Gompers* (Port Washington, NY: Kennikat Press, 1966), 54–88, 93–96, 112–130; Ira Brown Cross, *A History of the Labor Movement in California* (Berkeley: University of California Press, 1965), 224–27.

5. Herreshoff, *Disciples of Marx*, 123; Fine, *Farmer and Labor Parties*, 141–65; Commons, *History of Labour*, 2:509–20; Quint, *Forging of American Socialism*, 144–57.

6. Quint, *Forging of American Socialism*, 280–318; Fine, *Farmer and Labor Parties*, 184–96; Herreshoff, *Disciples of Marx*, 181; Ginger, *Bending Cross*, 187–215.

7. *San Francisco Chronicle* (August 3 and 23, 1893); *Cleveland Plain Dealer* (September 1 and October 17, 1894); *(Salt Lake City) Deseret Weekly* (August 25 and September 28, 1895); *Philadelphia Public Ledger* (January 26, 1897).

8. *New York Times* (July 10 and 24, 1893, and February 17 and 18, 1895); *Appleton's Annual Cyclopedia, 1894*; John D. Barnhart, "Rainfall and the Populist Party," *The American Political Science Review* 19 (August 1925), 527–40; Fite, *Farmers' Frontier*, 127–35; Woodward, *Origins of the New South*, 269–70.

9. C. W. Macune's controversial subtreasury plan was the means favored to expand the currency. Opposed by many Southerners as paternalistic, it called for the establishment of government warehouses in agricultural areas. Farmers were to be allowed to store crops in them in return for loans, in fiat currency, of up to 80 percent of current market value.

10. Hicks, *Populist Revolt*, 54–237 and 442–43; Woodward, *Origins of the New South*, 188–204 and 269; Theodore Saloutos, *Farmer Movements in the South, 1865–1933* (Berkeley: University of California Press, 1960), 69–97 and 102–52; Hackney, *Populism to Progressivism in Alabama*, 3–121; Norman Pollack, *The Populist Response to Industrial America: Midwestern Populist Thought* (Cambridge, MA: Harvard University Press, 1962); Walter T. K. Nugent, *The Tolerant Populists: Kansas Populism and Nativism* (Chicago: University of Chicago Press, 1963); C. Vann Woodward, "The Populist Heritage and the Intellectual," *The American Scholar* 29 (Winter 1959–60), 55–72; Theodore Saloutos, "The Professors and the Populists," *Agricultural History* 40 (October 1966), 235–55. See also Marion Knox Barthelme, *Women in the Texas Populist Movement: Letters to the Southern Mercury* (College Station: Texas A&M University Press, 1997); Peter H. Argersinger, *The Limits of Agrarian Radicalism: Western Populism and American Politics* (Lawrence: University Press of Kansas, 1995); Michael Kazin, *The Populist Persuasion: An American History* (New York: Basic Books, 1995); Robert C. McMath, *American Populism: A Social History, 1877–1898* (New York: Hill and Wang, 1993); Ostler, *Prairie Populism: The Fate of Agrarian Radicalism in Kansas, Nebraska, and Iowa, 1880–1892*; William Alfred Peffer, *Populism, Its Rise and Fall* (Lawrence: University Press of Kansas, 1992); Riddle, *The Old Radicalism: John R. Rogers and the Populist Movement in Washington*; Gene Clanton, *Populism: The Humane Preference in*

America, 1890–1900 (Boston: Twayne, 1991); Norman Pollack, *The Humane Economy: Populism, Capitalism, and Democracy* (New Brunswick, NJ: Rutgers University Press, 1990); William H. Riker, *Liberalism Against Populism: A Confrontation between the Theory of Democracy and the Theory of Social Choice* (Prospect Heights, IL: Waveland Press, 1982, 1988); Duncan Webster, *Looka Yonder! The Imaginary America of Populist Culture* (London: Routledge, 1988); McNall, *The Road to Rebellion: Class Formation and Kansas Populism, 1865–1900*; Theodore R. Mitchell, *Political Education in the Southern Farmers' Alliance, 1887–1900* (Madison: University of Wisconsin Press, 1987); Barnes, *Farmers in Rebellion: The Rise and Fall of the Southern Farmers Alliance and People's Party in Texas*; Shaw, *The Wool-Hat Boys: A History of the Populist Party in Georgia*; Pauline Adams and Emma S. Thornton, *A Populist Assault: Sarah E. Van De Vort Emery on American Democracy, 1862–1895* (Bowling Green, OH: Bowling Green State University Popular Press, 1982); Cherny, *Populism, Progressivism, and the Transformation of Nebraska Politics, 1885–1915*; Klepper, *The Economic Bases for Agrarian Protest Movements in the United States, 1870–1900*; Gerald H. Gaither, *Blacks and the Populist Revolt: Ballots and Bigotry in the "New South"* (University: University of Alabama Press, 1977); Robert C. McMath, *Populist Vanguard: A History of the Southern Farmers' Alliance* (New York: Norton, 1975, 1977); Muller, *New South Populism: North Carolina, 1884–1900*; Bicha, *Western Populism: Studies in an Ambivalent Conservatism*; Peter H. Argersinger, *Populism and Politics: William Alfred Peffer and the People's Party* (Lexington: University Press of Kentucky, 1974); Sheldon Hackney, *Populism: The Critical Issues* (Boston: Little, Brown, 1971); Allen Weinstein, *Prelude to Populism: Origins of the Silver Issue, 1867–1878* (New Haven, CT: Yale University Press, 1970); Thomas A. Clinch, *Urban Populism and Free Silver in Montana: A Narrative of Ideology in Political Action* (Missoula: University of Montana Press, 1970); Robert Miller Saunders, *The Ideology of Southern Populists, 1892–1895* (Charlottesville, VA: n.p., 1967, 1968); Sheldon, *Populism in the Old Dominion*: Robert Franklin Durden, *The Climax of Populism: The Election of 1896* (Lexington: University of Kentucky Press, 1965); and Clark, *Populism in Alabama*.

11. U.S. Congress, Senate, Senate Miscellaneous Document No. 12, 53d Cong., 2d sess., 1894, 290–97; Hicks, *Populist Revolt*, 238–73; Woodward, *Origins of the New South*, 258–63; and Faulkner, *Politics*, 119–40.

12. Morgan, *Hayes to McKinley*, 169–76.

13. *Washington Post* (April 14, 1894), in William Alexander Robinson, *Thomas B. Reed, Parliamentarian* (New York: Dodd, Mead, 1930), 321.

14. *Chicago Daily Tribune* (October 23, September 9 and 17, and October 8, 15, 27, 1894); *(Boise) Idaho Daily Statesman* (September 2, 26, 28, October 13, and November 1, 1894); *Seattle Post-Intelligencer* (August 24, 1894); *Cleveland Plain Dealer* (August 4 and 30, 1894); *St. Louis Post-Dispatch* (October 12, 14, 23, 29, 1894); Morgan, *Hayes to McKinley*, 180–81; Nevins, *Grover Cleveland*, 650–51.

15. "Editorial Summary," *Public Opinion* 17 (November 15, 1894), 783; *Chicago Daily Tribune* (November 9 and 14, 1894).

16. Kirk H. Porter, ed., *National Party Platforms* (New York: Macmillan, 1924), 201, 203; William Allen White, *The Autobiography of William Allen White* (New York: Macmillan, 1946), 277–78; Richard C. Bain, *Convention Decisions and Voting Records* (Washington, DC: Brookings, 1960), 153; Elmer Ellis, *Henry Moore Teller: Defender of the West* (Caldwell, ID: Caxton, 1941), 243–49; Herbert Croly, *Marcus Alonzo Hanna: His Life and His Work* (New York: Macmillan, 1912) 171, 184; Stanley L. Jones, *The*

Presidential Election of 1896 (Madison: University of Wisconsin Press, 1964), 91–157; Paul W. Glad, *McKinley, Bryan, and the People* (Philadelphia: J. B. Lippincott, 1964), 95–112; Morgan, *Hayes to McKinley*, 183–222.

17. *Washington Post* (February 23 and 24, 1893); *Chicago Daily Tribune* (August 2 and 3, 1893); *(Boise) Idaho Daily Statesman* and *New York Times* (July 13 and 24, 1893); *St. Louis Post-Dispatch* and *Chicago Daily Tribune* (October 3–8, 1893); Glad, *McKinley*, 112–117.

18. *Appleton's Annual Cyclopedia, 1895*, 265; *(Boise) Idaho Daily Statesman* (May 4 and 25, 1895); Barnes, *John G. Carlisle*, 434–43.

19. For a resume of 1895 silver conventions see *Appleton's Annual Cyclopedia, 1895*, 264–65, 268, 319, 428; Glad, *McKinley*, 118–20; *(Boise) Idaho Daily Statesman* (May 3, 1895); Nevins, *Grover Cleveland*, 675.

20. Elmer Ellis, "The Silver Republicans in the Election of 1896," *Mississippi Valley Historical Review* 17 (March 1932), 519–23; Glad, *McKinley*, 118–26; Nevins, *Grover Cleveland*, 675–89.

21. Porter, *Platforms*, 181–87; *New York Times* (July 10, 1896); Theodore Roosevelt to Henry Cabot Lodge, July 14, 1896, in Theodore Roosevelt, *The Letters of Theodore Roosevelt*, 1:547; William Jennings Bryan, *The First Battle: A Story of the Campaign of 1896* (Chicago: W. B. Conkey, 1896), 188–232; Jones, *Election*, 164–242; and Paola E. Coletta, *William Jennings Bryan: Political Evangelist* (Lincoln: University of Nebraska Press, 1964), 99–212.

22. Morgan, *Hayes to McKinley*, 241–42; Nevins, *Grover Cleveland*, 705–12.

23. Durden, *Climax of Populism*, 43, 23–119; Pollack, *Populist Response*, 103–43; Jones, *Election*, 74–90, 244–65; Porter, *Platforms*, 187–209; Bain, *Convention*, 157.

24. Bryan, *First Battle*, 315–37, 442 and passim; Jones, *Election*, 297–317; Coletta, *William Jennings Bryan*, 173–212.

25. Bryan, *First Battle*, 471–73; Gilbert C. Fite, "Republican Strategy and the Farm Vote in the Presidential Campaign of 1896," *American Historical Review* 65 (July 1960), 802, 787–806; Jones, *Election*, 276–96; Morgan, *Hayes to McKinley*, 222–42. What was to become of McKinley's silver dollar worth only fifty-three cents would have shocked the most ardent inflationist in the 1890s. In 1893 the mayor of Urbana, Illinois, placed an 1893-S Morgan silver dollar in a metal box that was then sealed in the cornerstone of the new city hall building. The coin was recovered in 1965 when the building was razed. In 1997 the value of the coin was placed between $40,000 and $75,000. *Columbus (Georgia) Ledger-Enquirer* (September 11, 1997), A2.

26. McSeveney, *Politics*, 433–34; Coletta, *William Jennings Bryan*, 173; Morgan, *Hayes to McKinley*, 521–23; Bryan, *First Battle*, 606–11.

27. White, *Autobiography*, 285; *St. Louis Post-Dispatch* (August 8, September 29, and October 5 and 13, 1896); *Raleigh (North Carolina) News & Observer* (August 2 and 11, and October 24, 1896); *Cleveland Plain Dealer* (October 18, 1896); Bryan, *First Battle*, 617–18; Coletta, *William Jennings Bryan*, 180–98; McSeveney, *Politics*, 434–37; Charles G. Dawes, *A Journal of the McKinley Years* (Chicago: R. R. Donnelley & Sons, 1950), 106, 97–110; Croly, *Hanna*, 212.

28. *Historical Statistics . . . to 1957*, 681–91; Edgar Eugene Robinson, *The Presidential Vote, 1896–1932* (Stanford, CA: Stanford University Press, 1934); Valdimer Orlando Key, Jr., "A Theory of Critical Elections," *Journal of Politics* 57 (February 1955), 3–18; Duncan Macrae, Jr., and James Meldrum, "Critical Elections in Illinois, 1888–1958," *American Political Science Review* 54 (September 1960), 669–83; Samuel P. Hayes, *New*

Possibilities for American Political History: The Social Analysis of Political Life (Ann Arbor, MI: The Inter-University Consortium for Political Research, n.d.), 46–47; William Diamond, "Urban and Rural Voting in 1896," *American Historical Review* 46 (January 1941), 281–305; McSeveney, *Politics*, 433–58; Hollingsworth, *Whirligig of Politics*, 92–107; Glad, *McKinley*, 189–209; Jones, *Election*, 332–46; Fite, "Republican Strategy," 803–7; Morgan, *Hayes to McKinley*, 517–18, 521–23.

29. Carl N. Degler, "American Political Parties and the Rise of the City," *Journal of American History* 51 (June 1964), 41–60; Hayes, *New Possibilities for American Political History*, 377–81; Morgan, *Hayes to McKinley*, 247.

A leading Italian paper, *Chicago Italia* (October 3, 1896), said that a Bryan win would entail such heavy losses to capital "as to bring starvation to hundreds of thousands of Italians in America." See Hollingsworth, *Whirligig of Politics*, 92–107.

30. Gilbert C. Fite, "William Jennings Bryan and the Campaign of 1896: Some Views and Problems," read at the Organization of American Historians meeting (April 29, 1966), 10, 17; and "Republican Strategy," 787–807; James A. Barnes, "Myths of the Bryan Campaign," *Mississippi Valley Historical Review* 34 (December 1947), 383–94; Coletta, *William Jennings Bryan*, 205; Daniel Roper, *Fifty Years of Public Life* (Durham, NC: Duke University Press, 1941), 87. Morgan, *Hayes to McKinley*, 247, suggests that Bryan may have campaigned too much in the Ohio Valley and too little in the middle border.

31. U.S. Congress, Senate, Senate Document No. 22, 55th Cong., 2d sess., 1899, 352–62.

32. Arnett, *Populist Movement in Georgia*, 156–84; Barnhart, "Rainfall and the Populist Party," 527–40; Durden, *Climax of Populism*, 143–47; Hallie Farmer, "The Economic Background of Frontier Populism," *Mississippi Valley Historical Review* 10 (March 1924), 406–27; Fite, *Farmers' Frontier*, 35–54, 210–24 and passim; and "Republican Strategy," 803–7; Hackney, *Populism to Progressivism in Alabama*, 89–121; Hicks, *Populist Revolt*; Roscoe C. Martin, *The People's Party in Texas* (Austin: University of Texas, 1933), 58–112; Nugent, *Tolerant Populists*, 35–54 and passim; Michael Paul Rogin, *The Intellectuals and McCarthy: The Radical Specter* (Cambridge, MA: MIT Press, 1967), 67–72, 109–16, and 140–44; Saloutos, *Farmer Movements*, 69–159; Sheldon, *Populism in the Old Dominion*; Woodward, *Origins of the New South*, 244–90; Hollingsworth, "Commentary. Populism: The Problem of Rhetoric and Reality," 81–85.

33. *A.F.L. Proceedings, 1894, 1895, 1896*; Mandel, *Gompers*, 152; Commons, *History of Labour*, 2:509–13; Chester McArthur Destler, *American Radicalism, 1865–1901* (Chicago: Quadrangle Books, 1966), 162–254; Glad, *McKinley*, 142–51; James Peterson, "The Trade Unions and the Populist Party," *Science and Society* 8 (Spring 1944), 143–60; Pollack, *Populist Response*, 43–82.

34. McSeveney, *Politics*, 474; Durden, *Climax of Populism*, 162; Hicks, *Populist Revolt*, 375; Woodward, *Origins of the New South*, 287.

In "Political Business Cycles before the Great Depression," Jac Heckelman and Robert Whaples ask whether "politicians attempt to boost their chances of reelection by stimulating the economy so that elections will be held in a favorable macroeconomic environment." Their investigation uncovered "only weak evidence of a political business cycle in the United States in the period between the Civil War and the Great Depression." *Economic Letters* 51 (1996), 247–51.

10

The Government Response: Cleveland Administration

*These men should not to be put in jail ... for no other reason than that
they are out of money.*
                    —Kansas Populist Governor Lorenzo D. Lewelling, 1893

The commercial, social, intellectual, and political manifestations of depression
inevitably required government action. From early spring 1893, fearful businessmen sent a growing torrent of mail beseeching the president to protect the
Treasury reserve. The coming of panic in May provoked widening waves of
anxiety and gloom. Within a month, an advertisement in a Midwestern newspaper heralded a panic clothing sale with a stark two and one-half inch lead,
"THE CRASH HAS COME." In midsummer an alarmed Charles Dawes confided
to his journal that the "number of unemployed ... is appalling." As winter
approached, worsening business and lengthening lines of the jobless forced a
belated general admission that "widespread distress" impended.[1] The eruption
of political upheavals from 1893 on, far-flung labor strife in 1894, and traumatic
social ferment throughout the era impelled people to look, even in a time of
limited government, for remedial public action. Deepening crisis demanded replies that only government had the resources to make. Responses involved every
level of public authority from local through national, and they extended from
fiscal retrenchment and relief for the jobless to controversial steps in national
finance, diplomatic measures, and innovations in national business labor policy.
    For local officials economic contraction translated into shrinking public re-
ceipts. Bookkeeping differences and difficulties of access make interpretation of

local public finances hazardous. Yet taking Baltimore, Boston, Chicago, Cincinnati, Columbus, Indianapolis, Philadelphia, Pittsburgh, and St. Louis as representative urban centers, receipts apparently at best steadied, as in Baltimore, or fell to troughs in 1894 or 1895 and again in 1897, 8 to 20 percent or more below former peaks. A prevailing determination to balance budgets forced proportionate cuts in spending, although expanded public works helped raise disbursements in Chicago, Indianapolis, and St. Louis through 1894. Retrenchment followed. Meanwhile the salary budget for certain Chicago officials was slashed 5 percent in 1894. Restrained outlays characterized some cities, including Cincinnati, Philadelphia, and St. Louis through the end of the decade.[2]

Just as revenues were declining, rising enrollments often dictated enlarged teaching staffs in city schools. However, average teacher's salaries, in current dollars, fell from 2 to 8 percent in Cincinnati, Columbus, New York, Philadelphia, and Pittsburgh—Columbus schools' adjusted pay dropped 10 percent in 1894. Annual reports of the United States Commissioner of Education—based on irregular and incomplete responses to inquiries sent to local school districts—revealed discouraging news for public education. Nationally, average monthly teachers' salaries in current dollars crept up until the 1895–96 school year, to $47.37 for men and $40.24 for women, sinking 5–6 percent over the succeeding year. Per capita annual expenditures from local funds and state appropriations per pupil of average daily attendance peaked at $18.62 in 1893–94, then fell to $18.41 the next year, and after a modest recovery dropped almost to the 1893–94 peak in 1896–97. Teacher salaries began to revive the year after and exceeded former figures only in 1898 or later.

The trend toward a longer average school term was interrupted, 1895–97 sessions falling from 141.4 to 140.4 days per year before spurting to 143.1 in 1897–98. National data obscure wide local variations, but proportionately, the less-developed sections of the country suffered most. Average sessions fell one day in the West, two in the South Atlantic, and seven in the even more educationally backward South Central states. In South Carolina they dropped to 141.5 in 1894, 106 in 1895, 93 in 1896, and 70 days in 1897. Hard hit industrial, mining, and cereal and fiber staple–growing districts, and drought or flood-devastated farm areas, were driven to even more desperate economies, with the children, as elsewhere, being the chief losers.[3]

While deepening depression in 1893 encouraged local authorities to retrench, increasing unemployment meant new demands on the public purse. Chicago estimated 180,000 unemployed—two-fifths of the local labor force; up to a hundred thousand were jobless in New York City; and perhaps 2.5 million nationally were out of work. The circumstances and unprecedented scope of joblessness undermined the prevailing tendency to hold the idle poor responsible for their own plight; they compelled recognition that most were "begging for work [not charity], and beggars in vain." Americans in the 1890s, like their heirs of the 1990s, blind to the immenseness of the poverty problem, delegated it to private charities.[4]

Public relief was confined largely to provisions (usually after an investigation and sometimes a work test) and to creating special emergency jobs. The volume of public assistance reportedly rose by 40 to 300 percent in a year in Lowell (Massachusetts), Taunton (New Jersey), Minneapolis, Detroit, Milwaukee, Omaha, and Yonkers (New York). New York City charitable expenditures rose from an average of about $1.3 million to nearly $7.5 million a year. Springfield, Massachusetts, and Boston established wayfarers' lodges and woodlots to afford temporary shelter and allow more effective work tests. Boston offered itinerants woodcutting jobs at $1.25 a day. It also surpassed most cities in differentiating between the hard-core poor and the temporarily jobless by refusing to enroll as paupers men hired to cut wood. New York, St. Louis, Chicago, Seattle, Dayton, Cincinnati, and other centers speeded public works to provide emergency employment in street maintenance and park, sewer, and other construction—marking the first extensive use of public work relief in a depression. In 1894 Mayor Hazen Pingree of Detroit allowed a thousand selected applicants to grow their own food on garden plots in vacant lots. Success was sufficient to inspire imitations in New York, Seattle, Boston, and elsewhere. Impressive as these efforts were, however, limited local resources held assistance far below need. A one-third increase in Boston's aid to impoverished families in December 1893 still reached only some 3,400 households, perhaps a twelfth of those requiring relief. The Cook County Board, at Chicago, had only a single distribution center, to which came twelve hundred applicants daily. "Waiting in line for hours, one woman was crushed to death and a man died from exposure." On extremely cold days many in need could not travel to the center.

In lieu of adequate public relief, private agencies struggled to fill the gap, following the lead of the Associated Charities or Charity Organization Societies. Spreading rapidly after their introduction from England to meet the business crisis of the 1870s, they elevated charity to a professional and scientific plane. After a work test, aid typically included supplies, loans of up to a hundred dollars "at a fair rate of interest," help in finding jobs, and temporary employment. Men were ordinarily set to chopping wood, women to sewing. After 1894 poverty and unemployment apparently became less visible, as public notice of it fell markedly, but charitable bodies continued to provide relief.

Churches, labor unions, and temporary committees tackled the emergency of the winter of 1893–94, drawing criticism from professional social workers by granting supplies or meals without imposing character or work tests. Churches raised funds or operated relief programs. Union hatters at Danbury, Connecticut, in December 1893 packed a special town meeting and voted fifty thousand dollars in unemployment relief for jobless hatters. In Chicago union pressure moved a mayor's committee to put several thousand men to work on the city drainage canal and streets. The cigar makers' union increased its unemployment payments five times, to ninety thousand dollars in 1892–93. The *New York World, St. Louis Globe-Democrat*, and other papers gaudily promoted circulation and relief by sponsoring funds for the poor. The Indianapolis Commercial Club in October 1893, after a grievance meeting of the unemployed, launched a comprehensive relief system that included operation of an employment bureau, street work, and the distribution of provisions to approved applicants. The Businessmen's Relief Committee of New York raised money to support the Industrial and Christian Alliance's seven restaurants and stores, which dispensed a million meals and food packages at five cents each. City Park Commissioner Nathan Strauss, a wealthy philanthropist, arranged for the sale at nominal prices of 41 million pounds of coal, 400,000 pounds of sugar, and 175,000 pounds each of flour and coffee, 50,000 of tea, and 400,000 loaves of bread, providing as well cheap lodging for ten thousand people, at a cost to himself of $100,000. The metropolis also boasted an Actor's Relief Fund and a hotel catering to impoverished intellectuals. Denver, Colorado, in summer 1893 added a camp for the jobless, who governed themselves through semimilitary rules until rail transport to the East was secured for them.[5]

Do state governments have any responsibility for helping the destitute? Is there federal responsibility? As always, distress collided with deficient revenues and retrenchment, and often with ideological obstacles to action as well. In February 1894 the mayor of Cleveland announced that local charitable resources were exhausted; state aid alone could meet the crisis. Yet weeks before, the Ohio legislature had spurned a state trades assembly proposal for work relief on grounds that insufficient funds were available and that such a program did not meet the requirement that revenues be expended only for "necessary" public purposes. Subsequently, Governor McKinley's 1895 appeal for gifts of supplies to aid coal miners in the anguished Hocking Valley revealed the essence of state action in Ohio.[6] A California state senator fruitlessly urged support for a system of county works, a foundation for a cooperative commonwealth. Edward Bellamy, author of *Looking Backward*, in 1894 advocated to the Massachusetts Board on the Unemployed a plan for state workshops to guarantee employment to all at a humane wage. The year before, New York's Governor Roswell P. Flower had expressed the conventional wisdom about such schemes. Rejecting as paternalistic and recklessly extravagant a works program to employ the jobless, he had observed that in this country "the people support the government," rather than the reverse.[7]

As autumn 1893 faded so did local aid for unemployed miners in Michigan's upper peninsula. They had become "practically impoverished and a charge on the public," and the governor appealed for gifts in their behalf.[8] To the west on the central plains, depression and drought struck so hard that some South Dakota counties made no efforts to collect taxes in 1894. Pleas for help brought forth money and supplies—ninety-nine rail-car loads of supplies were sent to Kansas farmers in one especially hard season. Yet more was needed. Overcoming concern that bolder steps might discourage potential settlers, several plains states governments followed precedents for direct action set in earlier crises. When rural distress swamped the governor's relief committee, Nebraska legislators appropriated $50,000 for coal and supplies and $200,000 for seed and feed. Kansas lawmakers in 1895 voted $100,000 for seed grain, to be distributed through county officials as loans. Several counties were also empowered to sell bonds for relief purposes. South Dakota solons authorized counties and townships to provide seed. Arkansas legislators in 1897 deferred tax payments of farmers in areas flooded by the Mississippi River. Louisiana lawmakers simultaneously allotted $96,000 to farmers in thirteen drought-blasted parishes.[9]

Late in 1893 Populist Governor Lorenzo D. Lewelling of Kansas issued a circular declaring his state's vagrancy law unconstitutional and directing police not to molest law-abiding tramps. Observing that he had been forced to become a tramp in 1865, Lewelling proclaimed that Kansas had "her share of 3,000,000 unemployed workingmen in the United States" and that "natural humanity" demanded that "these men should not to be put in jail . . . for no other reason than that they are out of money." It was "no crime to be without visible means of support." Tighter vagrancy laws approved in Maryland and Massachusetts better represented majority conservative opinion as to how to control tramps, especially after the industrial army movement.[10]

Staggering unemployment emphasized the need for precise social statistics. Early in the crisis, Maine, New York, New Hampshire, Connecticut, and West Virginia used sample questionnaires to supplement local and private estimates of unemployment. In 1894 Massachusetts charged a three-man commission to study the problem. Soon after, Kansas, Virginia, and other states joined in these important actions.[11] Closely related were steps taken to aid workers seeking jobs by creating or regulating employment agencies and by forming state labor or business bureaus to publish useful studies of industrial conditions. In 1893 Montana created a state Bureau of Agriculture, Labor, and Industry. During the succeeding four years troubled business conditions encouraged Indiana, Kentucky, Minnesota, New Hampshire, Massachusetts, Nebraska, Rhode Island, and Washington to institute, or extend the functions of, comparable bodies.[12]

Labor conflict, especially in 1894, accelerated a movement to adjust laws to new industrial conditions. Often measures took a repressive "law and order" cast. Alarm and anger led several states, among them Minnesota and Kentucky in 1894 and Indiana, Tennessee, and Washington in 1895, to toughen or add statutes governing interference with trains, riots, and liability for strike-caused damage. Concurrently union, agrarian, and reformist opposition to the use of military force against strikers waxed. The governors of Illinois, Kansas, Texas, Oregon, Idaho, and Colorado condemned the employment of federal troops in the Pullman boycott. Later, unionists agreed when the mildly radical editor of *The Arena* branded proposals to expand state militia forces as harbingers of Caesarism, and armories as "Plutocracy's Bastiles [*sic*]." Such fulminations bore little fruit in the face of determined opposition from the dominant conservatives.

When Oklahoma's lower house in 1897 voted to abolish the militia as an instrument of oppression, the territorial upper chamber refused to concur. There grew, nevertheless, a consensus that blacklisting, refusal to hire union members, yellow dog contracts, and similar discriminatory practices were unfair and intensified capital-labor strife. In 1894 and 1895, following the lead of other states, Indiana, Massachusetts, Montana, Nevada, Nebraska, and North Dakota initiated bans against discriminatory practices; Kansas and Colorado followed in 1897. Populist solons in Nebraska exempted unions from antitrust laws.[13]

Mounting hostility toward big business found expression in the passage of strict new regulatory measures, many of which conservative courts struck down. The *Commercial and Financial Chronicle* found it "almost incredible" that angry Nebraska farmers won a harsh maximum-railroad-rate law early in 1893, when poor earnings were buffeting the roads. Soon afterward a deadlocked legislature blocked a request of Colorado's Populist governor, Davis H. Waite, for a rate statute that would have forbidden court appeals from rulings of the state railroad commission. Lawmakers in the state of Washington enacted new regulations for rail rates for bulk grain shipments, and Minnesota extended state control of elevators before the year ended.

In 1895 Texas legislators placated militant farmers with an amended antitrust law that eased prosecution by providing, "The character of the trust . . . alleged may be established by proof of its general reputation as such." The following year Georgia closely copied the Texas act. In 1897 representatives of embattled farmers in Nebraska, Kansas, Alabama, Arkansas, South Carolina, Florida, and Tennessee legislated against trusts. Courts were often hostile and enforcement efforts lax, but at least ten more states passed antitrust acts before the end of the decade.[14]

Western and Southern state capitals spewed forth a growing stream of inflationist oratory, resolutions, petitions, and contract and financial laws of doubtful constitutionality. Kansas led off in 1893 with a law making all debts payable in silver as well as gold. Neighboring states followed, voiding exclusive gold contracts and, as did Arkansas and Texas in 1895, attacking the note issues of hated national banks. Although they were exercises in futility, such steps vividly charted the rising influence of silver inflationists.[15]

Conservative concerns for the Treasury reserve and specie payments, and Grover Cleveland's election, had assured national financial action to avert or combat the crisis even before it exploded. Steeped in cautious New York monetary views, Cleveland had opposed Treasury silver purchases during his first term. He was easily convinced that the Sherman Silver Act was the chief source of anxiety and contraction, and he was nearly persuaded by advisers to call a special congressional session at once upon resuming office in 1893, to repeal the act. However, he concluded that the time was wrong and instead quietly urged Democratic lawmakers to cooperate with Republicans seeking repeal in the last weeks of Harrison's presidency.

In his March 4 inaugural address, while promising beneficial tariff reductions, Cleveland made the financial situation his first concern. Warning that federal financial policies violated the "inexorable laws" of economics, he looked for "prudent and effective" remedial legislation.[16] Vigorous measures added millions of dollars to the Treasury reserve in March, but rising apprehension brought renewed withdrawals that carried it below one hundred million dollars for the first time on April 22. Advice poured in to the president. Andrew Carnegie proposed a public promise to defend specie payments, including a pledge that as long as Cleveland held office "the workingman is going to be paid in as good a dollar as the foreign banker."[17] Reassurances and a trip to New York with Treasury secretary Carlisle to discuss a bond issue with bankers failed to stem the tide.

With the panic, which struck in May, came insistent calls for relief. The *Chicago Daily Tribune* on May 5, and the St. Louis Commercial Club on the twentieth, led a growing clamor for repeal of the Sherman Silver Act. Cleveland was convinced that panic, bank failures, popular distress, and the June 27 announcement closing British mints in India to silver had created a favorable climate of opinion. On June 30 he summoned a special session of Congress for August 7, a month earlier than he had initially intended, to repeal the silver purchase clause of the offensive law. (A day later he underwent secret surgery to remove a malignant growth from his jaw.) The East and Northeast greeted news of the special session enthusiastically. Hundreds of newspapers praised the president—the news sent the *Chicago Daily Tribune* "LOOKING FOR A BOOM." Friends of silver met in Denver on July 12 to lay plans to seize Congress. A second, larger meeting was set for Chicago early in August. The Denver meeting issued a circular seeking Southern help and warning that if the silver law were repealed "the great bulk of us will be made paupers."

Repeal faced a perilous battle in Congress. On August 11, three days after receipt of Cleveland's forceful message blaming the country's financial ills on fears arising from the operation of the 1890 silver law, the House heard Ways and Means Chairman William L. Wilson report a bill halting silver purchases, followed by open debate. Nearly every member spoke before minority leader Tom Reed on the twenty-sixth closed debate for repeal, repeating that it was imperative to banish the distrust paralyzing business. On Monday, August 26, Wilson's generalship, Speaker Charles Robert Crisp's iron discipline, and Cleveland's determination won repeal, by a 239–108 sectional vote pitting Westerners and Southerners of both parties against Eastern goldbugs.

Unlimited debate and equal state representation, enhancing silverite power, made the Senate contest far more difficult than its counterpart in the House. Ten of twelve members from the states admitted in 1889–90, the Dakotas, Montana, Washington, Idaho, Wyoming, opposed repeal. Control of Indiana's patronage cemented the crucial support of Daniel Wolsey Voorhees, whose Finance Committee recommended repeal by a bare six-to-five vote. Silverites filibustered for two months. Kansas and Nebraska Populists William Peffer and William Allen, Tennessee and Missouri Democrats Harris and George Vest, and others spoke fiercely against the bill; Colorado Republican Teller wept at his own description of the misery it promised his state. An administration cloture attempt was lost in a thirty-eight-hour continuous session on October 11. Ten days later, thirty-

seven of forty-four Democrats broke for a compromise continuing silver purchases to July 1, 1894, and making silver certificates the sole currency in
denominations under ten dollars. An enraged Cleveland crushed the attempt, and
Southern Democratic silver men yielded. Administrative resolution and the leadership of Democrats Voorhees, Texas's Roger Quarles Mills, Kentucky's John
M. Palmer, Louisiana's Edward D. White, and New Jersey's John R. McPher-
son, with ranking Republicans including Sherman himself, brought a vote on
October 30. Before packed galleries silverites fired final, angry fusillades, then
bowed to a 43–32 repeal decision for which Republicans provided a vital
twenty-three votes. Cleveland signed the measure on November 1.[18]

The Cleveland administration's hopes that repeal of the silver purchase law
would spur recovery were unfilled. Year's end brought admissions of numbing
depression. Later, federal deficits compounded forces causing persistent Treasury gold losses. These developments and widening controversy over free silver
continued to focus the administration's response to depression primarily on
guarding the gold standard and Treasury while forcing it to seek an explanation
for continued hard times.[19]

In his December 4, 1893, annual message to Congress Cleveland remained
hopeful that repeal must improve trade. The president said little about business
conditions and stressed instead fulfilling election promises for tariff reform.
However, citing Carlisle's report of a $30 million deficit for the first five months
of fiscal 1894, he urged Congress to caution in spending "when many of our
people are engaged in a hard struggle for the necessaries of life." He approved
Carlisle's request for authority to sell $200 million of short-term, low-interest
bonds to protect the gold reserve and supply revenue deficiencies, or $50 million
of debt obligations to be used in lieu of cash for government payments.[20]

The Treasury lurched toward crisis. As panic eased, a high proportion of the
past summer's gold imports had temporarily flowed to the Treasury as customs
receipts—58 percent of September's payments were in specie. But short revenues and currency holdings obliged the Treasury to pay much of it out again,
and rising uneasiness later reduced the share of gold receipts. The reserve peaked
at only $103,683,000 on August 10, then fell to less than $66 million through
January even though currency redemption for specie for the five months ending
in January was a negligible $2.5 million. Income in fiscal 1894 was down $80
million, to $297 million. The year's deficit was nearly $70 million despite rigid
economies that included layoffs for several hundred war department and postal
workers and a 6 percent cut in spending. Dull trade and low merchandise imports
helped hold down customs and other receipts through fiscal 1896. Concurrently
spending dropped 8 percent from the 1893 level, surpassing pre-panic rates only
two years later. Curtailed expenditures and gradually rising revenues, led by a
ten-point growth of customs payments to $176.6 million (still 23 percent below
the 1890 high), cut the annual deficit to $18 million before the policies of the
McKinley administration and war with Spain reversed the trend.[21]

Vengeful silverites blocked a congressional grant of low-interest bonding authority, so Carlisle on January 17, 1894, announced the February $50 million bond sale. For weeks the issue hung in doubt. The Knights of Labor sought an injunction blocking it; the District of Columbia circuit court on January 30 denied the writ. As the deadline neared and 90 percent of the issue was not subscribed, Carlisle made a hasty trip to New York for secret talks with bankers. He probably minimized congressional opposition and doubts as to the sale's legality and may have threatened to coin Treasury silver bullion. Whatever he argued, he secured bankers' bids and saved the issue.[22]

The bonds provided but temporary relief and aggravated Cleveland's political problems. Some bidders redeemed notes to obtain Treasury gold with which to pay for bonds. Thus $24 million of $58,661,000 raised represented no gain. In June Cleveland cited a favorable shift in the trade balance and the end of silver purchases as encouraging events, but rising redemption and net monthly gold outflows of $9–23 million raged from April through July. For five months after May the reserve hovered below its February trough. Determined to uphold parity between gold and silver by redeeming in gold all notes offered, the administration could not ignore pleas such as the National City Bank's James Stillman's call for a second bond issue in November. Ten days after inviting bids, and following extensive conferences with bankers to assure success, the Treasury on November 24 sold the entire $50 million issue to a Stewart-Drexel-Morgan syndicate at 117.077, for $57,665,000. On November 26 hungry investors, lacking attractive alternatives, snapped up the bonds at 119. By November 30 a fourth of the issue had been marketed, and the syndicate had paid all but $2,665,000 to the Treasury. The reserve swelled briefly to $111 million in December.[23]

A new contest began in the House on February 7 when Bland offered a bill to coin the silver seignorage. The House approved 168–129 on March 1, with only forty-nine Democrats opposed, and the Senate soon after, 44–31. Moderates begged the chief executive to accept the bill as a reasonable compromise that might reunite his party, end the money controversy for a time, and add but $55 million to the $530 million of silver already in circulation. Warning that "our recovery being so well under way, nothing should be done to check our convalescence," on March 29 Cleveland vetoed the bill as threatening to revive the evils of the Sherman Act and agitation over money. He also pressed a reluctant Speaker Crisp to agree to recognize a motion for the previous question when the House took up the veto on April 4, to enable administration forces to sustain it. The tactic succeeded. But the cost, along with lingering bitterness over repeal and the first bond sale, was to alienate Democratic and other silver enthusiasts so hopelessly as to preclude passage of monetary reform measures for the remainder of Cleveland's presidency and beyond.[24]

As 1894 ended, demands for Treasury gold reached their depression height. Fear that the government would be compelled to abandon specie payments was the chief factor in a speculative outflow of $84 million from October 1994 to January 1895. Domestic and overseas investors liquidated bank balances and other short-term assets, and foreigners disposed of substantial holdings of railroad and other securities. The proceeds were transferred to London, even though call money and 60–90 day choice two-name paper there were ⅜ and ⅝ to ⅞ percent, as against 1 ⅛ and 2 ¾ to 3 percent in New York. A domestic gold drain that was both a cause and effect of the hot money movement aggravated affairs. Subscribers who had borrowed over $20 million of specie to buy bonds redeemed currency for gold late in December to repay their debts, adding to the pressure. January's redemptions reached $45 million, and shipments abroad $24.7 million.

Cleveland retained his conviction that a silver purchase policy violating immutable economic laws underlay the business collapse. Repeal and two bond issues had not, however, restored prosperity. In mid-November came reports that the president believed the country's currency system contradicted basic financial principles and must be changed. The new course linked government action to the broader impulse for currency reform incited by bad times, deepened political divisions over monetary policy, and reemphasized that the administration's main response to depression was financial.[25]

By the late 1880s profound criticisms of the banking system had won acceptance in financial circles—that note circulation was inelastic (contracting when interest rates rose and expanding when interest rates fell), causing seasonal stringency and unstable discount rates; that the banking industry lacked coherence; and that deposits needed greater security. Inelastic currency was barely critical in a country where 90 percent of business was conducted with checks—the supply of banknotes was important only in rural areas. National banknotes, backed by bonds deposited with the comptroller of the currency, were by nature inelastic. Banks were given 90 percent of the value of their bonds in notes. When interest rates rose (reflecting an increasing demand for currency), bond prices fell (because bonds pay a fixed return, rising interest rates force down the price of the bond to keep its effective rate competitive) and banks returned their currency, retrieved their bonds, and sold them to avoid capital losses in a declining bond market. The more bonds sold, of course, the lower the prices fell and the higher interest rates rose. Moreover an 1882 law forbade added issues for six months by banks that had reduced circulation by exchanging for bonds deposited in the Treasury legal tenders to the full value of notes retired.

The national banking laws had not created a system with central reserves and coordination but a pattern of free banking by independent units that met a few general legal requirements. Reserves were scattered, sometimes pyramided, and pyramiding was a structural problem not easily legislated away. Sound banking demanded careful management of deposits to maximize liquidity and profitability, opposite poles in the banking universe. A sound portfolio was a distribution of long-term (ten, fifteen, and twenty years), intermediate-term (three, five, ten years), short-term (one, two, and three years), near-term (three, six, nine months), and highly liquid, immediately redeemable (daily, weekly, thirty, sixty, and ninety days) investments and loans. The shorter the term the tighter the loan market. Banks had no problems putting long-term money to work in real estate and business loans, but shorter-term loans had to be vested in collateral that could be liquidated more quickly than land and factories. The nineteenth and early-twentieth-century banker had few secure outlets for money that had to be quickly available—there was no reliable market in highly liquid, short-term debt instruments.

Bankers faced the dilemma of idle funds (short-term) in one account and a shortage (long-term) in others. Real estate borrowers went wanting, while short-term funds sat in vaults. Opportunities for short-term loans were better in cities than in the country, and the larger the city the greater the opportunities. New York had the best options, because the New York Stock Exchange developed into the paramount equity market in the United States. New York banks found in call loans to brokers a highly liquid yet remunerative market. The broker secured the loans with stock, and stock could be liquidated rapidly in the active NYSE. So long as banks secured loans with stock of enough value to allow room for market ups and downs, stock-backed call loans were safe earning assets. The loans were popular with investors, too, because they let the buyer leverage the stock purchases. When New York banks exhausted their own short-term loanable funds, they turned to city banks for demand deposits to expand the call loan market. City banks directed their own excess reserves and those of their country bank correspondents to New York, where the stock market made money for banks across America. The flow of money from many country banks to a smaller number of city banks and then to larger (central) city banks, and finally to a few New York banks, shaped a triangle or pyramid—thus "pyramiding" of reserves.

The system was remunerative and workable. If a bank anywhere in the pyramid needed its reserves the call was directed up the chain to the broker who held the call loan. If the client who owned the stock held by the bank as collateral for the loan could not produce the funds on call the stock was sold and the money sent down the pyramid to the recalling bank. But what worked for any one bank might not work if many banks demanded funds at one time. If the market was swamped with stock sales to recover call loans, the market would fall. As the market fell, banks holding stocks as collateral watched, waiting to add to the sale offerings any stocks whose market value was falling and approaching the value of the loan. The chance of the stock market being inundated with collateral stock sales and collapsing under the weight increased as the margin between the value of the stocks and the value of the loans narrowed. Pyramiding remained a problem into the twentieth century, when Treasury bills and federal funds markets took the place of call loans as the primary highly liquid earning assets.[26]

Recurrent panics and depositors' losses did recommend efforts to provide greater security. Before 1890 bankers began to echo proposals of Treasury officials for sweeping change. They countered demands for free silver with plans for limited reform of note issues or repeal of laws discriminating against state banknotes. Silverites rejected the former and endorsed the latter. There were also a few suggestions for structural banking reform, allowing branching or central banking, and numerous calls for either a government guarantee of deposits or the creation of bank safety funds for that purpose.

Panic in 1893 inspired increased discussion of reform, although little was added to ideas already current. Most bankers remained aloof, but reform drew a growing corps of recruits. The Chicago meeting of the American Banking Association in October heard Comptroller Eckels advise prudent management and a revision so that banking laws would correspond to those of trade. Horace White, banking authority and financial writer for the *Nation* and *New York Evening Post*, followed, calling for the institution of branch banking and other changes. The next year Eckels and other writers warned that it was the soundness of money, not its quantity, that mattered most in any reform plan. Alexander Dana Noyes pointed out that during the 1893 crisis many national banks had hoarded funds or protected their own reserves rather than relieve the terrible stringency shackling trade.[27]

In 1895 mounting interest in reform inspired resolutions, as that of the New York Bankers' Association, calling for Congress to create a committee of experts ''to report . . . a comprehensive currency system adapted to the commercial needs and interests of the nation.'' Although reform sentiment swelled rapidly, bankers remained divided as to the proper approach. Progressives favored the divorce of note issue from the Treasury and a turn to a currency secured by the assets of banks as the best means toward a greater and more flexible circulation. Conservatives favored increasing note issues to the full par value of bonds national banks deposited in the Treasury, and special emergency issues bearing a high tax to assure elasticity.[28]

The reform program submitted to the Baltimore convention of the American Banking Association in October 1894 launched a major effort for change. New York's Third National Bank president, Alonzo Barton Hepburn, the most persistent advocate of reform during the 1890s, with president Charles C. Homer of Baltimore's Second National Bank and also Horace White, authored the plan. It proposed replacing bond-backed banknotes with an asset currency. Issues were to be limited to 50 percent of a national bank's paid-up, unimpaired capital and subject to a 1.5 percent annual tax. Emergency issues equal to an added fourth of the bank's capital could be circulated as needed, but they would bear both the regular tax and a special surtax to ensure speedy retirement. The United States was to be absolute guarantor of the notes, the Treasurer levying a yearly tax on notes outstanding to accumulate a guarantee fund of 5 percent of circulation.[29]

Favorable publicity and the interest of leading bankers in the Baltimore plan helped prompt the administration to make financial reform the core of its December 1894 legislative proposals. In the final weeks of November, although his physician advised against participation in at least three cabinet meetings because of a troublesome rheumatic foot, Cleveland plunged into cabinet discussions about banking proposals and worked on his annual message. Carlisle, who had been nurturing a plan for several years, shaped financial recommendations.[30]

Congress assembled on December 3 to receive the president's message. Despite Carlisle's belief that the Treasury's plight and the fall elections would chasten silverites and ease partisanship, the air rang with gloomy, and accurate, prophecies that the bitterly divided legislature had "not the slightest prospect" of acting on any but routine appropriation bills.[31] Cleveland's address energetically discussed Treasury specie losses and promised to defend gold payments. Required to redeem all government currency presented and to maintain parity with gold, the Treasury could not legally cancel or retire redeemed notes but had to recirculate them. The result was an endless chain of redemption and recirculation that had repeatedly threatened to exhaust the gold reserve, necessitating two bond sales to protect it and ease panic. Cleveland asked for authority to issue long-term, low-interest gold bonds to remedy the problem and increase confidence. He concluded with an unqualified endorsement of banking reform proposals contained in Carlisle's report.

The secretary elaborated the need for new bonding authority. Then, turning to the currency, he offered a plan designed to provide elasticity and a larger note circulation, safety, and to free the Treasury from the endless cycle of redemption. Clearly influenced by the Baltimore design, it proposed that national banks could issue notes valued at up to 75 percent of their capital, the notes to constitute a first lien on their assets. Issues were to be secured by a reserve of 30 percent, consisting of legal tenders withdrawn from circulation and deposited in the Treasury instead of federal bonds. The Treasury was to have discretionary authority to retire other government notes as well. An annual tax on bank issues was to create a 5 percent safety fund to redeem notes of failed banks, and all legal reserve requirements for national banks were to be repealed. State banks meeting the standards of the plan might issue notes exempt from the punitive 10 percent yearly tax enacted in 1866. Reflecting Cleveland's ideal of the "absolute divorcement of the Government from the business of banking," the plan amounted to a restatement of Jacksonian free banking principles.[32]

The House Banking and Currency Committee began to drafting a bill embodying Carlisle's ideas. The secretary on December 10 testified in a hearing that the threat of a "depreciated and fluctuating currency" had deranged business and provoked specie outflows. His schemes promised a safe, elastic currency that would restore confidence and halt gold losses. It was soon clear, however, that the program faced grave difficulty. A parade of hostile witnesses including Charles Homer, Horace White, the *Commercial and Financial Chronicle*'s William Buck Dana, Lyman J. Gage of Chicago's Chemical National Bank, and other prominent financial figures submitted statements preferring the Baltimore plan, doubting that Carlisle's scheme offered adequate security, attacking its legal tender deposit features for shifting the burden of redemption from government to banks and thereby tying up bank assets, and calling for either the funding of government note issues or their retirement. Republican committee members joined the fray, charging that the plan would precipitate a panic by forcing national banks to dump federal bond holdings on the market, or echoing press and even conservative Democratic warnings raising the specter of a revival of ''the chaotic conditions of the old state bank circulation'' should the state banks no longer have to pay a prohibitive tax on notes.[33]

The bill was reported Monday, December 17, with a minority attack attached. Banking and Currency chairman Springer opened debate the next day, and Massachusetts Republican Joseph Henry Walker reviewed the minority case. On the nineteenth Bland revealed the mood of the silver men when he announced that he planned to offer a free coinage substitute bill. After three days of debate Springer met with Carlisle to draft revisions to meet objections to the bill. He reported a revised measure on December 21 that omitted abolition of the legal reserve requirement and allowed national banks to choose to issue notes under existing legislation or under the new formula. Prospects for passage were slim. Republicans declared the measure unnecessary, that inadequate revenues under the 1894 Democratic tariff were the root of the Treasury's difficulty, and that the proper remedy was a new bond issue. When Congress reconvened after the holiday recess on January 3, Springer still expressed confidence.

Amid rumors that the administration would, if necessary to win a law without a special session, consider a compromise retiring the greenbacks, requiring customs payments in gold, and authorizing the issue of short-term Treasury debentures, House Democrats in caucus on January 7 endorsed the bill 81–59, but 75 members were absent. On January 9 the deadlocked representatives, to the professed surprise of Crisp, Springer, and Carlisle, killed the bill with a 122–129 decision against a rule to end debate and set a day for the vote.[34]

Division also doomed deliberations of both the Senate and its Finance Committee. In mid-January bimetallists blocked a Sherman proposal authorizing a 3 percent, five-year gold bond issue to protect the reserve. The impasse continued when Arkansas silver Democrat James Jones a week later offered a compromise that satisfied neither gold nor silver advocates, combining free coinage with an issue of $500 million of 3 percent ''coin'' bonds to protect the reserve, providing for the retirement of gold certificates, and allowing national banks to issue notes to the par value of bonds deposited in the Treasury.[35]

The Treasury crisis worsened after the defeat of Carlisle's plan. British, French, and American monetary authorities acted to restrain the gold flow to Europe. The Bank of England and the Bank of France in December, with ample reserves in dull money markets, reduced their prices for American bar gold. The Bank of England did so again on January 28, 1895. In December the Treasury had begun to redeem currency in lightweight gold coin. These steps tended to raise the gold export point. By late January sight sterling was $4.90, one cent above the arbitrary no-profit shipping point. However, the Treasury policy also incited near panic and hoarding that increased domestic gold holdings outside the Treasury by 10 percent between December and January, to $421 million.

Despite transfers of $29.5 million from other offices from January 12 to February 9, New York subtreasury gold fell by $7 million. On January 24 Cleveland read the famous "private & strictly confidential" Treasury memorandum that produced the February 1895 bond issue. The gold reserve was down to $68 million. A run on New York banks, which held $20 million of gold notes, could force specie suspension. Withdrawals—despite a large currency surplus—persuaded the president that a larger revenue would not solve the problem. Cleveland embodied the report's recommendations in a special message to Congress on January 28. He insisted again the problem was a lack of confidence in the Treasury's ability to pay its obligations in gold. He asked Congress for an issue of small denomination, 3 percent gold bonds to protect the reserve, redeem and retire the greenbacks and 1890 notes, and secure additional issues of national banknotes.[36]

Springer proposed a bill embracing the president's requests, but to no avail. At the end of January Assistant Treasurer Conrad Jordan in New York predicted that the reserve would last only until February 2. On January 30 Assistant Secretary of the Treasury William E. Curtis was sent to New York to consult about a bond issue. The next day he met with Jordan, August Belmont, and J. P. Morgan and obtained a tentative agreement for a sale of $100 million of bonds for gold to be imported from Europe. Carlisle, however, hesitated at the terms sought and at a private sale, and he rejected the plan on February 3. The defeat of the Springer bill on February 7 forced the administration to act. The next day Morgan, after his second trip to the capital in a week, with his junior partner Robert Bacon and counsel Francis L. Stetson, was ushered into Cleveland's workroom. The president preferred a sale by public subscription and balked at Morgan's terms of 3 ¾ percent. A telephone call from New York, though, forced him to relent; he was told that the city subtreasury had only $9 million in gold coin. When Morgan reported that Carlisle knew of one check outstanding for $12 million, Cleveland bowed to a private sale. The contract was signed that afternoon. It obliged a Morgan-Belmont syndicate to furnish 3.5 million ounces of gold, half of it from Europe, for $62 million of 4 percent bonds at 104 ½. Until the contract's expiration on September 30 the syndicate was to control the foreign exchange market to avert specie outflows. If Congress agreed within ten days to convert the bonds from "coin" to gold obligations, the interest rate was to fall to 3 percent.[37]

Congress rejected the terms. Despite furious silverite criticism, the sale accomplished its purpose. On the night of January 31, when the public first learned of bond negotiations, several million dollars of gold destined for export were taken ashore from ships. On February 1 only one million dollars actually went abroad, and the repatriation of securities from Europe slowed. As calm returned, monthly currency redemptions fell to a million dollars from March through June. The reserve passed $100 million when the syndicate made its final deposit on June 24. Through September 30 syndicate purchases of newly mined gold for deposit in the Treasury, manipulation of foreign exchange rates, and moral suasion held specie outflows to a minimum. Yet popular complaints and syndicate profits indicated that the cost was high. When the loan was offered for public purchase on February 20, hungry investors paid 110.460, or $68,833,591, versus $65 million paid the government. Half the issue was sold in Europe by overseas syndicate members J. P. Morgan & Co. and N. M. Rothschild & Sons. However, national bank purchases of $18 million of bonds first sold abroad, and changes in the contract reduced the amount of foreign gold delivered to $14,546,000.[38]

The president's stubborn defense of financial orthodoxy continued through the political upheavals of 1895 and 1896 to the end of his term. Ebbing business, then panicky new gold drains accompanying the Venezuela crisis brought, on December 20, 1895, another special appeal for power to issue gold bonds and retire the greenbacks. The House Republican majority, eager to embarrass the administration and publicize its faith that only a higher tariff would furnish revenue adequate to protect the Treasury, approved a bill advancing duties. Senate free silver substitutes, however, blocked both the tariff and an administration bond bill in February. Long before, attacks on the gold reserve had led the administration on January 6 to announce a fourth issue of $100 million of 4 percent bonds for February. By preference, and to avoid stirring popular outrage as great as that greeting the 1895 syndicate sale, the issue was let to public bidding. Enthusiastic buyers offered over 4,600 bids, enabling the Treasury to market the issue at 111.17. By March 1 the reserve had reached $124 million. Except for a brief dip after Bryan's nomination in July, repaired by concerted bank action, it thereafter remained at a safe level.[39]

In his last annual message to Congress, in December, Cleveland made a final and familiar plea for financial reform, which Congress ignored. As the close of his administration neared even his milder critics branded the president a friend of "dear money and cheap humanity." His financial policies had wrecked his popularity and his party without ending the depression. Cleveland could take satisfaction in one indisputable success: he had preserved the gold standard. No one could challenge his courage, whatever his wisdom. Moreover his struggle invigorated a movement for monetary reform that long outlasted the depression that gave it birth.[40]

NOTES

1. *St. Louis Post-Dispatch* (June 11, 1893); Dawes, *Journal of the McKinley Years*, 39–40, 43; *Chicago Daily Tribune* (November 21, 1893).

2. Annual reports, variously titled, for Baltimore, Boston, Cincinnati, New York, Philadelphia, Pittsburgh, Providence, Salt Lake City, Los Angeles, St. Louis, and Chicago.

3. Annual school reports, variously titled, for Baltimore, Boston, Cincinnati, New York, Philadelphia, Pittsburgh, Providence, Salt Lake City, Los Angeles, St. Louis, and Chicago.

4. Junius Henri Brown, "Succor for the Unemployed," *Harper's Weekly* 38 (January 6, 1894), 10; Closson, Jr., "The Unemployed in American Cities," 257; *New York Times* (January 13, 1894).

5. Leah Hanna Feder, *Unemployment Relief in Periods of Depression . . . 1857 . . .*

1920 (New York: Russell Sage Foundation, 1926), 71–188; Closson, Jr., "The Unemployed in American Cities," 456; Barnett Phillips, "Food, Fuel, Shelter," *Harper's Weekly* 38 (March 17, 1894), 255; William Alexander Platt, "The Destitute in Denver," ibid. (August 19, 1893), 787–88; Albert Shaw, "Relief for the Unemployed in American Cities," *Review of Reviews* 9 (January and February 1894), 29–37, 179–91; *New York Times* (December 31, 1893, January, February 24, and April 27, 1894); *Seattle Post-Intelligencer* (June 30, 1895); *San Francisco Chronicle* (December 2 and 21, 1896); Rezneck, "Unemployment," 324–32; Frank Dekker Watson, *The Charity Organization Movement in the United States* (New York: Macmillan Company, 1922), 248–308; Bremner, *From the Depths*, 3–85; Holli, *Reform in Detroit*, 56–73.

6. *Cleveland Plain Dealer* (February 24 and January 20, 1894); *Appleton's Annual Cyclopedia, 1895*, 623; Feder, *Unemployment Relief*, 185.

7. Rezneck, "Unemployment," 332; *New York Times* (January 3, 1894); *Appleton's Annual Cyclopedia, 1897*, 597–98.

8. *New York Times* (November 30, 1893); *Appleton's Annual Cyclopedia, 1893*, 494.

9. The most accessible guide to state action: *Appleton's Annual Cyclopedia, 1893–97*, under state entries. Also *New York Times* (November 12, 1893, February 17–18, 1895, and 1893–97); and Fite, *Farmers' Frontier*, 108–10, 130–32, and passim.

10. Closson, Jr., "The Unemployed in American Cities," 205–6; *Appleton's Annual Cyclopedia, 1894*, 458; *1896*, 457.

11. U.S. Congress, House, *Bulletin of the Department of Labor No. 18*, 55th Cong., 2d sess. (1898), House Document No. 206, 778–79; Rezneck, "Unemployment," 328–29.

12. U.S. Commissioner of Labor, *Labor Laws of the United States*, 2d ed. (Washington, DC: Government Printing Office, 1896), 666, 994–1010; U.S. Congress, House, *Bulletin of the Department of Labor No. 16*, 55th Cong., 2d sess. (1898), House Document No. 206, 500; state entries, *Appleton's Annual Cyclopedia, 1893–97*.

13. *Labor Laws of the United States*, 2d ed., 550, 354–69, 310, 1071, 1129–37; U.S. Congress, House, *Bulletin of the Department of Labor No. 13*, 55th Cong., 2d sess. (1898), House Document No. 206, 826; Benjamin Orange Flower, "Plutocracy's Bastiles: Or Why the Republic Is Becoming an Armed Camp," *The Arena* 10 (October 1894), 601–21; *A.F.L. Proceedings, 1896*, 75–76; *Appleton's Annual Cyclopedia, 1897*, 655; Rezneck, "Unemployment," 336; Lindsey, *Pullman Strike*, 261–63.

14. *Commercial and Financial Chronicle* (April 8, 1893); U.S. Industrial Commission, "Trust and Industrial Combinations," *Reports of the United States Industrial Commission* (Washington, DC: Government Printing Office, 1900), 2: 233, and passim; *New York Times* (July 31, 1893).

15. *Appleton's Annual Cyclopedia, 1893*, (Colorado) 178, (Georgia) 340–41, (Kansas) 420–23, and (Wyoming) 774; *1894*, (Colorado) 495; *1895*, (Arkansas) 30, (Idaho) 352, (Nevada) 527, (Tennessee) 263, (Texas) 719; *1897*, (Oklahoma) 297.

16. Richardson, *Messages and Papers of the Presidents*, 9: 389–93.

17. Carnegie to Cleveland, April 22, 1893, in Cleveland, *The Letters of Grover Cleveland, 1850–1908*, 324.

18. *Congressional Record*, 53d Cong., 1st sess. (1893), 25: 968, passim; Nevins, *Grover Cleveland*, 533–48; Barnes, *John G. Carlisle*, 263; White, *Recovery after 1893*, 23–35; Morgan, *Hayes to McKinley*, 451–60.

19. *Commercial and Financial Chronicle* (November 11, 1893); *Wall Street Journal* (October 30, 1893); *Cleveland Plain Dealer* (October 31, 1893); *St. Louis Post-Dispatch*

(October 29 and November 4, 1893); *Emporia (Kansas) Gazette* (November 18, 1893); *Boston Daily Advertiser* (November 6, 1893); *San Francisco Chronicle* (November 1, 1893); *(Boise) Idaho Daily Statesman* (November 3, 1893).

20. Richardson, *Messages and Papers of the Presidents*, 4: 434–60; U.S. Congress, House, *Annual Report of the Secretary of the Treasury 1894*, 53d Cong., 2d sess., House Executive Document No. 2; Donald R. Stabile, and Jeffrey A. Canton, *The Public Debt of the United States: An Historical Perspective, 1775–1990* (New York: Praeger, 1991).

21. U.S. Congress, House, *Report of the Secretary of the Treasury 1900*, 56th Cong., 2d sess., House Document No. 8; *Appleton's Annual Cyclopedia, 1894*, 261–63; *Historical Statistics . . . to 1957*, 712, 718.

22. Noyes, *Forty Years of American Finance*, 203–17.

23. *Commercial and Financial Chronicle* (June 30, November 17, and December 22, 1894); James Stillman to Grover Cleveland, November 1, 1894, Cleveland Papers, Series 2, 28, 177–78, Manuscript Division, Library of Congress; *Annual Report of the Secretary of the Treasury 1894*, lxvii; Noyes, *Forty Years of American Finance*, 231; Nevins, *Grover Cleveland*, 652–53.

24. Richardson, *Messages and Papers of the Presidents*, 9: 484; Nevins, *Grover Cleveland*, 600–603; Morgan, *Hayes to McKinley*, 458.

25. *New York Times* (November 14–18, 1894); *Washington Post* (November 10, 1894).

26. See Myers, *Financial History*, 124–28, 184–89.

27. *Chicago Daily Tribune* (October 19 and 20, 1893); James Herron Eckels, "How to Prevent a Currency Famine," *North American Review* 67 (January 1894), 50–56; Noyes, "Banks and the Panic," 12–30.

28. *Commercial and Financial Chronicle* (July 13 and October 19, 1895, December 12, 1896, January 16 and August 21, 1897); George Ernest Barnett, *State Banks and Trust Companies since the Passage of the National Banking Act* (Washington, DC: Government Printing Office, 1911), pp. 42–66; "Amendments to the National Banking Law," editorial, *Bankers' Magazine* 48 (October 1893), 241–43; John M. C. Marble, "The Best Banking," ibid. (September 1893), 217–18; C. C. Hemming, "An Elastic Currency," ibid. (June 1894), 910–20; J. C. Adams, A. K. Miller, and Hugh Craig, "Reform of the Currency," *North American Review* 163 (December 1896), 743–52; James H. Eckels, "The Duty of the Republican Administration," ibid., pp. 696–702; Redlich, *Molding of American Banking*, 2: 194–95, 208–10; Friedman and Schwarz, *Monetary History*, 117–18.

29. *Commercial and Financial Chronicle* (October 20, 1894); also James Laurence Laughlin, "The Baltimore Plan of Bank-Issues," *Journal of Political Economy* 3 (December 1894), 101–5.

30. See Carlisle to Richard Olney, November 26, 1894, Olney Papers, General Correspondence, 20: 3472, Manuscript Division, Library of Congress; also numerous letters in the Cleveland Papers including, notably, [John De Witt] Warner to Cleveland, undated, Series 2, 28,838–40. Also *New York Times* (November 15 and 16, 1894); *Washington Post* (November 16, 1894).

31. "Editorial Summary," *Public Opinion* 17 (November 22, 1894), 808.

32. Richardson, *Messages and Papers of the Presidents*, 9: 553–56; *Report of the Secretary of the Treasury 1894*, lxxvi–lxxxii. Comptroller Eckels offered a slightly different plan: U.S. Congress, House, *Annual Report of the Comptroller of the Currency*, 53d Cong., 3d sess., House Executive Document No. 3, 1:31–36.

33. U.S. Congress, House, *Notes of Hearings. The National Currency and Banking System*, 53d Cong., 3d sess., House Report No. 1508; *Philadelphia Public Ledger* (December 4, 1894); *Emporia (Kansas) Gazette* (December 11, 17–21, 1894); *Chicago Daily Tribune* (December 17, 1894); "Editorial Summary," *Public Opinion* 17 (December 13, 1894), 883, and (December 27, 1894), 931.

34. *Congressional Record*, 53d Cong., 3d sess. (1894), 232, 372–403, 545–46, 787–88, and passim; *Washington Post* (December 4, 1894–January 10, 1895); *New York Times* (December 16, 1894–January 10, 1895); "The Substitute for the Carlisle Currency Bill," *Public Opinion* 17 (December 27, 1894), 935; *Commercial and Financial Chronicle* (January 12, 1895).

35. *Congressional Record*, 53d Cong., 3d sess. (1894), 452–53, 1055, 1247–48, and passim; *Washington Post* (January 11–14, 1895).

36. "Private & strictly confidential," January 23, 1895, Cleveland Papers, Series 2, 28–29, 129–31, 912–15; Richardson, *Messages and Papers of the Presidents*, 9: 561–65; *Washington Post* (January 11–29, 1895); "From Our Own Point of View," *Public Opinion* 19 (December 12, 1895), 765.

37. Nevins, *Grover Cleveland*, 654–62; Matthew Simon, "The Morgan-Belmont Syndicate of 1895 and Intervention in the Foreign Exchange Market," *Business History Review*, 42 (Winter 1968), 385–417.

38. *Commercial and Financial Chronicle* (January, February, and June 29, 1895, and January 4, 1896); Alexander Dana Noyes, "The Late Bond Syndicate," *Political Science Quarterly* 10 (December 1895), 573–602.

39. Richardson, *Messages and Papers of the Presidents*, 9: 626–40, 659–60; Nevins, *Grover Cleveland*, 686–88; Barnes, *John G. Carlisle*, 412–16.

40. Richardson, *Messages and Papers of the Presidents*, 9: 743; Faulkner, *Politics*, 156–57.

11

The Government Response: McKinley Administration

. . . Manufacturers are "squatting behind the tariff like a lot of God damn rabbits."
    —McKinley presidential advisor Marcus Alonzo "Mark" Hanna, 1897

At his inauguration in March 1897, William McKinley identified tariff revision as the first task of the new administration. He skirted the monetary problem, promising only that it would receive early attention. Yet before the year was over there were major business and government attempts at comprehensive currency reform.

Soon after the November 1896 balloting quashed bimetallic hopes, the Indianapolis Board of Trade issued invitations for a major monetary reform meeting in the Hoosier capital in January. Three hundred delegates, mostly mercantile but including such prominent bankers as Charles Homer, attended, representing a hundred cities. When Senate obstruction and hasty adjournment at the end of the special tariff session in July prevented congressional authorization of a commission to propose financial reforms, the Indianapolis movement's leaders appointed an independent commission. Its director was eminent economist and gold standard advocate James Laurence Laughlin of Chicago. Henry Parker Willis, who later helped frame the Federal Reserve Act, served as research assistant. A preliminary report published in January 1898 won prompt endorsement from the reassembled Indianapolis convention. It recommended consolidation of the gold standard, separation of Treasury fiscal and redemption functions, authority to sell bonds to protect the reserve, creation of regional redemption centers, and largely adhered to the Baltimore plan for an asset currency.[1]

Within weeks of his election, silverites began pressing McKinley to fulfill his platform pledge to seek an international bimetallic agreement. Against the advice of conservatives, including Connecticut Senator Orville Platt, the president on April 12, 1897, named a three-man commission for the undertaking. At its head was Colorado's mustachioed junior Senator Edward Oliver Wolcott, who had already traveled to Europe in anticipation of the assignment. His colleagues, also bimetallists, were former vice president Adlai Ewing Stevenson and Charles J. Paine of Massachusetts. It was obvious by July that French unhappiness with the pending American tariff was a serious obstacle to success and that neither France nor England would agree unless the other assented. The mission ended in October when England refused to reopen mints in India to silver. McKinley, who thought the negotiation one of his "greatest efforts," was disappointed but recognized, with all save the staunchest silverites, that there was no longer any alternative to a single gold standard.

Warned that currency proposals might incite Senate Democrats and silver Republicans to talk the tariff to death, McKinley withheld a request for creation of a monetary commission until he signed the tariff, on July 24.[2] However, the administration had begun earlier to react to waxing business sentiment for financial reform with reassuring statements designed to widen support. In May Treasury Secretary Gage in the first of several such declarations told a Cincinnati businessmen's meeting that a comprehensive plan for financial reform was being readied. In December the president's annual message departed from the customary review of the work of various executive departments. Stressing that with the tariff settled "the question next pressing for consideration" was the currency, it was addressed substantially to monetary reform.

Gage's annual report as Secretary of the Treasury set out the administration's reform proposals in detail. It echoed the Indianapolis plan's call for solidification of the gold standard, separation of Treasury fiscal and redemption functions, and authorization for gold bond issues to fund a $125 million Treasury reserve. Redeemed federal notes were to be recirculated only in exchange for gold. Recognizing the futility of proposing to cancel the greenbacks or reduce monetary circulation, Gage offered a compromise formula to mitigate the cycle of redemption. National banks were to deposit $200 million of legal tenders in the Treasury, withdrawing them from circulation, and should in turn be allowed to expand their note circulation to the full par value of gold bonds received therefor. Elasticity was to be assured by allowing emergency, high-taxed asset note issues, secured by a safety fund.[3]

In mid-December the House Committee on Banking and Currency began consideration of Gage's recommendations, and in January it received a bill embodying the Indianapolis plan, but no proposal could win passage. Bankers were divided, as before, about reform itself, the degree of federal regulation needed, and the importance of security (assured by bond-backed notes), and about elasticity (derived from an asset currency). War with Spain diverted congressional attention. And adamantine Bryan supporters were in control of the Senate, where in January 1898 they forced adoption of a Teller resolution that federal bonds were redeemable in silver. An enlarged Republican majority did not pass a revised Gold Standard Act until 1900. Pressures generated in depression in the 1890s continued to ferment, maturing at last in the 1913 Federal Reserve Act. Cleveland's campaign to maintain gold payments and limit federal economic intervention by divorcing government from banking, with other contemporary proposals, resulted at length in a banking system that extended intervention by tempering private ownership with a measure of public control.[4]

The same economic verities that impelled a vigorous defense of gold payments and conservative fiscal policies, along with scruples about constitutional authority, prevented serious consideration of a federal works-relief program for the jobless or of direct national assistance to stricken farmers. After the repeal of the Sherman Silver Purchase Act in 1893, Senator Call spoke in favor of an unsuccessful movement to extend the special congressional session to allow action on the tariff and other important pending bills. He observed that serious unemployment promised a degree of distress during the coming winter "that will require consideration on the part of Congress." His argument went unheeded.

In the regular session in December Peffer offered a federal relief bill, pointing out that the time was near when new industrial conditions must make traditional jurisdictional limits unimportant where national problems such as relief were involved. He sought grants of $6.3 million in silver money for local authorities whose funds were exhausted. The bill was shelved. The following February, Bland advanced as one argument for the seignorage bill that it would provide money for public works to employ the jobless. Congress sustained Cleveland's veto of the measure. Coxey's pathetic spring trek elicited sympathy from only the handful of Populists in Congress. Two Peffer bills embodying Coxey's good-roads plan were summarily buried. So were Peffer and Allen resolutions asking the appointment of a congressional commission to hear the industrials and affirm their right to assemble at the Capitol. Allen and Ohio Representative Tom Johnson later demanded investigations of the violent police action against Coxey and his followers. Angry rejoinders and sarcastic comments about the lawless industrials, symptomatic of a repressive conservative reaction, quickly squelched both proposals.[5]

Evidently the peculiar version of laissez faire prevailing in and out of Congress allowed federal assistance for the jobless only if they could be helped indirectly by measures benefiting business. A proponent of the 1895 appropriation for naval expansion warned that the past decade's shipbuilding program had fostered a large industrial establishment: "Unless this appropriation be made, all of these industries will follow, and at least 100,000 employees will be affected, and perhaps go entirely out of employment." The following year California Republican Grove Johnson exhorted the House: "A large increase in the Navy, in building more ships . . . will give employment to thousands of workingmen and thus help the country. God knows we have too many idle men on the pavements of every city of this nation, striking terror to the heart of the taxpayer and causing sorrow to every lover of humanity.'' Both appropriations passed.[6]

Measures to deal with agrarian distress got no farther than federal work-relief proposals. In February 1895 South Dakota Senator Richard Pettigrew tried un-successfully to secure a $300,000 appropriation for seed for drought-struck Western farmers. Drought extending through the depression years also strength-ened Western interest in federal aid for irrigation farming. Nebraska's governor in an 1895 address to the legislature advised that national appropriations for irrigation works were as sensible as those for levee construction. Notwithstand-ing, federal action was confined to studies and to the inadequate Carey Act of 1894, which granted a million acres each to public-lands states if part of the land was irrigated and cultivated. Arkansas Senator James Henderson Berry spoke for those faithful to contemporary canons when he castigated proposals for federal work relief, saying, ''My idea is that each individual citizen . . . should look to himself, and it is not the purpose of this Government to give work to individuals by appropriating money which belongs to other people.'' Cleveland agreed, remaining faithful to the spirit of his famed 1887 veto of a bill granting seed money to needy Texas farmers, admonishing that ''though the people support the Government, the Government should not support the peo-ple.'' His official response to distress was to call upon fortunate citizens to aid the needy, in his annual Thanksgiving proclamations.[7]

On December 19, 1893, following weeks of preparation, William Wilson reported a tariff bill to the House of Representatives. It passed easily, 204–140, on February 1, 1894. As approved it moderately cut duties on manufacturers; placed iron ore, coal, sawed lumber, pig copper, wool, hemp, flax, and raw sugar on the free list; and pleased agrarians including eight of eleven Ways and Means Committee Democrats with an amendment laying a 2 percent annual tax on personal and corporate incomes over four thousand dollars, partly to offset revenue losses from reduced duties and partly to reform the country's regressive tax structure.

The opposition of several Democrats in the precariously divided Senate, where forty-four Democrats faced thirty-eight Republicans and three Populists, placed the bill in jeopardy. New York's David B. Hill attacked the income tax, Louisiana's senators demanded a sugar tariff, and Calvin S. Brice (Ohio) and Arthur Pue Gorman (Delaware) and others solicited higher duties for manufac-turers. Republicans joined the opposition, Matt Quay offering one twelve-day speech that filled 235 pages in the *Congressional Record*. Administration sup-porters sought compromise. A party conference accepted 408 protectionist amendments to ensure needed votes. Recalcitrants raised the total to 634, despite sordid revelations of influence peddling by the sugar trust and senatorial spec-ulation in its stock while adjusting sugar duties, before passing the bill. The president insisted on the original Wilson bill, but protectionist Senate Democrats held firm, and the House capitulated on August 13. The bill became law without Cleveland's signature. As amended it levied a 40 percent duty on raw sugar, left only raw wool, hides, lumber, and pig copper and minor items on the free list, and cut duties on manufactures by perhaps a fifth, to about 40 percent.[8] Until 1897 the United States imported more manufactures than it exported. In 1893 imports, at $365 million, were twice the value of exports, but the balance shifted as industrial exports helped spark recovery. Shipments of $485 million in 1900 were worth 40 percent more than imports, and net exports were about 5 percent of manufacturing output.[9]

Tariffs were not Cleveland's first priority. No free trader, he advocated moderate industrial duties and free raw materials to allow cheaper goods at home and more effective competition abroad. Republicans held that cheap raw materials and lower duties must deepen depression by enabling foreign manufacturers to compete in America, forcing domestic manufacturers to cut wages and production costs and thus purchasing power and consumption. Democrats asserted that excess industrial capacity underlay hard times and that foreign markets were the remedy.[10]

Protectionists hoped that settlement of the tariff would end economic uncertainty. After its passage they joined briefly with the Wilson bill's proponents in thinking that business must soon improve;[11] persistent stagnation, however, eroded optimism. Republicans capitalized on protectionist appeals in their 1894 election sweep and thereafter used the Treasury's embarrassments as a springboard for arguing that deficient revenues from a faulty tariff were the source of economic difficulty and that protection would revive industry and the economy. Federal deficits fell after 1894, and Treasury cash balances approached normal figures. But receipts that were $100 million below Carlisle's estimates for fiscal 1894–96, a third of the difference existing because the Supreme Court in 1895 invalidated the income tax, lent credence to Republican claims. Republicans ended the session by stepping up attacks on the Wilson Act in anticipation that the tariff would be the leading issue in the presidential election.[12]

In his last annual message Cleveland stubbornly if dispiritedly defended the 1894 tariff, well aware that the central position of protection in the program of the triumphant McKinley augured revision. Designed "primarily" for revenue, the Wilson Act would yield an adequate return "if allowed a fair opportunity." Moreover lower duties liberalized trade and "thus furnished a wider market for our products," while cutting living costs. Carlisle's report added, significantly, that since 1892 many American industries, mature and not dependent on tariff protection, had become exporters. The time must soon come when the United States would be the world's great exporting nation.[13]

Although the campaign had turned on the money question, McKinley moved first to tariff revision. His inaugural address emphasized the devastating impact of depression and a need for "friendly legislation" to encourage business, promising to call a special congressional session solely to raise the tariff. Congress

met on March 15, 1897. Nelson Dingley, who had prepared through the past
session, promptly introduced a bill. The House approved it on March 31. Senate
protectionists added 872 amendments, leading Mark Hanna to observe that manufacturers were "squatting behind the tariff like a lot of God damn rabbits."
Senate passage came on July 7, and after a conference committee resolved differences, the bill became law on July 24. In final form the Dingley tariff con-
ciliated Westerners by reimposing wool, hides, and sawed timber duties. It hiked
rates on woolens, silks, linens, and finished metal goods, restored 1890 levies
for China and glassware, and replaced the 1894 duty with a one-eighth cent per
pound differential tax on refined sugar while doubling that on raw sugar. The
president was empowered to negotiate reciprocity agreements cutting rates up
to 20 percent, subject to congressional approval. The new sugar and hides duties
made it unlikely that Latin American producing countries would seek agreements as they had under the more liberal reciprocity provisions of the 1890
tariff. There was little discussion of the bill's revenue features.[14]

The making of the 1897 tariff mimicked the 1894 experience. The general
manager of the American Iron and Steel Association, James M. Swank, had
earlier ascribed depression to overproduction. In a Ways and Means subcom-
mittee hearing about the desirability of reciprocal trade agreements he expressed
the prevailing business view, emphasizing the home market: "The old school
of protectionists always taught that foreign markets were to be captured by the
excellence and cheapness of our products after protection had built up our industries. We prefer the old way." National Cash Register Company officials
concurred, and a representative of the Crane Company thought it the "height
of absurdity to talk about . . . the export of manufactures" when it was not possible to supply "the home market if it is not liberally protected." Spokesmen
for Cudahy Packing, a stove manufacturer, the National Association of Wool
Manufacturers, and baling materials and bronze industries agreed, although they
advocated reciprocity. Protection for the home market subsequently dominated
full committee hearings and then GOP statements in Congress.[15]

Democratic opposition countered with free trade commonplaces. Protection
was "paternalism of the rankest character. . . . [It was] communism." It nurtured
oppressive trusts. In frustrated impotence Democrats directed mordant humor
against a free list that included acorns, ashes, asafetida, beeswax, stuffed birds,
dry blood, clay, dandelion roots, dragon's blood, fossils, ice, leeches, rags, teeth,
tobacco stems, and turtles. Yet as before there were growing, if subordinate,
pressures for access to overseas markets. Livestock, flour milling, and steel
industry figures conspicuously expressed the need for foreign markets for surplus output. While not generally maintaining that excess capacity required foreign sales to end depression, businessmen nevertheless rarely denied the
attractiveness of new markets or that industrial capacity was not 5 to 20 percent
greater than home consumption.[16]

Commercial crisis accelerated the program on naval construction that had
begun in 1883. The realization that several European and Latin American navies

could destroy America's fleet or endanger its growing hemispheric interests had inspired the program initially. Vigorous administrators carried it forward, earning industrial support by adopting a policy of using only steel of domestic manufacture. By the beginning of Cleveland's second term some three dozen modern vessels had been authorized. However, prevailing strategic concepts emphasized defense; before 1893 only four seagoing battleships were authorized.

Crushing depression discouraged Cleveland and Congress from appropriations for new ships in 1893, but the next year brought an abrupt change. The president supported Secretary of the Navy Hillary Herbert's request for funds for three new battleships and ten or twelve torpedo boats. The country, he said, now needed a navy for "offensive and defensive" operations, as unusual demand for vessels "to guard American interests" during the past year illustrated. Congress authorized two new battleships that session. In 1895 Herbert requested two more battleships and fifteen torpedo boats. The House approved four capital vessels, but the economy-minded Senate forced a reduction to three. In 1896 Herbert sought three more; Congress did not act. But Cleveland in his last annual message proudly reviewed naval progress since he had taken office. Five new battleships had been authorized; three first-class and two second-class battleships and two cruisers had been commissioned. The *Iowa*, begun in 1892, would be ready in 1897. The fleet that would defeat Spain in 1898 was nearing completion.[17]

While increasing use of the fleet underscored for many the need for naval expansion, proposals and debate centered on national honor, defense needs, and expense. Depression was mentioned most by opponents, who damned large naval expenditures when hardship urged easing the tax burden, and who ridiculed claims that a large navy was required to win needed foreign markets. Herbert and several congressmen, though, drew strength from Alfred Thayer Mahan, to whom the secretary had once written that the nation would follow his policy of using offensive capital ships to protect its expanding commerce. Mississippi Representative Hernando De Soto Money in 1895 warned that "without a fleet . . . to protect our harbors, our ports, and our commerce . . . the stagnation and decay of American industries" must attend any blockade by a belligerent power. Iowa Republican Johnathan Dolliver endorsed Mahan. He maintained that "the basis of a successful navy is a merchant fleet," adding that it was wise to support during depression the industries that the new navy had called into being. A leading senator reflected the sense of crisis born of the belief that the frontier was gone, declaring, "The opportunity for the adventurous spirit of our citizens . . . is being limited as we are settling our lands, and it is to the ocean that our children must look." Henry Cabot Lodge summed up burgeoning enthusiasm for the navy as a lever to open foreign markets with a blunt statement of an oft-quoted position that the House Committee on Naval Affairs used in its 1896 report: "Commerce follows the flag."[18]

The growing lure of foreign markets evident in business opinion, tariff debates, consideration of naval expansion, and elsewhere was a bridge between domestic and foreign affairs, reinforcing the swelling current of contemporary expansionism. Expansionism itself, of course, had always been one of the principal strands of national thought and policy. By the 1890s it combined a battery of influences. It was nurtured in part by a sense of special national mission, often tempered by humanitarian and reform impulses. A feeling of social crisis during the depressed and turbulent nineties, along with diplomatic confrontations with Chile, Italy, and England, strengthened it further by exciting nativist and jingoist outbursts. Mahan's neomercantilism, Josiah Strong's missionary pleadings, and fears that the closing of the frontier promised class or social strife unless surrogate sources of opportunity were found were added stimuli. Social Darwinism, as proclaimed by philosopher John Fiske and political scientist John W. Burgess, offered still more impetus. Fiske and Burgess easily showed that Charles Darwin's concept of "natural selection" among species applied as well to races of men, which were involved in a struggle for survival. They concluded with others, including Lodge, Roosevelt, and proponents of missionary Christianity, that the Anglo-Saxon race was destined by its proven colonizing ability and the genius of its institutions to dominate the world. Panic and depression in the nineties added an intensified desire for overseas outlets for industrial surpluses, helping push expansionism to flood tide. Although the government and people retained their usual primary preoccupation with domestic affairs, American diplomacy was catalyzed to heightened assertiveness in its efforts to extend the country's political and commercial interests.[19]

Key figures in the Cleveland administration shared many elements of expansionist thought. Cleveland, of course, drew back from the aggressive expansionism of Harrison's Secretary of State, James Gillespie Blaine, who had vigorously broadened American influence in Samoa, Hawaii, and especially Latin America. Finding a treaty for Hawaiian annexation pending in the Senate when he took office in 1893, Cleveland, aware that American residents in the islands with the aid of American naval forces and the country's minister to Hawaii had fomented revolution as a prelude to annexation, withdrew it and sent James H. Blount as a special agent to investigate the affair.

Administrative economic views occasionally contributed to restraint. In the 1894 fight for tariff reform the president scuttled Blaine's Republican policy of linking provision for reciprocal trade agreements with higher duties to open overseas markets. Two years later, in November 1896, the government promptly rejected a Russian secret proposal for joint action to organize an international wheat corner to raise prices and restore farm prosperity. Recommending against the scheme, Secretary of Agriculture J. Sterling Morton with characteristic unconcern for troubled farmers claimed that cheap wheat, reducing the cost of living, was "cause for congratulation." He added, typically, that in any case wheat prices were determined by the law of supply and demand and that it was "not the business of government to attempt . . . to override the fixed laws of economics . . . or mitigate . . . [their] operation."[20]

Yet expansionist ideas sharply challenged restraint. In arguing for the Wilson tariff Cleveland did hold that it would encourage exports. Reaffirming his 1887 claim that cheap raw materials would lower the domestic cost of manufacture, he concluded that American enterprise would thereby be enabled to penetrate new markets abroad and avoid gluts and depression at home. Navy Secretary Herbert, a forceful supporter of Mahan, won Cleveland to the cause of quickened naval expansion. Secretary of State Walter Quintin Gresham had been a lifelong Republican and even a contender for the 1888 GOP presidential nomination. Increasingly sensitive to unemployment and labor strife as serious social ills, he concluded in 1892 that a low tariff promised relief and changed parties. As Secretary of State his acute sense of crisis alerted him to the growing dangers of unemployment in a nation where "mills and factories can supply home demand by running six or seven months in the year." The answer to American unemployment, then, was expanded markets overseas, a conclusion also reached in 1895 by the newly organized National Association of Manufacturers (N.A.M.).[21]

Commercial expansionism shaped Cleveland's foreign policy and paved the way for a swift extension of American power at the decade's end. Cleveland's decision to recognize the Hawaii republican government in 1894, rather than restore the deposed monarchical regime or annex the island, enabled the United States to avoid the burden of governing extracontinental territory while retaining a favored commercial and political position. American planters dominated the insular republic. The Wilson tariff, in reimposing sugar duties, restored to Hawaiian sugar the preference in the American market granted it by an 1884 reciprocity treaty which had also given the country an exclusive right to a fortified naval base at Honolulu. Hawaii was left to ripen for annexation in 1898.[22]

The administration also guarded national interests in Latin America. Elements of the Brazilian navy revolted in September 1893, planning to win by cutting off foreign trade in Rio de Janeiro and thus vital government customs revenues. American policy, nominally impartial, determined the outcome of the insurrection. Gresham withheld recognition of belligerent status from the rebels, denying them the right to establish a blockade, and strenuously defended American shipping rights. On January 29 an insurgent ship fired on an American merchantman, and the USS *Detroit* threatened to sink the rebels. European powers, rather than challenge the United States, followed its example, and the revolution sputtered to failure in April. Events in Nicaragua in 1894 also illustrated a determination to advance U.S. commercial interests. Gresham intervened there to safeguard American citizens and trade, and an 1887 isthmian canal concession helped supplant British with American influence on the Mosquito Coast.[23]

Asian trade was not neglected. It was widely recognized that China's surprising collapse in the Sino-Japanese War of 1894–95 portended sweeping political and commercial changes in that country. The United States added five ships to its Asian squadron and offered its good offices, desiring to restore peace before commercial rivals intervened. The administration withheld aid for businessmen seeking foreign commercial concessions, but figures such as Charles

Denby, minister to China, partially offset its reticence with a consistent advocacy of greater trade. Although exports to China were a minuscule part of America's foreign trade, they trebled from 1890 to 1897, to $13 million a year, as the Cramp Shipbuilding, Union Iron, and American China Development companies and financial, railroad, and other firms became active in Asia. A leading business journal further confirmed the lure of oriental commerce with its boast that the United States "more than any other power" would control Pacific traffic.[24]

No event of the depression years better illustrated or excited jingoism and expansionism than the Venezuelan boundary crisis of December 1895. A year before, Venezuelan pleas had led Cleveland to repeat, again fruitlessly, an invitation tendered Great Britain in his first administration for an arbitral settlement. Public opinion was already agitated over British moves in the Brazilian revolution and Nicaragua. It was inflamed further as Britain aggressively pressed claims to the contested area, extending them in 1895 to the mouth of the Orinoco River. Concern moved Congress that February to resolve for arbitration. Henry Cabot Lodge in two articles attacked administrative inaction and cited the Monroe Doctrine to support a demand that the country not yield its hemispheric supremacy to colonial powers. Nor were economic pressures absent. An influential pamphlet by a former American minister hired to plead Venezuela's case appealed to mercantile interests by describing the Orinoco as the commercial key to a quarter of South America. By late spring Cleveland was ready to act, probably chiefly to uphold the Monroe Doctrine. With Gresham's death on May 28 Richard Olney, also a protagonist of American overseas interests, became Secretary of State. In July he sent a note to Great Britain demanding arbitration of the boundary controversy. Invoking the Monroe Doctrine, he asserted that "today the United States is practically sovereign on this continent, and its fiat is law." He continued that Britain's refusal to arbitrate violated the Doctrine and American interests by placing Venezuela "under virtual duress."[25]

A tardy and unsatisfactory British reply provoked from Cleveland a forthright message to Congress on December 17. Arguing that under the Monroe Doctrine "we have clear rights and undoubted claims," he requested authorization and funds for a commission to determine the border and—if the findings were contested—to enforce it. Congress shouted approval in three days, appropriating a million dollars, while the country luxuriated in jingoistic outbursts. Fortunately Britain, faced with problems elsewhere, accepted arbitration within a few weeks on the basis of a draft treaty prepared by the American boundary commission. Excitement waned, but the episode was a powerful stimulus to assertive nationalism.[26]

As the Venezuelan controversy receded, attention shifted to Cuba. Temptingly close, the island had been the object of strong annexationist pressures in the 1850s and again twenty years later. Cubans had long been unhappy with Spanish taxes, commercial regulations, and misrule. Late 1894 brought crushing depression as well—the Wilson tariff set aside a reciprocity agreement admitting certain Cuban goods to the United States on a favored basis; removed sugar, the island's major product, from the free list; and imposed a high 40 percent duty on it. Revolution erupted in February 1895. It quickly became the decisive outlet for a surging American expansionism, bringing war against Spain, with her vast overseas territorial acquisitions, in 1898.

War came months after American business had begun to recover, and its history thus lies beyond the limits of this study. But it drew on tendencies evident during the depression. Popular and governmental responses to the tragic events in Cuba, pointing clearly toward intervention in the island, promised to consummate the expansionism that developments accompanying hard times had done so much to encourage.

Americans instinctively sympathized with the rebels, who seemed to aspire to their own republican ideals. Cuban revolutionary committees in the United States sought funds, solicited support from organized labor, and wooed the press with free copy. Before 1895 ended, trade unions were resolving in favor of the rebels. The unionization of exile cigar makers was a factor in the A.F.L.'s declaration of support at its December convention. Meanwhile business, reform, and other groups arranged for a sympathy rally that drew four thousand to Chicago's Central Music Hall in September. Similar meetings were held in New York, Philadelphia, Kansas City, Cleveland, and elsewhere. Aggressive expansionists such as Roosevelt, Lodge, Mahan, Senators Platt and Allen, and the *New York Herald*'s Whitelaw Reid clamored for action. By early 1898 humanitarian and missionary impulses were moving many clergymen and religious journals to contend that the country had a moral obligation to end the savagery in Cuba. Some papers stressed that the Spanish monarchy was a "political anachronism," whose ownership of Cuba jeopardized basic American political, strategic, and economic concerns. Sensational New York dailies, especially the *World Journal* and *Herald*, distributing over wire services dispatches from correspondents in Cuba, helped excite a uniformity of opinion seldom attained in comparable past crises. Exaggerated reports of Spanish villainy and atrocities inflamed popular emotions.

Many agrarian radicals in Congress favored war with Spain in the hope that it would be necessary to coin silver to meet resultant expenses. Business opinion formed slowly. American investors in Cuba opposed recognition of rebel insurgency, fearing that it would absolve Spain of responsibility for protection of American property there. Business hung between fear that international crisis might renew depression and recognition of an expansionist potential. The time could come—and did in 1898—when protection of American trade or property in Cuba might require action, or when war would seem preferable to endless uncertainty. Thus nearly irresistible pressures were building for intervention long before war finally broke out.[27]

Cleveland and Olney pursued a cautious course toward the Cuban conflict, wishing to avoid direct intervention while protecting American interests. In June 1895 the president announced a policy of neutrality. Subsequently, mounting and well organized public sympathy for Cuba, and the bloody progress of the insurrection, eroded Cleveland's position. Every congressional session through the outbreak of the Spanish-American War produced a rush of pro-Cuba resolutions, which the administration resisted with growing difficulty. Early in 1896 the Senate overwhelmingly approved a resolution offered by Morgan of Alabama that called for recognition of Cuban belligerency. In the debates Lodge eagerly declared that a free Cuba meant ''a great market to the United States,'' and Vest added that failure to act would betray America's destiny. The House approved a resolution calling for ''intervention if necessary,'' 262–17, before accepting a milder concurrent substitute.[28]

In April the administration shifted. Still hopeful for a settlement combining Spanish sovereignty with Cuban autonomy, it doubted Spain's ability to subdue the rebels and feared anarchy if Spain should withdraw. Olney sent Spain an offer to mediate the war. Spain declined, replying that the matter was an internal affair. In his December message Cleveland, certain that Spain could not win and doubtful that the rebels could govern, edged closer to intervention. He rejected recognition of Cuban independence or belligerency, or intervention, for the present. However, after rehearsing the struggle and American investments and trade in Cuba, he warned that the time could come when a wish to avert the complete devastation of the island ''will constrain our Government to such action as will subserve the interests thus involved . . . and promise to Cuba . . . the blessings of peace.'' Olney's report, after illustrating the strength of American interest in Cuba by estimating investments there at an (overstated) $50 million, also suggested that the country's policy might soon have to change.

Although the 1896 Republican platform had spoken at length and sympathetically about Cuba, McKinley tried to follow Cleveland's course of seeking a peaceful outcome for the revolution. At the same time, he stiffened demands for reform in the troubled island. By early 1898 inadequate Spanish responses and rising domestic militancy and expansionism had brought the country to the brink of war and a swift fulfillment of hopes for the acquisition of far-flung overseas markets and territories. After the mysterious sinking of the battleship *Maine* in Havana harbor, a crystalization of business opinion, and other events, war was declared in April.[29]

Depression shock waves spread beyond foreign affairs. Intensifying popular antagonism toward big business appeared in congressional debates, influenced monetary measures and the tariff, complicated consideration of proposals eventuating in the 1898 federal bankruptcy law, and inhibited the legalization of railroad pooling. Agrarian radicals, with Populists in the fore, offered an unremitting barrage of proposals to tighten antitrust laws, expedite prosecution of violators, regulate or forbid shipment in interstate commerce of trust property or products, void trust-held patents, and deny tariff protection to trusts.[30] Mounting ire toward railroads, especially after the Pullman conflict, won similar expression as radicals pushed for government ownership, tighter control, regulation of sleeping car companies, expanded state regulatory authority, and investigation of railroad traffic associations.[31]

The same spirit obstructed congressional approval of plans for settling the Central and Union Pacific subsidy debts to the government after the Union Pacific entered receivership in October 1893. Between December 1893 and January 1897 Congress rejected several plans offered by reorganization committees. Radicals advocated government ownership, conservatives wanted to divorce the Union Pacific from the government by extending the road's mortgage at low interest or allowing it to issue securities to raise funds to pay the mortgage, and moderates sympathized with a proposal to give the government a majority on the Union Pacific board of directors and use a federal bond issue to retire the company's debts and provide working capital. Cleveland, despairing of congressional action, opened direct negotiations with the current reorganization committee. It was decided to sell the Union Pacific in foreclosure, the committee agreeing to bid at least $47,754,000 to satisfy federal claims against the property. Arrangements were perfected after McKinley took office. The road was sold at a series of foreclosure sales beginning in November 1897. The government received all principal and interest due until October 1, 1897 ($74,591,046), and the Union Pacific was afterward reorganized.[32]

Finally government had to contend with the unprecedented industrial warfare and dismaying marches of the unemployed that accompanied shrinking trade, falling wages and employment, and rising labor militancy. The crisis cut in two directions, both important. It provoked a definition of the basis of a national railroad strike policy and efforts to ameliorate industrial relations. Concurrently, with fearful contemporary class and political tensions, it sharpened a conservative reaction.

Federal action focused on the railroads, whose size, crucial role in interstate commerce (where there was clear government regulatory authority under the Constitution), and political influence made strikes emergencies with serious national implications. Government intervention dated from the first great rail strike in 1877, when troops quelled turmoil and enforced court orders against interference with mail shipments, rail property, and traffic. But interest receded between emergencies, and despite a proliferation of proposals, there was no agreement on how to meet the problem. Thus no national strike policy developed before the 1890s. By default local federal courts, often presided over by frightened antilabor judges, were left to draft legal guidelines for dealing with rail strikes.

Following recent precedents courts turned to the injunction as the first line of defense against labor unrest. In doing so they merged two streams of jurisprudence: the power of courts of equity to enjoin a nuisance and prevent irreparable injury to property, and the common law of conspiracy as used at the time, which held punishable as crimes combinations effected for unlawful purposes or to attain even lawful ends by illegal means. Neither stream by itself was sufficient.

The law could act against criminal conspiracies only after the fact, juries were fickle, and it was impractical to try large numbers of strikers on criminal charges. Equity courts could enjoin threatened acts and try violators in summary contempt proceedings conducted by judges without juries, but equity jurisdiction obtained only if threatened acts were wrong at law and admitting of suits for damages. A connection, allowing an equity court to enjoin a threatened strike, was possible if it could be shown that the impending outbreak was unlawful. In the 1890s federal courts found in the Interstate Commerce and Sherman Antitrust acts tools to broaden the scope of the unlawful and in turn the list of enjoinable offenses, to include strikes disrupting interstate commerce.

Judges William Howard Taft of the Sixth Circuit Court and Augustus J. Ricks of the Northern District Court of Ohio in the spring of 1893 helped set the direction of legal development with pivotal rulings in cases arising from a locomotive engineers' strike. Upholding injunctions against a boycott of traffic from a struck railroad, Taft recognized the right to strike. However, businessmen learned with satisfaction, the boycott had worked "criminal and unlawful injury" to the struck road, for the Interstate Commerce Act required common carriers to accept traffic from one another without discrimination. Ricks dealt with the question of contempt. He admitted that railroad employees were free to quit their jobs outright. But those who merely pretended to quit, so as to effectuate the boycott, by violating an injunction against an illegal conspiracy, became guilty of contempt.[33]

Catastrophic railroad failures that resulted in court-protected receiverships, and rapidly spreading strikes, provoked increasing litigation during the depression. In December 1893 Judge James Jenkins of the Seventh Circuit Court upon petition from receivers of the Northern Pacific authorized wage cuts and issued an injunction. Later he issued even more sweeping orders forbidding employees from "combining and conspiring to quit with or without notice," jointly or singly, from striking, from hindering operations, and from interfering with replacement workers. On April 6, 1894, Jenkins upheld his own writs, arguing that strikes were necessarily violent and that it was the duty of courts to restrain the warring factions of society. Duty to the public tempered the liberty of contract of railroad employees, and in extreme cases a court could order performance of a particular service to prevent a threatened injury to property or public rights.[34] An appeal a few weeks later clarified the right of individuals to quit work, when it was ruled that an injunction could not force a person to labor unwillingly, in involuntary servitude. Strikes were legal, but only as long as they were not conspiracies intended to injure railroad property.[35]

Concurrently the advent of Coxeyism and a strike on the Great Northern drew the Cleveland administration into the maelstrom of labor strife. In responding, the administration, even less friendly toward labor unions than most administrations of the era, perfected measures later used to combat the Pullman upheaval. By the end of April Olney had found a formula for dealing with train-stealing contingents of the industrial armies. After the industrials had violated injunctions issued to guard railroads in receivership under federal court protection, and United States marshals had reported that insurrection prevented them from executing court orders in the ordinary manner, federal troops were dispatched under Section 5298 of the Revised Statutes of the United States. The Great Northern's James J. Hill, meanwhile, failed to secure troops to crush a strike. But the Solicitor General did issue a ruling that any interference with any train carrying mail was illegal.

When the American Railway Union launched its great effort, Olney added only a reluctant use of the Sherman Antitrust Act to the means of resistance already at hand. Olney did not enforce the 1890 trust law with any vigor. During Cleveland's second term only eight antitrust suits were initiated, half of them against labor leaders. Determined to crush the Pullman strike at its center in Chicago, Olney sought injunctions under the Sherman Act and used the army as well. The court orders obtained July 2, 1894, forbade striker interference with the movement of mail and with railroad operations in interstate commerce. Instructions to deploy troops soon after were couched in similar terms. In December, in sentencing strike leader Debs to six months in prison for violating the injunction, Judge William A. Woods upheld the writ on the basis that the boycott was an illegal conspiracy in restraint of interstate commerce under the Sherman Act. In May 1895 the Supreme Court ruled on the case on appeal, holding that the strike was enjoinable because it interfered with the federal mails. Furthermore, Congress in passing the Interstate Commerce Act had conferred on the United States the duty of protecting the free flow of interstate traffic. The government could use its full power, including court orders and military force, to that end.[36]

Conservative jurists opposed other manifestations of radicalism as well. In doing so they speeded a process, under way for a decade, that forged the basis for the advanced judicial supremacy and obstructionism that so often thwarted reform efforts in the 1920s and '30s. In 1895 the Supreme Court dismissed proceedings against the sugar trust, thereby gutting the Sherman law and frustrating the intent of Congress. It solemnly intoned that the trust act forbade only combinations in restraint of interstate trade, while the defendants were engaged in sugar manufacturing, which bore "no direct relation to commerce."[37] The court defined commerce so narrowly as to restrict the Sherman law practically to the railroads, but it was not until the Trans-Missouri freight case two years later that it even applied the statute to the railroads and ordered the dissolution of a traffic association.[38] Meanwhile the justices determinedly overrode both Congress and the executive branch by striking down the 1894 income tax. But political dissent and clamorous pressures for change ultimately won a sixteenth constitutional amendment permitting an income tax, in 1913. Not until its Trans-Missouri judgment did the court hearten proponents of change, pervasive hostility toward railroad and other combinations stimulating general satisfaction with the ruling and a hope that it portended a revitalization of the trust law.[39]

Cleveland's and Olney's actions during the Pullman crisis established the principle that a nationwide rail strike would not be tolerated. The administration soon afterward began to move away from a policy of suppression. By September 1894 Olney had severed connections with several railroads, endorsed arbitration to settle labor disputes, and acknowledged the right to unionize. In the meantime Cleveland had selected Commissioner of Labor Carroll D. Wright to head a commission to investigate and report on the conflict. The commission heard witnesses throughout the summer and released its findings early in November. It assigned blame for the tragedy to all concerned. Pullman had been unreasonable and stubborn, the A.R.U. foolish for admitting manufacturing workers to membership, the General Managers' Association "arrogant and absurd" in refusing to bargain with the union, and the Justice Department wrong in deputizing railway employees. To avoid a repetition the commission proposed recognition of unions, banning contracts forbidding union membership, and compulsory arbitration.[40] The House Judiciary Committee investigated the Northern Pacific injunctions, concluded that Judge Jenkins had the authority to issue the writs, but recommended censure.[41]

Agitation continued after the boycott was subdued. In his first term Cleveland supported the 1888 law that permitted federal investigation of railway labor controversies and empowered the president to appoint the Chicago strike commission six years later. The strike commission's report reinforced swelling reform sentiment. The Chicago Civic Federation called an arbitration congress for November 13–14, 1894. Attended by such luminaries as Samuel Gompers, Lyman Gage, Carroll Wright, and Henry C. Adams of the Interstate Commerce Commission, it framed resolutions advocating a wider adoption of arbitration in labor disputes. Before the end of the depression at least eight states provided for voluntary arbitration.[42] With the approval of Cleveland, Olney helped revise for submission to Congress a voluntary arbitration bill drafted by Carroll Wright. It was considered early in 1895, passing the House after one day's debate only to expire in the Senate at the end of the session.[43]

The Debs decision, months later, provoked a new outcry from labor and agrarians. The "hand of the federal government," it was charged, had "been raised to crush labor." The *American Federationist* in June termed the ruling the "worst ever made by such a court, so far as the interests of labor are concerned." After noting how recent injunctions and contempt actions had restricted labor's freedom, the *Federationist* added, "By reason of the supreme court's decision, federal judges can now issue any kind of injunction restraining men from doing anything, and then rob them of their liberty, after going through the farce of trying them for contempt before the same judge issuing the injunction."

The A.F.L. launched a campaign to limit the use of injunctions and guarantee jury trials in contempt proceedings initiated under them. In response to public sentiment the 1896 Democratic platform denounced "government by injunction" as a "new and highly dangerous form of oppression" and called for legislation to curb the abuse.[44] Pressure for change bore fruit in May 1898 with passage of the Erdman Act and creation of the United States Industrial Commission. Designed to investigate industrial conditions, business combination, and relations between capital, labor, and agriculture, the commission was to recommend legislation as suggested by its findings, particularly to harmonize rival economic interests. Its nineteen-volume report, published 1900–1902, is an invaluable source of information about the national economy at the turn of the century.[45]

The Erdman Act was modelled on the Wright-Olney proposals. It authorized federal mediation and voluntary arbitration in railroad labor contests, made arbitral awards enforceable in equity proceedings and binding for one year, outlawed blacklists and contracts banning union membership in the railroad industry, and forbade the use of injunctions against individual workingmen. With its approval the first phase of the evolution of federal railroad strike policy ended. It solidified the principle that great railroad strikes were national emergencies not to be tolerated. Repression, however, had approached its limits in the savage Chicago fight. The Erdman law, to avert a repetition of the agonies of 1894, pointed away from suppression and toward amelioration. The government still dealt more with the symptoms than the causes of industrial strife, and prevailing opinion still inclined to favor the rights of property over those of labor. But depression experiences with labor disputes of railroads, which led in the process of industrialization, held lessons and precedents that were applied repeatedly during the twentieth century.[46]

NOTES

1. Richardson, *Messages and Papers of the Presidents*, 10:11–19; [James Laurence Laughlin], *Report of the Monetary Commission of the Indianapolis Convention* (Indianapolis: Hollebeck Press, 1900), 1–74; *Commercial and Financial Chronicle* (December 5, 1896, January 16 and August 21, 1897); Frederick A. Cleveland, "The Final Report of the Monetary Commission," *Annals of the American Academy of Political and Social Science* 13 (January 1899), 31–56; Charles Newell Fowler, "Financial and Currency Reform Imperative," *Forum* 22 (February 1897), 713–21; William Alfred Peffer, "The Cure for a Vicious Monetary System," ibid., 722–30; and "The Report of the Indianapolis Monetary Commission," *Public Opinion* 24 (January 13, 1898), 37–39.

2. William McKinley to John Hay, July 27, 1897, Hay Papers, Library of Congress, cited, with work of the commission, in H. Wayne Morgan, *William McKinley and His America* (Syracuse, NY: Syracuse University Press, 1963), 281–86; Richardson, *Messages and Papers of the Presidents*, 10:25–26.

3. Richardson, *Messages and Papers of the Presidents*, 10:27; *Annual Report of the Secretary of the Treasury 1897*, lxxii–lxxvi; Morgan, *McKinley and His America*, 286–87; *Commercial and Financial Chronicle* (June 5 and July 31, 1897).

4. Administration currency bills (H. R. 5181, 10289): *Congressional Record*, 55th Cong., 2d sess., 234, 4828, 6020, 6291; Indianapolis bill (H. R. 5855) in ibid., 413; U.S. Congress, House Report No. 1575, 55th Cong. 2d sess.; *New York Times* (December 16–18, 1897, May 16 and June 16, 1898). Teller resolution, *Congressional Record*, 55th

Cong., 2d sess., 311, 717, 788–1231, 1308. See also Alfred L. Ripley, "Two Plans for Currency Reform,"*Yale Review* 7 (May 1898), 50–71; James Laurence Laughlin, *The Federal Reserve Act: Its Origin and Problems* (New York: Macmillan, 1933), 3; Henry Parker Willis, *The Federal Reserve* (Garden City, NY: Doubleday, Page, 1917), 24–25; Redlich, *Molding of American Banking*, 2:208–9; Friedman and Schwartz, *Monetary History*, 118–19; Morgan, *McKinley and His America*, 286–87.

5. *Congressional Record*, 53d Cong., 1st sess., 3, 11–12; ibid., 53d Cong., 2d sess., 321, 385–88, 2435, 2752, 3076, 4442, 4562.

6. *Congressional Record*, 54th Cong., 1st sess., 2307, 3248.

7. *Congressional Record*, 53d Cong., 2d sess., 979; Richardson, *Messages and Papers of the Presidents*, 8:557–78, 9:433, 511, 593, 695–96, 677–79; Wallace Stegner, *Beyond the Hundredth Meridian: John Wesley Powell and the Second Opening of the West* (Boston: Houghton Mifflin, 1962), 294; White, *Recovery after 1893*, 36–43; Sproat, *Best Man*, 143–68.

8. *New York Times* (November 11, 28, 29, 1893, and January 26, 1894); George Tunnell, "The Legislative History of the Second Income Tax," *Journal of Political Economy* 3 (June 1895), 311–37; Nevins, *Grover Cleveland*, 563–88.

9. White, *Recovery after 1893*, 57–71; La Feber, *New Empire*, 159–72; *Historical Statistics . . . to 1957*, 544–45.

10. Faulkner, *Politics*, 157–62.

11. *Commercial and Financial Chronicle* (August 18, 1894); *Boston Daily Advertiser* (August 16, 1894); *St. Louis Post-Dispatch* (January 1, April 22, and August 16–23, 1894); *Raleigh (North Carolina) News & Observer* (February 2 and October 20, 1894); *Cleveland Plain Dealer* (April 30, 1894); "The Tariff Bill Passed," *Public Opinion* 17 (August 23 and September 6, 1894), 485–89.

12. *Congressional Record*, 53d Cong., 3d sess., 1503, 1580, 1797; *Congressional Record*, 54th Cong., 1st sess., 308, 456, 460, 484, 1267, 6441, and passim.

13. Richardson, *Messages and Papers of the Presidents*, 9:741; *Annual Report of the Secretary of the Treasury 1896*, lxxi–xcii.

14. Morgan, *McKinley and His America*, 278; Frank W. Taussig, *Tariff History of the United States*, 7th ed. (New York: G. P. Putnam's Sons, 1923), 322–60; James Laurence Laughlin and H. Parker Willis, *Reciprocity* (New York: Baker & Taylor, 1903), 177–307.

15. U.S. Congress, House, *Reciprocity and Commercial Treaties*, 54th Cong. 1st sess., 1895, House Report No. 2263, 470, 420, 357–59, 393, 171, 394, 461; ibid., *Tariff Hearings*, 54th Cong., 2d sess., 1896, House Document No. 338, 1:174–83, 2:212, 1240, 1334, 1368, 1602, and passim.

16. The strongest enthusiasm for foreign markets came from industries long dependent on overseas sales; iron was an important newcomer whose claims related to the current economic transformation. *Congressional Record*, 54th Cong., 1st sess., 308, 456, 460, 484, 1267, 6441, and passim. *Congressional Record*, 55th Cong., 1st sess., 175, 177, passim; U.S. Congress, *Reciprocity and Commercial Treaties*, 54th Cong., 1st sess., 1895, House Report No. 2263, 178, 321, 472, 442, 387, 414, 193, 428, 372, 395; *Tariff Hearings*, 54th Cong., 2d sess., 1896, House Document No. 338, 1:481, 174–83, 642–66, 801, 2:1840; *Proposed Revision of Tariff*, 55th Cong., 1st sess., 1897, House Report No. 1.

17. Richardson, *Messages and Papers of the Presidents*, 9:434, 540, 541, 640, 732; U.S. Congress, *Annual Reports of the Secretary of the Navy*, 1893, 53d Cong., 2d and

3d sess., 1894, House Executive Document No. 1, Part 3; *Annual Reports of the Secretary of the Navy, 1893–96*, 54th Cong., 1st and 2d sess., 1895–96, House Document No. 3; also Robert Seager II, "Ten Years before Mahan: The Unofficial Case for the New Navy, 1880–1890," *Mississippi Valley Historical Review* 40 (December 1953), 491–512; Harold and Margaret Sprout, *The Rise of American Naval Power, 1776–1918* (Princeton, NJ: Princeton University Press, 1939), 165–222.

18. *Congressional Record*, 53d Cong., 3d sess., 2242, 2252, 2249, 3045, 3107; also 54th Cong., 1st sess., 3141–3257, 3277, 4456; 2d sess., 2066, 2113; U.S. Congress, 53d Cong., 3d sess., House Report No. 1675 and Senate Report No. 1020; 54th Cong., 1st sess., House Report No. 3009 and Senate Report No. 1556; La Feber, *New Empire*, 58–60, 229–41.

19. Albert Katz Weinberg, *Manifest Destiny* (Baltimore: Johns Hopkins Press, 1935); Richard Hofstadter, *Social Darwinism in American Thought, 1860–1915* (Philadelphia: University of Pennsylvania Press, 1945), and *Paranoid Style in American Politics*, 145–62; Thomas J. McCormick, *China Market* (Chicago: Quadrangle Books, 1967), 21–52; Faulkner, *Politics*, 213–18; La Feber, *New Empire*, 1–149.

20. Quotes, Morton to Richard Olney, November 5, 1896, in J. D. Whelpley, "An International Wheat Corner," *McClure's Magazine* 15 (August 1900), 363–68; White, *Recovery after 1893*, 144–46.

21. Gresham to Judge Charles E. Dyer, May 2, Gresham to Colonel John S. Cooper, July 26, both 1894, Letterbook Gresham Papers, Manuscript Division, Library of Congress; *Annual Report of the Secretary of the Treasury 1894*, lxxxii–lxxxiii; U.S. Congress, *Notes of Hearings. The National Currency and Banking System*, 53d Cong., 3d sess., 1894, House Report No. 1508, 5.

22. *Papers Relating to the Foreign Relations of the United States, 1894* (Washington, DC: Government Printing Office, 1895), 358 and Appendix II; Nevins, *Grover Cleveland*, 549–62; Julius W. Pratt, *Expansionists of 1898* (Chicago: Quadrangle Books, 1964), 1–200; La Feber, *New Empire*, 203–9.

23. *Foreign Relations, 1894*, 115, 120, 234–336, and 433–80.

24. Ibid., 95–179 and Appendix I, 5–106; *Foreign Relations, 1895*, 1:87–203; *Commercial and Financial Chronicle* (August 18, 1894); McCormick, *China Market*, 53–89; and La Feber, *New Empire*, 210–29, 300–311.

25. Quotes, Olney to Thomas F. Bayard, July 20, 1895, *Foreign Relations, 1895*, I: 558, 562; Nelson M. Blake, "Background of Cleveland's Venezuelan Policy," *American Historical Review* 47 (January 1942), 259–77; and La Feber, *New Empire*, 243–70.

26. Quote, Richardson, *Messages and Papers of the Presidents*, 9:655; *Foreign Relations, 1895*, 1:563–76, *1896*, 240–55; Nevins, *Grover Cleveland*, 64; Ernest R. May, *Imperial Democracy* (New York: Harcourt, Brace & World, 1961), 33–65; Samuel Flagg Bemis, *A Diplomatic History of the United States*, 4th ed. (New York: Holt, Rinehart and Winston, 1960), 415–22.

27. Pratt, *Expansionists*, 279–316, 230–78; Charles W. Auxier, "Middle Western Newspapers and the Spanish-American War," *Mississippi Valley Historical Review* 26 (March 1940), 525; Joseph E. Wisan, *The Cuban Crisis as Reflected in the New York Press* (New York: Columbia University Press, 1934), 21–38 and passim; *Commercial and Financial Chronicle* (March 21 and December 26, 1896, and January 1, 1898); La Feber, *New Empire*, 285–300, 370–79; *A.F.L. Proceedings, 1895*, 81; May, *Imperial Democracy*, 69–82; Faulkner, *Politics*, 223–30; Ray Allen Billington, "The Origins of Middle Western Isolationism," *Political Science Quarterly* 60 (March 1945), 44–49.

28. *Foreign Relations, 1895*, 1194–95; Richardson, *Messages and Papers of the Presidents*, 9:636; *Congressional Record*, 54th Cong., 1st sess., 1065–3541, 3628.

29. Richardson, *Messages and Papers of the Presidents*, 9:716–22; *Foreign Relations, 1896*, lxxx–lxxxvii, 582, 846; *1897*, 540–47; *1898*, 558–78; *Congressional Record*, 54th Cong., 2d sess., 39, 326, 1118, 1151, 1612, and passim; La Feber, *New Empire*, 290–300, 333–406 and passim; Pratt, *Expansionists*, 317; May, *Imperial Democracy*, 78; Nevins, *Grover Cleveland*, 713–19; Walter Millis, *The Martial Spirit* (Boston: Houghton Mifflin, 1931), 1–145; H. Wayne Morgan, *America's Road to Empire* (New York: Wiley, 1965); and Morgan, *McKinley and His America*, 326–78.

30. *Congressional Record*, 53d Cong., 1st sess., 666, 1272, 1274, 1496, 1700; 2d sess., 11, 819, 6607, 7609, 8010; 3d sess., 193, 231, 234, 310; 54th Cong., 1st sess., 22, 27, 98, 192, 606; 2d sess., 38, 1603, 2591; 55th Cong., 1st sess., 21, 421, 425, 562, 2198; 2d sess., 13, 192, 319, 1604, 4688.

31. Ibid., 53d Cong., 2d sess., 6923, 6979, 7082, 7399, 7663; 3d sess., 16; 54th Cong., 1st sess., 286, 810, 1270, 1573; 2d sess., 40; 55th Cong., 1st sess., 91, 2303; 2d sess., 255, 3821.

32. *Congressional Record*, 54th Cong., 2d sess., 554, 573, 581, 596; *Commercial and Financial Chronicle* (June 15 and October 19, 1895; January 30, March 20, and October 30, 1897; and January 1, 1898); *Wall Street Journal* (January 7–12, 1897); Campbell, *Reorganization of the American Railroad System*, 233–55.

33. *Toledo, A[nn] A[rbor] & N[orthern] M[ichigan] Ry. Co. v Pennsylvania Co., et al.*, 54th Fed., 740–43, 746 (1893); *Commercial and Financial Chronicle* (April 8, 1893); Commons et al., *History of Labour*, 2:501–9; Felix Frankfurter and Nathan Greene, *The Labor Injunction* (New York: Macmillan, 1930); Edwin E. Witte, *The Government in Labor Disputes* (New York: McGraw-Hill, 1932); P. F. Brissenden, "The Labor Injunction," *Political Science Quarterly* 48 (September 1933), 413–50; also *Appleton's Annual Cyclopedia, 1894*, 262; *1895*, 262, 265; *1896*, 373; and Frederick Jessup Stimson, "Democracy and the Laboring Man," *Atlantic Monthly* 80 (November 1897), 605–19.

34. *Farmers' Loan & Trust Co. v N. P. R. Co.*, 60 Fed. 803 (1894).

35. *Arthur et al. v Oakes et al.*, 63 Fed. 310 (1894).

36. U.S. Congress, 53d Cong., 2d sess., *Annual Report of the Attorney-General, 1893*, House Executive Document No. 7, xxvi–xxviii; Sproat, *Best Man*, 166–68; *U.S. v Debs et al.*, 64 Fed. 724 (1894); *Debs*, 158 U.S. 564 (1895); Eggert, *Railroad Labor Disputes*, 1–197.

37. *U.S. v E. C. Knight C.*, 156 U.S. 1 (1895).

38. *U.S. v Trans-Missouri Freight Association*, 166 U.S. 290 (1897). After Judson Harmon became Attorney General in 1895 the administration showed some energy in enforcing the Antitrust Act, and Cleveland's last annual message devoted a paragraph to the problem. Richardson, *Messages and Papers of the Presidents*, 9:745; Nevins, *Grover Cleveland*, 722–24; Hans Birger Thorelli, *The Federal Anti-Trust Policy* (Baltimore: Johns Hopkins Press, 1955), 380–98.

39. *Pollock v Farmers' Loan and Trust Company*, 157 U.S. 429 (1895), 158 U.S. 601 (1895); *Philadelphia Inquirer, Salt Lake City Tribune*, and *Indianapolis Independent* in "The Supreme Court's Decision against the Income Tax," *Public Opinion* 18 (May 30, 1895), 595–69; "The Supreme Court's Decision against Railway Pooling," *Public Opinion* 22 (April 1, 1897), 389–90; Arnold M. Paul, *Conservative Crisis and the Rule of Law: Attitudes of Bar and Bench, 1887–1895* (Ithaca, NY: Cornell University Press, 1960), 82–158; and Eggert, *Railroad Labor Disputes*, 108–35.

40. *Report on the Chicago Strike*, xxxi; "Olney on Unionism," *American Federationist* 1 (December 1894), 229–30; Eggert, *Railroad Labor Disputes*, 197–216.

41. U.S. Congress, 53d Cong. 2d sess., 1894, *Report Submitting Resolutions Declaring Injunction against Employees of Northern Pacific Railroad Unwarranted*, House Report No. 1049.

42. "The Arbitration Congress at Chicago," *Public Opinion* 17 (November 29, 1894), 832; U.S. Congress, 55th Cong., 2d sess., 1898, *Bulletin of the Department of Labor No. 14*, House Document No. 206, 118–39; U.S. Industrial Commission, *Reports*, 17:423–64; *Appleton's Annual Cyclopedia, 1897*, 412; Eggert, *Railroad Labor Disputes*, 54–80.

43. *Congressional Record*, 53d Cong., 3d sess., 1092, 1712, 2789, 2797–2805, 2881, 2961, 3075; Eggert, *Railroad Labor Disputes*, 218–24.

44. *Jacksonville (Florida) Times-Union* in "The Supreme Court and the Debs Injunction," *Public Opinion* 17 (June 6, 1895), 629; "The Debs Case," *American Federationist* 2 (June 1895), 68; Porter, *Platforms*, 185; *A.F.L. Proceedings, 1894*, 48; *1895*, 14; *1896*, 17.

45. *Congressional Record*, 53d Cong., 3d sess., 964, 1226, 1640, 2808; 54th Cong., 1st sess., 26, 33, 387, 6059; 2d sess., 189, 233; 55th Cong., 1st sess., 259, 2664; 2d sess., 353, 1486, 4861–4988, 5086, 5800; *Proceedings of the General Assembly of the Knights of Labor ... 1894*, 175–76; *A.F.L. Proceedings, 1897*, 17–22; Thorelli, *Anti-Trust Policy*, 510–12.

46. Eggert, *Railroad Labor Disputes*, 224–41 and passim; *Congressional Record*, 53d Cong., 3d sess., 478, 670; 54th Cong., 1st sess., 23, 49, 51, 958, 3463, 5466; 2d sess., 703, 2164, 2387, 3402; 55th Cong., 1st sess., 21, 38, 90, 93, 117, 880, 1215; 2d sess., 74, 192, 456, 1749–4638, 4638, 4659, 6045.

Epilogue

There is nothing more difficult to take in hand, more perilous to conduct,
or more uncertain in its success, than to take the lead in the introduction
of a new order of things.

—Niccolò Machiavelli
The Prince (1532, ch. 6)

Government responses to depression during the 1890s exhibited elements of
complexity, confusion, and contradiction. Yet they also showed a pattern that
confirmed the transitional character of the era and clarified the role of the business crisis in the emergence of modern America. Hard times, intimately related
to developments issuing in an industrial economy characterized by increasingly
vast business units and concentrations of financial and productive power, were
a major influence on society, thought, politics, and thus, unavoidably, government. Awareness of, and proposals for adapting to, deep-rooted changes attending industrialization, urbanization, and other dimensions of the current
transformation of the United States long antedated the economic contraction of
the nineties.

As the nineteenth century flowed into the twentieth, however, social problems,
seriously aggravated, demanded greater recognition and action. The effects of
commercial crisis were traceable in such important things as family life, heightened class tension as farmers and industrial labor perceived more clearly the
importance of collective action, flare-ups of nativism and jingoism, and significant intellectual and political developments. Prevailing opinion emphasized fi-

nancial explanations and remedies, but a growing and influential minority of people blamed excessive industrial capacity for depression and looked for new foreign markets to absorb surplus output and thus restore prosperity.

Fear spread that the passing of the frontier and the opportunities it had provided presaged harsh difficulties for the country unless some surrogate were found. Attitudes about such matters as poverty, relief, and industrial relations, confronting staggering hardship and social stress, underwent important modifications. Growing scholarly debate on urgent contemporary issues occasionally provoked sharp controversy.

Imaginative literature and some of the arts displayed a heightened sensitivity to the circumstances of industrial life. The election of 1896 saw voters increasingly mindful of depression and the industrial character of American society complete the forging of a new political balance by choosing a candidate and program representative of the rising urban nation rather than the waning agrarian order. New conditions and problems intensified by depression finally aroused mounting demands for public action on a variety of fronts, extending from relief measures to financial reform, the amelioration of industrial relations, business regulation, and foreign policy.

Old attitudes and values—the individualism, administrative minimalism, and minimum government cherished by nineteenth-century liberalism and Social Darwinism—yielded grudgingly, to resurge at any crisis that might require public aid to a disconsolate cohort of the commonweal. A conservative reaction to contemporary turmoil delayed for a decade the implementation of many proposals for reform and sometimes took the form of repression, as against strikers and Coxey's pathetic marchers. Still, few persons forsook confidence for despair, and depression accelerated an irresistible gross movement of government toward the interventionist, activist, administrative state and mildly collectivist measures of an urban, industrial, twentieth-century United States.

Hard times contained difficulties that nurtured agitation for reform consummated in key measures of the Progressive Era, including the income tax amendment, the Federal Reserve System, railroad labor, farm credit, business consolidation, and a variety of other pivotal issues. Moreover, the commercial contraction was a signal stimulus for the naval construction program and expansionist mood and foreign policy that preceded the war with Spain and the advent of the country as a great power and indeed, by the middle of the twentieth century, a superpower. Throughout, the business crisis operated as a catalyst accelerating the processes of social transformation. It was a crucible in which the elements of the modern United States were clarified and refined. The nation that emerged from depression in 1897 and afterward was distinctly different from that of 1893. The changes so widely evident did indeed make the nineties the divide, however gentle, between a passing agrarian America and an emerging industrial power, and depression was so conspicuous in the timing, amplitude, and content of those changes as to mark perhaps better than any other event the boundary between the old and new orders.[1]

NOTE

1. Ballard C. Campbell, *The Growth of American Government: Governance from the Cleveland Era to the Present* (Bloomington: Indiana University Press, 1995); Richard A. Easterlin, *Growth Triumphant: The Twenty-First Century in Historical Perspective* (Ann Arbor: University of Michigan Press, 1996). Succinct essays on many people and issues set forth in the foregoing text—for example, Alexander Hamilton, John Sherman, Populism and greenbacks, silver issue and the gold standard—is readily accessible in Larry Schweikart, *Banking and Finance to 1913, Encyclopedia of American Business History and Biography* (New York: Facts on File, 1990).

Selected Bibliography

Adams, Brooks. *The Law of Civilization and Decay*. New York: Macmillan, 1896.

Adams, Edward F. "Cooperation among Farmers." *Forum* 20 (November 1895): 364–76.

Adams, Henry. *The Education of Henry Adams*. New York: Random House, 1931.

————. "The Tendency of History." *Annual Report of the American Historical Association, 1894*. Washington: Government Printing Office, 1895.

Adams, J. C., A. K. Miller, and Hugh Craig. "Reform of the Currency." *North American Review* 163 (December 1896): 743–52.

Adams, Pauline, and Emma S. Thornton. *A Populist Assault: Sarah E. Van De Vort Emery on American Democracy, 1862–1895*. Bowling Green, OH: Bowling Green State University Popular Press, 1982.

Allman, James. *Carmina Noctis and Other Poems*. New York: W. Hammer, 1898.

"Amendments to the National Banking Law." *Bankers' Magazine* 48 (October 1893): 241–43.

Anderson, Thornton. *Brooks Adams: Constructive Conservative*. Ithaca, NY: Cornell University Press, 1951.

"The Anglo-Venezuelan Boundary Dispute." *Public Opinion* 19 (December 26, 1895): 838–44.

Appleton's Annual Cyclopedia and Register of Important Events for the Year 1897. Third Series. New York: D. Appleton, 1898.

"The Arbitration Congress at Chicago." *Public Opinion* 17 (November 29, 1894): 832.

Argersinger, Peter H. *The Limits of Agrarian Radicalism: Western Populism and American Politics*. Lawrence: University Press of Kansas, 1995.

————. *Populism and Politics: William Alfred Peffer and the People's Party*. Lexington: University Press of Kentucky, 1974.

Arnett, Alex Mathews. *The Populist Movement in Georgia.* New York: Columbia University, 1922.

Atkinson, Edward. "The Benefits of Hard Times." *Forum* 20 (September 1895): 79–90.

———. "The True Meaning of Farm-Mortgage Statistics." *Forum* 17 (May 1894): 310–25.

Atlanta Constitution, 1891–1900.

Auxier, Charles W. "Middle Western Newspapers and the Spanish-American War." *Mississippi Valley Historical Review* 26 (March 1940): 525.

Bain, Richard C. *Convention Decisions and Voting Records.* Washington, DC: Brookings, 1960.

Baird, Charles W. "Labor Law Reform: Lessons from History." *Government Union Review* 12, no. 1 (Winter 1991): 22–55.

Bald, Ralph Dewar, Jr. "The Development of Expansionist Sentiment in the United States, 1885–1895, As Reflected in Periodical Literature." Ph.D. diss.: University of Pittsburgh, 1953.

Bankers' Magazine, 1891–1900.

"The Bank Failures." *Bankers' Magazine* 48 (July 1893): 1–5.

Barnes, Donna. *Farmers In Rebellion: The Rise and Fall of the Southern Farmers Alliance and People's Party in Texas.* Austin: University of Texas Press, 1985.

Barnes, James A. *John G. Carlisle: Financial Statesman.* New York: Dodd, Mead, 1931.

———. "Myths of the Bryan Campaign." *Mississippi Valley Historical Review* 34 (December 1947): 383–94.

Barnett, George Ernest. *State Banks and Trust Companies since the Passage of the National Banking Act.* Washington, DC: Government Printing Office, 1911.

Barnett, Paul. *Business Cycle Theory in the United States, 1860–1900.* Chicago: University of Chicago Press, 1941.

Barnhart, John D. "Rainfall and the Populist Party." *The American Political Science Review* 19 (August 1925): 527–40.

Barr, Robert. *The Victors.* New York: Frederick A. Stokes, 1901.

Barthelme, Marion Knox. *Women in the Texas Populist Movement: Letters to the Southern Mercury.* College Station: Texas A&M University Press, 1997.

Bates, Stockton. "How to Prevent Strikes and Lockouts." *North American Review* 160 (March 1895): 171–74.

Bauer, John Ireland Howe. *New Art in America: Fifty Painters of the Twentieth Century.* New York: Praeger, 1957.

Baum, Lyman Frank. *The Wonderful Wizard of Oz.* Chicago: George M. Hill, 1900.

Beardsley, Charles, Jr. "The Effect of an Eight Hours' Day on Wages and the Unemployed." *Quarterly Journal of Economics* 9 (July 1895): 450–59.

Bemis, Samuel Flagg. *A Diplomatic History of the United States.* 4th ed. New York: Holt, Rinehart and Winston, 1960.

Benson, Lee. "An Approach to the Scientific Study of Past Public Opinion." *Public Opinion Quarterly* 31 (Winter 1967–1968): 522–67.

Beringause, Arthur F. *Brooks Adams: A Biography.* New York: Knopf, 1955.

Berthoff, Rowland T. "Southern Attitudes toward Immigration, 1865–1914." *Journal of Southern History* 39 (August 1951): 328–60.

Bicha, Karel D. *Western Populism: Studies in an Ambivalent Conservatism.* Lawrence: Coronado Press, 1976.

Billington, Ray Allen. *America's Frontier Heritage*. New York: Holt, Rinehart & Winston, 1966.

―――. "The Origins of Middle Western Isolationism." *Political Science Quarterly* 60 (March 1945): 44–49.

Blake, Nelson M. "Background of Cleveland's Venezuelan Policy." *American Historical Review* 47 (January 1942): 259–77.

Blank, David M. *The Volume of Residential Construction, 1889–1950*. New York: National Bureau of Economic Research, 1954.

Bogue, Allan G. *Money at Interest: The Farm Mortgage on the Middle Border*. Ithaca, NY: Cornell University Press, 1955.

(Boise) Idaho Daily Statesman, 1891–1900.

Boston Daily Advertiser, 1891–1900.

Bremner, Robert H. *From the Depths: The Discovery of Poverty in the United States*. New York: New York University Press, 1956.

Brice, Lloyd Stephens, and James J. Wait. "The Railway Problem." *North American Review* 164 (March 1897): 327–48.

Brossenden, P. F. "The Labor Injunction." *Political Science Quarterly* 48 (September 1933): 413–50.

Brown, Junius Henri. "Succor for the Unemployed." *Harper's Weekly* 38 (January 6, 1894): 10.

Bruchey, Stuart. *Enterprise: The Dynamic Economy of a Free People*. Cambridge, MA: Harvard University Press, 1990.

Bryan, William Jennings. *The First Battle: A Story of the Campaign of 1896*. Chicago: W. B. Conkey, 1896.

Bryce, Lloyd Stephens. "The Trusts and the Workingman." *North American Review* 159 (June 1897): 719–31.

Buder, Stanley. *Pullman: An Experiment in Industrial Order and Community Planning, 1880–1930*. New York: Oxford University Press, 1967.

Buell, Carl J. "A Partial Solution to the Railway Problem." *Arena* 12 (May 1895): 321–22.

Burns, Arthur Frank. "New Facts on Business Cycles." *Business Cycle Indicators*. Edited by Geoffrey H. Moore. 2 vols. Princeton, NJ: Princeton University Press, 1961.

Burns, Arthur F., and Wesley Clair Mitchell. *Measuring Business Cycles*. New York: National Bureau of Economic Research, 1946.

Byrnes, Thomas. "The Menace of Coxeyism." *North American Review* 158 (June 1894): 697.

Cady, Edwin H. *The Realist at War: The Mature Years 1885–1920 of William Dean Howells*. Syracuse, NY: Syracuse University Press, 1958.

Campbell, Ballard C. *The Growth of American Government: Governance from the Cleveland Era to the Present*. Bloomington: Indiana University Press, 1995.

Campbell, Edward Gross. *Reorganization of the American Railroad System, 1893–1900*. New York: Columbia University Press, 1938.

Cell, John. *The Highest Stage of White Supremacy: The Origins of Segregation in South Africa and the American South*. New York: Cambridge University Press, 1982.

Chafe, William H. "The Negro and Populism: A Kansas Case Study." *Journal of Southern History* 34 (August 1968).

Chandler, Alfred D., Jr. "The Beginnings of 'Big Business' in American History." *Business History Review* 33 (Spring 1959).

———. *Scale and Scope: The Dynamics of Industrial Capitalism*. Cambridge, MA: Harvard University Press, 1990.

———. *Strategy and Structure: Chapters in the History of the Industrial Enterprise*. Cambridge, MA: MIT Press, 1962.

———. *The Visible Hand: The Managerial Revolution in American Business*. Cambridge, MA: Harvard University Press, 1977.

Cherny, Robert W. *Populism, Progressivism, and the Transformation of Nebraska Politics, 1885–1915*. Lincoln: University of Nebraska Press for Center for Great Plains Studies, University of Nebraska–Lincoln, 1980.

Chetwood, John. "Immigration, Hard Times, and the Veto." *Arena* 18 (December 1897): 788–801.

Chicago Daily Tribune, 1891–1900.

Christian Advocate, 1891–1900.

Clanton, Gene. *Populism: The Humane Preference in America, 1890–1900*. Boston: Twayne, 1991.

Clark, James Gowdy. "The Coming Industrial Order." *Arena* 40 (January 1895): 239–40.

Clark, John Bunyan. *Populism in Alabama*. Auburn, AL: Auburn Printing Company, 1927.

Clark, Victor S. *History of Manufactures in the United States*. 3 vols. New York: McGraw-Hill, 1929.

Clemen, Rudolf Alexander. *The American Livestock and Meat Industry*. New York: Ronald Press, 1923.

Cleveland, Frederick A. "The Final Report of the Monetary Commission." *Annals of the American Academy of Political and Social Science* 13 (January 1899): 31–56.

Cleveland, Grover. *The Letters of Grover Cleveland, 1850–1908*. Edited by Allan Nevins. New York: Houghton Mifflin, 1933.

Cleveland Plain Dealer, 1891–1900.

Clews, Henry. *Fifty Years on Wall Street*. New York: Irving Publishing, 1908.

Clinch, Thomas A. *Urban Populism and Free Silver in Montana: A Narrative of Ideology in Political Action*. Missoula: University of Montana Press, 1970.

Closson, Carlos C., Jr. "The Unemployed in American Cities." *Quarterly Journal of Economics* 8 (January, April, 1894): 168–217, 257–60, 453–77.

Cochran, Thomas Childs, and William Miller. *The Age of Enterprise: A Social History of Industrial America*. New York: Macmillan, 1942.

Coletta, Paolo E. *William Jennings Bryan: Political Evangelist*. Lincoln: University of Nebraska Press, 1964.

"Collapse of the National Cordage Company." *Public Opinion* 15 (May 20, 1893): 155–57.

Commager, Henry Steele. *The American Mind: An Interpretation of Thought and Culture since the 1880s*. New Haven, CT: Yale University Press, 1950.

Commercial and Financial Chronicle, 1890–1900.

Commons, John R. "The Day and Contract Systems of Municipal Works." *Yale Review* 5 (February 1897): 428–45.

———. *The Distribution of Wealth*. New York: Macmillan, 1893.

————. *Myself*. Madison: University of Wisconsin Press, 1963.

Commons, John Rogers, et al. *The History of Labour in the United States*. 4 vols. New York: Macmillan, 1918–1935.

Conant, Luther, Jr. "Industrial Consolidations in the United States." *Quarterly Publications of the American Statistical Association* 8 (March 1901).

Constantine, J. Robert. *Gentle Rebel: Letters of Eugene V. Debs*. Urbana: University of Illinois Press, 1995.

Corey, Lewis. *Meat and Man: A Study of Monopoly Unionism, and Food Policy*. New York: Viking, 1950.

Cowles, Alfred A., III, et al. *Common Stock Indexes, 1871–1937*. Bloomington, IN: Principia Press, 1938.

Croly, Herbert. *Marcus Alonzo Hanna: His Life and His Work*. New York: Macmillan, 1912.

Cross, Ira Brown. *A History of the Labor Movement in California*. Berkeley: University of California Press, 1965.

Cunnliffe, Marcus. "American Watersheds." *American Quarterly* 13 (Winter 1961): 480–94.

Curti, Merle E. *The Growth of American Thought*. 2d ed. New York: Harper & Brothers, 1951.

Cutler, James Elbert. *Lynch Law: An Investigation into the History of Lynching in the United States*. New York: Longmans, Green, 1905.

Davies, Glyn. *A History of Money from Ancient Times to the Present Day*. Cardiff: University of Wales Press, 1994.

Dawes, Charles G. *A Journal of the McKinley Years*. Chicago: R. R. Donnelley & Sons, 1950.

Degler, Carl N. *The Age of the Economic Revolution, 1876–1900*. 2nd ed. Glenview, IL: Scott, Foresman, 1967.

————. "American Political Parties and the Rise of the City." *Journal of American History* 51 (June 1964): 41–60.

Demarest, David P., Jr. *"The River Ran Red": Homestead 1892*. Pittsburgh: University of Pittsburgh Press, 1992.

Denny, C. S. "The Whipping Post for Tramps." *Century Magazine*, n.s., 27 (April 1895): 794.

Destler, Chester McArthur. *American Radicalism, 1865–1901*. Chicago: Quadrangle Books, 1966.

Dewey, Davis Rich. *Financial History of the United States*. New York: Longmans, Green, 1903.

Diamond, William. "Urban and Rural Voting in 1896." *American Historical Review* 46 (January 1941): 281–305.

Donnelly, Ignatius. *Caesar's Column: A Story of the Twentieth Century*. Chicago: F. J. Schulte, 1891.

Dorfman, Joseph Harry. *The Economic Mind in American Civilization*. 5 vols. New York: Viking, 1949.

Douglas, Paul Howard. *Real Wages in the United States, 1890–1926*. Boston: Houghton Mifflin, 1934.

Durden, Robert Franklin. *The Climax of Populism: The Election of 1896*. Lexington: University of Kentucky Press, 1965.

Easterlin, Richard A. *Growth Triumphant: The Twenty-First Century in Historical Perspective*. Ann Arbor: University of Michigan Press, 1996.

Eckels, James H. "The Duty of the Republican Administration." *North American Review* 163 (December 1896): 696–702.

———. "How to Prevent a Currency Famine." *North American Review* 67 (January 1894): 50–56.

Eckler, Ross. "A Measure of the Severity of Depression, 1873–1932." *Review of Economics and Statistics* 15 (May 15, 1933): 75–81.

Edgerton, Charles E. "The Wire-Nail Association of 1895–96." In *Trusts, Pools, and Combinations*, edited by William Zebina Ripley. Rev. ed. Boston: Ginn, 1916.

Edwards, Louise Betts. "Step Brothers to Dives." *Harper's New Monthly Magazine* 89 (August 1894): 436–40.

Ellis, Elmer. *Henry Moore Teller: Defender of the West*. Caldwell, ID: Caxton, 1941.

———. "The Silver Republicans in the Election of 1896." *Mississippi Valley Historical Review* 17 (March 1932): 519–23.

Ely, Richard Theodore. "Natural Monopolies and the Workingman: A Programme of Social Reform." *North American Review* 147 (March 1894): 294–303.

Emporia (Kansas) Gazette, 1891–1898.

Evans, George Heberton. *Business Incorporation in the United States, 1800–1943*. New York: National Bureau of Economic Research, 1948.

Ewen, David. *Complete Book of American Musical Theatre*. New York: Henry Holt, 1958.

Farmer, Hallie. "The Economic Background of Frontier Populism." *Mississippi Valley Historical Review* 10 (March 1924): 406–27.

Faulkner, Harold Underwood. *Politics, Reform, and Expansion, 1890–1900*. New York: Harper, 1959.

Feder, Leah Hanna. *Unemployment Relief in Periods of Depression . . . 1857 . . . 1920*. New York: Russell Sage Foundation, 1926.

Fels, Rendigs. *American Business Cycles, 1865–1897*. Chapel Hill: University of North Carolina Press, 1959.

Fender, Ann Harper. "Iron and Steel Foundries." In *Extractives, Manufacturing, and Services: A Historiographical and Bibliographical Guide*. Vol. 2, *Handbook of American Business History*, edited by David O. Whitten and Bess E. Whitten. Westport, CT: Greenwood Press, 1997.

Fine, Nathan. *Farmer and Labor Parties in the United States, 1828–1928*. New York: Rand School of Social Sciences, 1928.

Fisher, Sidney George. "Has Immigration Increased Population?" *Popular Science Monthly* 47 (December 1895 and January 1896): 244–55, 412.

Fisher, Willard. " 'Coin' and His Critics." *Quarterly Journal of Economics* 10 (January 1896): 187–208.

Fishlow, Albert. *American Railroads and the Transformation of the Ante-Bellum Economy*. Cambridge, MA: Harvard University Press, 1965.

Fite, Gilbert C. *The Farmers' Frontier, 1865–1890*. New York: Holt, Rinehart & Winston, 1966.

———. "Republican Strategy and the Farm Vote in the Presidential Campaign of 1896." *American Historical Review* 65 (July 1960): 787–806.

———. "William Jennings Bryan and the Campaign of 1896: Some Views and Problems.'' Paper presented at the Organization of American Historians' meeting, April 29, 1966.

Fletcher, Henry J. ''The Railway War.'' *Atlantic Monthly* 74 (October 1894): 534–41.

Flower, Benjamin Orange. ''Plutocracy's Bastiles: Or Why the Republic Is Becoming an Armed Camp.'' *Arena* 10 (October 1894): 601–21.

Fogel, Robert. *Railroads and American Economic Growth: Essays in Econometric History.* Baltimore: Johns Hopkins Press, 1964.

Ford, Worthington Chauncey. ''Foreign Exchange and the Movement of Gold, 1894–1895'' *Yale Review* 4 (August 1895): 128–48.

———. ''The Turning of the Tide.'' *North American Review* 161 (August 1895): 187–95.

Fowler, Charles Newell. ''Financial and Currency Reform Imperative.'' *Forum* 22 (February 1897): 713–21.

Frankfurter, Felix, and Nathan Greene. *The Labor Injunction.* New York: Macmillan, 1930.

Frederickson, George M. *The Black Image in the White Mind: The Debate on Afro-American Character and Destiny, 1817–1914.* New York: Harper & Row, 1971.

Frickey, Edwin. *Production in the United States, 1860–1914.* Cambridge, MA: Harvard University Press, 1947.

Friedman, Milton, and Anna Jacobson Schwartz. *A Monetary History of the United States, 1867–1960.* Princeton, NJ: Princeton University Press, 1963.

Gabriel, Ralph Henry. *The Course of American Democratic Thought: An Intellectual History since 1815.* New York: Ronald Press, 1940.

Gaither, Gerald H. *Blacks and the Populist Revolt: Ballots and Bigotry in the ''New South.''* University: University of Alabama Press, 1977.

Galbraith, John Kenneth. *A Short History of Financial Euphoria.* Knoxville, TN: Whittle Direct Books, 1990.

Gardiner, Martin, and Russell P. Nye. *The Wizard of Oz and Who He Was.* East Lansing: Michigan State University Press, 1957.

Garland, Hamlin. *Crumbling Idols.* Gainesville, FL: Scholars' Facsimiles & Reprints, 1957.

———. ''The Land Question and Its Relation to Art and Literature.'' *Arena* 9 (January 1894): 174.

Garraty, John A. *The New Commonwealth, 1877–1890.* New York: Harper & Row, 1968.

Ginger, Ray. *The Bending Cross: A Biography of Eugene Victor Debs.* New Brunswick, NJ: Rutgers University Press, 1949.

Glad, Paul W. *McKinley, Bryan, and the People.* Philadelphia: J. B. Lippincott, 1964.

Gladden, Washington. ''Relief Work—Its Principles and Methods.'' *Review of Reviews* 9 (January 1894): 38–40.

Glasner, David. *Business Cycles and Depressions: An Encyclopedia.* New York: Garland, 1997.

Godkin, Edwin Lawrence. ''What to Do with the Unemployed.'' *Nation* 57 (December 28, 1893): 401–2.

Goldberg, Michael L. *An Army of Women: Gender and Politics in Gilded Age Kansas.* Baltimore: Johns Hopkins University Press, 1997.

Goldman, Emma. *Living My Life.* 2 vols. New York: Alfred A. Knopf, 1931.

Goodwyn, Lawrence. *Democratic Promise: The Populist Movement in America.* New York: Oxford University Press, 1976.

————. *The Populist Moment: A Short History of the Agrarian Revolt in America.* New York: Oxford University Press, 1978.

Gould, E. R. L. "How Baltimore Banished the Tramps and Helped the Idle." *Forum* 19 (June 1894): 487–504.

Grant, H. Roger. *Self Help in the 1890s Depression.* Ames: Iowa State University Press, 1983.

Grantham, Dewey W. *The South in Modern America: A Region at Odds.* New York: HarperCollins, 1994.

Greenway, John. *American Folksongs of Protest.* Philadelphia: University of Pennsylvania Press, 1953.

Hackney, Sheldon. *Populism: The Critical Issues.* Boston: Little, Brown, 1971.

————. *Populism to Progressivism in Alabama.* Princeton, NJ: Princeton University Press, 1969.

Hale, David D. "The Panic of 1893." *Across the Board* 25 (January 1988): 24–32.

Handlin, Oscar. "American Views of the Jew at the Opening of the Twentieth Century." American Jewish Historical Society *Publications* 40 (June 1951): 323–44.

Hansen, Alvin Harvey. "Industrial Class Alignments in the United States." *Quarterly Publications of the American Statistical Association* 17 (December 1920): 417–22.

Harben, William Nathaniel. *The Land of the Changing Sun.* New York: Merriam, 1894.

Harter, Michael D. "Free Coinage, the Blight of Our Commerce." *Forum* 13 (May 1892): 281–84.

Harvey, William Hope. *Coin's Financial School.* Chicago: Coin Publishing Company, 1894.

Haven, Emerson, and Harriet E. Hughes. *Population, Births, Notifiable Diseases and Deaths Assembled for New York City, New York, 1866–1938.* New York: Columbia University, n. d.

Hayes, Samuel P. *New Possibilities for American Political History: The Social Analysis of Political Life.* Ann Arbor: The Inter-University Consortium for Political Research, n. d.

————. "Political Parties and the Community-Social Continuum." In *The American Party Systems*, edited by William Nisbet Chambers and Walter Dean Burnham. New York: Oxford University Press, 1967.

————. "The Social Analysis of American Political History, 1880–1920." *Political Science Quarterly* 80 (September 1965): 384–88.

Heald, Morrell. "Business Attitudes toward European Immigration, 1890–1900." *Journal of Economic History* 13 (Summer 1953): 291–304.

Hemming, C. C. "An Elastic Currency." *Bankers' Magazine* 49 (June 1894): 910–20.

Hemphill, J. C. "Free Coinage and the Loss of Southern Statesmanship." *Forum* 13 (May 1892): 295–99.

Herreshoff, David. *American Disciples of Marx: From the Age of Jackson to the Progressive Era.* Detroit: Wayne State University Press, 1967.

Herrick, Robert. *The Web of Life.* New York: Macmillan, 1900.

Hicks, John Donald. *The Populist Revolt: A History of the Farmers' Alliance and the People's Party.* Minneapolis: University of Minnesota Press, 1931.

Higgs, Robert. *The Transformation of the American Economy, 1865–1914.* New York: Wiley, 1971.

Higham, John. "Anti-Semitism in the Gilded Age—A Reinterpretation." *Mississippi Valley Historical Review* 43 (March 1957): 559–78.

———. *Strangers in the Land: Patterns of American Nativism, 1860–1925*. New York: Athenaeum, 1963.

Himmelberg, Robert F. *The Rise of Big Business and the Beginnings of Antitrust and Railroad Regulation, 1870–1900*. New York: Garland, 1994.

Himmelfarb, Gertrude. "Revolution in the Library." *The American Scholar* 66 (Spring 1997): 197–204.

Hoffmann, Charles. "The Depression of the Nineties." *Journal of Economic History* 16 (June 1956): 137–64.

———. *The Depression of the Nineties: An Economic History*. Westport, CT: Greenwood Publishing, 1970.

Hofstadter, Richard. *The Age of Reform: From Bryan to F.D.R.* New York: Vintage Books, 1960.

———. *The Paranoid Style in American Politics*. New York: Vintage Books, 1967.

———. *The Progressive Historians: Turner, Beard, Parrington*. New York: Alfred A. Knopf, 1968.

———. *Social Darwinism in American Thought, 1860–1915*. Philadelphia: University of Pennsylvania Press, 1945.

Hofstadter, Richard, and Walter P. Metzger. *The Development of Academic Freedom in the United States*. New York: Columbia University Press, 1955.

Holli, Melvin G. *Reform in Detroit: Hazen S. Pingree and Urban Politics*. New York: Oxford University Press, 1969.

Hollingsworth, J. Rogers. "Commentary. Populism: The Problem of Rhetoric and Reality." *Agricultural History* 39, no. 2 (April 1965): 81–85.

———. *The Whirligig of Politics: The Democracy of Cleveland and Bryan*. Chicago: University of Chicago Press, 1963.

Holt, Marilyn Irvin. *Linoleum, Better Babies and the Modern Farm Woman, 1880–1930*. Albuquerque: University of New Mexico Press, 1995.

Howard, Oliver Otis. "The Menace of Coxeyism." *North American Review* 158 (June 1894): 687–96.

Howells, William Dean. *A Traveler from Altruria*. New York: Harper & Brothers, 1894.

Hubbard, Elbert. *No Enemy (But Himself): The Story of a Gentleman Tramp*. New York: G. P. Putnam's Sons, 1894.

Hutt, W. M. "The Tramp and the Reform School." *Century Magazine* 26 (December 1894): 311.

Hyde, Charles K. "Metal Mining." In *Extractives, Manufacturing, and Services: A Historiographical and Bibliographical Guide*. Vol. 2, *Handbook of American Business History*, edited by David O. Whitten and Bess E. Whitten. Westport, CT: Greenwood Press, 1997.

Imlah, Albert H. "British Balance of Payments and Export of Capital, 1816–1913." *Economic History Review* 5, no. 2 (1952): 208–39.

Jensen, Richard. *The Winning of the Midwest: Social and Political Conflict, 1888–1896*. Chicago: University of Chicago Press, 1971.

Jones, Eliot. *The Trust Problem in the United States*. New York: Macmillan, 1929.

Jones, Stanley L. *The Presidential Election of 1896*. Madison: University of Wisconsin Press, 1964.

Journal of the 22d General Conference of the Methodist Episcopal Church. New York: Eaton & Mains, 1896.

Juglar, Clement. *A Brief History of Panics and Their Periodical Occurrence in the United States.* Edited and translated by De Courcy W. Thom. 4th ed. New York: G. P. Putnam's Sons, 1916.

Kazin, Alfred. *On Native Ground: An Interpretation of Modern American Prose Literature.* New York: Reynal & Hitchcock, 1942.

Kazin, Michael. *The Populist Persuasion: An American History.* New York: Basic Books, 1995.

Kemball, Edward, et al. "The Business Revival." *North American Review* 49 (November 1894): 613.

Kenkel, Joseph B. *The Cooperative Elevator Movement.* Washington: Catholic University of America, 1922.

Key, Valdimer Orlando, Jr. "A Theory of Critical Elections." *Journal of Politics* 57 (February 1955): 3–18.

Kindleberger, Charles Poor. *Manias, Panics, and Crashes: A History of Financial Crises.* Rev. ed. New York: Basic Books, 1989.

King, Charles. "A Tame Surrender. A Story of the Chicago Strike." *Lippincott's Monthly Magazine* 4 (March 1895): 376.

Kinzer, Donald L. *An Episode in Anti-Catholicism: The American Protective Association.* Seattle: University of Washington Press, 1964.

Kirkland, Edward Chase. *Industry Comes of Age, 1860–1897.* New York: Holt, Rinehart & Winston, 1961.

Klepper, Robert. *The Economic Bases for Agrarian Protest Movements in the United States, 1870–1900.* New York: Arno Press, 1978.

Kolko, Gabriel. *Railroads and Regulation, 1877–1916.* Princeton, NJ: Princeton University Press, 1965.

Kovaleff, Theodore P. *The Antitrust Impulse: An Economic, Historical, and Legal Analysis.* 2 vols. Columbia University Seminar Series. Armonk, NY: M. E. Sharpe, 1994.

Krause, Paul. *The Battle for Homestead, 1880–1892: Politics, Culture, and Steel.* Pittsburgh: University of Pittsburgh Press, 1992.

Kuznets, Simon Smith. *National Product since 1869.* New York: National Bureau of Economic Research, 1946.

Kyun, Kim. *Equilibrium Business Cycle Theory in Historical Perspective.* New York: Cambridge University Press, 1988.

La Feber, Walter. *The New Empire: An Interpretation of American Expansion, 1860–1898.* Ithaca, NY: Cornell University Press, 1963.

Lamoreaux, Naomi R. *The Great Merger Movement in American Business, 1895–1904.* New York: Cambridge University Press, 1985.

Larkin, Oliver W. *Art and Life in America.* New York: Rinehart, 1949.

Lauck, William Jett. *The Causes of the Panic of 1893.* New York: Houghton Mifflin, 1907.

Laughlin, James Laurence. "The Baltimore Plan of Bank-Issues." *Journal of Political Economy* 3 (December 1894): 101–5.

———. *Facts about Money.* Chicago: E. A. Weeks, 1895.

———. *The Federal Reserve Act: Its Origin and Problems.* New York: Macmillan, 1933.

————. *Report of the Monetary Commission of the Indianapolis Convention*. Indianapolis: Hollebeck Press, 1900.

Laughlin, James Laurence, and H. Parker Willis. *Reciprocity*. New York: Baker & Taylor, 1903.

Lebergott, Stanley. "Earnings of Nonfarm Employees in the U.S. 1890–1946." American Statistical Association *Journal* 43 (March 1948): 74–93.

Lewis, W. David. *Sloss Furnaces and the Rise of the Birmingham District: An Industrial Epic*. Tuscaloosa: University of Alabama Press, 1994.

Lightner, Otto C. *The History of Business Depressions*. New York: Northeastern Press, 1922.

Lindsey, Almont. *The Pullman Strike*. Chicago: University of Chicago Press, 1942.

Littlefield, Henry. "The Wizard of Oz: Parable on Populism." *American Quarterly* 16 (Spring 1964): 47–58.

Lloyd, Henry Demarest. *Wealth against Commonwealth*. New York: Harper & Brothers, 1894.

Lloyd, William. *Wind Harp Songs*. Buffalo: Peter Paul, 1895.

Lockwood, V. H. "How to Reform Business Corporations." *North American Review* 164 (March 1897): 294–304.

Lodge, Henry Cabot. "The Census and Immigration." *Century Magazine* 46 (September 1893): 737–39.

London, Jack. "Hoboes That Pass in the Night." *Cosmopolitan* 44 (December 1907): 190–97.

Long, Clarence D., Jr. *Building Cycles and the Theory of Investment*. Princeton, NJ: Princeton University Press, 1940.

Lowell, Josephine Shaw. "Methods of Relief for the Unemployed." *Forum* 16 (February 1894): 660.

Macrae, Duncan, Jr., and James Meldrum. "Critical Elections in Illinois, 1888–1958." *American Political Science Review* 54 (September 1960): 669–83.

Maddison, Angus. *Phases of Capitalist Development*. New York: Oxford University Press, 1982.

Mahan, Alfred Thayer. *The Influence of Sea Power upon History, 1660–1783*. Boston: Little, Brown, 1890.

————. *The Interest of America in Sea Power, Present and Future*. New York: Little, Brown, 1885.

Mandel, Bernard. *Samuel Gompers: A Biography*. Yellow Springs, Ohio: Antioch Press, 1963.

Marble, John M. C. "The Best Banking." *Bankers' Magazine* 48 (September 1893): 217–18.

Martin, Roscoe C. *The People's Party in Texas*. Austin: University of Texas, 1993.

May, Ernest R. *Imperial Democracy*. New York: Harcourt, Brace & World, 1961.

May, Henry Farnham. *Protestant Churches and Industrial America*. New York: Harper & Brothers, 1949.

McCormick, Thomas J. *China Market*. Chicago: Quadrangle Books, 1967.

McCurdy, Rahno Mabel. *The History of the California Fruit Growers' Exchange*. Los Angeles: G. Rice & Sons, 1925.

McMath, Robert C., Jr. *American Populism: A Social History*. New York: Hill and Wang, 1993.

————. *Populist Vanguard: A History of the Southern Farmers' Alliance*. New York: Norton, 1975, 1977.

McMurry, Donald LeCrone. *Coxey's Army: A Study of the Industrial Army Movement of 1894*. Boston: Little, Brown, 1924.

McNall, Scott G. *The Road to Rebellion: Class Formation and Kansas Populism, 1865–1900*. Chicago: University of Chicago Press, 1988.

McSeveney, Samuel Thompson. *The Politics of Depression: Political Behavior in the Northeast, 1893–1896*. New York: Oxford University Press, 1972.

McSpadden, Joseph Walker. *Light Opera and Musical Comedy*. New York: Thomas Y. Crowell, 1936.

Means, David MacGregor. "The Dangerous Absurdity of State Aid." *Forum* 17 (May 1894), 286–96.

Melvin, A. D. "The Federal Meat-Inspection Service." Published in U.S. Dept. of Agriculture, *Twenty-third Annual Report of the Bureau of Animal Industry for the Year 1906*. Washington, DC: Government Printing Office, 1908, 65–100.

Mendelowitz, Daniel. *A History of American Art*. New York: Holt, Rinehart & Winston, 1960.

Mercer, Lloyd D. "Railroad Transportation." In *Extractives, Manufacturing, and Services: A Historiographical and Bibliographical Guide*. Vol. 2, *Handbook of American Business History*, edited by David O. Whitten and Bess E. Whitten. Westport, CT: Greenwood Press, 1997: 313–53.

Michaels, Walter Benn. *The Gold Standard and the Logic of Naturalism: American Literature at the Turn of the Century*. Berkeley: University of California Press, 1987.

Millis, Walter. *The Martial Spirit*. Boston: Houghton Mifflin, 1931.

Minutes of the Ninth Session of the National Council of the Congregational Churches. Boston: Congregational Sunday School and Publishing Society, 1896.

Mitchell, B. R., with Phyllis Deane, *Abstract of British Historical Statistics*. Cambridge, UK: Cambridge University Press, 1962.

Mitchell, Edmund. "Co-operation and the Agricultural Depression." *Westminster Review* 142 (September 1894): 241–49.

Mitchell, Theodore R. *Political Education in the Southern Farmers' Alliance, 1887–1900*. Madison: University of Wisconsin Press, 1987.

Moody, John. *The Truth about the Trusts*. New York: Moody, 1904.

Morgan, H. Wayne. *America's Road to Empire*. New York: Wiley, 1965.

————. *From Hayes to McKinley: National Party Politics, 1877–1896*. Syracuse, NY: Syracuse University Press, 1969.

————. *William McKinley and His America*. Syracuse, NY: Syracuse University Press, 1963.

Morton, J. Sterling, et al. "The Financial Muddle." *North American Review* 160 (February 1895): 151.

Moses, Montrose J. "The Drama, 1860–1918." In William Peterfield Trent et al. *The Cambridge History of American Literature*. 4 vols. New York: G. P. Putnam's Sons, 1917–1921.

Muller, Philip Roy. *New South Populism: North Carolina, 1884–1900*. Chapel Hill: n.p., 1971, 1972.

Murrell, William [James Guy Fisher]. *A History of American Graphic Humor*. 2 vols. New York: Macmillan, 1938.

Myers, Margaret G. *A Financial History of the United States.* New York: Columbia University Press, 1970.

"A National Transportation Department." *Atlantic Monthly* 76 (July 1895): 119–26.

Nelson, David. *Farm and Factory: Workers in the Midwest, 1880–1990.* Bloomington: Indiana University Press, 1995.

Nelson, Nelson O. "Organized Labor." *New England Magazine* 13 (November 1895): 338–45.

Nelson, Ralph L. *Merger Movements in American Industry, 1895–1916.* Princeton, NJ: Princeton University Press, 1959.

Nerlove, Marc. "Railroads and Economic Growth." *Journal of Economic History* 26 (March 1966): 109–15.

Nevins, Allan. *Grover Cleveland: A Study in Courage.* New York: Dodd, Mead, 1932.

———. *John D. Rockefeller: The Heroic Age of American Enterprise.* 2 vols. New York: Scribner's, 1940.

(New York) Christian Advocate, 1891–1899.

(New York) Churchman, 1891–1899.

New York Times, 1891–1900.

Nicholls. W. T. "The Strike at Barton's." *Lippincott's Monthly Magazine* 9 (October 1897).

Nichols, Jeanette P. "Bryan's Benefactor: Coin Harvey and His World." *Ohio Historical Quarterly* 47 (October 1958): 299–325.

"No Help from Europe." *Harper's Weekly* 34 (December 31, 1892): 1250.

"Notes and Memoranda." *Quarterly Journal of Economics* 7 (July 1893): 494–95.

Noyes, Alexander Dana. "The Banks and the Panic." *Political Science Quarterly* 9 (March 1894): 12–28.

———. "The Late Bond Syndicate." *Political Science Quarterly* 10 (December 1895): 573–602.

———. *Forty Years of American Finance.* New York: Putnam's Sons, 1906.

———. *Thirty Years of American Finance.* New York: Putnam's Sons, 1896.

Nugent, Walter T. K. *The Tolerant Populists: Kansas Populism and Nativism.* Chicago: University of Chicago Press, 1963.

Ogden, Rollo. "The Real Problem of the Unemployed." *Nation* 59 (July 5, 1894): 6.

———. "Vagabonds' Disease: Coxey's Army." *Nation* 58 (April 12, 1894): 266.

"Olney on Unionism." *American Federationist* 1 (December 1894): 229–30.

Ostler, Jeffrey. *Prairie Populism: The Fate of Agrarian Radicalism in Kansas, Nebraska, and Iowa, 1880–1892.* Lawrence: University Press of Kansas, 1993.

Papers Relating to the Foreign Relations of the United States, 1894. Washington, DC: Government Printing Office, 1895.

Parrington, Vernon Louis. *Main Currents in American Thought.* 3 vols. New York, 1927–1930.

Patton, Spiro G. "Blast Furnaces and Steel Mills." In *Manufacturing: A Historiographical and Bibliographical Guide.* Vol. 1, *Handbook of American Business History,* edited by David O. Whitten and Bess E. Whitten. Westport, CT: Greenwood Press, 1990.

———. "Local and Suburban Transit." In *Extractives, Manufacturing, and Services: A Historiographical and Bibliographical Guide.* Vol. 2, *Handbook of American Business History,* edited by David O. Whitten and Bess E. Whitten. Westport, CT: Greenwood Press, 1997, 357–74.

Paul, Arnold M. *Conservative Crisis and the Rule of Law: Attitudes of Bar and Bench, 1887–1895*. Ithaca, NY: Cornell University Press, 1960.

Paullin, Charles O. *Atlas of the Historical Geography of the United States*. Baltimore: Carnegie Institution of Washington and American Geographical Society of New York, 1932.

Peffer, William Alfred. "The Cure for a Vicious Monetary System." *Forum*: 722–30.

———. *Populism, Its Rise and Fall*. Lawrence: University Press of Kansas, 1992.

Peterson, Lt. James. "The Trade Unions and the Populist Party." *Science and Society* 8 (Spring 1944): 143–60.

Philadelphia Public Ledger, 1891–1900.

Philbrick, Frank S. "The Mercantile Conditions of the Crises of 1893." *University Studies* 2, no. 4. Lincoln: University of Nebraska, 1902.

Phillips, Barnett. "Food, Fuel, Shelter." *Harper's Weekly* 38 (March 17, 1894): 255.

Pierce, H. A. "A Review of Finance and Business." *Bankers' Magazine and Statistical Register* 47 (February 1893): 561–72.

Platt, William Alexander. "The Destitute in Denver." *Harper's Weekley* 38 (August 19, 1893), 787–88.

Pollack, Norman. *The Humane Economy: Populism, Capitalism, and Democracy*. New Brunswick, NJ: Rutgers University Press, 1990.

———. *The Populist Response to Industrial America: Midwestern Populist Thought*. Cambridge, MA: Harvard University Press, 1962.

Poor, Henry Varnum, and Henry W. Poor. *Poor's Manual of Railroads, 1892*. New York: Henry Varnum Poor and Henry W. Poor, 1893.

Porter, Glenn. *The Rise of Big Business, 1860–1910*. Arlington Heights, IL: Harlan Davidson, 1973.

Porter, Kirk H. *National Party Platforms*. New York: Macmillan, 1924.

Powderly, Terence V. *The Path I Trod*. New York: Columbia University Press, 1940.

Pratt, Julius W. *Expansionists of 1898*. Chicago: Quadrangle Books, 1964.

The President's Report to the Board of Regents . . . 1891–1899. Ann Arbor: University of Michigan Press, 1891–1899.

"The Problem of the West." *Atlantic Monthly* 78 (September 1896): 287–97.

Proceedings of the General Assembly of the Knights of Labor. Seventeenth Regular Session. 1893. Philadelphia: Journal of the Knights of Labor, 1893.

Pusateri, C. Joseph. *Big Business in America: Attack and Defense*. Itasca, IL: F. E. Peacock, 1975.

"The Question of the Trusts." *Public Opinion* 21 (December 10, 1896): 757–59.

Quint, Howard H. *The Forging of American Socialism: Origins of the Modern Movement*. Columbia: University of South Carolina Press, 1953.

Rabinowitz, Howard. "More Than the Woodward Thesis: Assessing *The Strange Career of Jim Crow*." "Perspectives: *The Strange Career of Jim Crow*." *Journal of American History* 75 (December 1988): 842–56.

Rader, Benjamin O. *The Academic Mind and Reform: The Influence of Richard T. Ely in American Life*. Lexington: University of Kentucky Press, 1966.

Raleigh (North Carolina) News & Observer, 1891–1900.

Redlich, Fritz. *The Molding of American Banking: Men and Ideas*. Part 2, *1840–1910*. New York: Hafner, 1951.

Reed, Louis S. *The Labor Philosophy of Samuel Gompers*. Port Washington, NY: Kennikat Press, 1966.

Rees, Albert. *Real Wages in Manufacturing, 1890–1914*. Princeton, NJ: Princeton University Press, 1961.

Report of Proceedings of the American Federation of Labor, 1893. Bloomington, IN: American Federation of Labor, 1893.

"The Report of the Indianapolis Monetary Commission." *Public Opinion* 24 (January 13, 1898): 37–39.

Rezneck, Samuel S. "Unemployment, Unrest, and Relief in the United States during the Depression of 1893–97." *Journal of Political Economy* 61 (August 1953): 345. Quoted from *Iron Age* 60 (December 23, 1897): 19.

Richardson, James Daniel. *A Compilation of the Messages and Papers of the Presidents, 1789–1902*. 11 vols. Washington, DC: Bureau of National Literature and Arts, 1897.

———. *A Supplement to "A Compilation of the Messages and Papers of the Presidents, 1789–1902."* Compiled and arranged by George Raywood Devitt. Washington, D.C.: Published by Authority of Bureau of National Literature and Art, 1904.

Riddle, Thomas W. *The Old Radicalism: John R. Rogers and the Populist Movement in Washington*. New York: Garland, 1991.

Riggleman, John R. "Building Cycles in the United States, 1875–1932." *American Statistical Journal* 28 (June 1933): 174–83.

"The Right to Work." *Arena* 21 (February 1899): 131–42.

Riker, William H. *Liberalism against Populism: A Confrontation between the Theory of Democracy and the Theory of Social Choice*. Prospect Heights, IL: Waveland Press, 1982, 1988.

Ripley, Alfred L. "Two Plans for Currency Reform." *Yale Review* 7 (May 1898): 50–71.

Ritter, Gretchen. *Goldbugs and Greenbacks: The Antimonopoly Tradition and the Politics of Finance in America*. New York: Cambridge University Press, 1997.

Robinson, Edgar Eugene. *The Presidential Vote, 1896–1932*. Stanford, CA: Stanford University Press, 1934.

Robinson, William Alexander. *Thomas B. Reed, Parliamentarian*. New York: Dodd, Mead, 1930.

Rogin, Michael Paul. *The Intellectuals and McCarthy: The Radical Specter*. Cambridge, MA: MIT Press, 1967.

Roosevelt, Theodore. *Letters of Theodore Roosevelt*. Edited by Elting E. Morison et al. 8 vols. Cambridge, MA: Harvard University Press, 1951–1954.

Roper, Daniel. *Fifty Years of Public Life*. Durham, NC: Duke University Press, 1941.

Rose, Lisle Abbot. "A Bibliographical Survey of Economic and Political Writings, 1865–1900." *American Literature* 15 (January 1944): 381–410.

Ross, Robert J. S., and Kent C. Trachte. *Global Capitalism: The New Leviathan*. Albany: State University of New York Press, 1990.

Salom, A. B. "Truth and the Trusts." *Scientific American* 76 (June 5, 1897): 362.

Saloutos, Theodore. *Farmer Movements in the South, 1865–1933*. Berkeley: University of California Press, 1960.

———. "The Professors and the Populists." *Agricultural History* 40 (October 1966): 235–55.

(Salt Lake City) Deseret Weekly, 1891–1899.

Salvatore, Nick. *Eugene V. Debs: Citizen and Socialist*. Urbana: University of Illinois Press, 1982.

San Francisco Chronicle, 1891–1900.

Saunders, Robert Miller. *The Ideology of Southern Populists, 1892–1895*. Charlottesville, VA: n.p. 1967, 1968.

Scharf, J. Thomas. "The Farce of the Chinese Exclusion Laws." *North American Review* 146 (December 1898): 85–97.

Schindler, Solomon. *Young West: A Sequel to Edward Bellamy's Celebrated Novel, Looking Backward*. Boston: Ticknor, 1894.

Schumpeter, Joseph A. *Business Cycles: A Theoretical, Historical, and Statistical Analysis of the Capitalist Process*. 2 vols. New York: McGraw-Hill, 1939.

Schuster, Eunice Marie. *Native American Anarchism: A Study of American Left Wing Individualism*. Northampton, MA: Smith College, 1931.

Schwantes, Carlos A. *Coxey's Army: An American Odyssey*. Lincoln: University of Nebraska Press, 1985.

Schweikart, Larry. *Banking and Finance to 1913: Encyclopedia of American Business History and Biography*. New York: Facts on File, 1990.

Seager, Robert, II. "Ten Years before Mahan: The Unofficial Case for the New Navy, 1880–1890." *Mississippi Valley Historical Review* 40 (December 1953): 491–512.

Seattle Post-Intelligencer, 1891–1900.

Seavoy, Ronald E. *The Origins of the American Business Corporation, 1784–1855: Broadening the Concept of Public Service during Industrialization*. Contributions in Legal Studies no. 19. Westport, CT: Greenwood Press, 1982.

Sedgewick, Arthur George. "Bankruptcy in the United States." *Nation* 45 (December 1897): 135–43.

———. "Pools, Trusts, and Combinations." *Nation* 65 (December 16, 1897): 471–72.

Shannon, Fred Albert. *The Farmer's Last Frontier: Agriculture, 1860–1897*. New York: Holt, Rinehart & Winston, 1945.

———. "The Homestead Law and the Labor Surplus." *American Historical Review* 41 (January 1936): 637–51.

Shaw, Albert. "Relief for the Unemployed in American Cities." *Review of Reviews* 9 (January and February 1894): 29–37, 179–91.

Shaw, Barton C. *The Wool-Hat Boys: A History of the Populist Party in Georgia*. Baton Rouge: Louisiana State University Press, 1984.

Shaw, William Howard. *Value of Commodity Output since 1869*. New York: National Bureau of Economic Research, 1946.

Sheldon, Charles Monroe. *In His Steps: "What Would Jesus Do?"* Chicago: Advance, 1897.

Sheldon, William Du Bose. *Populism in the Old Dominion: Virginia Farm Politics, 1885–1900*. Gloucester, MA: Peter Smith, 1935, 1967.

"The Significance of the Frontier in American History." *Annual Report of the American Historical Association, 1893*. Washington, D.C.: Government Printing Office, 1984: 199–227.

Simon, Matthew. *Cyclical Fluctuations and the International Capital Movements of the United States, 1865–1897*. New York: Arno Press, 1979.

———. "The Morgan-Belmont Syndicate of 1895 and Intervention in the Foreign Exchange Market." *Business History Review* 42 (Winter 1968): 385–417.

Simons, Algie Martin. *Social Forces in American History*. New York: Macmillan, 1912.

Smith, Charles Stewart, and Francis B. Thurber. "What Will Bring Prosperity?" *North American Review* 164 (April 1897): 428–30.

Smith, Susan L. *Sick and Tired of Being Sick and Tired: Black Women's Health Activism in the United States, 1890–1950*. Philadelphia: University of Pennsylvania Press, 1995.

Sobel, Robert. *They Satisfy: The Cigarette in American Life*. New York: Anchor, 1978.

Soper, John Charles. *The Long Swing in Historical Perspective: An Interpretive Study*. New York: Arno Press, 1978.

Spaeth, Sigmund. *A History of Popular Music in America*. New York: Random House, 1948.

Spahr, Charles Barzillai. *An Essay on the Present Distribution of Wealth in the United States*. New York: T. Y. Crowell, 1896.

"The Spanish War and the Equilibrium of the World." *Forum* 25 (August 1898): 641–51.

Sprague, Oliver Mitchell Wentworth. *History of Crises under the National Banking System*. 61st Cong. 2d sess. 1910. S. Doc. 538.

Sproat, John G. *The Best Man! Liberal Reformers in the Gilded Age*. New York: Oxford University Press, 1968.

Sprout, Harold, and Margaret Sprout. *The Rise of American Naval Power, 1776–1918*. Princeton, NJ: Princeton University Press, 1939.

Stabile, Donald R., and Jeffrey A. Canton. *The Public Debt of the United States: An Historical Perspective, 1775–1990*. New York: Praeger, 1991.

Stead, William Thomas. "Coxeyism: A Character Sketch." *Review of Reviews* 10 (July 1894): 56.

Stegner, Wallace. *Beyond the Hundredth Meridian: John Wesley Powell and the Second Opening of the West*. Boston: Houghton Mifflin, 1962.

Steigerwalt, Albert Kleckner. *The National Association of Manufacturers, 1895–1914: A Study in Business Leadership*. Michigan Business Studies 16, no. 2. Ann Arbor: Bureau of Business Research, Graduate School of Business Administration, University of Michigan, 1964.

Stern, Richard. "The Ward-Ross Correspondence, 1891–1896." *American Sociological Review* 3 (June 1938): 362–401.

Stevens, Albert Clark. "An Analysis of the Phenomena of the Panic in the United States in 1893." *Quarterly Journal of Economics* 8 (January 1894): 117–48.

Stimson, Frederick Jessup. "Democracy and the Laboring Man." *Atlantic Monthly* 80 (November 1897): 605–19.

St. Louis Globe-Democrat, 1893–1894.

St. Louis Post-Dispatch, 1891–1900.

Strong, Josiah. *Expansion under New World Conditions*. New York: Baker & Taylor, 1900.

———. *The New Era; or, the Coming Kingdom*. New York: Baker & Taylor, 1893.

———. *Our Country: Its Possible Future and Its Present Crisis*. New York: Baker & Taylor, 1885.

"The Substitute for the Carlisle Currency Bill." *Public Opinion* 17 (December 27, 1894): 935.

Sullivan, J. W. *So the World Goes*. Chicago: Charles H. Kerr, 1897.

"The Supreme Court's Decision against Railway Pooling." *Public Opinion* 22 (April 1, 1897): 389–90.

Swinton, John. *A Momentous Question: The Respective Attitudes of Capital and Labor.* Philadelphia: Keller, 1895.

"The Tariff Bill Passed." *Public Opinion* 17 (August 23 and September 6, 1894): 485–89.

Taus, Esther Rogoff. *Central Banking Functions of the United States Treasury, 1789–1941.* New York: Columbia University Press, 1943.

Taussig, Frank W. *Tariff History of the United States.* 7th ed. New York: G. P. Putnam's Sons, 1923.

Taylor, Walter Fuller. *The Economic Novel in America.* Chapel Hill: University of North Carolina Press, 1942.

Thelen, David. "Introduction." "Perspectives: *The Strange Career of Jim Crow.*" *Journal of American History* 75 (December 1988): 841.

———. *The New Citizenship: Origins of Progressivism, 1885–1900.* New York: Columbia University Press, 1972.

Thorelli, Hans Birger. *The Federal Anti-Trust Policy.* Baltimore: Johns Hopkins Press, 1955): 380–98.

Thorp, Willard. "American Writers on the Left." In *Socialism in American Life*, edited by Donald Drew Egbert and Stow Persons. 2 vols. Princeton, NJ: Princeton University Press, 1952.

———. *Business Annals.* New York: National Bureau of Economic Research, 1926.

Torrey, Jay Linn. "The Torrey Bankrupt Bill." *Forum* 23 (March 1897): 42–49.

Tourgee, Albion Winegar. "The Anti-Trust Campaign." *North American Review* 157 (July 1893): 30–41.

Tufano, Peter. "Business Failure, Judicial Intervention, and Financial Innovation: Restructuring U.S. Railroads in the Nineteenth Century." *Business History Review* 71 (Spring 1997): 1–40.

Tunnell, George. "The Legislative History of the Second Income Tax." *Journal of Political Economy* 3 (June 1895): 311–37.

Turner, Frederick Jackson. *The Significance of the Frontier in American History.* Madison: State Historical Society of Wisconsin, 1894.

Ulmer, Melville J. *Trends and Cycles in Capital Formation by United States Railroads, 1870–1950.* New York: National Bureau of Economic Research, 1954.

U.S. Bureau of the Census. *Compendium of the Eleventh Census, 1890.* 3 vols. Washington, DC: Government Printing Office, 1897.

———. *Eleventh Census of the United States: 1890, Population.* 15 vols. Washington, DC: Government Printing Office, 1895–97.

———. *Historical Statistics of the United States, 1789–1945.* Washington, DC: Government Printing Office, 1949.

———. *Historical Statistics of the United States, Colonial Times to 1957.* Washington, DC: Government Printing Office, 1960.

———. *Twelfth Census of the United States: 1900, Manufacturers.* 10 vols. Washington, DC: U.S. Census Office, 1902.

U.S. Bureau of Education. *Report of the Commissioner of Education on the Years 1893–94—1898–99.* Washington, DC: Government Printing Office, 1896–1900.

U.S. Bureau of Statistics. *Statistical Abstract of the United States: 1900.* Washington, DC: Government Printing Office, 1901.

U.S. Commissioner of Labor. *Second Annual Report: Labor Laws of the United States.* 2d ed. Washington, DC: Government Printing Office, 1896.

————. *Labor Laws of the United States*. 2d ed. Washington, DC: Government Printing Office, 1896.

U.S. Congress. *Congressional Record*. 54th Cong., 1st sess. Washington: Government Printing Office, 1896.

————. House. *Annual Report of the Comptroller of the Currency*. 56th Cong., 2d Sess., 1900. House Document 10.

————. House. *Annual Reports of the Secretary of the Navy, 1893*. 53d Cong., 2d–3d sess., 1894. House Executive Document No. 1, Part 3.

————. House. *Bulletin of the Department of Labor No. 15*. 55th Cong., 2d sess., 1898. House Document No. 206.

————. House. *Bulletin of the Department of Labor No. 16*. 55th Cong., 2d sess., 1898. House Document No. 206.

————. House. *Monthly Summary of Commerce and Finance of the United States 1901*. 56th Cong., 2d sess., 1901. House Document 15.

————. House. *Notes of Hearings. The National Currency and Banking System*. 53d Cong., 3d sess. House Report No. 1508.

————. House. *Report of the Comptroller of the Currency*. 54th Cong., 2d sess., 1896. House Document 10.

————. House. *Report of the Secretary of the Treasury*. 53d Cong., 3d sess., 1894. House Executive Document 2.

————. House. *Report of the Secretary of the Treasury*. 56th Cong., 2d sess., 1900. House Document 8.

————. House. *Report Submitting Resolutions Declaring Injunction against Employees of Northern Pacific Railroad Unwarranted*. 53d Cong., 2d sess. 1894. House Report No. 1049.

————. House. *Sixteenth Annual Report of the Commissioner of Labor. 1901. Strikes and Lockouts*. 57th Cong., 1st sess., 1901. House Document 18.

————. National Monetary Commission. *Statistics for the United States, 1867–1909*. 61st Cong., 2d sess., 1911. Senate Document 570.

————. Senate. *Report on the Chicago Strike of June–July, 1894, by the United States Strike Commission*. 53d Cong., 3d sess., 1894.

————. Senate. *Reports of the Immigration Commission*. 61st Cong., 3d Sess., 1911. Senate Document 756. "Statistical Review of Immigration, 1820–1910." "Distribution of Immigrants, 1850–1900."

U.S. Department of Agriculture. *Yearbook of the Department of Agriculture 1901*. Washington, DC: Government Printing Office, 1902.

U.S. Federal Trade Commission. *Report of the Federal Trade Commission on the Meat-Packing Industry*. Part 2, *Evidence of Combination among Packers*. Washington, DC: Government Printing Office, 1918.

U.S. Industrial Commission. "Trust and Industrial Combinations." *Reports of the United States Industrial Commission*. 19 vols. Washington, DC: Government Printing Office, 1900.

U.S. Interstate Commerce Commission. *Eighth Report*. Washington, DC: Government Printing Office, 1894.

————. *Twelfth Annual Report, 1898*. Washington, DC: Government Printing Office, 1899.

U.S. v E. C. Knight Company. 156 U.S. 1 (1895).

Van Slyck, Abigail A. *Free to All: Carnegie Libraries & American Culture, 1890–1920.* Chicago: University of Chicago Press, 1995.

Veblen, Thorstein. "The Army of the Commonweal." *Journal of Political Economy* 2 (June 1894): 456–61.

Vilas, William F. "The Threat of the Present Coinage Law." *Forum* 13 (May 1892): 285–94.

Voss, Kim. *The Making of American Exceptionalism: The Knights of Labor and Class Formation in the Nineteenth Century.* Ithaca, NY: Cornell University Press, 1993.

Walch, Carolyn C. *Dr. Sphinx: A Novel.* New York: F. Tennyson Neely, 1896. *Wall Street Journal,* 1893–1900.

Walsh, Margaret. *The Rise of the Midwestern Meat Packing Industry.* Lexington: University of Kentucky Press, 1982.

Ward, Robert David, and William Warren. *Labor Revolt in Alabama: The Great Strike of 1894.* University: University of Alabama Press, 1965.

Warren, Charles. *Bankruptcy in American History.* Cambridge, MA: Harvard University Press, 1935.

Washington Post, 1891–1900.

Watson, Frank Dekker. *The Charity Organization Movement in the United States.* New York: Macmillan Company, 1922.

Watson, Thomas E. "The Negro Question in the South." *Arena* 6 (October 1982): 254–368.

Weberg, Frank Paul. *The Background of the Panic of 1893.* Washington, DC: Catholic University Press of America, 1929.

Webster, Duncan. *Looka Yonder! The Imaginary America of Populist Culture.* London: Routledge, 1988.

Weinberg, Albert Katz. *Manifest Destiny.* Baltimore: Johns Hopkins Press, 1935.

Weinstein, Allen. *Prelude to Populism: Origins of the Silver Issue, 1867–1878.* New Haven, CT: Yale University Press, 1970.

Weir, Robert E. *Beyond Labor's Veil: The Culture of the Knights of Labor.* University Park: Pennsylvania State University Press, 1996.

Welcome, S. Byron. *From Earth's Center: A Polar Gateway Message.* Chicago: Charles H. Kerr, 1894.

Whelpley, J. D. "An International Wheat Corner." *McClure's Magazine* 15 (August 1900): 363–68.

White, Eugene N., ed. *Crashes and Panics: The Lessons from History.* Homewood, IL: Dow Jones-Irwin, 1990.

White, Gerald Taylor. *The United States and the Problems of Recovery after 1893.* University: University of Alabama Press, 1982.

White, Hervey. *Differences.* Boston: Small, Maynard, 1899.

White, Horace. *Coin's Financial Fool.* New York: J. S. Ogilvie, 1895.

White, William Allen. *The Autobiography of William Allen White.* New York: Macmillan, 1946.

Whitten, David O. "Anthracite Coal." In *Extractives, Manufacturing, and Services: A Historiographical and Bibliographical Guide.* Vol. 2, *Handbook of American Business History,* edited by David O. Whitten and Bess E. Whitten. Westport, CT: Greenwood Press, 1997, 112–14.

———. *Emergence of Giant Enterprise, 1860–1914: American Commercial Enterprise and Extractive Industries*. Contributions in Economics and Economic History No. 54. Westport, CT: Greenwood Press, 1983.

Williams, George Fred. "Imminent Anger from the Silver Purchase Act." *Forum* 14 (February 1893): 789–96.

Williams, Willard F., and Thomas T. Stout. *Economics of the Livestock-Meat Industry*. New York: Macmillan, 1964.

Williamson, Joel. *The Crucible of Race: Black-White Relations in the American South since Emancipation*. New York: Oxford University Press, 1984.

———. "Wounds, Not Scars: Lynching, the National Conscience, and the American Historian." *Journal of American History* 83 (March 1997): 1221–53.

Willis, Henry Parker. *The Federal Reserve*. Garden City, NY: Doubleday, Page, 1917.

Windmüller, Louis. "The Folly of the Silver Agitation." *Forum* 13 (August 1892): 718–24.

Wisan, Joseph E. *The Cuban Crisis as Reflected in the New York Press*. New York: Columbia University Press, 1934.

Witte, Edwin E. *The Government in Labor Disputes*. New York: McGraw-Hill, 1932.

Woirol, Gregory R. *In the Floating Army: F. C. Mills on Itinerant Life in California, 1914*. Champaign: University of Illinois Press, 1992.

Wollman, Henry. "The Bane of Friendly Receiverships." *North American Review* 157 (March 1897): 250–51.

Wolman, Leo. *The Growth of American Unions, 1880–1923*. New York: National Bureau of Economic Research, 1924.

Woodcock, George. *Anarchism: A History of Libertarian Ideas and Movements*. Cleveland: World, 1962.

Woodward, C. Vann. *Origins of the New South, 1877–1913*. Baton Rouge: Louisiana State University Press, 1951.

———. "The Populist Heritage and the Intellectual." *American Scholar* 29 (Winter 1959–60): 55–72.

———. "*Strange Career* Critics: Long May They Persevere." "Perspectives: *The Strange Career of Jim Crow*." *Journal of American History* 75 (December 1988): 857–68.

———. *The Strange Career of Jim Crow*. 4th ed. New York: Oxford University Press, 1974.

Wright, Carroll Davidson. "Steps toward government Control of Railroads." *Forum* 18 (February 1895): 704–13.

Wyckhoff, Walter A. *The Workers: An Experiment in Reality*. 2 vols. New York: Charles Scribner's Sons, 1898.

Yeager, Mary. *Competition and Regulation: The Development of Oligopoly in the Meat Packing Industry*. Greenwich, CT: JAI Press, 1981.

Index

About the Authors

DOUGLAS STEEPLES, dean, college of liberal arts and professor of history at Mercer University, is editor of *Institutional Revival: Case Histories* (1986), *Successful Strategic Planning: Case Studies* (1988), *Managing Change in Higher Education* (1990), and associate editor (history) for *Business Library Review*. Recent articles by Steeples include "Young Will Dana: The Education of an Entrepreneur," *Essays in Economic and Business History* (1993); "William Dana: Man of Enterprise," *Essays in Economic and Business History* (1994); "Calico Silver and the Fabric of Western Development," *Essays in Economic and Business History* (1995); and "Origins of the Depression of the 1890s: An Economy in Transition," *Essays in Economic and Business History* (1996). Steeples is president of the Economic and Business Historical Society for 1998–99.

DAVID O. WHITTEN, professor of economics at Auburn University, is author of *The Emergence of Giant Enterprise, 1860–1914: American Commercial Enterprise and Extractive Industries* (1983), *A History of Economics and Business at Auburn University* (1992), and *Andrew Durnford, A Black Sugar Planter in the Antebellum South* (1995). He is editor (with Bess E. Whitten) of *Business Library Review*; *Manufacturing: A Historiographical and Bibliographical Guide*, Vol. 1, *Handbook of American Business History* (1990); *Eli Whitney's Cotton Gin, 1793–1993* (1995); and *Extractives, Manufacturing, and Services: A Historiographical and Bibliographical Guide*, Vol. 2, *Handbook of American Business History* (1997).